BURUNDI

D1826429

COUNTRY STUDY GUIDE

International Business Publications, USA
Washington, DC- Bujumbura

BURUNDI
COUNTRY STUDY GUIDE

Editorial content: International Business Publications, USA

Editor-in-Chief:	Dr. Igor S. Oleynik
Editor:	Natasha Alexander
Managing Editor:	Karl Cherepanya

Published by
International Business Publications, USA
P.O.Box 15343, Washington, DC 20003
Phone: (202) 546-2103, Fax: (202) 546-3275.
E-mail: rusric@erols.com

UPDATED ANNUALLY

We express our sincere gratitude to all government agencies and international organizations which provided information and other materials for this guide

Databases & Information: International Business Publications, USA
Cover Design: International Business Publications, USA

International Business Publications, USA. has used its best efforts in collecting, analyzing and preparing data, information and materials for this unique guide. Due to the dynamic nature and fast development of the economy and business environment, we cannot warrant that all information herein is complete and accurate. IBP does not assume and hereby disclaim any liability to any person for any loss or damage caused by possible errors or omissions in the guide.
This guide is for individual use only. Use this guide for any other purpose, included but not limited to reproducing and storing in a retrieval system by any means, electronic, photocopying or using the addresses or other information contained in this guide for any commercial purposes requires a special written permission from the publisher.

2004 International Business Publications, USA
ISBN 0-7397-9407-8
For customer service and information, please contact:

in the USA: International Business Publications, USA
                P.O.Box 15343, Washington, DC 20003
                Phone: (202) 546-2103, Fax: (202) 546-3275.
                E-mail: rusric@erols.com

Printed in the USA

For additional analytical, marketing, investment and business opportunities information, please contact
Global Investment & Business Center, USA
(202) 546-2103. Fax: (202) 546-3275. E-mail: rusric@erols.com

BURUNDI

COUNTRY STUDY GUIDE

TABLE OF CONTENTS

For additional analytical, marketing, investment and business opportunities
information, please contact
Global Investment & Business Center, USA
(202) 546-2103. Fax: (202) 546-3275. E-mail: rusric@erols.com

For additional analytical, marketing, investment and business opportunities
information, please contact
Global Investment & Business Center, USA
(202) 546-2103. Fax: (202) 546-3275. E-mail: rusric@erols.com

For additional analytical, marketing, investment and business opportunities information, please contact
Global Investment & Business Center, USA
(202) 546-2103. Fax: (202) 546-3275. E-mail: rusric@erols.com

**For additional analytical, marketing, investment and business opportunities
information, please contact
Global Investment & Business Center, USA
(202) 546-2103. Fax: (202) 546-3275. E-mail: rusric@erols.com**

For additional analytical, marketing, investment and business opportunities
information, please contact
Global Investment & Business Center, USA
(202) 546-2103. Fax: (202) 546-3275. E-mail: rusric@erols.com

**For additional analytical, marketing, investment and business opportunities
information, please contact
Global Investment & Business Center, USA
(202) 546-2103. Fax: (202) 546-3275. E-mail: rusric@erols.com**

STRATEGIC AND DEVELOPMENT PROFILES

GENERAL OVERVIEW

Official name: Republika y'Uburundi (The Republic of Burundi)
Head of State: President Major Pierre Buyoya (Tutsi); Vice President Domitien Ndayizeye (Hutu) (from Nov 2001) (the presidency will be assumed by Ndayizeye after 18 months) *President Pierre Nkurunziza*
Head of government: President Major Pierre Buyoya
Ruling party: Three-year Transitional Government of National Unity (installed 1 Nov 2001; the cabinet is almost equally split between Tutsi and Hutu). *CNDD*
Area: 27,834 square km
Population: 6.61 million (2000)
Capital: Bujumbura
Official language: Kirundi and French
Currency: Burundi franc (Buf) = 100 centimes
Exchange rate: Buf867.58 per US$ (Aug 2002)
GDP per capita: US$126 (2000)
GDP real growth: -2.30% (2000); 3.3% (2001)
Inflation: 24.30% (2000); 8.0% (2001)
Balance of trade: -US$58.80 million (2000)
Foreign debt: US$1.11 billion (2000)

GEOGRAPHY

Location: Central Africa, east of Democratic Republic of the Congo

Geographic coordinates: 3 30 S, 30 00 E

Map references: Africa

Area:
total: 27,830 sq km
land: 25,650 sq km
water: 2,180 sq km

Area—comparative: slightly smaller than Maryland

For additional analytical, marketing, investment and business opportunities information, please contact
Global Investment & Business Center, USA
(202) 546-2103. Fax: (202) 546-3275. E-mail: rusric@erols.com

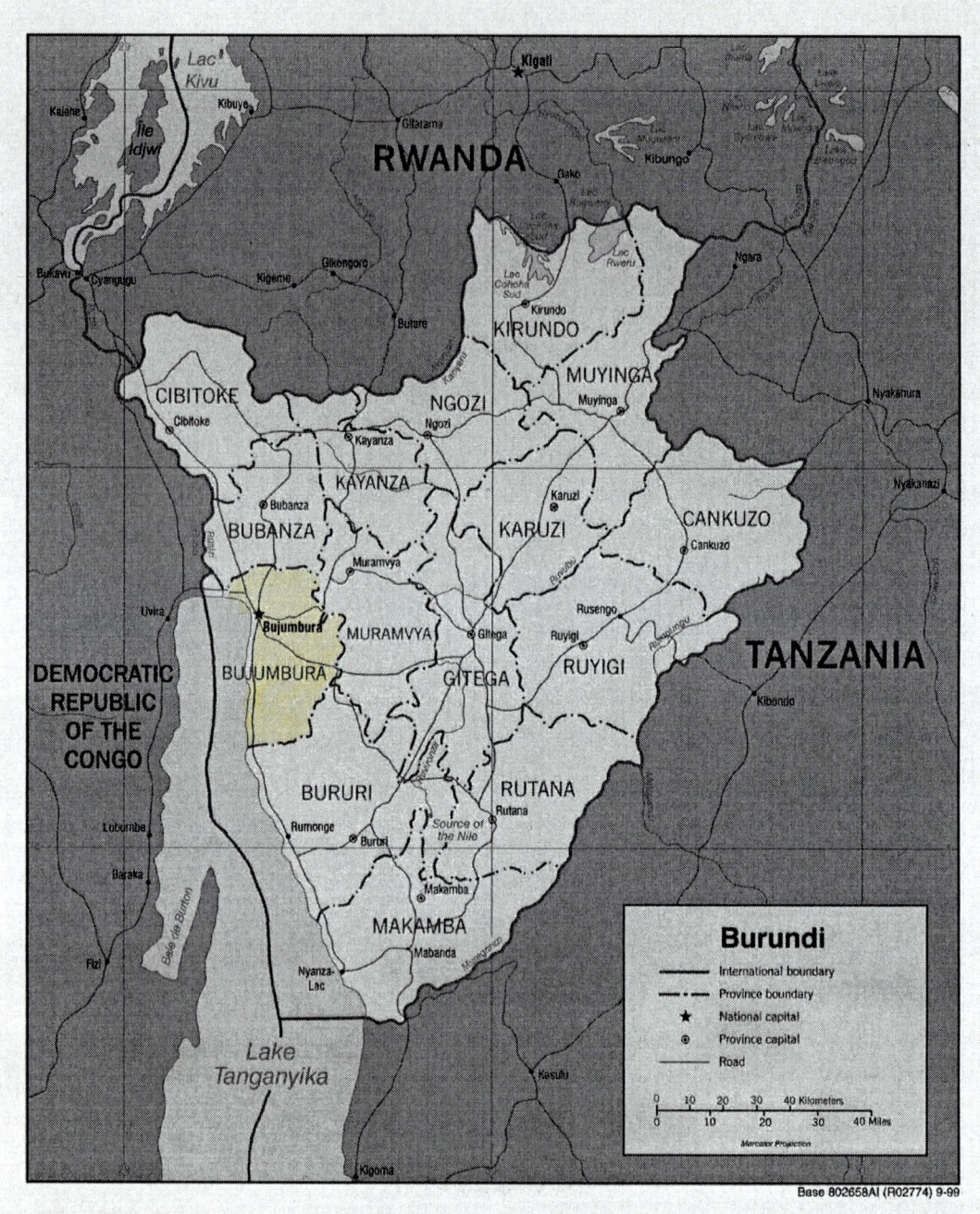

For additional analytical, marketing, investment and business opportunities
information, please contact
Global Investment & Business Center, USA
(202) 546-2103. Fax: (202) 546-3275. E-mail: rusric@erols.com

Rwanda and Burundi

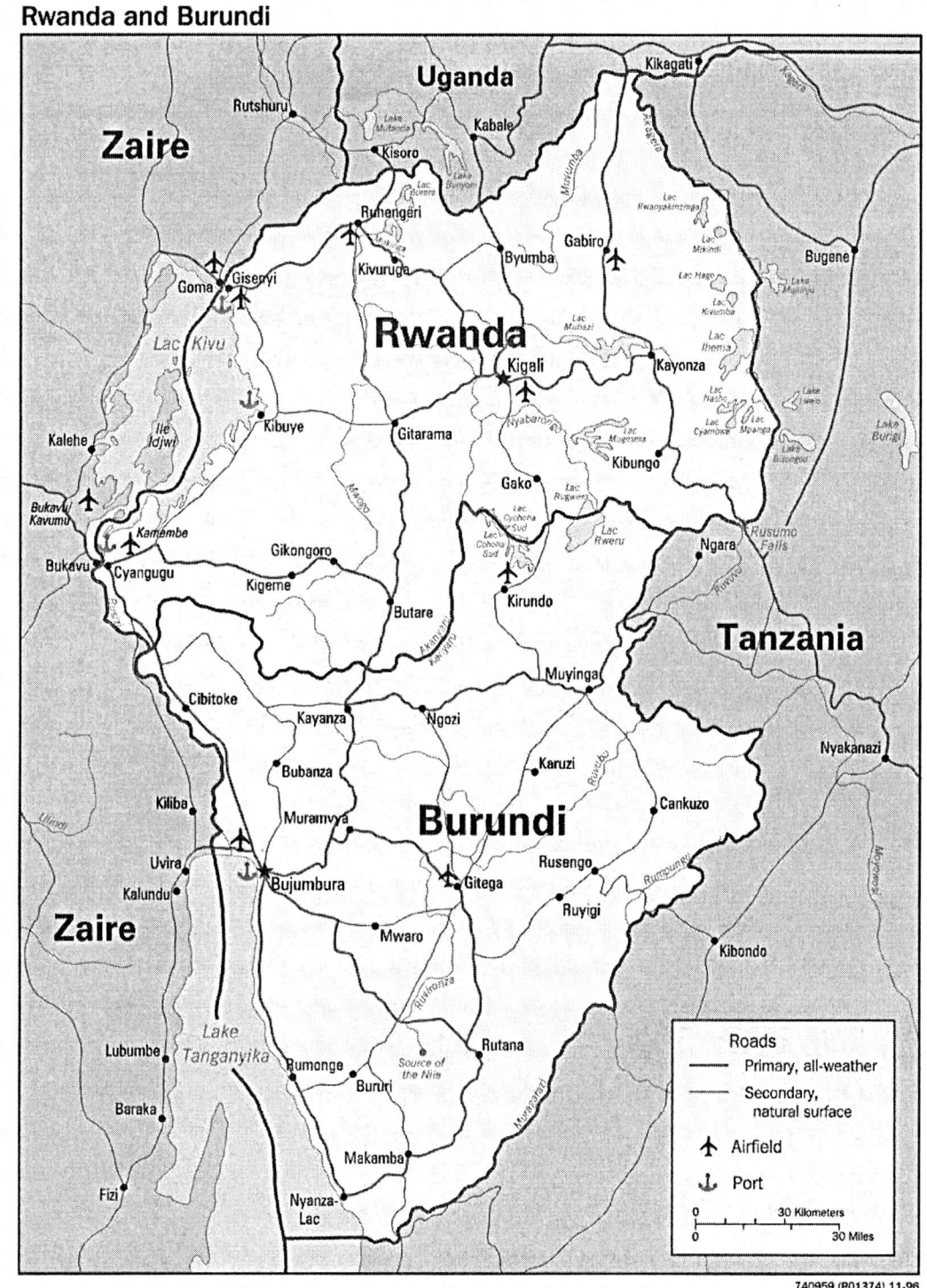

740959 (R01374) 11-96

For additional analytical, marketing, investment and business opportunities
information, please contact
Global Investment & Business Center, USA
(202) 546-2103. Fax: (202) 546-3275. E-mail: rusric@erols.com

Land boundaries:
total: 974 km
border countries: Democratic Republic of the Congo 233 km, Rwanda 290 km,
Tanzania 451 km

Coastline: 0 km (landlocked)

Maritime claims: none (landlocked)

Climate: equatorial; high plateau with considerable altitude variation (772 m to
2,760 m); average annual temperature varies with altitude from 23 to 17 degrees
centigrade but is generally moderate as the average altitude is about 1,700 m;
average annual rainfall is about 150 cm; wet seasons from February to May and
September to November, and dry seasons from June to August and December to
January

Terrain: hilly and mountainous, dropping to a plateau in east, some plains

Elevation extremes:
lowest point: Lake Tanganyika 772 m
highest point: Mount Heha 2,670 m

Natural resources: nickel, uranium, rare earth oxides, peat, cobalt, copper,
platinum (not yet exploited), vanadium

Land use:
arable land: 44%
permanent crops: 9%
permanent pastures: 36%
forests and woodland: 3%
other: 8% (1993 est.)

Irrigated land: 140 sq km (1993 est.)

Natural hazards: flooding, landslides

Environment—current issues: soil erosion as a result of overgrazing and the
expansion of agriculture into marginal lands; deforestation (little forested land
remains because of uncontrolled cutting of trees for fuel); habitat loss threatens
wildlife populations

Environment—international agreements:
party to: Biodiversity, Climate Change, Desertification, Endangered Species,

For additional analytical, marketing, investment and business opportunities
information, please contact
Global Investment & Business Center, USA
(202) 546-2103. Fax: (202) 546-3275. E-mail: rusric@erols.com

Hazardous Wastes, Ozone Layer Protection
signed, but not ratified: Law of the Sea, Nuclear Test Ban

Geography—note: landlocked; straddles crest of the Nile-Congo watershed

PEOPLE

Population: 5,735,937 (July 1999 est.)

Age structure:
0-14 years: 47% (male 1,349,995; female 1,345,201)
15-64 years: 50% (male 1,392,880; female 1,479,835)
65 years and over: 3% (male 69,748; female 98,278) (1999 est.)

Population growth rate: 3.54% (1999 est.)

Birth rate: 41.27 births/1,000 population (1999 est.)

Death rate: 17.23 deaths/1,000 population (1999 est.)

Net migration rate: 11.33 migrant(s)/1,000 population (1999 est.)

Sex ratio:
at birth: 1.03 male(s)/female
under 15 years: 1 male(s)/female
15-64 years: 0.94 male(s)/female
65 years and over: 0.71 male(s)/female
total population: 0.96 male(s)/female (1999 est.)

Infant mortality rate: 99.36 deaths/1,000 live births (1999 est.)

Life expectancy at birth:
total population: 45.44 years
male: 43.54 years
female: 47.41 years (1999 est.)

Total fertility rate: 6.33 children born/woman (1999 est.)

Nationality:
noun: Burundian(s)
adjective: Burundi

Ethnic groups: Hutu (Bantu) 85%, Tutsi (Hamitic) 14%, Twa (Pygmy) 1%, Europeans 3,000, South Asians 2,000

For additional analytical, marketing, investment and business opportunities information, please contact
Global Investment & Business Center, USA
(202) 546-2103. Fax: (202) 546-3275. E-mail: rusric@erols.com

Religions: Christian 67% (Roman Catholic 62%, Protestant 5%), indigenous beliefs 32%, Muslim 1%

Languages: Kirundi (official), French (official), Swahili (along Lake Tanganyika and in the Bujumbura area)

Literacy:
definition: age 15 and over can read and write
total population: 35.3%
male: 49.3%
female: 22.5% (1995 est.)

GOVERNMENT

Country name:
conventional long form: Republic of Burundi
conventional short form: Burundi
local long form: Republika y'u Burundi
local short form: Burundi

Data code: BY

Government type: republic

Capital: Bujumbura

Administrative divisions: 15 provinces; Bubanza, Bujumbura, Bururi, Cankuzo, Cibitoke, Gitega, Karuzi, Kayanza, Kirundo, Makamba, Muramvya, Muyinga, Ngozi, Rutana, Ruyigi
note: there may be a new province named Mwaro

Independence: 1 July 1962 (from UN trusteeship under Belgian administration)

National holiday: Independence Day, 1 July (1962)

Constitution: 13 March 1992; provided for establishment of a plural political system; supplanted on 6 June 1998 by a Transitional Constitution which enlarged the National Assembly and created two vice presidents

Legal system: based on German and Belgian civil codes and customary law; does not accept compulsory ICJ jurisdiction

Suffrage: NA years of age; universal adult

For additional analytical, marketing, investment and business opportunities information, please contact
Global Investment & Business Center, USA
(202) 546-2103. Fax: (202) 546-3275. E-mail: rusric@erols.com

Executive branch:
chief of state: President Pierre BUYOYA (interim president since 27 September 1996 and officially sworn in on 11 June 1998) is chief of state and head of government and is assisted by First Vice President Frederic BAMVUGINYUMVIRA (since NA) and Second Vice President Mathias SINAMENYA (since NA); note—former President NTIBANTUNGANYA was overthrown in a coup on 25 July 1996
head of government: President Pierre BUYOYA is both chief of state and head of government; assisted by First Vice President Frederic BAMVUGINYUMVIRA (since NA) and Second Vice President Mathias SINAMENYA (since NA)
cabinet: Council of Ministers appointed by president
elections: NA

Legislative branch: unicameral National Assembly or Assemblee Nationale (81 seats; note—new Transitional Constitution calls for 121 seats; members are elected by popular vote on a proportional basis to serve five-year terms)
elections: last held 29 June 1993 (next was scheduled to be held in 1998, but suspended by presidential decree in 1996)
election results: percent of vote by party—FRODEBU 71%, UPRONA 21.4%; seats by party—FRODEBU 65, UPRONA 16; other parties won too small shares of the vote to win seats in the assembly

Judicial branch: Supreme Court or Cour Supreme

Political parties and leaders: Unity for National Progress or UPRONA [Luc RUKINGAMA, president]; Burundi Democratic Front or FRODEBU [Jean MINANI, president]; Socialist Party of Burundi or PSB [leader NA]; People's Reconciliation Party or PRP [leader NA]
note: opposition parties, legalized in March 1992, include Burundi African Alliance for the Salvation or ABASA; Rally for Democracy and Economic and Social Development or RADDES [Cyrille SIGEJEJE, chairman]; and Party for National Redress or PARENA [Jean-Baptiste BAGAZA]

International organization participation: ACCT, ACP, AfDB, CCC, CEEAC, CEPGL, ECA, FAO, G-77, IBRD, ICAO, ICRM, IDA, IFAD, IFC, IFRCS, ILO, IMF, Intelsat (nonsignatory user), Interpol, IOC, ITU, NAM, OAU, OPCW, UN, UNCTAD, UNESCO, UNIDO, UPU, WHO, WIPO, WMO, WToO, WTrO

Diplomatic representation in the US:
chief of mission: Ambassador Thomas NDIKUMANA
chancery: Suite 212, 2233 Wisconsin Avenue NW, Washington, DC 20007
telephone: [1] (202) 342-2574
FAX: [1] (202) 342-2578

For additional analytical, marketing, investment and business opportunities information, please contact
Global Investment & Business Center, USA
(202) 546-2103. Fax: (202) 546-3275. E-mail: rusric@erols.com

Diplomatic representation from the US:
chief of mission: Ambassador Morris N. HUGHES, Jr.
embassy: Avenue des Etats-Unis, Bujumbura
mailing address: B. P. 1720, Bujumbura
telephone: [257] (2) 223454
FAX: [257] (2) 222926

Flag description: divided by a white diagonal cross into red panels (top and bottom) and green panels (hoist side and outer side) with a white disk superimposed at the center bearing three red six-pointed stars outlined in green arranged in a triangular design (one star above, two stars below)

ECONOMY

Economy—overview: Burundi is a landlocked, resource-poor country with a poorly developed manufacturing sector. The economy is predominately agricultural with roughly 90% of the population dependent on subsistence agriculture. Its economic health depends on the coffee crop, which accounts for 80% of foreign exchange earnings. The ability to pay for imports therefore rests largely on the vagaries of the climate and the international coffee market. Since October 1993 the nation has suffered from massive ethnic-based violence which has resulted in the death of perhaps 250,000 persons and the displacement of about 800,000 others. Foods, medicines, and electricity remain in short supply.

GDP: purchasing power parity—$4.1 billion (1998 est.)

GDP—real growth rate: 4.5% (1998 est.)

GDP—per capita: purchasing power parity—$740 (1998 est.)

GDP—composition by sector:
agriculture: 58%
industry: 18%
services: 24% (1997 est.)

Population below poverty line: 36.2% (1990 est.)

Household income or consumption by percentage share:
lowest 10%: NA%
highest 10%: NA%

Inflation rate (consumer prices): 17% (1998 est.)

Labor force: 1.9 million

For additional analytical, marketing, investment and business opportunities information, please contact
Global Investment & Business Center, USA
(202) 546-2103. Fax: (202) 546-3275. E-mail: rusric@erols.com

Labor force—by occupation: agriculture 93%, government 4%, industry and commerce 1.5%, services 1.5% (1983 est.)

Unemployment rate: NA%

Budget:
revenues: $NA
expenditures: $165 million, including capital expenditures of $42.6 million (1998 est.)

Industries: light consumer goods such as blankets, shoes, soap; assembly of imported components; public works construction; food processing

Industrial production growth rate: NA%

Electricity—production: 122 million kWh (1996)

Electricity—production by source:
fossil fuel: 1.64%
hydro: 98.36%
nuclear: 0%
other: 0% (1996)

Electricity—consumption: 152 million kWh (1996)

Electricity—exports: 0 kWh (1996)

Electricity—imports: 30 million kWh (1996)
note: imports some electricity from Democratic Republic of the Congo

Agriculture—products: coffee, cotton, tea, corn, sorghum, sweet potatoes, bananas, manioc (tapioca); beef, milk, hides

Exports: $49 million (f.o.b., 1998)

Exports—commodities: coffee, tea, cotton, hides

Exports—partners: UK, Germany, Benelux, Switzerland (1997)

Imports: $102 million f.o.b., 1998)

Imports—commodities: capital goods, petroleum products, foodstuffs, consumer goods

For additional analytical, marketing, investment and business opportunities information, please contact
Global Investment & Business Center, USA
(202) 546-2103. Fax: (202) 546-3275. E-mail: rusric@erols.com

Imports—partners: Benelux, France, Germany, Japan (1997)

Debt—external: $1.1 billion (1995 est.)

Economic aid—recipient: $286.1 million (1995)

Currency: 1 Burundi franc (FBu) = 100 centimes

Exchange rates: Burundi francs (FBu) per US$1—508 (January 1999), 477.77 (1998), 352.35 (1997), 302.75 (1996), 249.76 (1995), 252.66 (1994)

Fiscal year: calendar year

COMMUNICATIONS

Telephones: 7,200 (1987 est.)

Telephone system: primitive system
domestic: sparse system of open wire, radiotelephone communications, and low-capacity microwave radio relay
international: satellite earth station—1 Intelsat (Indian Ocean)

Radio broadcast stations: AM 2, FM 2, shortwave 0 (1998)

Radios: NA

Television broadcast stations: 1 (1997)

Televisions: 4,500 (1993 est.)

TRANSPORTATION

Railways: 0 km

Highways:
total: 14,480 km
paved: 1,028 km
unpaved: 13,452 km (1996 est.)

Waterways: Lake Tanganyika

Ports and harbors: Bujumbura

Airports: 4 (1998 est.)

For additional analytical, marketing, investment and business opportunities information, please contact
Global Investment & Business Center, USA
(202) 546-2103. Fax: (202) 546-3275. E-mail: rusric@erols.com

Airports—with paved runways:
total: 1
over 3,047 m: 1 (1998 est.)

Airports—with unpaved runways:
total: 3
914 to 1,523 m: 2
under 914 m: 1 (1998 est.)

MILITARY

Military branches: Army (includes naval and air units), paramilitary Gendarmerie

Military manpower—military age: 16 years of age

Military manpower—availability:
males age 15-49: 1,260,909 (1999 est.)

Military manpower—fit for military service:
males age 15-49: 658,115 (1999 est.)

Military manpower—reaching military age annually:
males: 73,271 (1999 est.)

Military expenditures—dollar figure: $25 million (1993)

Military expenditures—percent of GDP: 2.6% (1993)

For additional analytical, marketing, investment and business opportunities
information, please contact
Global Investment & Business Center, USA
(202) 546-2103. Fax: (202) 546-3275. E-mail: rusric@erols.com

IMPORTANT INFORMATION FOR UNDERSTANDING BURUNDI

GEOGRAPHY

Burundi is a land-locked country in the heart of Africa, a little south of the equator, on the eastern shore of Lake Tanganyika. It is bordered by Rwanda to the north, by Tanzania to the south and by the Democratic Republic of Congo to the west. The interior is a broken plateau sloping east to Tanzania and the valley of the River Malagarasi. The southern tributary of the Nile system rises in the south of the country. The landscape is characterized by hills and valleys covered with eucalyptus trees, banana groves, cultivated fields and pasture. In the east, the fertile area gives way to savannah grassland, and tea and coffee are now grown on mountainsides.

CLIMATE

Burundi has a "moderate" tropical climate with average temperatures between 23 and 24°C. This is a gift from nature to have such an average near the Equatorial area known for its heat and humidity. In Bujumbura city where it is hotter, average temperatures are about 25 ° C.

The country has two important seasons: the dry season from June to September and the rainy season from February to May. The remaining time is made up of middle seasons - half dry and half rainy - with a short rainy season between September and December, and a short dry season between January and February. The vegetation is lush and agriculture important.

HISTORY

CHRONOLOGY OF BURUNDIAN HISTORY

14th to 18th Centuries: Waves of cattle-herders, perhaps originating in the north and east [note: some sources claim the Tutsis are of Hamitic (east African/Ethiopian) origin, but Lemarchand rejects this conclusion], settle in the area of modern Burundi. Gradually, the "Tutsi" cattle-herders establish a feudal system over the "Hutu" cultivators. Hutus had arrived in the area several centuries before the Tutsis.

1550 (approximately): The unified kingdom of Burundi is formed.

1885: The Conference of Berlin awards Rwanda and Burundi to German East Africa.

For additional analytical, marketing, investment and business opportunities information, please contact
Global Investment & Business Center, USA
(202) 546-2103. Fax: (202) 546-3275. E-mail: rusric@erols.com

1916: Belgian forces easily displace the German administration in Burundi (then known as Ruanda-Urundi, an area which included Rwanda).

1921: The League of Nations awards Belgium a mandate over Rwanda and Burundi.

1929-1933: Seeking to impose greater administrative rationality, Belgian colonial authorities reorganize the system of chiefdoms, reducing their total number from 133 to 46. Significantly, Hutus lose almost all of their positions as local leaders, although Tutsi incumbents are also displaced. The greatest beneficiaries of this measure are the "Bezi," a regional/princely faction composed of both Hutus and Tutsis (the Bezi are rivals of another mixed Hutu-Tutsi regional/princely faction known as the "Batare").

1934: Amid poor economic conditions caused by the Great Depression, a typhus epidemic spreads through Burundi. Deteriorating economic and social conditions prompt a revolt by discontented Hutu peasants.

November 1959: A Hutu revolt in Rwanda causes a major refugee flow of Tutsis into Burundi, heightening ethnic tensions in Burundi.

January 1961: A Hutu coup d'etat occurs in Rwanda, the monarchy is abolished, and a Republic is established.

June 20, 1962: The UN General Assembly votes to accept the partition of Ruanda-Urundi into two independent states.

July 1, 1962: Burundi declares independence.

September 1962: Burundi joins the United Nations.

1963-1965: The Tutsi king (note: although the king was a Tutsi the royal court in Burundi, unlike in Rwanda, was not associated with Tutsi dominance) attempts to balance competing ethnic interests by dividing top government posts between Hutus and Tutsis.

May 1963: Burundi is a founding member of the Organization of African Unity (OAU).

January 1965: The first Hutu Prime Minister is assassinated by a Tutsi refugee from Rwanda.

For additional analytical, marketing, investment and business opportunities information, please contact
Global Investment & Business Center, USA
(202) 546-2103. Fax: (202) 546-3275. E-mail: rusric@erols.com

May 1965: A Hutu electoral victory in parliamentary elections is nullified when the king refuses to accept the Hutu Prime Minister-designate. Instead, the king appoints a Tutsi as Prime Minister.

October 1965: A failed coup attempt by Hutu members of the army and gendarmerie is staged. The royal palace is attacked. The coup is prompted by attempts to transfer powers from parliament to the (Tutsi) king after Hutus, for the first time, gained a majority in the legislature.

November 1965: The Tutsi monarch is overthrown and flees to Europe. A military-dominated (also meaning a Tutsi-dominated) republic is declared.

October-November 1965: Civil war follows a revolt by Hutu military units. In Muramvya province (near Rwanda) Hutu peasants kill about 500 Tutsi. Hutus burn Tutsi houses near the capital. Most Hutu members of the army and gendarmerie are killed, as are Hutu political leaders. Uncoordinated Hutu attacks are followed by organized Tutsi counter-strikes. The number of Hutu deaths is estimated at 5,000. By the end of 1965, a distinct Hutu political consciousness crystallizes in the face of their increasing exclusion from politics.

July 1966: (Tutsi) King Mwambutsa IV (reigned 1915-1966) is deposed by his son Charles Ndizeye, who becomes king Ntare III. The constitution is suspended.

November 1966: Tutsi army officers abolish the monarchy, thus depriving the country of a potentially stabilizing arbiter between competing ethnic factions.

After the second coup of 1966, all public references to ethnic identities are suppressed.

1968: Hutus are no longer eligible to receive scholarships to study abroad. An unusual 'girth by height' requirement is introduced in order to exclude Hutu recruits from the military.

1968-69: More executions of Hutu officers occur, with other Hutu leaders arrested. These measures bolster Tutsi control over army and political structures.

1971: A number of Tutsi-Abanyaruguru (a Tutsi sub-group) officials are arrested and charged with plotting to overthrow the government. In this period (1970-71) President Micombero (a Tutsi-Hima) attempts to purge Abanyaruguru from his government.

1972: Hutu insurgents attempt a coup and attack Tutsi civilians, leading to systematic massacres of Hutus by the Tutsi-dominated army (thus this violence was the result of an organized conspiracy against the state by Hutu militants).

For additional analytical, marketing, investment and business opportunities
information, please contact
Global Investment & Business Center, USA
(202) 546-2103. Fax: (202) 546-3275. E-mail: rusric@erols.com

The estimated number of deaths is 80,000 to 100,000 (this is a conservative figure). Educated Hutus are especially targeted in this genocide in order to incapacitate a future Hutu leadership cadre. The violence is particularly harsh in Bururi province (where Tutsi-Hima dominance is strong), hence most refugees flee to adjacent Tanzania.

As a result of the events of 1972, Belgium terminates its security cooperation pact with Burundi. However, during and after the killings France provides military assistance to the military.The government conducts no official inquiry into the events of 1972 nor are reconciliation measures implemented.

It appears that after the violence of 1972, a systematic effort is made to recruit only Tutsis into the officer and enlisted ranks of the military. Previously, most officers were Tutsis while the enlisted ranks were filled mostly by Hutus.

1976: Army units led by General Bagaza stage a bloodless coup and overthrow President Micombero. The sole political party is abolished. A Supreme Revolutionary Council under military control is established to rule the country.

1977: President Bagaza initiates land reforms ending the system of Tutsi feudal landlords.

1980s: President Bagaza launches a vigorous drive against the Catholic Church. This anti-Catholic campaign is seen as an effort to undermine Hutus, who despite widespread discrimination maintain significant influence in Church affairs. The Church also serves as a counterweight and potential rival of the government by educating and providing medical treatment to poor Hutus, which the minority government apparently views as a threat.

1987: France and Burundi announce that they will continue their military training agreement.

September 1987: Bagaza is overthrown by Major Pierre Buyoya. The civilian constitution of 1981 is abrogated and a 31 member Military Committee for National Salvation is formed to rule the country.

1988: As a result of disorganized rural violence by politically and socially discontented Hutus against local Tutsi officials, notables, and civilians in the northern Ntega and Marangara communes, the Tutsi-dominated army conducts unpremeditated massacres of Hutus. Deaths are estimated to be between 5,000 and 20,000, or as high as 50,000.

For additional analytical, marketing, investment and business opportunities
information, please contact
Global Investment & Business Center, USA
(202) 546-2103. Fax: (202) 546-3275. E-mail: rusric@erols.com

In 1988, Burundi is in the midst of an effort sponsored by the World Bank to move away from a subsistence economy by boosting private investment and diversifying exports.

After the 1988 massacres, the following reform measures are implemented by Buyoya: an equal number of cabinet positions go to Hutus and Tutsis; more Hutus are recruited into the civil service; a Hutu Prime Minister is named; a national commission to study ethnic violence (described as a commission on "national unity", the euphemism for problems of ethnicity) is established with an equal number of Hutus and Tutsis; anti-Catholic Church policies are repealed; ethnic Hutu soldiers are assigned to the president's personal guard.

Buyoya's reform measures, although limited and cautious, raise the ire of Tutsi hardliners even as they increase Hutu expectations to new heights. However, as during previous reform efforts, local Tutsi administrators continue repressive measures against Hutus.

After the 1988 massacres, Hutu militants are put on trial but Army officers who may have exceeded their authority are not similarly charged. At an aid conference in 1988, the Government of Burundi raised 100 million more in aid than it had requested.

August 1988: The European Community calls on Burundi to allow international observers to investigate ethnic clashes. Canada calls for an independent investigation of Burundi's ethnic violence. The Canadian foreign minister says his diplomats will meet with Burundian officials as well as representatives of the Hutu tribe to discuss the situation.

A US State Department spokesperson states that it appears that the army of Burundi is not responsible for initiating the latest cycle of killings.

October 1988: The US State Department departs from its previous statements blaming both sides for killing civilians, and specifically charges the army with initiating large scale killings. The US House of Representatives votes 415-0 for a non-binding resolution which condemns ethnic violence in Burundi and urges the government to step up efforts at achieving national reconciliation. After the US Congress and State Department exert considerable pressure, President Buyoya acknowledges that an investigation of Burundi's ethnic situation is needed.

1989: In a policy opposed by World Bank advisors (who are pushing for austerity measures including reductions in government expenditures), Buyoya recruits more Hutus into the civil service.

For additional analytical, marketing, investment and business opportunities information, please contact
Global Investment & Business Center, USA
(202) 546-2103. Fax: (202) 546-3275. E-mail: rusric@erols.com

May 1989: President Buyoya pledges to give Hutus more influence in governing Burundi, but rejects Hutu domination based on their numerical strength.

1990: A report by the Population Crisis Committee (Washington, DC) on the challenge to democracy caused by population growth, cites Burundi as one of the most unstable countries in the world due to its population problems.

A National Security Council is formed to oversee operations of the security forces, and as a gesture of reconciliation President Buyoya appoints an equal number of Hutus and Tutsis to this body.

February 1991: A "National Unity Charter" is endorsed by 89.1% of voters. The Charter calls for ending military rule, restoring the constitution, and ensuring harmony between Hutu and Tutsi.

May 16, 1991: A National Unity Code is issued which pledges equal rights for Hutus, Tutsis, and Twas and condemns political violence. The Code is prepared by a committee of national reconciliation composed of politicians, church figures, and ordinary citizens.

August 1991: Small-scale incursions are carried out by Hutu exiles operating from Tanzania.

Burundi accuses the Rwandan press of orchestrating a propaganda campaign against the country.

October 1991: The State Security Court (for cases of threats to internal and external security, insurrection, treason, and espionage) is abolished and replaced with a common-law court. Military offenses are to be dealt with under military courts.

November 1991: The radical Party for the Liberation of the Hutu People (Palipehutu), which was founded in the 1980s, launches attacks in northern towns in the hope of provoking a general Hutu uprising (300 Tutsi civilians are left dead and 1,000 Hutus are killed by the army).

In a joint statement Burundi's two human rights leagues condemn violence, but apparently make no mention of ethnic groups and utilize the government rhetoric by appealing for "national unity."

December 1991: Burundi accuses Rwanda of supporting the Palipehutu rebels.

1992: A government minister claims that the security situation has improved because people (probably meaning Hutus) were no longer fleeing abroad for

For additional analytical, marketing, investment and business opportunities
information, please contact
Global Investment & Business Center, USA
(202) 546-2103. Fax: (202) 546-3275. E-mail: rusric@erols.com

protection during ethnic violence, but were placing themselves under the protection of the security services.

February 1992: A decree on the press is promulgated calling for a pluralistic media operating under the framework of democracy. A new National Council for Communications is established to oversee the new system of press freedom, but objective information flow continues to be hampered by lack of resources and political intimidation.

A new constitution is adopted which vests executive power in a directly-elected president who serves for 5 years. The official political monopoly enjoyed by UPRONA for 26 years is ended. Ethnically-based political movements are banned under this constitution, hence parties must pledge support for the concept of "national unity," recruit membership from every province, and reflect the ethnic diversity of Burundi. With the new constitution in place, the framework for elections is set, and they are held the following year.

April 1992: Palipehutu rebels invade Cibitoke province from their sanctuaries in Rwanda. In response, the government initiates a large-scale anti-rebel offensive. Small-scale incursions have also been made into Burundi by Hutu exiles operating out of Tanzania.

A government minister claims that rebels are receiving arms, training, and safehaven from Rwanda. The BBC reports on government claims that "sophisticated guns and grenades were seized" from rebel forces operating in Cibitoke province.

The government establishes a human rights center under the Ministry of Justice with responsibility for educating Burundians regarding their rights and responsibilities in the area of human rights.

May 1992: The government puts down a coup attempt by rebellious soldiers.

February 19, 1993: At the OAU meeting in Addis Ababa, Burundian ministers in Addis Ababa seek agreement on the deployment of an OAU force in their country for the protection of government officials.

June 1, 1993: Democratic elections are held in which a Hutu, Melchoir Ndadaye, wins the presidency with 71 percent of the vote, mostly from Hutus. Thus the ruling Tutsi elite are clearly rejected by the electorate (the Tutsi dominated UPRONA loses to the Front for Democracy in Burundi - FRODEBU)

For additional analytical, marketing, investment and business opportunities information, please contact
Global Investment & Business Center, USA
(202) 546-2103. Fax: (202) 546-3275. E-mail: rusric@erols.com

In the weeks following his victory, Ndadaye seeks to transforms the country's political structures by naming a female Tutsi Prime Minister and opening the government to all groups. Nine out of 23 cabinet seats are held by Tutsis.

June 3, 1993: Rwandan (Hutu) president Habayarimana salutes (Hutu) Ndadaye after his victory in the presidential election.

June 4, 1993: Tutsi students and civil servants demonstrate in Bujumura, the capital, to protest the "ethnic sentiments" of the vote.

June 18, 1993: President Ndadaye's FRODEBU sweeps legislative elections winning 65 of 81 seats in parliament.

July 1993: A coup is attempted by supporters of the former (Tutsi) president from the Second Commando Battalion.

October 21, 1993 and after: Disaffected military forces revolt, resulting in the death of President Ndadaye (a Hutu). Clashes between Hutus and Tutsi, including Tutsi-dominated military units, begin.

After massacres occur, the UN refuses to send peacekeepers to Burundi. In the Security Council, the US argues against such a mission, fearing it will be an open-ended commitment with no definite plan for withdrawal.

Three waves of killings are reported: Tutsi soldiers against Hutu civilians, Hutus against Tutsi, and Tutsi against Hutus. Both Hutus and Tutsi's engage in the massacre of innocent civilians with an estimated number of deaths of 150,000 plus an additional 800,000 to one million refugees fleeing into Rwanda, Tanzania, Zaire. 100,000 are internally displaced. The coup receives widespread condemnation and quickly collapses. Loyal military officers urge civilians to resume control. A period of extreme unease with isolated killings prevails.

The coup attempt is strongly condemned by the UN, OAU, and EC, which threatened sanctions. The CEPGL (a regional economic cooperation union) also endorses dispatching a multi-national force of African troops to help restore order in Burundi.

October 22, 1993: Ugandan President Museveni blames foreign pressure for bringing about the coup in Burundi.

October 28, 1993: France offers military advisors to the Burundi government to help set up a new security system.

For additional analytical, marketing, investment and business opportunities information, please contact
Global Investment & Business Center, USA
(202) 546-2103. Fax: (202) 546-3275. E-mail: rusric@erols.com

November 1, 1993: Burundi asks for 1,000 OAU troops as a protection force. Later in the month the OAU dispatches a small force to Burundi to protect the government and the UN sends a fact finding mission to clarify the events surrounding the coup.

The Burundi army displays its political clout and challenges the government's call for a foreign military force, denouncing it as external intervention in Burundi affairs. The Tutsi Prime Minister, Kinigi, says that the government does not control the security forces.

November 16, 1993: Following ethnic clashes, UN envoys report that Tutsi ministers, not fearing the army, have returned home while Hutu ministers have remained in hiding.

November 20, 1993: The British charity Actionaid warns of a Bosnia or Somalia like tragedy in Burundi.

Communications Minister Ngedahayo says that the proposed OAU force of 180 troops is too small for their mission of protecting government officials.

November 27, 1993: Belgium decides to provide logistical support to the OAU forces planned for Burundi.

December 1993: An OAU summit decides to send a protection force to Burundi.

Agence France Presse reports that 700,000 Burundian are refugees in Rwanda, Tanzania, and Zaire (500,000 in Tanzania).

January 1994: The Catholic Church, often divided along ethnic lines during violence, brokers a constitutional settlement between competing factions. After prolonged negotiations the Hutu dominated FRODEBU (Front for Democracy in Burundi, legalized in 1992) and the Tutsi dominated UPRONA (Party for Unity and Progress in Burundi, the former ruling group) agree to share power. Under the accord, Hutu Cyprien Ntaryamira becomes President, but substantial concessions are made for UPRONA representation at the highest levels of government.

OAU General Secretary Salim arrives in Burundi to convince Tutsi leaders to accept an OAU protection force for government ministers. Meanwhile, security forces, allegedly sympathetic to protesters, do not clear barricades erected by opposition forces in the capital to protest possible foreign intervention in Burundi.

For additional analytical, marketing, investment and business opportunities information, please contact
Global Investment & Business Center, USA
(202) 546-2103. Fax: (202) 546-3275. E-mail: rusric@erols.com

January 25, 1994: The government backs away from supporting an OAU intervention force, reportedly in response to strong protests by the army and opposition groups.

March 1994: The army chief refuses to furnish an ethnic breakdown of his troops and claims that in ongoing communal clashes the military remains neutral.

Press stories claim that Rwandan Tutsi refugees are assisting the Burundi army (composed of Tutsis) to commit killings in the capital.

March 8, 1994: Amnesty International urges Burundi to set up a commission of inquiry into mass killings.

March 24, 1994: (Hutu) President Ntaryamira accuses the army of stirring up trouble with Hutu elements. The army reportedly protests the government's decision to punish officers involved in violence against Hutus.

March 30, 1994: The government fails to support a call by Interior and Public Security Minister Leonard Nyangoma (probably a Hutu) for an international peacekeeping force for the country.

April 1994: Presidents Ntaryamira of Burundi and Habyarimana of Rwanda (both Hutus) are killed when the airplane they are aboard is shot down by a rocket near Kigali, capital of Rwanda. While genocide sweeps through Rwanda, smaller-scale and sporadic violence occurs in Burundi.

Following the assassination of President Ntaryamira, media reports cite the existence of an apparently newly formed Hutu "Armee Populaire" (People's Army) operating in the Kamenge region north of the capital. In many cases, the sinister strategy of Hutu extremists is to target Tutsi civilians with the knowledge that the Tutsi security forces will respond with massive attacks on Hutu civilians, thus provoking a cycle of violence.

Hutu and Tutsi extremists each circulate tracts in the capital urging rejection of any compromise with the other side.

May 1, 1994: 10,000 persons are arrested in a massive operation to confiscate illegal arms in the Kamenge region. The government claims the measure is aimed at checking tribal violence. News services do not report on the ethnicity of those arrested, although the area is a Hutu stronghold.

September 1994: Following a lengthy series of talks begun after the assassination of the president in October 1993, an agreement is

For additional analytical, marketing, investment and business opportunities information, please contact
Global Investment & Business Center, USA
(202) 546-2103. Fax: (202) 546-3275. E-mail: rusric@erols.com

reached on the appointment of Hutu Sylvestre Ntibantuganya as the new president. In parliament, FRODEBU (majority Hutu) controls 65 out of a total of 85 seats, while UPRONA (majority Tutsi) has 16 delegates. This distribution of deputies reflects the results of July 1993 parliamentary elections in which the FRODEBU won 80 percent of the vote.

1995: Throughout the year, an extremely chaotic security situation prevails amid a low intensity ethnic war between Hutu rebels and the Tutsi-dominated army and security units. News services report individual killings and assassinations of government officials at the local, provincial, and national levels. Small scale massacres of up to 400 (including women and children) also occur routinely (Hutus and Tutsis are both perpetrators and victims of such killings, but the Hutus seem to be the victims more often than are Tutsis). Hutu exiles from Rwanda (veteran perpetrators of the 1994 genocide) operate alongside Burundi's Hutu rebels. Tutsi militias and military forces also engage in killings of Hutu civilians, sometimes separately and perhaps in concert.

June 27, 1995: The EU calls for the convocation of a peace conference on Burundi under the auspices of the UN and OAU.

July 11, 1995: UPRONOA, Burundi's chief Tutsi opposition political force, states that it will not participate in peace talks aimed at ending the country's communal warfare.

July 17, 1995: UN General Secretary Boutros Ghali announces that the UN will conduct an inquiry into the violence in Burundi.

August 1995: A high ranking Hutu politician alleges that Tutsi extremists are instituting a coordinated plan to assassinate Hutu officials at the provincial and local levels.

October 27, 1995: President Ntibantunhanya of Burundi asks former US President Jimmy Carter to convene a peace conference on his country as soon as possible.

November 21, 1995: Jimmy Carter states that he has received the support of the government of Burundi for a draft agenda for a summit meeting on ethnic conflict in Rwanda and Burundi.

December 1995: A report by the medical charity Doctors Without Frontiers states that hundreds of people are dying each month in ethnic clashes, with women and children constituting forty percent of the casualties. In addition to random acts of violence, there is some evidence of a more systematic pattern of murders.

For additional analytical, marketing, investment and business opportunities information, please contact
Global Investment & Business Center, USA
(202) 546-2103. Fax: (202) 546-3275. E-mail: rusric@erols.com

Late 1995: Only one suburb of the capital remains ethnically mixed.

February 22, 1996: The OAU's Committee for Conflict Prevention, Management and Resolution releases a statement crediting international pressure with preventing a total collapse in Burundi.

May 1996: The UN notes that the security situation in Burundi is deteriorating, while the US State Department declares that the violence in Burundi constitutes genocide.

In a controversial statement, US Ambassador to Burundi Robert Krueger estimates that 2,500 people are dying per month in the violence.

June 11, 1996: Tanzania's President Julius Nyerere, mediating between rival Burundi ethnic factions, calls on the country's Tutsi minority to make political concessions to Hutus.

July 10, 1996: An OAU summit meeting endorses dispatching a peacekeeping force to Burundi composed of troops from neighboring states. The initiative is somewhat unusual for the degree of consensus found in the OAU, which in previous years strongly opposed intervention in the internal affairs of member states.

July 25, 1996: The military, on the pretext of stabilizing the security situation, carries out a coup d'etat against Ntibantunganya. Burundi's former military ruler, Buyoya, again takes power.

The coup is met with a mixed international reaction: both Belgium and the US negotiate with the coup leaders, but by the end of the month economic sanctions are imposed on Burundi by other African countries.

July-August 1996: In follow-up operations after the military coup, government troops kill some 6,000 Hutus according to Amnesty International.

9 September 1996: Burundi's Archbishop Joachim Ruhuna, a Tutsi, and several others were killed in an ambush. The government and CNDD (National Council for the Defense of Democracy), an armed Hutu group, blamed each other for the attack. Ruhuna had condemned all violence in the country.

23 September 1996: Lt. Col. Longin Minani, spokesman for the army, said sanctions were hurting the weak and the country would soon explode if they were not lifted. The embargo was imposed by states in the region and cut off oil imports and blocked coffee exports.

For additional analytical, marketing, investment and business opportunities
information, please contact
Global Investment & Business Center, USA
(202) 546-2103. Fax: (202) 546-3275. E-mail: rusric@erols.com

FRODEBU Secretary General Augustin Nzojibwami said that the party was committed to peaceful resolution of the conflict in Burundi. FRODEBU split after the July coup. One faction elected rebel leader Leonard Nyangoma as its president and endorsed armed struggle against the government. The other faction, led by Nozojibwami, backed exiled party president Jean Minani and is committed to peaceful resolution of the conflict.

1 October 1996: The FDD(Forces for the Defence of Democracy)/CNDD said it would only talk about a cease-fire if the rule of law and democracy were first restored in Burundi. Large areas of the country are no-go areas plagued by violence.

10 October 1996: President Buyoya held talks with international mediator Julius Nyerere in northern Tanzania. He had agreed to restore the national assembly and lifted a ban on political parties last month.

12 October 1996: African leaders agreed to maintain their economic embargo against Burundi despite suggestions from the United States that sanctions should be eased. They had received a letter from President Buyoya which stated that he was committed to unconditional negotiations with the CNDD and other armed Hutu groups.

30 January 1997: President Buyoya promised to investigate reports by the United Nations that the army killed 1000 civilians in November-December 1996. Increased violence in Burundi in recent months was accompanied by an army policy to forcefully relocate Hutu peasants and an increased use of mines in the conflict. Another report said 3000 had been killed in the November-December 1996 period.

21 February 1997: At least 1700 Burundians refugees left a camp in southwest Rwanda and returned to Burundi's Cibitoke province, considered the most dangerous province in the country. The UNHCR maintains a policy of not helping to repatriate Burundian refugees because civilians are frequently massacred.

April 1997: Regional governments eased sanctions against Burundi and invited President Buyoya to their regional summit in Arusha.

May 1997: Fighting has been intense around Rutana in recent days. An attack on a school in early May resulted in the deaths of 36 students. At least 20 villagers were killed and 15 kidnaped in another attack on Rutana by Hutu rebels.

17 May 1997: It was revealed that the government and CNDD had been meeting secretly in Rome over the past months under the auspices of Sant Egidio Community, a Catholic Peace group. They agreed to work to restore peace

For additional analytical, marketing, investment and business opportunities
information, please contact
Global Investment & Business Center, USA
(202) 546-2103. Fax: (202) 546-3275. E-mail: rusric@erols.com

- 33 -

through direct talks with a seven point agenda. An accord signed in Rome in March included agreement on the seven points: restoration of constitutional and institutional order; issued relating to the armed forces and police; a suspension of hostilities; justice, including the creation of an international tribunal to judge acts of genocide and political crimes; identification and involvement of other parties in the peace process; a cease-fire; and guarantees of how the overall accord should be carried out and respected.

23 May 1997: The CNDD turned down the invitation to a peace conference in Geneva in June. It said it was already in talks with the government and did not believe UNESCO was the right negotiator for the conflict.

27 May 1997: A wing of FRODEBU, led by Jean Minani who is based in Tanzania, threatened to resort to force to restore constitutional rule to Burundi. FRODEBU's other wing led by Leonard Nyangoma is fighting the Tutsi-dominated army in Burundi.

The UNHCR reported the massacre of 60 people, mostly returning refugees, in northwest Cibitoke province on May 18. Burundi's military continues to forcibly relocate tens of thousands of Hutus.

1 June 1997: Burundi called for a total lifting of sanctions against it. External Affairs and Cooperation Minister Luc Rukingama said the sanctions were hurting civilians and hindering peace negotiations.

7 June 1997: Deposed President Slyvestre Ntibantunganya came out of hiding. His appearance is likely to rekindle the struggle within the FRODEBU leadership which split following his overthrow.

14 June 1997: The governor of Cibitoke Province has said that the security situation in the province had greatly improved in some communes. There have been arrests of Interahamwe militiamen in the region, but Mabayi, Murwi, and Buganda communes remained rebel strongholds.

17 July 1997: The United Nations Security Council discusses establishing an international criminal tribunal for Burundi. It would be responsible for judging crimes of genocide and political assassinations carried out since the country gained independence.

28 July 1997: Burundian parties agreed to peace talks to be chaired by Julius Nyerere and to take place in mid-August. However, the talks never got under way because of the refusal of the Burundian government to participate after rising tensions between Burundi and Tanzania.

For additional analytical, marketing, investment and business opportunities information, please contact
Global Investment & Business Center, USA
(202) 546-2103. Fax: (202) 546-3275. E-mail: rusric@erols.com

28 August 1997: Tanzanian soldiers killed 20 Burundian government troops who planted land mines along the border. There was no independent confirmation of the report from either country. Last week, Burundi accused Tanzania of harboring Hutu rebels among the 300,000 refugees in the country. Tanzania accused Burundi of crossing into its territory in pursuit of rebels. Tensions between the two countries have risen since Tanzania put pressure on regional government to continue economic sanctions against Burundi. This led to Buyoya to refuse to participate in peace talks with rebel groups this month.

20 September 1997: Authorities arrested UPRONA party leader Charles Mukasi as he held a press conference. UPRONA opposes negotiations between the government and rebel groups.

6 October 1997: The government announced it had freed more than 3000 people taken hostage by armed gangs in Cibitoke Province. The armed men withdrew towards the hills bordering on Buganda.

22 November 1997: FROLINA spokesman Venerand Ndegeya announced that its armed wing, the People's Liberation Army, had resumed its armed struggle against the government. FROLINA had been observing an 18 month unilateral cease-fire in order to allow international mediation to work. The group claimed to have the localities of Mukereyi, Gisenga, Kabonga, Gihoro, Nyabigina, Gasaba, and Mugina under its control.

8 December 1997: The Burundian army captured a number of Ugandan mercenaries fighting alongside rebels in Cibitoke and Gitega provinces.

6 December 1997: A dispute between FRODEBU and the government began when the party reappointed to its leadership persons not currently residing in the country. Party leader Jean Minani lives in Dar es Salaam where he is illegally occupying the Burundian embassy. Burundi's law governing political parties states that party leaders must reside in Burundi. The government suspended the party for 10 months, and the case has been referred to the Supreme Court.

12 January 1998: The government denied accusations that it carried out a massacre at Rukaramu on 1 January 1998. At least 280 people, Hutus, were killed. Most people were killed by blows from machetes or hoes, not by bullets, supporting the government claim that the rebels were the perpetrators. The CNDD has called for an international inquiry into the massacre, but the Burundi Human Rights League has blamed the CNDD for the killings.

20 January 1998: Rebel attacks have intensified since the beginning of the year around the capital Bujumbura. At lease 82 rebels and 7 soldiers were killed in clashes last week. Rebels hold no territory nor have they captured any strategic

For additional analytical, marketing, investment and business opportunities
information, please contact
Global Investment & Business Center, USA
(202) 546-2103. Fax: (202) 546-3275. E-mail: rusric@erols.com

points in the country despite operating in an environment with most of the population sympathetic to their cause.

27 February 1998: Over two hundred seventy Burundian refugees left Tanzania for Burundi following an agreement between the two governments and the UNHCR. Over 180 returned to their homes in January.

18 March 1998: Army spokesman Lt-Col. Isaie Nibizi told the press that arms, including land mines, belonging to the CNDD had been seized by Zambian police in Lusaka.

30 March 1998: The government lifted a travel ban against the President of the National Assembly, Leonce Ngendakumana, after dropping charges of genocide against him.

28 April 1998: The International Crisis Group released the report A Burundi Under Siege. Among its findings:

-Since the 1996 coup, there has been a radicalization of some elements of the army and Tutsi community who fear pressure from the region may force the government to make concession compromising the security of the Tutsi minority;

-The government=s political base has fragmented with deep divisions within UPRONA. Those who oppose negotiations with rebels are led by Charles Mukasi;

-The military presently has about 60,000 men and its equipment is sophisticated;

-About 350,000 people were in armed camps during 1997. The government decided to let some people back into their villages in late 1997, but many farmers found their land had been occupied in their absence, so most returned to the camps or fled to Bujumbura;

-The civil war in Zaire forced rebel groups based there to flee and move their bases to Tanzania. The rebels are reportedly becoming less popular with the general population since being cut off from their supplies and using pressure tactics on civilians in order to maintain their positions. Armed groups are becoming more violent and uncontrolled;

-There are divisions within FRODEBU and the CNDD, and between FRODEBU and CNDD and between CNDD, Palipehutu and FROLINA;

-Collaboration between rebel groups in the Great Lakes region appears to be on the rise. Rebel groups cooperating include Burundian groups ex-FAR,

For additional analytical, marketing, investment and business opportunities information, please contact
Global Investment & Business Center, USA
(202) 546-2103. Fax: (202) 546-3275. E-mail: rusric@erols.com

Interahamwe, Mobutu's ex-special presidential division, Mai-Mai warriors of Kivu, and Ugandan rebels.

15 May 1998: Army spokesman Isaie Nibizi said the security situation throughout Burundi had improved markedly due to dwindling arms supplies and internal disputes within rebel groups. A rift within the CNDD emerged last week when a group of top CNDD officials announced they had toppled chairman Leonard Nyagoma who they accused of corruption and dictatorship for sacking a number of top CNDD members in November. A split was also reported in FRODEBU. A group in Burundi led by Leonce Ngendakumana reportedly favors negotiations with the government while the wing led by Minani in exile opposes negotiations.

Fighting between the CNDD and Palipehutu has continued over the past several months in Cibitoke and Buyanza provinces.

21 June 1998: The Arusha peace talks got underway 15 June. These are the first all-party peace talks since the 1996 military coup, and include the five main political parties, three rebel groups, civic and religious organizations, and outside mediators.

At the end of the first session, all groups attending had agreed to a cease-fire to begin by 21 July 1998 when the second round of peace talks are to begin. An agenda for the next round was also agreed to.

In mid-June, Buyoya named a 22 member cabinet, including 12 Hutus, in the hopes that the new political arrangement would convince regional leaders to lift economic sanctions.

The external peace process is running parallel to an internal peace dialogue between Buyoya and the parliament. A transition constitution was agreed to 6 June 1998 and provides for an enlarged parliament (121 MPs) and two vice presidents while reducing the overall size of the government.

26 June 1998: The FDD rejected the Arusha-agreed cease-fire by July 20th as unrealistic. The FDD and CNDD are at odds over participation in the Arusha peace talks. The FDD is at the talks as an unofficial delegations without the right to sign any agreements. While Buyoya's delegation signed the cease-fire agreement, it also added a caveat effectively exempting the army from any cease-fire.

1999 began with feelings of optimism for Burundi. On 23 January, the political leaders of the Great Lakes region unanimously suspended the economic sanctions imposed on Burundi in July 1996, and the foreign affairs ministers of Burundi and Tanzania took the initiative to revive the tripartite mechanism

For additional analytical, marketing, investment and business opportunities information, please contact
Global Investment & Business Center, USA
(202) 546-2103. Fax: (202) 546-3275. E-mail: rusric@erols.com

(UNHCR-Burundi-Tanzania) on the issue of repatriation. Meanwhile, the external peace process in Arusha witnessed a number of positive developments when the 18 parties involved regrouped into 3 factions and different proposals for future transition were tabled. However, this positive climate was dampened when the tripartite meeting, announced for March 1999, was unilaterally postponed sine die by the Tanzanian Government.

A series of rebel attacks in the eastern province of Ruyigi in April 1999 seriously hindered repatriation operations in an area that had been calm for two years. Additionally, an increased violence in the outskirts of Bujumbura, which since July 1999 has claimed many civilian lives, plus the issue of the possible inclusion of rebel leader Jean-Bosco Ndayikengurukiye in Arusha have combined to slow down the talks. NGOs and UN agencies now fear that the political process in Arusha has absorbed the humanitarian debate.

Overall, repatriation figures remain below expectations. In this context, UNHCR believes that major repatriation movements will only occur after the implementation of a peace agreement. On a positive note, a meeting between the Tanzanian and Burundi defense ministers in August concerning the issue of border security indicates a better degree of collaboration between the two countries.

The majority of Congolese refugees who fled the DRC in 1998 and came to Burundi have now returned home, but the conflict is still an important factor in the continued instability of the region.

PRE-COLONIAL PERIOD

Without going into theories of occupation of the present Burundi territory through various migrations, the most spread of which is that the "Batwa" were the first to arrive,then the " Bahutu " ,and finally the "Batutsi "who infiltrated the country and astutely usurped power, we may say that the present territory of Burundi is occupied, since the 16th Century, by a population assimilated to the current human groups.

Initially organized in familial and clanic groupings,the social evolution has given birth to principalities using the names of various chiefs of lineages . With King Ntare Rushatsi,an attempt was made to regroup peoples around a central power of feudal type, and the said power was concentrated in an hereditary dynasty.In the long run, the power came to rotate between four main historic dynasties,each of them being vested with symbolic missions. Ntare was the warrior King who worked hard to expand the territory, Mwezi was the Sovereign of stability inside

For additional analytical, marketing, investment and business opportunities
information, please contact
Global Investment & Business Center, USA
(202) 546-2103. Fax: (202) 546-3275. E-mail: rusric@erols.com

the territory, the mission of Mutaga was to bring prosperity,while mwambutsa has been the Sovereign of a transition to a new era.

All historians who have carried out a research give the following chronology :

Name	Deceased	Reign
Ntare Rushatsi	No data	around the 16th century
Ntare Ruyenzi	around 1850	between 1800 - 1850
Mwezi Gisabo	21.08.1908	between 1850 - 1908
Mutaga Mbikije	30.11.1915	end of 1908 - 30.11.1915
Mwambutsa Bangiricenge	26.04.1977	16.12.1915 - 05.07.1966
Ntare Ndizeye	29.04.1972	01.09.1966 - 28.11.1966

With the historic evolution ,a blind magico-religious belief became the mark of the royal power, making the king Father of the Nation. The princely aristocracy in power edified a mystic of power whereby the " Baganwa " constitute a super-class of people who are neither " Batutsi",nor " Bahutu ".The power, symbolically concentrated in the king, is structured on this special class. Within the same logic begins a stratification of different clans and lineages of " hutu " and "tutsi" in order to establish the distinction between the very good, good, ordinary and people of bad luck.

This is how, for example, within the tutsi ethnic group the distinction between the "Banyaruguru" and the "Bahima" is so pronounced that the "Bahima " were despised by everybody to such an extent that they were not allowed to milk others' cows. This logic of identification induces superiority or inferiority complexes useful for the mechanisms of power, but which are inevitably time bombs.

Within the realism of politico-religious power, one can find a princely aristocracy (the Baganwa) and an elite composed of "bahutu " and "batutsi" from lineages considered as prestigious. In its stratification, that pre-colonial society experienced a web of statutory or individual antagonisms of ethnic, clanic, lineal and territorial type. In reaction to that potentiality for diffuse violence, it was brought about a strategy of power and survival devised on the basis of a network of links of reciprocity and clientelism, the most known of which are " ubugabire-bondage contract born of a donation of a cow "and "ubugererwa-bondage contract born of a domanial exploitation".

For additional analytical, marketing, investment and business opportunities information, please contact
Global Investment & Business Center, USA
(202) 546-2103. Fax: (202) 546-3275. E-mail: rusric@erols.com

The pacts of blood and the formulas of redemption are part of the same logic.Those links were particularly useful in the different fights for power.This created solidarity at the time of rebellions, dynastic quarrels, frontier wars with the neighboring kingdoms of North, West and East. Burundians were a people in arms. That latent violence ended up in a cultural integration leading to the logic of being suspicious of others or of any stranger. Many dictums and proverbs also induced constant vigilance in people so as not to be surprised by the enemy. Some of them invited hutu to beware of Tutsi and vice versa, even if no great confrontation of an ethnic character was recorded during the pre-colonial period. Nevertheless, it remains true that whole lineages could be subjected to persecutions similar to a real cleansing.

The case of "Abasapfu"and "Abavubikiro" has become a legendary example. According to historian André GUICHAOUA,"the practice of eliminating the enemy, quite common in certain wars opposing kingdoms, is confirmed on several occasions by dynastic quarrels, but in a particular totalitarian form: this time it is the family and lineal group extended to the neighbouring relatives which is targetted in the name of a conception derived from the preeminence of "collective I "over the individual, a conception according to which the culpability of an individual is paid by the group which must disappear.

Such a practice is confirmed by certain etiologic stories or names of certain lineages close to high political circles and the court: the lineage of Abasapfu, condemned by the King, was saved from extinction because one of its members miraculously escaped the massacre... More recently in 1915,it is the extermination of Abavubikiro, a princely lineage, following the accusation by the soothsayers and mother-queen of a Muvubikiro chief from the North that he had poisoned King Mutaga Mbikije; finally, by extension, other lineages have been collectively subjected to such royal condemnations which have provoked their exclusion or their statutory degradation (André Guichaoua, The political crisis in Burundi and Rwanda 1993-1994,pge 65).

The remedy for this system of violence in bundle seemed to be the work of an institution of "Abashingantahe Council of wisemen " vested with a check and balance power born of discussions at the public place, whereby the truth was to be deducted from contradictory statements of facts and a consensus re-establishing social harmony.

The pre-colonial history presents to us a unitarian Burundi Nation, having the same culture, the same religious believes and the same language. The whole country was ruled by a sovereign- " Mwami" (king) incarnating the law and customs, exercising a power of life and death over his subjects.
However, that apparent organization had internal weaknesses which became

For additional analytical, marketing, investment and business opportunities information, please contact
Global Investment & Business Center, USA
(202) 546-2103. Fax: (202) 546-3275. E-mail: rusric@erols.com

time bombs as the society learned another logic resulting from the contact with the Arab and Western worlds.

THE COLONIAL PERIOD

1899 Burundi and its neighbour, Rwanda, were incorporated into German East Africa.

After the Second World War both countries were transferred from Germany to Belgium under the joint name of Ruanda-Urundi; they then became independent separately.

The Tutsis, although comprising only 14 per cent of the population, dominated through their control of the army and the fact that the royal family and surrounding princes were Tutsis. Tutsis and Hutus (85 per cent of the population) intermarried.

1961 Prince Rwagasore, the unifying pre-independence figure, was killed.
1962 Burundi received independence from Belgium as a kingdom.

1965 Tutsi-Hutu coalitions ruled, but a Hutu prime minister was killed and replaced by a Tutsi prince. The Hutus attemped a coup and failed. Instead, the Tutsis massacred the Hutu elite.

1966 After the king was deposed by his son, who was deposed by the army, Burundi was declared a republic.

1972 After another abortive coup attempt, between 200,000 and 400,000 Hutus were killed.

1976-87 The government of Tutsi Colonel Jean-Baptiste Bagaza was notorious for its violations of human rights.

1992 The constitution was adopted by referendum on 9 March.

1993 Tutsi Major Pierre Buyoya ousted Bagaza and permitted Burundi's first multi-party election. The victor was Melchior Ndadaye who was committed to reforming the Tutsi-dominated army. Ndadaye was assassinated. Civil war began in October between the Tutsi-led army and Hutu rebels.

1994 Cyprien Ntaryamira, a Hutu, was elected president by the National Assembly. He was killed in a plane crash on 6 April, together with the Hutu President of Rwanda. Sylvestre Ntibantuganya, a Hutu, took over the presidency.

For additional analytical, marketing, investment and business opportunities information, please contact
Global Investment & Business Center, USA
(202) 546-2103. Fax: (202) 546-3275. E-mail: rusric@erols.com

1995 A coalition government was formed under Antoine Nduwayu, a Tutsi.

1996 Major Pierre Buyoya seized power in a coup on 25 July.

1997 President Buyoya banned political parties and dissolved the National Assembly.

1999 Regional sanctions were suspended in January. By December it was estimated that more than 250,000 Burundians had been killed in the ethnic conflict.

2000 President Pierre Buyoya and 13 political parties signed a peace deal on 28 August. An ethnically balanced government is to be put in place as a preliminary to a three-year transition to full democracy.

2001 An attempted coup in April failed

THE GERMAN OCCUPATION

At the time of Berlin Conference 1884-1885 on the division of Africa, Burundi was granted to Germany and was part of the German East Africa (the Deutsche-Ost-Afrika), together with Rwanda and Tanganyika. Burundi was officially recognized as "German Protectorate of East Africa " in 1890. There were many punitive expeditions conducted by German Officers in order to subjugate this small kingdom of Burundi which had resisted against Arab slavery. King Mwezi Gisabo tried but in vain to resist against the German occupation until his surrender which ended up with the Kiganda Treaty of June 1903. This Treaty was about the free passage of caravans, the recognition of Bujumbura military base, the promise to open up the Bujumbura - Muyaga road (West- East).

The Germans promised to King Mwezi Gisabo a support and recognized him as King of Burundi in 1905. The King died in 1908. Mutaga IV succeeded to him. He died in 1915,leaving the throne to his 3 years old son Bangiricenge who reigned until 1966 using the name of Mwambutsa IV.

THE BELGIAN MANDATE AND TRUSTEESHIP

After the first World War, Germany lost all its colonies and protectorates. Burundi became an " Occupation Territory " placed under the Administration of Belgium by the Society of Nations. In 1924, Belgium accepted the mandate on Burundi. After the second World War, the Society of Nations turned into an Organization of the United Nations. The mandate regime was replaced by the trusteeship. In 1953, Belgium reorganized the Burundi politics. There was notably the creation of Councils of chiefdoms, sub-chiefdoms, territory, as well as a Supreme Council

For additional analytical, marketing, investment and business opportunities information, please contact
Global Investment & Business Center, USA
(202) 546-2103. Fax: (202) 546-3275. E-mail: rusric@erols.com

of the country. At the Bandoeng Conference in 1955,the third world countries claimed for independence. Nationalist parties were created almost everywhere in Africa. Burundi was not an exception.

Prince Rwagasore founded the Uprona party (Union for the National Progress) which asked for an immediate independence. He won legislative elections organized on 18.09.1961. He was assassinated on October 13[th]1961, victim of princely conspiracy. At the end of many and stormy debates at the United Nations, a resolution was passed on June 27th 1962 by the General Assembly ,setting July 1st 1962 as the end of the Belgian trusteeship on Rwanda-Urundi and consecrated their accession to independence.

Hence, Burundi attained independence on July 1st 1962. During the whole period of occupation, Germans and Belgians applied the principle of indirect rule, by maintaining the traditional authority found in place, although the King, chiefs, sub-chiefs were progressively stripped of their power.
On top of that, the Belgian colonizers aggravated ethnic differences by excluding Hutu from educational and administrative fields to the advantage of the Tutsi minority branded as a superior race. The consequences of these policies were felt three years after independence.

THE POST COLONIAL PERIOD

THE LAST YEARS OF THE MONARCHY: 1962-1966

Burundi attained independence on July 1st 1962 although remaining under the authority of King Mwambutsa IV. The assassination of his son, Prince Rwagasore, then Prime Minister of Burundi generated internal conflicts within UPRONA party. UPRONA split into two tendencies called moderate (Monrovia headed by Thaddée Siryuyumunsi - a Tutsi, Speaker of the National Assembly) ,and extremist (Casablanca led by André Muhirwa - former Prime Minister,successor of Rwagasore, and Nyamoya Albin- who was Prime Minister in 1963). The year of 1965 is the turning point. It was marked by the assassination of Prime Minister Pierre Ngendandumwe - a Hutu, two days after the nomination of his cabinet, and by an attempted coup d'état wrongly or rightly attributed to Hutu army officers. There has been a judicial parody whereby all suspects (Army Officers, Ministers and Functionaries) were sentenced to death and immediately executed. Prime Minister Léopold Biha, appointed by the King in violation of the laws in force, escaped by a narrow margin and went to undergo medical treatment in Europe.

The King joined him there, abandoning the country to Cpt. Michel Micombero-Secretary of State responsible of Defense and Arthémon Simbananiye- State Secretary for Justice. It is worth stressing that Michel Micombero and Arthémon

For additional analytical, marketing, investment and business opportunities information, please contact
Global Investment & Business Center, USA
(202) 546-2103. Fax: (202) 546-3275. E-mail: rusric@erols.com

Simbananiye are from the tusi-hima clan which was to prepare a revenge. In reaction against that usurpation of power born of the polls, Paul Mirerekano- Vice President of Uprona, organized a popular resistance in his Busangana-Muramvya Province, leading to inter-ethnic massacres. The repression was bloody. For the first time in the history of Burundi, Burundians were being killed because of their ethnic origin. And the year 1965 is the first notch of chain of cyclical massacres that Burundi continues to experience due to the obvious will of the tutsi-hima to monopolize the power.

THE MILITARY REGIME (1966 -1993)

THE FIRST REPUBLIC (1966 - 1976)

In 1966,there were so many intrigues at the royal Court that Micombero team persuaded king Mwambutsa IV to retire and leave the throne to his son Prince Charles Ndizeye who will be enthronised on September 1st 1966,under the name of Ntare V. While on visit in Kinshasa , the young king was deposed by his Prime Minister Cpt. Michel Micombero who proclaimed himself President of the 1st Republic on 28.11.1966, hence abolishing the monarchy.
He set up a political regime based on the exclusion of Bahutu in particular, then came the turn of Batutsi not originating from his Bururi province in the South of the country. His rule was characterized by clientelism, regionalism and corruption with repetitive massacres and political assassinations. It was during Micombero regime that the army carried out the genocide against Hutu in 1972,resulting in more than 300,000 killed and 500,000 refugees. Since that drama, the army, the judiciary and the economy have become private hunting grounds and repressive instruments at the service of the tutsi-hima power.

THE SECOND REPUBLIC (1976 - 1987)

On November 1st 1976,Col. Jean Baptiste Bagaza -a Tutsi-hima from Rutovu commune and relative of Micombero - made a coup d'état ,a palace revolution which was smoothly executed. Cpt. Micombero,by then self-promoted General ,was arrested and put under house arrest at Ngozi in the North of the country.Thereafter, he was exiled to Somalia where he died. Col. Bagaza exercised a dictatorial power, putting under his control the unique UPRONA party which he restructured and the army which he modernized. Inside the country, he continued to apply the exclusionist and regional policy like his predecessor. He came into conflict with the Catholic Church of which he closed churches,jailed priests and expulsed missionaries.

His conflicting relations with the church led the Western countries to isolate him on the international scene. His ethnic group and his army considered him as embarrassing. He was chased away from power by his relative major Pierre Buyoya while he was taking part in a Francophone Summit in Quebec-Canada.

For additional analytical, marketing, investment and business opportunities information, please contact
Global Investment & Business Center, USA
(202) 546-2103. Fax: (202) 546-3275. E-mail: rusric@erols.com

Troughout the 11 years of power, Col.Jean Baptiste Bagaza officially denied the existence of ethnic groups in Burundi. However, it was during his rule that his Minister of Education perfected the system of excluding Hutu from secondary and high schools by initiating what was termed as the intellectual genocide of Hutu. He ordered the extermination of many Hutu and Tutsi opponents in prisons by inanition.

THE THIRD REPUBLIC (1987 - 1993)

Taking advantage of the worsening and decadence of Col. Bagaza's policy marked by the persecution of the churches, the catholic church in particular and the limitation of fundamental liberties, Major Buyoya staged a coup d'état against Col. Bagaza, although being himself a Tutsi-Hima from the same Rutovu commune. The change took place without bloodshed. It was a palace revolution, since everything was decided by army officers having blood ties in most cases and originating from the same province.

Major Buyoya normalized the relations between the Church and the State, and this earned him a big credit in ecclesiastic circles. The catholic hierarchy adhered to his policy. As far as thorny question of Bahutu and Batutsi is concerned, Buyoya gave the same answer as Col. Bagaza i.e. this is no more a problem. One year after his seizure of power (August 1988), inter-ethnic clashes broke out in Ntega and Marangara communes in the north of the country. The army intervened in a murderous way.

The power in place which opposed the setting up of a commission of inquiry gave an official death toll of 5,000, while independent sources reported more than 20,000 killed, the majority of them being Hutu, and tens of thousands of refugees. He realized that the cohabitation of Bahutu and Batutsi could not be taken for granted. Then, he initiated a policy of national unity, materialized by the appointment in October 1988 of a Hutu Prime Minister (Adrien Sibomana) at the head of a government with equal representation of both sides. He created a National Commission charged with studying the question of the national unity; its work was sanctioned by a referendum on 5.2.1991 on the Charter of National Unity. After the adoption of this text which became a reference ,Major Buyoya put the country on the path of democracy . He appointed a Constitutional Commission which wrote down a Constitution authorizing the multipartism and which was submitted to the people's referendum on March 9th 1992,and promulgated on March 13th 1992.

Soon after, the political parties were registered and started the campaign for election. Presidential elections putting face to face 3 candidates : Major Buyoya of UPRONA party, Melchior Ndadaye of FRODEBU party and Pierre Claver Sendegeya of PRP (royalist party), were held on June 1st 1993 . FRODEBU candidate, Melchior Ndadaye won them by 65% of the votes. In legislative

For additional analytical, marketing, investment and business opportunities information, please contact
Global Investment & Business Center, USA
(202) 546-2103. Fax: (202) 546-3275. E-mail: rusric@erols.com

elections of June 29th 1993, FRODEBU won 65 out of 81 seats of the National Assembly . The former unique party UPRONA got 16 seats only. These polls put an end to the military regime in place since 1966, spread over 3 Republics and monopolized by the tutsi-hima clan. A page had therefore been turned in the history of Burundi.

THE DEMOCRATIC BURUNDI AND THE CIVIL WAR

THE SHORT REGIME OF NDADAYE (07.10.1993 TO 10.21.1993)

Melchior Ndadaye, first President of Burundi, elected by universal suffrage, was sworn in on July 10th 1993. He appointed as Prime Minister – Mrs. Sylvie Kinigi from the Tutsi ethnic group, member of UPRONA party. In the composition of the government, the winner party and its allies got 60% of the ministerial posts, while the new opposition obtained 40% . President Ndadaye formed an open Government, although he had an overwhelming majority which would have allowed his party FRODEBU to rule alone ,without sharing power with others. President Ndadaye was assassinated on October 21st 1993 in a military camp of the capital. Other high level officials were tortured and executed the same night: Pontien Karibwami and Gilles Bimazubute, respectively Speaker and Deputy-Speaker of the National Assembly, the Interior Minister Juvénal Ndayikeza and the Administrator General of the National Security - Richard Ndikumwami. For two days, the country was plunged in a total chaos. In certain areas, Hutu avenged the death of the President and his colleagues by killing Tutsi of UPRONA. The putschists came up against the resistance of the people and were compelled to return the power to the surviving members of the Democratic Government who had taken refuge in embassies.

THE RAMPANT PUTSCH (10.21.1993 TO 07.25.1996)

Instead of restoring order and security, the army indulged in massacres of Hutu all over the country irrespective of their political parties. There were hundreds of thousands killed refugees and internally displaced persons. On February 5th 1994,Cyprien Ntaryamira became President of the Republic, replacing President Ndadaye. In his turn, he was killed on April 6th 1994 when the aircraft of the Rwandese President was shot down over Kigali soon after a summit held in Dar-es-Salaam - Tanzania.

The Speaker of the National Assembly, Sylvestre Ntibantunganya acted as President until his investiture in October 1994 within the framework of a Government Convention negotiated between political parties and the putschist army. Considering that the Government Convention as a legitimatization of the October 1993 coup d'état, the former Interior Minister Léonard Nyangoma created the National Council for the Defence of Democracy-CNDD with its armed wing: the Forces for the Defense of Democracy. On their side, the army and the

For additional analytical, marketing, investment and business opportunities information, please contact
Global Investment & Business Center, USA
(202) 546-2103. Fax: (202) 546-3275. E-mail: rusric@erols.com

opposition parties set up para-military militias " sans -échecs " which have played a dominating role in the ethnic "purification " of Bujumbura town and in the political assassinations.

On July, 25th 1996, Major Buyoya finalized the coup d'état, rampant since October of 1993, by overthrowing the democratic institutions in place which had become fragile due to permanent state of insecurity. He abolished the Constitution, suspended the National Assembly and the political parties. The countries of the Great Lakes Region imposed economic embargo on Burundi in order to compel the putschists to restore democracy and engage in negotiations. The embargo remains in force, even if some relaxations were decided on humanitarian grounds. The putschists and presumed assassins of President Ndadaye, the authors of different massacres committed since 1965 to date are still politically and economically so strong that they rather prefer war to negotiations because they want to enjoy a total impunity.

POPULATION AND SOCIETY

Annual population growth 2.3 per cent in 1992-98. Population density: 250 inhabitants per square km (1997). Urban population: 8 per cent (1992-98). Approximately 46 per cent of the total population is under 15 years.

The Hutu people are believed to comprise 85 per cent of the population, the Tutsi 14 per cent and the Twa 1 per cent, but there have never been any census statistics on ethnic groups.

MAIN CITIES

Bujumbura (estimated population 310,000 in 1997), Gitega (30,000), Rumonge (15,000).

PEOPLE

One of the first problems encountered when surveying press accounts of communal conflict in Rwanda and Burundi, not surprisingly, is an oversimplification of its nature. It is often described as a contest between two tribes with markedly different physical characteristics. Tutsis are depicted as tall, lighter-skinned, with long necks and narrow noses, and Ethiopian or more European in appearance. Hutus are described as short, squat, broad featured, with darker skin tone. Indeed, it is not unusual for marauding gangs in both countries to kill based on the perceived physical characteristics of their enemies. Yet, more sober and detached analysis leads to the conclusion that while a small percentage of individuals may fit the ideal body type of their communal group, these people are the exception rather than the rule.

For additional analytical, marketing, investment and business opportunities information, please contact
Global Investment & Business Center, USA
(202) 546-2103. Fax: (202) 546-3275. E-mail: rusric@erols.com

There are some people who are clearly distinguishable as Tutsi. There are other people who are clearly distinguishable as Hutu. And then there are the great mass of people in between, who are not immediately distinguishable as one or the other. In general they know who is who. But they know more because they know the person and his personal family history. If they see someone walking down the street, they cannot immediately tell you, in most cases, whether that person is Hutu or Tutsi. While long ago Hutus and Tutsis had different genetic pools, similar lifestyles and intermarriage promoted genetic resemblance over time.

Just as physical characteristics are an unreliable guide for identifying individuals as Hutu or Tutsi in Rwanda and Burundi, so too is geography. In neither country is there a particular region which can be described as a historical Hutu or Tutsi homeland. Of course, there are sections in both Rwanda and Burundi in which one group is more prominent. In Rwanda, for example, about 45 percent of Tutsis inhabit a region in the center of the country around Nyabisindu, which was once the seat of power of the Tutsi monarchy.

Turning to the question of language, this attribute again fails to divide Hutus and Tutsis within the two countries. Hutus and Tutsis in Rwanda both speak Kinyarwanda, which is closely related to the language spoken by the Tutsi and Hutu of Burundi, namely Kirundi. Other aspects of culture, such as dance and music, are also shared by the two groups.

In short, if one accepts the standard definition of a tribe as "a territorially bounded and culturally discrete entity," then the Hutus and Tutsis of Rwanda and Burundi are quite clearly not different tribes. On the other hand, while the media's use of the phrase "tribal warfare" may be uninformed, it is true that in both countries the two groups perceive of themselves as distinct and competitive. Hence, at least in times of extreme danger, people have a conscious desire to identify themselves as Hutu or Tutsi. One reason, of course, is fear and the hope of finding safety in numbers. After the April 1994 violence, Tutsi refugees in Benaco, Tanzania established a separate camp apart from that of their Hutu countrymen. However, observers note that Rwanda's resident and expatriate Tutsis, although they lost their elite status decades ago, remain a fiercely proud people.

THE TWA

Approximately (less than) one percent of the population in both Rwanda and Burundi consists of the Twa, a pygmoid people. Although the Twa share social structures and language with their Hutu and Tutsi countrymen, they are decidedly third-class citizens who exist on the very margins of society. International observers documented Twas voting in Burundi's 1993 elections, but in Rwanda and Burundi pygmies enjoy no access to education and hence are barred from government service and meaningful political participation. Under Habyarimana,

For additional analytical, marketing, investment and business opportunities information, please contact
Global Investment & Business Center, USA
(202) 546-2103. Fax: (202) 546-3275. E-mail: rusric@erols.com

Rwanda had a system of ethnic quotas which, in theory, granted Tutsi proportional access to education and jobs, but no provision was made for the Twa. Today, as in previous decades, Twa greivances focus on securing land and improved housing. While Hutus and Tutsis discriminate against Twa, their complete lack of economic, social, or political standing may to some extent insulate pygmies from direct attack during ethnic explosions.

Although for convenience the Twa are often cited as constituting about one percent of the population in both Rwanda and Burundi, it is likely that their numbers fall below this level. For example, some sources, including a Twa spokesman, state that there were 30,000 Twa in Rwanda before the 1994 genocide, which would place their percentage at approximately 0.4. The Twa of Rwanda and Burundi are severely discriminated against, but they are not coded as part of the Minorities at Risk dataset for two reasons: they probably fall under the project's population thresholds (100,000 or one percent of the population), and information about them is extremely sparse and contradictory.

For example, the US Department of State concluded that "there is no reliable information on specific human rights abuses perpetuated against the Batwa population during the April 1994 upheaval. A group of several hundred Rwandan Batwa refugees were discovered living in a forested area outside of Goma, Zaire, deeply traumatized by the events they had witnessed. They did not clarify, however, that they or other Batwa had been caught up on either side of the massacres."

Journalistic reporting has supported the State Department's authoritative assertion of ambiguity regarding Rwanda's Twa. One account from August 1994 indicated that Twa were targeted for extermination by Hutu death squads. The following month, however, a different news service asserted that the Twa had sided with the Hutu against the Tutsi by joining the army and militias, and had fled into exile after the Hutu defeat as a result. Later, a Twa "spokesman" and "leader," touring Western capitals in search of support for his people, claimed that two-thirds of Rwanda's 30,000 Twa had died in the civil war and genocide, although he apparently indicated that they were largely bystanders and not direct participants or intended victims of the violence.

LANGUAGES

Republic of Burundi. Republika y'Uburundi. Formerly part of Ruanda-Urundi. The number of languages listed for Burundi is 3.

French. Indo-European, Italic, Romance, Italo-Western, Western, Gallo-Romance. National language.

For additional analytical, marketing, investment and business opportunities information, please contact
Global Investment & Business Center, USA
(202) 546-2103. Fax: (202) 546-3275. E-mail: rusric@erols.com

Hima(UROHIMA) 7,000 in all countries. Also in Zaïre and Rwanda. Niger-Congo, Atlantic-Congo, Benue-Congo, Bantoid, Southern, Narrow Bantu. Dialects: ORUHEMA (HEMA), ORUHIMA (HIMA), ORUHUMA (HUMA), KIHEMA. Survey needed.

Rundi(KIRUNDI, URUNDI) 5,400,000 in Burundi (1996); 120,903 in Uganda (1996); 100,000 in Tanzania (1996 Johnstone); 6,200,000 in all countries (1996 WA). Also in Tanzania, Rwanda. Niger-Congo, Atlantic-Congo, Volta-Congo, Benue-Congo, Bantoid, Southern, Narrow Bantu, Central, J, Rwanda-Rundi (J.60). Ethnic groups: Hutu 80% to 85%, Tutsi 14% to 15%, Twa (Gesera, pygmy) 1%. Dialects of the Hutu and Tutsi are similar. Twa is more distinct but all are inherently intelligible, and also intelligible with Kinyarwanda (Rwanda). About 55% are literate in Kirundi (MARC 1978). Some speakers use Swahili as a lingua franca. National language. Christian, traditional religion, Muslim; Twa: traditional religion, Christian.

EDUCATION

UNIVERSITY OF BURUNDI

 The University of Burundi was created in 1965, and at that time, it was called "Institut Agronomique du Rwanda-Urundi" with its home at Bujumbura. And in 1968 it became the "Institut Facultaire du Burundi" with two main entities : the "Ecole Normale Supérieure" (E.N.S.) and the "Université Officielle du Burundi" (U.O.B.). Only in 1979, the two institutes were gathered in the current "Université du Burundi".

- Financially supported by the Burundian Government
- Located in the capital and partly in the second city of Burundi : Gitega.
- Five (5) Campuses : Mutanga (the main Campus), Kiriri, Kamenge, and Rohero at Bujumbura ; and the Campus of Zege at Gitega, holding the Institute of Agriculture.

UNIVERSITY FACULTIES

Faculty of Agricultural Sciences
Faculty of health and Medical Sciences
Faculty of Sciences
Faculty of Arts and Social Sciences
Faculty of Applied Sciences
Faculty of Economics and Business Administration
Faculty of Psychology and Educational Sciences
Faculty of Law

For additional analytical, marketing, investment and business opportunities
information, please contact
Global Investment & Business Center, USA
(202) 546-2103. Fax: (202) 546-3275. E-mail: rusric@erols.com

UNIVERSITY INSTITUTES

Institute of Agriculture
Institute of Applied Pedagogy
Institute of Business
Institute of Sport and physical Education
Institute of Technology and Civil Engineering

- 20 Specialized Research Centers;
- 6 000 Students and 1000 entries per year;
- 350 Permanent Faculty members (professors, associate professors, junior lecturers and assistants)
- 130 Part-time lecturers;
- 40 Animation teams of researchers;
- Cooperation with France, Belgium, Germany, China, Egypt, UNDP, AUPELF.

For additional analytical, marketing, investment and business opportunities information, please contact
Global Investment & Business Center, USA
(202) 546-2103. Fax: (202) 546-3275. E-mail: rusric@erols.com

POLITICAL AND GOVERNMENT SYSTEM

S. E. Major Pierre BUYOYA, PRESIDENT

POLITICAL STRUCTURE

CONSTITUTION

A Transitional Constitution replaced the 1992 constitution in 1998. Under the terms of the Transitional Constitutional Act in 1998, Buyoya was sworn in as President on 11 June and appointed a 117-member National Assembly on 18 July.

FORM OF STATE

Burundi became a republic after a military coup in 1966.

THE EXECUTIVE

The constitution vests executive power in a directly elected president who serves a five-year term.

NATIONAL LEGISLATURE

For additional analytical, marketing, investment and business opportunities information, please contact
Global Investment & Business Center, USA
(202) 546-2103. Fax: (202) 546-3275. E-mail: rusric@erols.com

Legislative power is vested in a National Assembly, elected for a five-year term by universal suffrage.

LAST ELECTIONS

June 1993.

POLITICAL PARTIES

RULING PARTY

Coalition of the Front pour la Démocratie au Burundi (Frodebu) (Front for Democracy) and the Union pour le Progrès National (Uprona) (Union for National Progress)

MAIN OPPOSITION PARTY

Inama y'Igihugu Igwanira Demokarasi/Conseil National pour la Défense de la Démocratie (National Council for the Defence of the Democracy)

PRESS

Main newspapers are Le Renouveau du Burundi (French daily) and Ubumwe (Kirundi weekly) - both are government-controlled. Many other newspapers have emerged since 1992, including Carrefour des Idées, Le Citoyen (twice monthly), l'Indépendant (weekly), l'Aube de la Démocratie (published twice monthly by the Frodebu party), Intahe, Burakeyei and Kanura.

Dailies: The main government controlled daily newspaper in French is Le Renouveau du Burundi.

Weeklies: Weeklies include Ubumwe (Kirundi weekly) that is government-controlled and l'Indépendant.

Periodicals: Periodicals include Carrefour des Idées, Le Citoyen (twice monthly), l'Aube de la Démocratie (published twice monthly by the Frodebu party), Intahe, Burakeyei and Kanura.

BROADCASTING

Radio: Radio service in Kirundi, KiSwahili, French and English operated by the state broadcasting station Voix de la Révolution.

Television: TV service established in 1984.

For additional analytical, marketing, investment and business opportunities information, please contact
Global Investment & Business Center, USA
(202) 546-2103. Fax: (202) 546-3275. E-mail: rusric@erols.com

CABINET

President	**Buyoya,** Pierre
Vice President	**Ndayizeye,** Domitien
Min. of Agriculture & Livestock	**Ndikumagenge,** Pierre
Min. of Civil Service	**Ntanyungu,** Festus
Min. of Communal Development	**Ngendanganya,** Casimir
Min. of Communications & Government Spokesman	**Mbonerane,** Albert
Min. of Development Planning & Reconstruction	**Wakana,** Seraphine
Min. of Energy & Mines	**Nkundikije,** Andre
Min. of External Relations & Cooperation	**Sinunguruza,** Terence
Min. of Finance	**Kadigiri,** Edouard
Min. of Good Government & Privatization	**Kiganahe,** Didace
Min. of Handicrafts, Vocational Training, & Adult Literacy	**Hakizimana,** Godefroy
Min. of Institutional Reforms, Human Rights, & Relations with Parliament	**Barancira,** Alphonse
Min. of Interior & Public Security	**Ntihabose,** Salvator
Min. of Justice & Keeper of the Seals	**Dwima Bakana,** Fulgence
Min. of Labor, Employment, & Professional Training	**Nditabiriye,** Dismas
Min. of National Defense	**Ndayirukiye,** Cyrille, Maj. Gen.
Min. of National Education	**Mpawenayo,** Prosper
Min. of Public Health	**Kamana,** Jean, M. D.
Min. of Public Works & Equipment	**Bigirimana,** Balthazar
Min. of Reintegration & Resettlement of Displaced Persons & Repatriates	**Ngendahayo,** Francoise
Min. of Social Action & Promotion of Women	**Nduwimana,** Marie-Goretti

For additional analytical, marketing, investment and business opportunities information, please contact
Global Investment & Business Center, USA
(202) 546-2103. Fax: (202) 546-3275. E-mail: rusric@erols.com

Min. of Territorial Development, Environment, & Tourism	**Nikobamye**, Gaetan
Min. of Trade & Industry	**Karikurubu**, Charles
Min. of Transport, Posts, & Telecommunications	**Ndikumugongo**, Severin
Min. of Youth, Sports, & Culture	**Muteragiranwa**, Barnabe
Min. in Charge of Mobilization for Peace & Natl. Reconciliation	**Rukingama**, Luc
Min. in the Office of the President in Charge of AIDS Control	**Sindabizera**, Genevieve
Governor, Central Bank	**Bayiyezako**, Greogiore
Ambassador to the US	**Ndikumana**, Thomas
Permanent Representative to the UN, New York	**Nteturuye**, Marc

BURUNDI GOVERNMENT BUILDING

The Arusha Agreement for peace and reconciliation in Burundi, which has been torn by several years of political instability and civil war, was signed by all political parties on September 20th, 2000. It was ratified by the National Assembly.

Two important points remain to be settled before the Agreement can be implemented :

1. The cessation of hostilities, still in negotiation,
2. The composition of the transitional government.

Among other things, the Peace Agreement lays down the principles according to which the future institutions should be organised.

The new State institutions must be organised so as to "be able to integrate and reassure every category of Burundi society".

The main principle governing the Agreement is respect of ethnic and religious diversity. It acknowledges the Bahutu, the Batutsi and the Batwa as categories of Burundi national society.

The Agreement provides for the creation of a bicameral system, where the Senate would represent and safeguard the multi-ethnic nature of Burundi society (I).

For additional analytical, marketing, investment and business opportunities information, please contact
Global Investment & Business Center, USA
(202) 546-2103. Fax: (202) 546-3275. E-mail: rusric@erols.com

During the transitional period before the new institutions are set up, a Senate will also be instituted. (II).

Organisation of the legislative power

The legislative power is exercised by the National Assembly and, in the domains provided by the Peace Agreement, by the National Assembly and the Senate.

I - THE SENATE

1) Composition

The Senate is composed of two delegates from each province, elected by an electoral college composed of members from the district councils in the province concerned, deriving from the various ethnic communities and elected by separate elections.

Former presidents are entitled to sit in the Senate. The Senate may co-opt up to three members of the Batwa to ensure that this community is represented.

The Senate bureau will be multi-ethnic.

2) Powers

a) To approve the amendments to the Constitution and organic laws, including laws governing the electoral process :

- the Constitution may be amended only by a majority of four fifths of the National Assembly and two thirds of the Senate ;

-organic laws may be amended only by a majority of two thirds of the National Assembly, with the agreement of the Senate.

b) To be sent the ombudsman's reports on any aspect of State administration.

c) To institute enquiries into State administration and, as the case may be, to make recommendations to ensure that no region or group is excluded from the benefits of State services.

d) To check the application of the constitutional provisions in respect of representation, or balanced composition of any section of the civil services or defense and security organizations.

For additional analytical, marketing, investment and business opportunities information, please contact
Global Investment & Business Center, USA
(202) 546-2103. Fax: (202) 546-3275. E-mail: rusric@erols.com

For a period fixed by the Senate, not more than 50% of members of the army may belong to a single ethnic group.

e) To ensure that the district councils reflect the ethnic make up of their electoral roll as a general rule. In the event that the composition of a district council does not reflect this ethnic diversity, the Senate may order the co-optation of persons from an under-represented ethnic group to the council, provided that such persons do not represent more than one fifth of the members on the council. The persons to be co-opted are nominated by the Senate from a list of names provided by the district council or by a hill chief from the district concerned.

f) To advise the President and the National Assembly on all issues, more particularly legislative issues.

g) To supervise the application of the Arusha Agreement.

h) To make observations or suggest amendments to legislation voted by the National Assembly, and draw up and introduce bills for examination by the National Assembly.

The National Assembly must examine the draft amendments and may, if it so decides, include them in the bill submitted for the approval of the President.

l) To approve bills on the definition and allocation of power to the provinces, districts and hills.

j) To approve nominations :

The Senate approves the following nominations :

a. Chief of the defence forces, police and intelligence services ;

b. Governors of the provinces nominated by the President of the Republic ;

c. The Ombudsman ;

d. Members of the Higher Council of Judges ;

e. Members of the Supreme Court ;

f. Members of the Constitutional Court (with a 2/3 majority) ;

g. The Head of Public Prosecutions and the judges of the Public Prosecution Department ;

For additional analytical, marketing, investment and business opportunities information, please contact
Global Investment & Business Center, USA
(202) 546-2103. Fax: (202) 546-3275. E-mail: rusric@erols.com

h. The President of the Court of Appeal and the President of the Administrative Court ;

i. The Attorney General for the Court of Appeal ;

j. The Presidents of the higher civil courts, the commercial courts and the labour court ;

k. The Public Prosecutors ;

l. The Vice-Presidents of the Republic (two) (this power is also vested in the National Assembly, but the two chambers vote separately).

II - THE TRANSITION SENATE

During the transitional period, to begin 3 to 6 months following signature of the Arusha Agreement, and to end when the new President is elected, the transition legislature will be composed of a National Assembly and a Senate :

1) Composition of the transition Senate

The Senate is to be set up by the President of the Republic and the Bureau of the National Assembly, paying careful attention to political, ethnic and regional balances.

It is to comprise, among others, former Heads of State, three persons from the Twa people, and members from the transition National Assembly co-opted by the President of the Republic and the Bureau of the transition National Assembly.

Those members of the transition National Assembly that have been co-opted for the transition Senate will not be replaced.

2) Powers of the transition Senate

The Transition Senate will exercise the powers expressly provided in the constitutional principles laid down by the Agreement.

3) Adoption of the Constitution

The transition National Assembly and Senate will adopt a post-transition Constitution, as provided for by the principles in Chapter I of the Arusha

For additional analytical, marketing, investment and business opportunities information, please contact
Global Investment & Business Center, USA
(202) 546-2103. Fax: (202) 546-3275. E-mail: rusric@erols.com

Agreement, keeping the same terms, not later than eighteen months following their creation, by a two-thirds majority.

ARUSHA PEACE AND RECONCILIATION AGREEMENT FOR BURUNDI

We, the representatives of:

- The Government of the Republic of Burundi,
- The National Assembly,
- The Alliance Burundo-Africaine pour le Salut (ABASA),
- The Alliance Nationale pour le Droit et le Développement (ANADDE),
- The Alliance des Vaillants (AV-INTWARI),
- The Conseil National pour la Défense de la Démocratie (CNDD),
- The Front pour la Démocratie au Burundi (FRODEBU),
- The Front pour la Libération Nationale (FROLINA),
- The Parti Socialiste et Panafricaniste (INKINZO),
- The Parti pour la Libération du Peuple Hutu (PALIPEHUTU),
- The Parti pour le Redressement National (PARENA),
- The Parti Indépendant des Travailleurs (PIT),
- The Parti Libéral (PL),
- The Parti du Peuple (PP),
- The Parti pour la Réconciliation du Peuple (PRP),
- The Parti Social-Démocrate (PSD),
- The Ralliement pour la Démocratie et le Développement Economique et Social (RADDES),
- The Rassemblement du Peuple Burundais (RPB) and
- The Union pour le Progrès National (UPRONA),

Hereinafter referred to as "the Parties",

Considering the rounds of talks held in Mwanza in 1996,

Having participated in the negotiations held in Arusha pursuant to the Declaration by the Participants in the Burundi Peace Negotiations involving all the Parties of the Burundi Conflict signed at Arusha on 21 June 1998 ("the Declaration of 21 June 1998") under the facilitation of the late Mwalimu Julius Kambarage Nyerere, and subsequently of Mr. Nelson Rolihlahla Mandela, on behalf of the States of the Great Lakes region and the international community,

For additional analytical, marketing, investment and business opportunities information, please contact
Global Investment & Business Center, USA
(202) 546-2103. Fax: (202) 546-3275. E-mail: rusric@erols.com

Expressing our deep appreciation for the persistent efforts of the Facilitators, the late Mwalimu Julius Kambarage Nyerere and Mr. Nelson Rolihlahla Mandela, the States of the Great Lakes region and the international community with a view to assisting the people of Burundi to return to peace and stability,

Determined to put aside our differences in all their manifestations in order to promote the factors that are common to us and which unite us, and to work together for the realization of the higher interests of the people of Burundi,

Aware of the fact that peace, stability, justice, the rule of law, national reconciliation, unity and development are the major aspirations of the people of Burundi,

Reaffirming our unwavering determination to put an end to the root causes underlying the recurrent state of violence, bloodshed, insecurity, political instability, genocide and exclusion which is inflicting severe hardships and suffering on the people of Burundi, and seriously hampers the prospects for economic development and the attainment of equality and social justice in our country,

Reaffirming our commitment to shape a political order and a system of government inspired by the realities of our country and founded on the values of justice, democracy, good governance, pluralism, respect for the fundamental rights and freedoms of the individual, unity, solidarity, mutual understanding, tolerance and cooperation among the different ethnic groups within our society,

In the presence of:

- Jean-Baptiste Bagaza and Sylvestre Ntibantunganya, former Presidents of Burundi.
- The representatives of Burundian civil society and women's organizations and Burundian religious leaders,
- H. E. Mr. Nelson Rolihlahla Mandela, Facilitator,
- H. E. General Gnassingbé Eyadéma. President of the Republic of Togo and current Chairman of the Organization of African Unity,
- H. E. Yoweri Kaguta Museveni, President of the Republic of Uganda,
- H. E. Daniel T. arap Moi, President of the Republic of Kenya,
- H. E. Benjamin William Mkapa, President of the United Republic of Tanzania,

For additional analytical, marketing, investment and business opportunities information, please contact
Global Investment & Business Center, USA
(202) 546-2103. Fax: (202) 546-3275. E-mail: rusric@erols.com

- H. E. Frederick J. T. Chiluba, President of the Republic of Zambia,
- H. E. Major-General Paul Kagame, President of the Republic of Rwanda,
- H. E. Laurent Désiré Kabila, President of the Democratic Republic of the Congo,
- H. E. Meles Zenawi, Prime Minister of the Republic of Ethiopia,
- H. E. Mr. Kofi Annan, Secretary-General of the United Nations,
- H. E. Dr. Salim Ahmed Salim, Secretary-General of the Organization of African Unity,
- Hon. Charles Josselin, Minister of Cooperation of the French Republic, representing the European Union,
- H. E. Dr. Boutros Boutros Ghali, Secretary-General of the International Organization of la Francophonic, and
- Mr. Joseph Waryoba Butiku, Executive Director of the Mwalimu Nyerere Foundation,

Do hereby resolve and commit ourselves to be bound by the provisions of the Arusha Peace and Reconciliation Agreement for Burundi, hereinafter referred to as "the Agreement".

Article 1

The Parties accept as binding the following Protocols and Annexes thereto, which form an integral part of the Arusha Peace and Reconciliation Agreement for Burundi:

PROTOCOL I:	**NATURE OF THE CONFLICT, PROBLEMS OF GENOCIDE AND EXCLUSION AND THEIR SOLUTIONS;**
Protocol II:	**Democracy and good governance;**
Protocol III:	**Peace and security for all;**
Protocol IV:	**Reconstruction and development;**

For additional analytical, marketing, investment and business opportunities information, please contact
Global Investment & Business Center, USA
(202) 546-2103. Fax: (202) 546-3275. E-mail: rusric@erols.com

| Protocol V: | Guarantees on the implementation of the Agreement. |

ANNEXES

Annex I:	Pledge by participating parties;
Annex II:	Structure of the National Police Force;
Annex III:	Ceasefire agreement;
Annex IV:	Report of Committee IV;
Annex V:	Implementation timetable.

2. The Parties, recognizing the need to provide in the Agreement for contingencies unforeseen at the time that the protocols were finalized, agree that the provisions of the Agreement over-ride any contrary provisions within the protocols, and further agree as follows.

    a. Where the Protocols of the Agreement contemplates that decision was to be taken by the Parties at the time of signature of the Agreement, and such matters or decisions have not been so taken at the date of signature of the Agreement, they shall be taken by the signatory parties, with or without the assistance of the Facilitator, within 30 days of signature.

    b. Any provision of the Agreement or the protocols may be amended as provided for in article 20 of Protocol II or, pending the establishment of the Transitional National Assembly, with the consent of nine-tenths of the Parties;

    c. Pending the negotiation and agreement of a comprehensive cease-fire agreement with the armed wings of non-signatory parties, Chapter III of Protocol III to the Agreement shall not come into effect; following the conclusion of the ceasefire agreement, it shall be deemed to be amended so as to be consistent with the provisions thereof.

For additional analytical, marketing, investment and business opportunities information, please contact
Global Investment & Business Center, USA
(202) 546-2103. Fax: (202) 546-3275. E-mail: rusric@erols.com

Members of the parties to the Burundi Peace Negotiations in Arusha which do not sign the Agreement shall not be entitled to participate or hold office in the transitional Government or the transitional Legislature unless such parties are admitted as participating parties in accordance with article 14 of Protocol II to the Agreement with the consent of four-fifths of the Parties.

Article 2

1. The Parties acknowledge the need for the Agreement to be accompanied by and to be a condition for lasting peace and a cessation of violence in Burundi.
2. The Parties accordingly call upon armed wings of non-signatory parties to suspend hostilities and violent actions immediately, and invite such non-signatory parties to participate in or engage in serious negotiations towards a cease-fire. The Parties agree that in addition to this public invitation included herein, they will as a priority take all reasonable and necessary steps to invite such Parties to participate in cease-fire negotiations.
3. The Parties pledge that in the event of belligerent parties spurning or refusing such an invitation and continuing their belligerent activities against the people of Burundi, or any section of them, the violent acts of such parties will be deemed to be constitute an attack on all the Parties comprising this national platform of the Burundian people, as well as on this endeavour to establish an inclusive democratic Burundian state. In such an event the Parties agree to call collectively, through the appropriate agencies including the Implementation Monitoring Committee, upon the Governments of neighbouring States, the international agencies which are guarantors of the Agreement and other appropriate national and international bodies to take the necessary steps to prohibit, demobilize. disarm, and if necessary arrest, detain and repatriate, members of such armed groups, and further to take such steps as are appropriate against any Party which encourages or supports such activities.

Article 3

The Parties commit themselves to refrain from any act or behaviour contrary to the provisions of the Agreement, and to spare no effort to ensure that the said provisions are respected and implemented

For additional analytical, marketing, investment and business opportunities information, please contact
Global Investment & Business Center, USA
(202) 546-2103. Fax: (202) 546-3275. E-mail: rusric@erols.com

in their letter and spirit in order to ensure the attainment of genuine unity, reconciliation, lasting peace, security for all, solid democracy and on equitable sharing of resources in Burundi.

Article 4

The Agreement shall be signed by the Parties. The Facilitator, the President of the Republic of Uganda as the Chairman of the Regional Peace Initiative on Burundi, the President of the Republic of Kenya as the region's elder statesman and the President of the United Republic of Tanzania as the host, and the representatives of the United Nations, the Organization of African Unity, the European Union and the Mwalimu Nyerere Foundation shall also affix their signatures hereto as witnesses and as an expression of their moral support for the peace process.

Article 5

The Agreement shall enter into force on the date of its signature.

Article 6

All of the final documents shall be drawn up in English, French and Kirundi. The English and French texts be equally authentic. The French text, being the original, shall be deposited with the Secretary-General of the United Nations, the Secretary-General of the Organization of African Unity and the Government of Burundi, and certified true copies thereof shall be transmitted by the Government to all Parties.

Signed in Arusha on the 28th day of the month of August 2000.

SIGNATORY PARTIES

For the **Government of Burundi**

Name of Representative: Mr. Ambroise NIYONSABA

Title: Minister for the Peace Process

For the **National Assembly**

Name of Representative: Hon. Léonce NGENDAKUMANA

For additional analytical, marketing, investment and business opportunities information, please contact
Global Investment & Business Center, USA
(202) 546-2103. Fax: (202) 546-3275. E-mail: rusric@erols.com

Title: Speaker of the National Assembly

For **ABASA**

Name of the Party's representative: Amb. Térence NSANZE
Title: Chairman

For **ANADDE**

Name of the Party's representative: Prof. Patrice NSABABAGANWA
Title: Chairman

For **AV-INTWARI**

Name of the Party's representative: Prof. André NKUNDIKIJE
Title: Chairman

For **CNDD**

Name of the Party's representative: Mr. Leonard NYANGOMA
Title: Chairman

For **FRODEBU**

Name of the Party's representative: Dr. Jean MINANI
Title: Chairman

For **FROLINA**

Name of the Party's representative: Mr. Joseph KARUMBA
Title: Chairman

For **INKINZO**

For additional analytical, marketing, investment and business opportunities
information, please contact
Global Investment & Business Center, USA
(202) 546-2103. Fax: (202) 546-3275. E-mail: rusric@erols.com

Name of the Party's representative: Dr. Alphose RUGAMBARARA
Title: Chairman

For PALIPEHUTU

Name of the Party's representative: Dr. Etiénne KARATASI
Title: Chairman

For PARENA

Name of the Party's representative: H. E. Jean-Baptiste BAGAZA
Title: Chairman

For PIT

Name of the Party's representative: Prof. Nicéphore NDIMURUKUNDO
Title: Chairman

For PL

Name of the Party's representative: Mr. Gaëtan NIKOBAMYE
Title: Chairman

For PP

Name of the Party's representative: Mr. Shadrack NIYONKURU
Title: Chairman

For PRP

Name of the Party's representative: Mr. Mathias HITIMANA
Title: Chairman

For PSD

For additional analytical, marketing, investment and business opportunities
information, please contact
Global Investment & Business Center, USA
(202) 546-2103. Fax: (202) 546-3275. E-mail: rusric@erols.com

Name of the Party's representative: Mr. Godefroy HAKIZIMANA

Title: Chairman

For **RADDES**

Name of the Party's representative: Mr. Joseph NZEYIMANA

Title: Chairman

For **RPB**

Name of the Party's representative: Mr. Balthazar BIGIRIMANA

Title: Chairman

For **UPRONA**

Name of the Party's representative: Mr. Lib??re BARARUNYERETSE

Title: Chairman

COSIGNATORIES

H. E. Mr. Nelson Rolilhalha Mandela, Facilitator;

H. E. Yoweri Kaguta Muscveni, President of the Republic of Uganda,

H. E. Daniel T. arap Moi, President of the Republic of Kenya,

H. E. Benjamin William Mkapa, President of the United Republic of Tanzania

H. E. Mr. Kofi Annan, Secretary-General of the United Nations,

H. E. Dr. Salim Ahmed Salim, Secretary-General of the Organization of African Unity,

Hon. Charles Josselin, Minister of Cooperation of the French Republic, representing the European Union,

For additional analytical, marketing, investment and business opportunities information, please contact
Global Investment & Business Center, USA
(202) 546-2103. Fax: (202) 546-3275. E-mail: rusric@erols.com

Mr. Joseph Waryoba Butiku, Executive Director of the Mwalimu Nyerere Foundation

PROTOCOL I NATURE OF THE BURUNDI CONFLICT, PROBLEMS OF GENOCIDE AND EXCLUSION AND THEIR SOLUTIONS

PREAMBLE

We, the Parties,

Having analysed the historical causes of the conflict in Burundi during the precolonial, colonial and post-colonial periods,

Having engaged in a lengthy, exhaustive, introspective and frank debate on the perceptions, root causes, practice and ideology of genocide, war crimes and other crimes against humanity, the role of the national political class and institutions in this regard, the regional and international context in which they occur and their manifestation in Burundi,

Having also discussed the origins and evolution, causes and manifestations of exclusion in Burundi,

Resolved to eradicate genocide and to reject all forms of division, discrimination and exclusion,

Motivated by the concern to work towards national reconciliation,

Have agreed as follows:

CHAPTER I NATURE AND HISTORICAL CAUSES OF THE CONFLICT

Article 1
Precolonial period

1. During the precolonial period, all the ethnic groups inhabiting Burundi owed allegiance to the same monarch, Umwami, believed in the same god, Imana, had the same culture and the same language, Kirundi, and lived together in the same territory. Notwithstanding the migratory movements that accompanied the settlement of the various groups in Burundi, everyone recognized themselves as Barundi.

For additional analytical, marketing, investment and business opportunities information, please contact
Global Investment & Business Center, USA
(202) 546-2103. Fax: (202) 546-3275. E-mail: rusric@erols.com

2. The existence of Bashingantahe who came from among the Baganwa, the Bahutu and the Batutsi and were judges and advisors at all levels of power was, inter alia, a factor in promoting cohesion.
3. As a result of the mode of management of national affairs, there were no known ethnic conflicts between the various groups during this period.
4. Nevertheless, certain traditional practices such as Ukunena, Ukwihutura, Ubugeregwa, Ubugabire, Ukunyaga, Ukwangaza, Ugutanga ikimazi-muntu, Ugushorerwako inka and others could, depending on the circumstances, constitute sources of injustice and of frustration both among the Bahutu and the Batutsi and among the Batwa.

Article 2
Colonial period

1. The colonial administration, first German and then Belgian under a League of Nations mandate and United Nations trusteeship, played a decisive role in the heightening of frustrations among the Bahutu, the Batutsi and the Batwa, and in the divisions which led to ethnic tensions.
2. In the context of a strategy of "divide and rule", the colonial administration injected and imposed a caricatured, racist vision of Burundian society, accompanied by prejudices and clichés relating to morphological considerations designed to set the different components of Burundi's population against one another on the basis of physical characteristics and character traits.
3. It also introduced an identity card which indicated ethnic origin, thus reinforcing ethnic awareness to the detriment of national awareness. This also enabled the colonizer to accord specific treatment to each ethnic group in accordance with its theories.
4. It manipulated the existing system to its advantage by resorting to discriminatory practices.
5. Moreover, it undertook to destroy certain cultural values that until then had constituted a factor for national unity and cohesion.
6. On the eve of independence the colonizer, sensing that its power was threatened, intensified divisionist tactics and orchestrated socio-political struggles. However, the charismatic leadership of Prince Louis Rwagasore and his colleagues made it possible for Burundi to avoid political confrontation based on ethnic considerations and enabled it to attain independence in peace and national harmony.

Article 3
Post-colonial period

1. Since independence, and throughout the different regimes, there have been a number of constant phenomena which have given rise to the

For additional analytical, marketing, investment and business opportunities information, please contact
Global Investment & Business Center, USA
(202) 546-2103. Fax: (202) 546-3275. E-mail: rusric@erols.com

conflict that has persisted up to the present time: massive and deliberate killings, widespread violence and exclusion have taken place during this period.

2. Views differ as to the interpretation of these phenomena and their influence on the current political, economic and socio-cultural situation in Burundi, as well as of their impact on the conflict.

3. Nevertheless, without prejudice to the results and conclusions of the International Judicial Commission of Inquiry and National Truth and Reconciliation Commission to be established pursuant to Chapter II of the present Protocol in order to shed light on these phenomena, the Parties recognize that acts of genocide, war crimes and other crimes against humanity have been perpetrated since independence against Tutsi and Hutu ethnic communities in Burundi.

Article 4
Nature of the Burundi conflict

With regard to the nature of the Burundi conflict, the Parties recognize that:

a. The conflict is fundamentally political, with extremely important ethnic dimensions;
b. It stems from a struggle by the political class to accede to and/or remain in power.

In the light of the foregoing, the Parties undertake to abide by the principles and implement the measures set forth in Chapter II of the present Protocol.

CHAPTER II SOLUTIONS

Article 5
General political measures

1. Institution of a new political, economic, social and judicial order in Burundi, in the context of a new constitution inspired by Burundian realities and founded on the values of justice, the rule of law, democracy, good governance, pluralism, respect for the fundamental rights and freedoms of the individual, unity, solidarity, equality between women and men, mutual understanding and tolerance among the various political and ethnic components of the Burundian people.

2. A reorganization of the State institutions to make them capable of integrating and reassuring all the ethnic components of Burundian society.

3. Speedy establishment of the transitional institutions pursuant to the provisions of Protocol II to the Agreement.

For additional analytical, marketing, investment and business opportunities information, please contact
Global Investment & Business Center, USA
(202) 546-2103. Fax: (202) 546-3275. E-mail: rusric@erols.com

4. Orientation of political parties' programmes towards the ideals of unity and national reconciliation and of socio-economic development rather than the protection of a specific component of the Burundian people.
5. Adoption of constitutional provisions embodying the principle of separation of powers (executive, legislative and judicial), pursuant to the provisions of Protocol II to the Agreement.
6. Enactment of an electoral law that takes into account the concerns and interests of all components of the nation on the basis of the provisions of Protocol II to the Agreement.
7. Prevention of coups d'état.

Article 6
Principles and measures relating to genocide, war crimes and other crimes against humanity

Political principles and measures

1. Combating the impunity of crimes.
2. Prevention, suppression and eradication of acts of genocide, war crimes and other crimes against humanity, as well as violations of human rights, including those which are gender-based.
3. Implementation of a vast awareness and educational programme for national peace, unity and reconciliation.
4. Establishment of a national observatory for the prevention and eradication of genocide, war crimes and other crimes against humanity.
5. Promotion of regional cooperation to establish a regional observatory for the prevention and eradication of genocide, war crimes and other crimes against humanity.
6. Promotion of a national inter-ethnic resistance front to combat genocide, war crimes and other crimes against humanity, as well as generalization and collective attribution of guilt.
7. Erection of a national monument in memory of all victims of genocide, war crimes and other crimes against humanity, bearing the words "NEVER AGAIN".
8. Institution of a national day of remembrance for victims of genocide, war crimes and other crimes against humanity, and taking of measures that would facilitate the identification of mass graves and ensure a dignified burial for the victims.

Principles and measures in the area of justice

9. Enactment of legislation to counter genocide, war crimes and other crimes against humanity, as well as human rights violations.

For additional analytical, marketing, investment and business opportunities information, please contact
Global Investment & Business Center, USA
(202) 546-2103. Fax: (202) 546-3275. E-mail: rusric@erols.com

10. Request by the transitional Government for the establishment by the United Nations Security Council of an International Judicial Commission of Inquiry on genocide, war crimes and other crimes against humanity responsible for:
    a. Investigating and establishing the facts relating to the period from independence to the date of signature of the Agreement;
    b. Classifying them;
    c. Determining those responsible;
    d. Submitting its report to the United Nations Security Council;
    e. The Commission shall make use of all the reports that already exist on this subject, including the 1985 Whitaker report, the 1994 non-governmental organizations' report, the 1994-1994 report by ambassadors and the 1996 report of the United Nations International Commission of Inquiry.

11. Request by the Government of Burundi for the establishment by the United Nations Security Council of an international criminal tribunal to try and punish those responsible should the findings of the report point to the existence of acts of genocide, war crimes and other crimes against humanity.

Article 7
Principles and measures relating to exclusion

1. Constitutional guarantees of the principle of the equality of rights and duties for all citizens, men and women, and all the ethnic, political, regional and social components of Burundian society.
2. Combating conflict-generating injustices of all kinds.
3. Banning of all political or other associations advocating ethnic, regional, religious or gender discrimination or ideas contrary to national unity.
4. Deliberate promotion of disadvantaged groups, particularly the Batwa, to correct the existing imbalances in all sectors. This exercise shall be conducted, while maintaining professionalism and avoiding the quota system, in accordance with a timetable starting at the same time as the transition period.

Principles and measures relating to public administration

5. A qualified, efficient and responsible administration that shall work in the general interest and promote balance, including gender balance.
6. A transparent administration committed to the sound management of public affairs.
7. Training, in such a way as to include all the components of Burundian society, of civil servants, particularly for regional and local government, by establishing a national school of administration.

For additional analytical, marketing, investment and business opportunities information, please contact
Global Investment & Business Center, USA
(202) 546-2103. Fax: (202) 546-3275. E-mail: rusric@erols.com

8. Equal opportunities of access to this sector for all men and women through strict respect for, or the introduction of, laws and regulations governing the recruitment of State personnel and the staff of public and parastatal enterprises, as well as through transparency of competitive entrance examinations.
9. Depoliticization of the public administration to ensure its stability; in this respect, there is a need for legislation that will distinguish between political and technical functions; staff in the first category may change with the Government, whereas the technical staff must be guaranteed continuity.
10. Reinstatement of former refugees, taking into account experience gained before and during their exile.

Principles and measures relating to education

11. Equitable regional distribution of school buildings, equipment and textbooks throughout the national territory, in such a way as to benefit girls and boys equally.
12. Deliberate promotion of compulsory primary education that ensures gender parity through joint financial support from the State and the communes.
13. Transparency and fairness in non-competitive and competitive examinations.
14. Restoration of the rights of girls and boys whose education has been interrupted as a result of the Burundi conflict or of exclusion, by effectively reintegrating them into the school system and later into working life.

Principles and measures relating to the defence and security forces

15. Clear definition of the roles of the defence and security forces.
16. Organization of the defence and security forces as a voluntary and professional entity, and their modernization.
17. Relevant reforms to correct the ethnic, gender and regional imbalances within these forces pursuant to the relevant provisions of Protocol III to the Agreement.

Principles and measures relating to justice

18. Pursuant to the relevant provisions of Protocol II to the Agreement:
    a. Promotion of impartial and independent justice. In this respect, all petitions and appeals relating to assassinations and political trials shall be made through the National Truth and Reconciliation Commission established pursuant to the provisions of article 8 of the present Protocol;

For additional analytical, marketing, investment and business opportunities information, please contact
Global Investment & Business Center, USA
(202) 546-2103. Fax: (202) 546-3275. E-mail: rusric@erols.com

b. Reform of the judicial machinery at all levels, inter alia with a view to correcting ethnic and gender imbalances where they exist;

c. Amendment of laws where necessary (Criminal Code, Code of Criminal Procedure, Civil Code, Nationality Act, etc.);

d. Reform of the Judicial Service Commission so as to ensure its independence and that of the judicial system;

e. Organization of a judicial training programme, inter alia through the establishment of a National School for the Magistracy;

f. Provision of adequate human and material resources for the courts;

g. Establishment of the post of Ombudsperson.

Principles and measures relating to the economy

19. Equitable apportionment and redistribution of national resources throughout the country.

20. Urgent implementation of an economic recovery programme with a view to combating poverty and raising the income of the people and of a programme for the reconstruction of destroyed economic infrastructures.

21. Legislation and structures for combating financial crime and corruption (tax legislation, customs legislation, legislation on public markets, etc.).

22. Recovery of State property plundered by some citizens.

23. Introduction of incentives for economic development in the context of fairness and harmony.

24. Development of the private sector by means of incentives with a view to creating new jobs and reducing the burden and pressures on the public sector.

Principles and measures relating to social services

25. Pursuant to the relevant provisions of Protocol IV to the Agreement:

a. Equitable distribution of and access to social infrastructures, particularly schools and hospitals;

b. Promotion of a policy of assumption by the communes of responsibility for their own affairs, in the context of decentralization;

c. Definitive resolution of the issues relating to refugees, displaced persons, regrouped persons, dispersed persons and other sinistrés: rehabilitation, resettlement, reintegration and compensation for plundered property;

d. Return to the rightful successors of the victims of the various crises of property confiscated by certain bodies or by the State or stolen by third parties: movable and immovable property, bank and Savings Bank (CADBU) assets, contributions to the Social Security Fund (INSS);

For additional analytical, marketing, investment and business opportunities information, please contact
Global Investment & Business Center, USA
(202) 546-2103. Fax: (202) 546-3275. E-mail: rusric@erols.com

e. Establishment of a National Commission for the Rehabilitation of Sinistrés to benefit the victims of the various crises;

f. Establishment by the State of mechanisms to facilitate the recovery and repatriation of refugees' assets abroad.

Cultural principles and measures

26. Education of the population, particularly of youth, in positive traditional cultural values such as solidarity, social cooperation, forgiveness and mutual tolerance, Ibanga (discretion and sense of responsibility), Ubupfasoni (respect for others and for oneself) and Ubuntu (humanism and character).

27. Rehabilitation of the institution of Ubushingantahe.

Article 8
Principles and measures relating to national reconciliation

1. A national commission known as the National Truth and Reconciliation Commission shall be established. This Commission shall have the following functions:

a. Investigation

The Commission shall bring to light and establish the truth regarding the serious acts of violence committed during the cyclical conflicts which cast a tragic shadow over Burundi from independence (1 July 1962) to the date of signature of the Agreement, classify the crimes and establish the responsibilities, as well as the identity of the perpetrators and the victims. However, the Commission shall not be competent to classify acts of genocide, crimes against humanity and war crimes;

b. Arbitration and reconciliation

The Burundian crisis is a profound one: the task of reconciliation will be long and exacting. There are still gaping wounds which will need to be healed.

To this end the Commission shall, upon completion of its investigations, propose to the competent institutions or adopt measures likely to promote reconciliation and forgiveness, order indemnification or restoration of disputed property, or propose any political, social or other measures it deems appropriate.

For additional analytical, marketing, investment and business opportunities information, please contact
Global Investment & Business Center, USA
(202) 546-2103. Fax: (202) 546-3275. E-mail: rusric@erols.com

In this context, the transitional National Assembly may pass a law or laws providing a framework for granting an amnesty consistent with international law for such political crimes as it or the National Truth and Reconciliation Commission may find appropriate;

c. Clarification of history

The Commission shall also be responsible for clarifying the entire history of Burundi, going as far back as possible in order to inform Burundians about their past. The purpose of this clarification exercise shall be to rewrite Burundi's history so that all Burundians can interpret it in the same way.

2. Membership of the commission
    a. Source

    Candidates for membership of the Commission shall be put forward by civil society associations, political parties, religious denominations or women's organizations, or may stand as individual candidates.

    b. Appointing body

    Members of the Commission shall be appointed by the transitional Government in consultation with the Bureau of the transitional National Assembly.

    c. Profile and selection of candidates

    Members of the Commission must show probity, integrity and ability to rise above divisions of all kinds. In the selection of candidates, balance must be taken into account, and the following criteria shall apply:

    i.   Age of members: at least 35 years;
    ii. Level of education: at least a full secondary education certificate or equivalent.

3. Functioning of the Commission

The Commission must have the leeway to work independently, inter alia through autonomy in managing the material and financial resources to be allocated to it.

For additional analytical, marketing, investment and business opportunities information, please contact
Global Investment & Business Center, USA
(202) 546-2103. Fax: (202) 546-3275. E-mail: rusric@erols.com

The Commission shall, whenever necessary, propose additional reconciliation mechanisms, and shall be free to set up sub-commissions as appropriate.

The public authorities shall have the obligation to do their utmost to enable the Commission to accomplish its mission without hindrance, by providing it with sufficient material, technical and financial resources.

4. Duration

The Commission shall conduct its work over a two-year period. At the end of two years, the appropriate transitional institutions shall assess the work done, and may decide on an extension for one year.

PROTOCOL II: DEMOCRACY AND GOOD GOVERNANCE

PREAMBLE

We, the Parties,

Aware of the vital need to promote lasting peace in Burundi and to put an end to the conflict, division and suffering inflicted on the Burundian people,

Reaffirming our commitment to a democratic system of government, inspired by the realities of our country, that guarantees security and justice for all, and is founded on the values of unity without exclusion,

Have agreed:

1. To ensure that a constitutional text for the people of Burundi is drafted during the transition period that is in conformity with the principles set forth in Chapter I of the present Protocol, and to ensure that such a text is adopted and brought into force in accordance with the time-frames and procedures herein, in conformity with a vision of democracy and good governance and the principles listed hereunder.
2. To provide for a transition period that is in conformity with the transitional arrangements set forth in Chapter II of the present Protocol.
3. To give effect, within the designated time limits, to the obligations set forth in this and other protocols with regard to the establishment of the transitional institutions.

CHAPTER I CONSTITUTIONAL PRINCIPLES OF THE POST-TRANSITION CONSTITUTION

For additional analytical, marketing, investment and business opportunities information, please contact
Global Investment & Business Center, USA
(202) 546-2103. Fax: (202) 546-3275. E-mail: rusric@erols.com

Article 1
Fundamental values

1. All Burundians are equal in value and dignity. All citizens are entitled to equal rights and to equal protection of the law. No Burundian shall be excluded from the social, economic or political life of the nation on account of her/his race, language, religion, gender, or ethnic origin.
2. All Burundians are entitled to live in Burundi in security and peace, and must live in harmony with one another while respecting one another's dignity and tolerating one another's differences.
3. Government shall be based on the will of the Burundian people, shall be accountable to them, and shall respect their fundamental rights and freedoms.
4. The Government of Burundi shall be so structured as to ensure that all Burundians are represented in and by it; that there is equal opportunity to serve in it; that all citizens have access to government services; and that the decisions and actions of government enjoy the widest possible level of support.
5. The task of government shall be to realize the aspirations of the Burundian people, and in particular to heal the divisions of the past, to improve the quality of life of all Burundians, and to ensure that all Burundians are able to live in Burundi free from fear, discrimination, disease and hunger.
6. The function of the political system shall be to unite, reassure and reconcile all Burundians while ensuring that the Government is able to serve the people of Burundi, who are its source of power and authority. In its functioning the Government shall respect the separation of powers, the rule of law, and the principles of good governance and transparency in the management of public affairs.

Article 2
General principles

1. Burundi shall be a sovereign independent nation, united but respecting its ethnic and religious diversity and recognizing the Bahutu, the Batutsi and the Batwa, who make up the one nation of Burundi.
2. The national territory of Burundi shall be inalienable and indivisible subject to the provisions of the Constitution. Its frontiers shall be those recognized by international law.
3. Burundi shall be divided into provinces, communes and collines or zones, and such other subdivisions as are provided for by law. Their organization and operation shall be determined by the Constitution and by law.
4. The National Assembly shall take a decision regarding the status and revival of the monarchy, and any party peacefully promoting the restoration of the monarchy shall be allowed to function.

For additional analytical, marketing, investment and business opportunities information, please contact
Global Investment & Business Center, USA
(202) 546-2103. Fax: (202) 546-3275. E-mail: rusric@erols.com

5. The national language of Burundi shall be Kirundi. The official languages shall be Kirundi and any other languages decided upon by the National Assembly.

Article 3
Charter of Fundamental Rights

1. The rights and duties proclaimed and guaranteed inter alia by the Universal Declaration of Human Rights, the International Covenants on Human Rights, the African Charter on Human and Peoples' Rights, the Convention on the Elimination of All Forms of Discrimination against Women and the Convention on the Rights of the Child shall form an integral part of the Constitution of the Republic of Burundi. These fundamental rights shall not be limited or derogated from, except in justifiable circumstances acceptable in international law and set forth in the Constitution.
2. All citizens shall have rights and obligations.
3. Human dignity shall be respected and protected.
4. All women and men shall be equal. No one may be discriminated against, inter alia, on grounds of origin, race, ethnicity, gender, colour, language, social situation, or religious, philosophical or political convictions, or by reason of a physical or mental handicap. All citizens shall enjoy equal protection of the law, as well as equal treatment under the law.
5. No person shall be arbitrarily dealt with by the State or its organs.
6. All women and men shall have the right to life.
7. All women and men shall have the right to personal freedom, including to physical and mental integrity, and to freedom of movement. Torture and any other kind of cruel, inhuman, degrading treatment or punishment shall be prohibited. Everyone shall have the right to be free from violence from either public or private sources.
8. No one shall be held in slavery or servitude. Slavery and the slave trade shall be prohibited in all their forms.
9. The State shall to the extent possible ensure that all citizens have the means to lead an existence consistent with human dignity.
10. All women and men shall have the right to respect for their private and family life, residence and personal communications.
11. There shall be freedom of marriage, including the right to choose one's partner. Marriage shall be entered into only with the free and full consent of the intending spouses.
12. The family, as the fundamental unit of society, shall be entitled to protection by society and the State.
13. Freedom of expression and of the media shall be guaranteed. The State shall respect freedom of religion, belief, conscience and opinion.

For additional analytical, marketing, investment and business opportunities information, please contact
Global Investment & Business Center, USA
(202) 546-2103. Fax: (202) 546-3275. E-mail: rusric@erols.com

14. Freedom of assembly and association shall be guaranteed, as shall freedom to form non-profit-making associations or organizations in conformity with the law.

15. All Burundian citizens shall have the right to move and settle freely anywhere in the national territory, as well as to leave it and return to it.

16. No one shall be arbitrarily deprived of her/his nationality or denied the right to change it.

17. No one may be denied access to basic education. The State shall organize public education, and shall develop and promote access to secondary and post-secondary education.

18. The State shall ensure the good management and utilization of the nation's natural resources on a sustainable basis, conserving such resources for future generations.

19. Property rights shall be guaranteed for all women and men. Compensation that is fair and equitable under the circumstances shall be payable in case of expropriation, which shall be allowed only in the public interest and in accordance with a law which shall also set forth the basis of compensation.

20. The right to form and join trade unions and to strike shall be recognized. The law may regulate the exercise of these rights and prohibit certain categories of persons from going on strike.

21. Everyone shall have the right, in judicial or administrative proceedings, for her/his case to be dealt with equitably and decided within a reasonable time limit. Everyone shall have the right to due process and a fair trial.

22. No one may be deprived of her/his liberty other than in conformity with the law.

23. The State shall be under an obligation to promote the development of the country, especially rural development.

24. Each individual shall have the duty to respect and show consideration for her/his fellow citizens without any discrimination.

25. All citizens shall be required to discharge their civic obligations, and to defend their homeland.

26. Every child shall have the right to special measures to protect or promote her/his care, welfare, health and physical security, and to be protected from maltreatment, abuse or exploitation.

27. No child shall be used directly in armed conflict, and children shall be protected in times of armed conflict.

28. No child shall be detained except as a measure of last resort, in which case the child may be detained only for the shortest appropriate period of time and shall have the right to be kept separately from detained persons over the age of 16 years and to be treated in a manner, and kept in conditions, that take account of her/his age.

For additional analytical, marketing, investment and business opportunities information, please contact
Global Investment & Business Center, USA
(202) 546-2103. Fax: (202) 546-3275. E-mail: rusric@erols.com

29. Any restriction of a fundamental right must have a legal basis; it must be justified by the public interest or by the protection of another person's fundamental right; it must be proportional to the objective pursued.
30. Fundamental rights must be respected throughout the legal, administrative and institutional order. The Constitution shall be the supreme law and must be upheld by the Legislature, the Executive and the Judiciary. Any law that is not in conformity with the Constitution shall be invalid.

Article 4
Political parties

1. The multiparty system shall be recognized in the Republic of Burundi.
2. Political parties may be formed freely in conformity with the law.
3. A political party shall be a non-profit association uniting citizens around a democratic blueprint for society founded on national unity, and having a political programme with precise objectives dictated by the desire to serve the public interest and ensure the development of all citizens.
4. Political parties must comply with democratic principles in their organization and functioning, be open to all Burundians and be national in character and leadership, and shall not promote ethnic, regional or religious violence and hatred.
5. Political parties - and coalitions of political parties - shall promote the free expression of suffrage and shall participate in political life by peaceful means.
6. For the purposes of promoting democracy, a national law may authorize the financing of political parties on an equitable basis in proportion to the number of seats they hold in the National Assembly. Such financing may apply both to the functioning of the political parties and to electoral campaigns, and shall be transparent. The law shall define the types of subsidies, benefits and facilities that the State may grant political parties.
7. Registration of political parties shall fall within the competence of the Ministry of the Interior.
8. The law shall guarantee non-interference by the public authorities in the internal functioning of political parties, save for such restrictions as may be necessary for the prevention of ethnic hatred and the maintenance of public order.
9. Political parties may form coalitions during elections in accordance with the electoral law.

Article 5
Elections

1. The right to vote shall be guaranteed.

For additional analytical, marketing, investment and business opportunities information, please contact
Global Investment & Business Center, USA
(202) 546-2103. Fax: (202) 546-3275. E-mail: rusric@erols.com

2. Elections shall be free, fair and regular in accordance with the electoral law and the law governing political parties.
3. Elections shall be organized impartially at the national, commune and colline levels and at other levels prescribed by the Constitution or by law.
4. Until amended in accordance with the post-transition Constitution, the rules relating to the electoral system shall be the same as those governing the elections for institutions at the national, commune and colline levels to be held during the transition period.
5. An Independent National Electoral Commission constituted in conformity with the provisions of article 20 of the present Protocol shall guarantee the freedom, impartiality and independence of the electoral process.

Article 6
The Legislature

1. Legislative power shall be exercised by the National Assembly and, where specified herein, by the National Assembly and the Senate. A law adopted by a legislative body or bodies may only be amended by the same body or bodies.
2. The nwnber of members of the National AssembJy shall be specified in the Constitution, and in the first instance shall be 100. The Constitution may allow for the number of members to be determined in accordance with a designated ratio per number ofinhabitants or by setting an absolute number.
3. The National Assembly shall pass legislation, oversee the actions of the Government and exercise all other functions assigned to it by the Constitution. The National Assembly shall be responsible for approving the national budget. This provision shall not preclude the submission of matters for popular approval by way of referendum.
4. A Court of Audit responsible for examining and certifying the accounts of all public services shall be established and organized by law. Its composition shall be specified in the post-transition Constitution. It shall be given the resources required for the performance of its duties. Administrative departments shall not withhold their co-operation from the Court of Audit. The Court of Audit shall submit to the National Assembly a report on the regularity of the general account of the State, and shall also ascertain whether public funds have been spent in accordance with the proper procedures and in accordance with the budget approved by the National Assembly.
5. The Constitution may not be amended except with the support of a **four-fifths** majority in the National Assembly and a **two-thirds** majority in the Senate.
6. Organic laws may not be amended except by a **three-fifths** majority in the National Assembly and with the approval of the Senate.

For additional analytical, marketing, investment and business opportunities information, please contact
Global Investment & Business Center, USA
(202) 546-2103. Fax: (202) 546-3275. E-mail: rusric@erols.com

7. Members of the National Assembly and the Senate may not be prosecuted, made the subject of a warrant, arrested, detained or subjected to a penalty for acts performed as a member of the National Assembly or of the Senate.

8. Any criminal case involving a person holding political office shall be referred to a Chamber of the Supreme Court, and in the event of conviction, any appeal shall be receivable by the Chambers of the Supreme Court sitting together.

9. During sessions, a member of the National Assembly or the Senate may be prosecuted in respect of acts other than those referred to in paragraph 7 above only with the authorization of the National Assembly or the Senate, as the case may be.

10. The mechanisms for replacing members of the National Assembly or the Senate in the event of the vacancy of a seat shall be determined by law.

11. The National Assembly and the Senate shall adopt the rules of procedure governing their respective organization and functioning and the election of their bureaux. The post-transition Constitution must specify the duties of the bureaux, when the National Assembly shall convene for the first time and who shall preside at the initial meeting. The National Assembly's Bureau shall have a multiparty character, while the Senate's Bureau shall be of a multi-ethnic character.

12. The compensation and benefits regime, as well as the incompatibility regime, for members of the National Assembly and of the Senate shall be established by law.

13. The opposition parties within the National Assembly shall participate by right in parliamentary commissions, whether sectoral or of inquiry.

14. There shall be a Senate having the functions set forth herein, and such other functions as are allocated to it in the Constitution or in any law. The Senate shall comprise two delegates from each province. They shall be elected by an Electoral College comprising members of the commune councils in the province in question, shall be from different ethnic communities and shall be elected in separate ballots.

15. A former president shall be entitled to sit in the Senate. The Senate may co-opt up to three members of the Batwa group so as to ensure representation of this community.

16. The Senate shall have the following functions:
    a. To approve constitutional amendments and organic laws, including laws governing the electoral process;
    b. To receive the report of the Ombudsperson on any aspect of the public administration;
    c. To conduct inquiries into the public administration and where necessary recommend action, to ensure that no region or group is excluded from the delivery of public services;

For additional analytical, marketing, investment and business opportunities information, please contact
Global Investment & Business Center, USA
(202) 546-2103. Fax: (202) 546-3275. E-mail: rusric@erols.com

    d. To monitor compliance with those prescripts of the Constitution requiring representativeness or balance in the composition of any part of the public service, including the defence and security forces;

    e. To advise the President and the National Assembly on any matter, including legislation;

    f. To monitor compliance with the present Protocol;

    g. To comment on or suggest amendments to legislation adopted by the National Assembly, as well as to initiate and introduce bills for consideration by the National Assembly;

    h. To approve laws dealing with the boundaries, functions and powers of provinces, communes and collines.

17. The Senate shall approve solely the following appointments:

    a. The heads of the defence forces, the police and the intelligence service;

    b. The provincial governors appointed by the President of the Republic;

    c. The Ombudsperson;

    d. The members of the Judicial Service Commission;

    e. The members of the Supreme Court;

    f. The members of the Constitutional Court;

    g. The Principal State Prosecutor and members of the National Department of Public Prosecutions;

    h. The presidents of the Court of Appeal and the Administrative Court;

    i. The principal State Prosecutor in the Court of Appeal;

    j. The presidents of the Court of First Instance, the Commercial Court and the Labour Court;

    k. The State Prosecutors.

18. The Senate shall ensure that commune councils in general reflect the ethnic diversity of their constituencies; if the composition of any Commune Council does not do so, it may order the co-optation of persons by the Commune Council from an underrepresented ethnic group to that Council, provided that no more than **one-fifth** of the Council may consist of such co-opted persons. The persons to be co-opted shall be identified by the Senate from a list of names supplied to it by the Commune Council or by any colline chief within the commune.

19. Where the Senate proposes amendments to laws other than those in respect of which its consent is necessary, the National Assembly must consider those proposed amendments, and may if it so chooses give effect to them, before referring the bill to the President for his formal assent.

20. Members of the National Assembly and of the Senate shall have the right to debate the Government's actions and policies.

21. The Constitution shall grant the Senate the powers and resources necessary to perform its functions.

For additional analytical, marketing, investment and business opportunities information, please contact
Global Investment & Business Center, USA
(202) 546-2103. Fax: (202) 546-3275. E-mail: rusric@erols.com

Article 7
The Executive

1.

   a. The Constitution shall provide that, save for the very first election of a President, the President of the Republic shall be elected by direct universal suffrage in which each elector may vote for only one candidate. The President of the Republic shall be elected by an absolute majority of the votes cast. If this majority is not obtained in the first round, a second round shall follow within 15 days.

   b. Only the two candidates who have received the greatest number of votes during the first round may stand in the second round. The candidate who receives the majority of votes cast in the second round shall be declared the President of the Republic.

   c. For the first election, to be held during the transition period, the President shall be indirectly elected as specified in article 20, paragraph 10 below.

2. The President of the Republic shall exercise regulatory power and shall ensure the proper enforcement and administration of legislation. She/he shall exercise her/his powers by decrees, countersigned, where required, by a Vice-President or a minister concerned.

3. She/he shall be elected for a term of five years, renewable only once. No one may serve more than two presidential terms.

4. In the exercise of her/his functions, the President of the Republic shall be assisted by two Vice-Presidents. They shall be appointed by the President of the Republic, who shall previously have submitted their candidacy for approval by the National Assembly and the Senate, voting separately, by a majority of their members. The President of the Republic may dismiss the Vice-Presidents. They shall belong to different ethnic groups and political parties.

5. The President of the Republic, after consultation with the two Vice-Presidents, shall appoint the members of the Government and terminate their appointments.

6. Parties or coalitions thereof shall be invited, but not obliged, to submit to the President a list of persons to serve as ministers if such parties or coalitions have received more than **one-twentieth** of the vote. They shall be entitled to at least the same proportion, rounded off downwards, of the total number of ministers as their proportion of members in the National Assembly. If the President dismisses a minister, she/he must choose a replacement from a list submitted by the party or coalition of the minister in question.

7. The President of the Republic shall be the Head of State and Commander-in-Chief of the defence and security forces. She/he shall

For additional analytical, marketing, investment and business opportunities information, please contact
Global Investment & Business Center, USA
(202) 546-2103. Fax: (202) 546-3275. E-mail: rusric@erols.com

declare war and sign armistices following consultation with the Government and the bureaux of the National Assembly and of the Senate.

8. The President of the Republic may be impeached for serious misconduct, impropriety or corruption by resolution of **two-thirds** of the members of the National Assembly and the Senate sitting together.

9. The President of the Republic may be charged only with the crime of high treason. The case shall be heard by the Supreme Court and the Constitutional Court sitting together and presided over by the President of the Supreme Court.

10. The Supreme Court shall receive a written statement of the assets and property of the President, the Vice-Presidents and members of the Government when they assume and relinquish office.

Article 8
Local government

1. The provinces shall be administered by civilian governors appointed by the President of the Republic and confirmed by the Senate.

2. Communes shall be decentralized administrative entities. They shall be the basis of economic and social development, and shall be divided into collines or zones and such other subdivisions as are provided for by law.

3. The law shall make provision for the circumstances under which a commune administrator may be dismissed or suspended, by the central authorities or by the Commune Council, for good cause including incompetence, corruption, gross misconduct or embezzlement.

Article 9
The Judiciary

1. The judicial authority of the Republic of Burundi shall be vested in the courts.

2. The Judiciary shall be impartial and independent and shall be governed solely by the Constitution and the law. No person may interfere with the Judiciary in the performance of its judicial functions.

3. The Judiciary shall be so structured as to promote the ideal that its composition should reflect that of the population as a whole.

4. The courts and tribunals shall operate in Kirundi and the other official languages. Laws shall be enacted and published in Kirundi and the other official languages.

5. The Constitution shall provide for a Supreme Court of Burundi. Its Rules of Procedure, composition and chambers, and the organization of its chambers, shall be determined by an organic law.

For additional analytical, marketing, investment and business opportunities information, please contact
Global Investment & Business Center, USA
(202) 546-2103. Fax: (202) 546-3275. E-mail: rusric@erols.com

6. The judges of the Supreme Court shall be appointed by the President from a list of candidates nominated by the Judicial Service Commission and approved by the National Assembly and the Senate.
7. There shall be a National Department of Public Prosecutions attached to the Supreme Court; its members shall be appointed in the same manner as the judges of the Supreme Court.
8. The other courts and tribunals recognized in the Republic of Burundi shall be the Court of Appeal, the High Courts, the Resident Magistrates' Courts and such other courts and tribunals as are provided for by law. The Ubushingantahe Council shall sit at the level of the colline. It shall administer justice in a conciliatory spirit.
9. The President of the Court of Appeal, the presidents of the High Courts, the public prosecutors and the state counsels shall be appointed by the President of the Republic following nomination by the Judicial Service Commission and confirmation by the Senate.
10. The Government, within the limits of its resources, shall ensure that magistrates possess the desired qualifications and necessary training for the performance of their duties, and that the resources needed by the Judiciary are made available to it.
11. No one shall be denied a post in the magistracy on grounds of ethnic origin or gender.
12. A Judicial Service Commission with an ethnically balanced composition shall be established. It shall be made up of five members nominated by the Executive, three judges of the Supreme Court, two magistrates from the National Department of Public Prosecutions, two judges from the resident magistrates' courts and three members of the legal profession in private practice. The judges, magistrates and members of the legal profession shall be chosen by their peers. All members of the Commission shall be approved by the Senate.
13. The Commission shall have a secretariat. It shall be chaired by the President of the Republic, assisted by the Minister of Justice. It shall meet on an ad hoc basis. Its members who are not members of the Judiciary shall not be construed as members of the Judiciary solely because they are members of this oversight commission.
14. The Judicial Service Commission shall be the highest disciplinary body of the magistracy. It shall hear complaints by individuals, or by the Ombudsperson, against the professional conduct of magistrates, as well as appeals against disciplinary measures and grievances concerning the career of magistrates. No magistrate may be dismissed other than for professional misconduct or incompetence, and solely on the basis of a finding by the Judicial Service Commission.
15. Trials shall be public except where the interests of justice or a compelling public interest require otherwise. Judgements shall be reasoned and shall be handed down in public.

For additional analytical, marketing, investment and business opportunities information, please contact
Global Investment & Business Center, USA
(202) 546-2103. Fax: (202) 546-3275. E-mail: rusric@erols.com

16. Magistrates shall be appointed by decree of the President on the proposal of the Judicial Service Commission. The presidents of resident magistrates' courts shall be appointed in the same manner except that the nominees shall be proposed to the President after obtaining the approval of the Senate.

17. The Constitutional Court shall be the highest court for constitutional matters. Its jurisdictions shall be those set forth in the 1992 Constitution. The organization of the Court shall be laid down in an organic law. Reference is made for this purpose to the elements contained in Chapter II of the present Protocol.

18. The members of the Constitutional Court, seven in number, shall be appointed by the President of the Republic and confirmed by the Senate by a **two-thirds** majority. They shall have a term of office of six years non-renewable. The first Constitutional Court shall be that established under Chapter II of the present Protocol for the transition period. The members shall have the qualifications set forth in Chapter II of the present Protocol.

19. Matters shall be referred to the Constitutional Court by the President of the Republic, the President of the National Assembly or the President of the Senate, by petition by **one quarter** of the Members of the National Assembly or **one quarter** of the Members of the Senate, or by the Ombudsperson. In addition, every natural person with a direct interest in the matter, as well as the Public Prosecutor, may request the Constitutional Court to rule on the constitutionality of laws, either directly by means of an action or by an exceptional procedure for claiming unconstitutionality raised in a matter which concerns that person before an authority.

20. The Constitutional Court may sit validly only if at least five of its members are present.

21. Decisions of the Constitutional Court shall be taken by an absolute majority of its members, except that the President of the Court shall have a casting vote if the Court is evenly split on any matter.

22. The Constitutional Court shall be competent to:
    a. Rule on the constitutionality of adopted laws and regulatory acts;
    b. Rule on the constitutionality of executive action;
    c. Interpret the Constitution and rule on vacancies in the posts of President of the Republic and President of the National Assembly if a dispute arises in regard thereto;
    d. Rule on the regularity of presidential and legislative elections;
    e. Administer the oath to the President of the Republic before she/he assumes office;
    f. Verify the constitutionality of organic laws before their promulgation, and of the Rules of Procedure of the National Assembly before their application;

For additional analytical, marketing, investment and business opportunities information, please contact
Global Investment & Business Center, USA
(202) 546-2103. Fax: (202) 546-3275. E-mail: rusric@erols.com

g. Rule on any other matters expressly provided for in the Constitution.

Article 10
The administration

1. The administration shall function in accordance with the democratic values and principles enshrined in the Constitution, and with the law.
2. The administration shall be so structured, and all civil servants shall so perform their duties, as to serve all users of public services with efficiency, courtesy, impartiality and equity. Embezzlement, corruption, extortion and misappropriation of all kinds shall be punishable in accordance with the law. Any state employee convicted of corruption shall be dismissed from the public administration following a disciplinary inquiry.
3. The administration shall be organized in ministries, and every minister in charge of a ministry shall report to the President of the Republic and to the National Assembly on the manner in which the ministry performs its functions and utilizes the funds allocated to it.
4. The administration shall be broadly representative and reflect the diversity of the components of the Burundian nation. The practices with respect to employment shall be based on objective and equitable criteria of aptitude and on the need to correct the imbalances and achieve broad representation.
5. A law shall specify the distinction between posts that are career or technical posts and those that are political posts.
6. No civil servant or member of the Judiciary may be accorded favourable or unfavourable treatment solely on grounds of her/his gender, ethnicity or political affiliation.
7. An independent Ombudsperson shall be created by the Constitution. The organization and functioning of her/his service shall be determined by law.
8. The Ombudsperson shall hear complaints and conduct inquiries relating to mismanagement and infringements of citizens' rights committed by members of the public administration and the judiciary, and shall make recommendations thereon to the appropriate authorities. She/he shall also mediate between the administration and citizens and between administrative departments, and shall act as an observer of the functioning of the public administration.
9. The Ombudsperson shall possess the powers and resources required to perform her/his duty. She/he shall report annually to the National Assembly and the Senate. Her/his report shall be published in the Official Gazette of Burundi.
10. The Ombudsperson shall be appointed by the National Assembly by a three-quarters majority. The appointment shall be subject to confirmation by the Senate.

For additional analytical, marketing, investment and business opportunities information, please contact
Global Investment & Business Center, USA
(202) 546-2103. Fax: (202) 546-3275. E-mail: rusric@erols.com

Article 11
Defence and security forces

1. The post-transition Constitution shall contain in full the principles relating to the defence and security forces and principles of organization of those forces set forth respectively in articles 10 and 11 of Protocol III to the Agreement.
2. An organic law shall determine the organization and functioning of the defence and security forces.
3. The military head of the defence force shall be appointed by the President, subject to confirmation by the Senate.
4.
    a. The defence and security forces shall be subordinate to the civil authority of the State, and shall uphold the Constitution and the law.
    b. The defence and security forces shall be professional and non-partisan, and shall not promote or disadvantage any political party or ethnic group.
    c. The defence and security forces shall be trained at all levels to respect international humanitarian law and the supremacy of the Constitution.
    d. For a period to be determined by the Senate, not more than 50% of the national defence force shall be drawn from any one ethnic group, in view of the need to achieve ethnic balance and to prevent acts of genocide and coups d'état.
    e. No civilian shall be subject to a military code of justice or tried by a military court.
5. Only the President may authorize the employment of the defence and security forces:
    a. In defence of the State;
    b. In the restoration of order and public safety;
    c. In the discharge of international obligations and commitments.

If the defence and security forces are employed in any of the capacities set forth above, the President shall promptly inform the National Assembly and the Senate of the nature, extent and reasons for this employment. If the National Assembly is not in session it shall be convened within seven days for the consideration of such matter, as specified in Protocol III to the Agreement.

CHAPTER II TRANSITIONAL ARRANGEMENTS

Article 12
Objectives

For additional analytical, marketing, investment and business opportunities information, please contact
Global Investment & Business Center, USA
(202) 546-2103. Fax: (202) 546-3275. E-mail: rusric@erols.com

1. Exceptional and special arrangements concerning the government of Burundi shall be made pending the adoption and entry into force of a Constitution that is in conformity with the constitutional principles set forth in Chapter I of the present Protocol.
2. The objectives of the transitional arrangements shall be:
    a. To ensure the adoption of a post-transition Constitution that is in conformity with the constitutional principles;
    b. To reconcile and unite Burundians and lay the foundations for a democratic and united Burundi, inter alia by promoting a broad programme of education in peace, democracy and ethnic tolerance;
    c. To ensure the repatriation, resettlement and reintegration of Burundians living outside the national territory and the rehabilitation of the sinistrés;
    d. To apply the measures and arrangements relating to the restoration of peace, the cessation of hostilities and the building of a professional army loyal to Burundi;
    e. To ensure the adoption of agreed measures to confront the consequences of the past and avoid any recurrence of genocide, exclusion and impunity;
    f. To implement the measures and carry out the reforms relating to the Judiciary, the administration and the defence and security forces in accordance with the Agreement;
    g. To adopt an electoral law, establish an independent electoral commission and ensure the holding during the transition period of elections at the local and national levels as provided for in article 20 below;
    h. To adopt laws on political parties, local administration, the press and other matters as required by the present Protocol and by the needs of the transitional institutions;
    i. To implement the Agreement in accordance with the implementation timetable in Annex V to the Agreement.

Article 13
Duration of the transition

1. The transition period shall commence from the time that the conditions necessary for installing the transitional Government in accordance with the applicable instruments have been met, which shall be as soon as possible after three months, and in any event not later than six months, from the date of signature of the Agreement. The Implementation Monitoring Committee alone shall determine this date, and may bring it forward if it decides that the necessary conditions exist. Until the transition period commences, all parties shall meet their obligations under the Agreement to establish or co-operate in establishing the agreed legal and institutional

For additional analytical, marketing, investment and business opportunities information, please contact
Global Investment & Business Center, USA
(202) 546-2103. Fax: (202) 546-3275. E-mail: rusric@erols.com

framework. The implementation Monitoring Committee, established as set forth in Protocol V, shall be the mechanism for guaranteeing compliance with the Agreement.

2. The transition period shall culminate upon the election of the new President. The presidential election shall take place after the first democratic election of the National Assembly. Both elections shall take place within 30 months of the commencement of the transition period.

Article 14
Political parties during the transition

1. The transitional National Assembly shall within twelve months of its installation adopt a law setting forth the qualifications and procedure for registration of political parties.
2. The said law shall specify a judicial authority which shall receive and adjudicate on applications by political parties for registration. Decision of the authority shall be posted in public places and published in the official Gazette of Burundi.
3. Pending the adoption of such a law, all political parties shall be entitled to function in accordance with the 1993 law on political parties.
4. The political parties shall commit themselves in writing to oppose any political ideology and any action that has at its purpose the promotion of violence, hatred or unlawful discrimination.
5. In order to promote national renewal, reconciliation and unity, no party shall be registered if it is established on the basis of ethnic or regional exclusivity. This sub-clause shall take effect nine months after the commencement of the transition period, in order to enable parties whose names or constitution do not satisfy this requirement to duly amend them so as to comply.
6. No political party may participate in the transitional arrangements, including those relating to the integration of the defence and security forces, if they do not respect the commitments embodied in the Agreement. Each such "participating party" must sign the pledge annexed hereto confirming its intention to participate in the transitional arrangements and its commitment to peace, reconciliation and democracy.
7. If political parties represented within the transitional National Assembly decide to merge, the merging parties shall retain the number of seats they had acquired initially.
8. Subject to the provisions of paragraphs 6 and 9 of this article, all Parties shall be entitled, but not obliged, to become participating parties.
9. The Government and National Assembly that are signatories to the Agreement shall not be participating parties unless specifically so provided in the Agreement.

For additional analytical, marketing, investment and business opportunities information, please contact
Global Investment & Business Center, USA
(202) 546-2103. Fax: (202) 546-3275. E-mail: rusric@erols.com

10. A non-signatory party may become a participating party subsequent to the date of signature of the Agreement if **four-fifths** of the Parties represented in the Implementation Monitoring Committee so agree.
11. If a non-signatory party is admitted as a participating party in accordance with the present Protocol, it shall be accorded the same entitlement to participate in the transitional institutions and the Implementation Monitoring Committee as the other participating parties.

Article 15
Transitional institutions

1. There shall be a transitional Legislature made up of a National Assembly and a Senate, a transitional Executive, a Judiciary and other transitional institutions as set forth in the present Protocol.
2. The constitutional provisions governing the powers, duties and functioning of the transitional Executive, the transitional Legislature and the Judiciary, as well as the rights and duties of citizens and of political parties and associations, shall be as set forth hereunder and, where this text is silent, in the Constitution of the Republic of Burundi of 13 March 1992. When there is any conflict between that Constitution and the Agreement, the provisions of the Agreement shall prevail. To give legal effect to this provision, the terms of the Agreement shall be appropriately adopted and promulgated within Burundi within four weeks of its signature.
3. The composition of the transitional National Assembly shall be as follows:

The National Assembly

   a. The Members of the National Assembly elected in 1993 shall retain or resume their seats. Where vacancies have occurred, the parties whose members occupied the vacant seats before the vacancy occurred shall fill them or allow those who have already filled them to remain;
   b. The transitional National Assembly shall be augmented so that each of the participating parties which are not represented under (a) will be entitled to at least three seats so as to be represented within the transitional National Assembly;
   c. It shall thereafter be augmented by the 28 members representing civil society currently sitting in the National Assembly;
   d. The appointed members of the National Assembly shall retain their seats in the transitional National Assembly regardless of the return from exile of the members of the National Assembly elected in 1993.

The Senate

For additional analytical, marketing, investment and business opportunities information, please contact
Global Investment & Business Center, USA
(202) 546-2103. Fax: (202) 546-3275. E-mail: rusric@erols.com

e. The Senate shall be put in place by the President of the Republic and the Bureau of the National Assembly, while ensuring respect for the political, regional and ethnic balances;

f. It shall include inter alia former heads of State, three individuals from the Twa ethnic group and members of the transitional National Assembly coopted by the President of the Republic and the Bureau of the transitional National Assembly;

g. No provision shall be made for replacement of the members of the transitional National Assembly coopted to sit in the transitional Senate;

h. The transitional Senate shall perform the functions provided for inter alia in article 6 paragraph 16, and all such other functions and are expressly provided for in the constitutional principles embodied in the Agreement;

i. The Senate shall draw up its rules of procedure, which shall go into effect following verification by the Constitutional Court of their conformity with the transitional arrangements. Its first session shall be devoted to drawing up its rules of procedure and establishing its bureau. This session shall be presided over by the oldest Senator;

j. Its Bureau shall consist of a Speaker, and a Deputy Speaker, a Secretary-General and a Deputy Secretary-General.

4. The transitional National Assembly and the traditional Senate shall within 18 months adopt in the same terms, by a **two-thirds** majority, a post-transition Constitution in conformity with the principles set forth in Chapter I of the present Protocol.

5. After such adoption, the text in question shall be submitted to the Constitutional Court for verification of its compliance with the principles set forth in Chapter I. If the text does not so comply, the Court shall indicate which provisions must be amended. If and whenever the Court declines to certify a text submitted to it pursuant to this provision, the transitional National Assembly and the transitional Senate shall within 30 days amend the text and resubmit it to the Court.

6. A text referred to above shall, if certified, be submitted for popular approval by way of referendum. A text which is so approved shall be the post-transition Constitution and shall come into force upon the termination of the transition period.

7. If no duly adopted text has been certified and approved by referendum within 23 months of the commencement of the transition, the Implementation Monitoring Committee may instruct experts - either national or international - to prepare a text in conformity with Chapter I of the present Protocol. The experts shall have regard to any judgements of the Constitutional Court and to any constitutional texts not certified by it. The text prepared by the experts shall be submitted for direct approval by way of referendum. If approved, it shall become the post-transition

For additional analytical, marketing, investment and business opportunities information, please contact
Global Investment & Business Center, USA
(202) 546-2103. Fax: (202) 546-3275. E-mail: rusric@erols.com

Constitution. If not approved, it shall serve provisionally as the Constitution for purposes of the Legislature and Executive elected during the transition period under the provisions of article 20 of the present Protocol. Such first elected Legislature shall draft a post-transition Constitution and adopt it in conformity with the procedure for amending the post-transition Constitution set forth in Chapter I of the present Protocol.

8.
   a. The rules of procedure of the transitional National Assembly shall be those of the National Assembly elected in 1993 until they are duly amended.
   b. The President and the Vice-President of the transitional National Assembly shall come from two different political families.

9. During the transition period, the National Assembly shall not pass a vote of no confidence and may not be dissolved.

10. A **two-thirds** majority shall be required for the adoption of legislation.

11. Any commission required under the present Protocol to be established by the transitional National Assembly shall be established by the Bureau of the transitional National Assembly unless otherwise indicated in the present Protocol.

12. The first transitional President and Vice-President of the Republic shall come from different ethnic groups and political parties. In the event of the death or incapacity of either of them, the new transitional President or Vice-President of the Republic shall be elected by the transitional National Assembly by a resolution which receives the support of **two-thirds** of the members. Pending the election of a new President, the President of the transitional National Assembly, assisted by the Vice-President of the Republic, shall act as President, The term of the transitional President and Vice-President shall terminate upon the election of the first President under the provisions of this Protocol.

13. During the transition period, there shall be a broad-based transitional Government of national unity. The Government shall include representatives of different parties in a proportion whereby more than **half** and less than **three-fifths** of the portfolios are allocated amongst the G-7 group of parties.

14. The precise identity of the members of the transitional Executive shall be decided by the transitional President and Vice-President after consultations with the heads of the parties participating in the transitional National Assembly.

15.
   a. There shall be between 24 and 26 members of the transitional Executive, in addition to the transitional President and Vice-President.
   b. The transitional President and Vice-President shall determine the initial function of each Minister when allocating the ministries to

For additional analytical, marketing, investment and business opportunities information, please contact
Global Investment & Business Center, USA
(202) 546-2103. Fax: (202) 546-3275. E-mail: rusric@erols.com

parties. The transitional President and Vice-President shall ensure that the minister in charge of the defence force belongs to a different family of parties from the minister responsible for the police.

16. The transitional Executive shall take its decisions and otherwise function in accordance with the spirit embodied in the concept of a Government of national unity, and shall make or propose appointments to the public administration and to diplomatic positions in the same spirit. It shall strive to take its decisions by consensus. It shall also take into account the need to reflect ethnic, religious, political, and gender balance in its decisions and appointments.

17. Any decision to be taken, by law or in accordance with the present Protocol, by the transitional President shall be taken only after consultation with the transitional Vice-President or the transitional Executive.

18. The transitional Executive shall confirm the appointment of the heads of the police and the defence force.

19. The transitional President, after consultation with the transitional Executive, shall within 30 days prepare for submission to the transitional Senate in accordance with the present Protocol a list of appointments for a period or periods specified by her/him to the offices listed below:
    a. Provincial governors;
    b. Judges of the Constitutional Court;
    c. Commune administrators.

20.
    a. The transitional Government shall within 30 days of the commencement of the transition establish a commission under the chairmanship of a judge to investigate, as a matter of urgency, and to make recommendations on:
        i. The conditions in jails, the treatment of prisoners and the training and conditions of service of warders;
        ii. The release of prisoners awaiting trial in respect of whom there has been an undue delay in the prosecution of their cases;
        iii. The existence of and release of any political prisoners.
    b. The establishment of this commission shall not preclude the transitional Government or the transitional National Assembly dealing with the above matters.

21. The transitional National Assembly and the transitional Executive may establish commissions with or without expert participation to assist in preparing texts or for any other purpose which is part of their respective missions during the transition.

For additional analytical, marketing, investment and business opportunities information, please contact
Global Investment & Business Center, USA
(202) 546-2103. Fax: (202) 546-3275. E-mail: rusric@erols.com

Article 16
Legal and administrative continuity

1. For purposes of continuity, all laws in force prior to the commencement of the transition shall remain in force until amended or repealed.
2. The transitional National Assembly shall as a priority review all legislation in force with a view to amending or repealing legislation incompatible with the objectives of the transitional arrangements and the provisions of the present Protocol.
3. The transitional National Assembly may pass laws with retrospective effect. However, no law may impose a penalty for conduct or action for which there was no penalty at the time it was committed, or provide for retrospective increase in a penalty.

Article 17
Judicial and administrative reforms

1. Within 30 days of the commencement of the transition period, a commission of the transitional National Assembly in which all the parties are represented shall be established to monitor the reforms of the public administration and of the administration of justice and to submit recommendations thereon to the transitional National Assembly and the transitional Executive.
2. The transitional National Assembly may for purposes of reforming the judicial sector amend by **two-thirds** majority any existing law, including the provisions of the 1992 Constitution, dealing with the structure and functioning of the Supreme Court.
3. For purposes of improving the judicial services in Burundi, the transitional Government shall implement the following reforms:
    a. The promotion of gender and ethnic balances in the Burundian judicial sector shall be undertaken, inter alia through recruitment and appointment;
    b. So as to correct the ethnic and gender imbalances in the Burundian judicial sector during and after the transition period, training colleges for employees of the judicial system shall be created, accelerated training shall be promoted, and the status and the internal promotion of magistrates shall be improved;
    c. Existing legislation relating to the organization of the Judiciary, the codes of criminal and civil procedure and the map of judicial jurisdiction shall be reviewed;
    d. All legislation shall be made available in Kirundi;
    e. Respect for the law shall be promoted;
    f. Steps shall be taken to discourage corruption, to denounce officials guilty of corruption, to enforce all legislation related to corruption, to

For additional analytical, marketing, investment and business opportunities information, please contact
Global Investment & Business Center, USA
(202) 546-2103. Fax: (202) 546-3275. E-mail: rusric@erols.com

establish effective oversight bodies, to improve working conditions in the judicial sector and to take necessary measures to require civil servants to report instances of corruption;

g. The necessary measures shall be taken, including those specified in Protocol I to the Agreement, to deal with the problem of impunity and take any other steps required to ensure that any travesties of justice are dealt with or re-opened;

h. The judicial sector shall be given the necessary resources so as to discharge its responsibilities impartially and independently.

4. Any appointment to the Judiciary required by Chapter I of the present Protocol to be made by the President shall, during the transition, be made by the transitional President and Vice-President in consultation with the Minister of Justice.

5. Any appointment to the Judiciary required by Chapter I of the present Protocol to be submitted for approval or confirmation to the National Assembly or the Senate shall, during the transition period, be required to be approved or confirmed by the transitional National Assembly by **two-thirds** majority.

6. There shall be a Constitutional Court possessing the jurisdiction and functions set forth in the 1992 Constitution of the Republic of Burundi.

7. The Constitutional Court shall be made up of seven members, two of whom shall be permanent (the President and Vice-President). They shall be appointed by the President of the Republic, subject to confirmation by the transitional National Assembly by a majority of **two-thirds**. Three of these judges shall be appointed for a period of three years only, and shall be replaced in the manner provided for in the post-transition Constitution. The remaining four shall be appointed for six years beginning at the commencement of the transition. The appointments shall be made within one month of the commencement of the transition. Judges of the Constitutional Court shall be persons of moral integrity and shall have legal training or experience. A member of a standing court must be amongst the nominees.

8. The Constitutional Court may sit validly only if at least five of its members, including its President or Vice-President, are present.

9. Decisions of the Constitutional Court shall be taken by an absolute majority of its members, except that the President of the Court shall have a casting vote if the Court is evenly split on any matter.

10. International co-operation and legal assistance will be required by the transitional Government to assist it in improving and reforming the legal system. Foreign jurists, including former Burundian nationals living outside the country, shall be requested to assist in the reform of the judicial system. The transitional Government may appoint any such persons to judicial positions so as to promote confidence in the Judiciary.

For additional analytical, marketing, investment and business opportunities information, please contact
Global Investment & Business Center, USA
(202) 546-2103. Fax: (202) 546-3275. E-mail: rusric@erols.com

11. Members of the public administration, including local government and the diplomatic corps, shall be so appointed by the transitional Executive as to ensure that imbalances observed in these sectors are corrected. The Government may appoint a commission with expert participation to assist it in making appointments.
12. Provincial governors and commune administrators shall be appointed by the President, subject to confirmation by the transitional National Assembly. They shall be natives of the territorial entity placed under their authority. They shall be civilians.

Article 18
Combating impunity during the transition

1. In accordance with Protocol I to the Agreement, the transitional Government shall request the establishment of an International Judicial Commission of Inquiry which will investigate acts of genocide, war crimes and other crimes against humanity and report thereon to the Security Council of the United Nations.
2. In accordance with Protocol I to the Agreement, a National Truth and Reconciliation Commission shall be established to investigate human rights abuses, promote reconciliation and deal with claims arising out of past practices relating to the conflict in Burundi.
3. The transitional Government shall scrupulously fulfil the commitments contained in Protocol IV to the Agreement concerning the repatriation and resettlement of refugees and sinistrés as well as the restitution of property, including land, belonging to such persons.

Article 19
Defence and security forces

1. Associations having the character of militias shall be prohibited.
2. The transitional arrangements regarding the defence and security forces, including the constitutional and legal framework governing such forces, shall be those set forth in Protocol III to the Agreement. Where that Protocol is silent, the provisions of the 1992 Constitution of the Republic of Burundi shall apply.

Article 20
Elections

1. Elections at the commune level and at the national level shall be held during the transition period in accordance with the provisions and within the time-frames set forth in the present Protocol.

For additional analytical, marketing, investment and business opportunities information, please contact
Global Investment & Business Center, USA
(202) 546-2103. Fax: (202) 546-3275. E-mail: rusric@erols.com

2. An Independent National Electoral Commission shall be established by the transitional Government as set forth hereunder.
3. The Commission shall be made up of five independent personalities and shall solicit advice from a multiparty commission of the transitional National Assembly. Its members shall be approved by a **three-fourths** majority of the transitional National Assembly, and may include non-Burundians who have expertise and integrity.
4. The Commission shall have as its functions:
   a. To organize elections at the national, commune and colline levels;
   b. To ensure that these elections are free, fair and transparent;
   c. To proclaim the results of the elections within a period determined by law, which shall be as short as possible;
   d. To promulgate the arrangements, the code of conduct, and the technical details, including the location of voting stations and times of voting;
   e. To hear and adjudicate on complaints regarding observance of the rules of the elections. The decisions of the commission shall be final;
   f. To ensure through appropriate rules that parties do not operate in a manner that incites ethnic violence or is otherwise not in conformity with the present Protocol;
   g. To ensure, and hear disputes regarding, compliance with the multiethnic requirements set forth in the present Protocol.
5. The transitional National Assembly shall within 12 months and by a **two-thirds** majority adopt a law regarding electoral rules.
6. The revised electoral code may set a threshold - up to 2% - below which no political party may be allocated seats if it has not won that percentage of the votes cast at the national level.
7. There shall be elections for the National Assembly, which shall take place after the commune elections and before the election of the President. The National Assembly shall have 100 directly elected members. As an exceptional measure and for the purpose of the first election only, and only if one party has received more than **three-fifths** of the directly elected seats, an additional 18 to 21 members in total shall be co-opted in equal numbers from the lists of all the parties that have obtained more than the threshold vote, or two persons per party if more than seven parties qualify.
8. The electoral system for the National Assembly shall be the system of blocked lists with proportional representation. The revised electoral code shall prescribe that lists be multi-ethnic in character and reflect gender representation. For each three names in sequence on a list, only two may belong to the same ethnic group, and for each five names at least one shall be a woman.

For additional analytical, marketing, investment and business opportunities information, please contact
Global Investment & Business Center, USA
(202) 546-2103. Fax: (202) 546-3275. E-mail: rusric@erols.com

9. The election of the President of the Republic shall take place after the National Assembly elections and before the end of the transition period.
10. The first post-transition President shall be elected by the National Assembly and Senate sitting together by a majority of **two-thirds** of the votes.
11. Any person who has served as President during the transition period shall be ineligible to stand for President in the first election. Candidates for the presidency must be Burundian citizens and over 35 years of age.
12. Elections at the commune level shall be held, in accordance with the procedures listed below, within eighteen months of the commencement of the transition period.
13.
    a. The collines shall be administered by colline councils of five members elected by direct universal suffrage. The councillor with the greatest number of votes shall become the chief of the colline. Elections for the colline chiefs shall, for the first elections, not be based on party political lists and all candidates shall stand as independents.
    b. The communes shall be administered by commune councils, which shall be elected by direct universal suffrage.
    c. For purposes of the first election, each Commune Council shall appoint a Commune Administrator and may dismiss her/him for good cause, including incompetence, corruption, misconduct or embezzlement. For subsequent elections, the National Assembly and the Senate may, after evaluation, legislate for the administrators to be elected by direct universal suffrage.
    d. At the national level, not more than 67% of commune administrators shall be from either of the two main ethnic components. The Senate shall ensure respect for this principle.

Article 21
Amendment of the transitional arrangements

Changes may be made to the transitional arrangements and the text of the Agreement with the consent of **nine-tenths** of the members of the transitional National Assembly.

Article 22
Interim period

1. The Parties agree to comply during the period between the signature of the Agreement and the installation of the transitional National Assembly with the obligations, arrangements and commitments set forth in Chapter II of the present Protocol.

For additional analytical, marketing, investment and business opportunities information, please contact
Global Investment & Business Center, USA
(202) 546-2103. Fax: (202) 546-3275. E-mail: rusric@erols.com

2. By its signature the National Assembly agrees, within four weeks, to:
   a. Adopt the present Protocol as the supreme law without any amendments to the substance of the Agreement;
   b. Repeal the provisions of any legislation which prevent free political activity, or which would hinder the implementation of the present Protocol;
   c. Pending the installation of a transitional Government adopt such legislation as is necessary for the granting of temporary immunity against prosecution for politically motivated crimes committed prior to the signature of the Agreement.
3. The parties wishing to participate in the transitional arrangements (the "participating parties") agree to file with the Implementation Monitoring Committee the following:
   a. Within seven days of the signature of the Agreement, a pledge, which appears as Annex I to the Agreement, committing the participating party to observe its commitments to democracy, peace and reconciliation, to reject all forms of violence and to participate in a public programme on peace and reconciliation;
   b. Within 60 days of signature, a document nominating the members representing the participating party in the transitional National Assembly.
4. The transitional President and Vice-President shall within 60 days of the signature of the Agreement submit to the Implementation Monitoring Committee a list identifying the members of the Cabinet.
5. Starting one month after the signature of the Agreement, the Implementation Monitoring Committee shall continuously review whether the conditions for the installation of a transitional Government have been met, and may direct the Government or any Party or participating party to undertake any steps which would enable those conditions to be met. It alone shall fix the date on which the transitional National Assembly and transitional Government shall be installed, and may postpone such date, provided the final date is not later than six months after the signature of the Agreement.
6. Between the date of signature of the Agreement and the installation of the transitional Government, the Government shall:
   a. Provide all necessary assistance and cooperation to international agencies, the political parties and the Implementation Monitoring Committee in regard to establishing structures and facilities and issuing the necessary documentation, including travel documents for all returning exiles, refugees and members of the armed groups as provided for in this and other protocols, as required by the international agencies or as directed by the Implementation Monitoring Committee;

For additional analytical, marketing, investment and business opportunities information, please contact
Global Investment & Business Center, USA
(202) 546-2103. Fax: (202) 546-3275. E-mail: rusric@erols.com

b. Compile, within 30 days of the signature of the Agreement, an inventory co-signed by the Minister of each ministry listing each of the assets owned by the State exceeding the value of US$ 250 in the possession of such ministry, and lodge a copy of such inventory with the Implementation Monitoring Committee;

c. Not destroy or allow the destruction of any record, file, or information or of any building or other property held by it during this period;

d. Take the necessary steps, including the signing of international agreements, to facilitate the entry and deployment of observers and members of forces or security personnel as agreed in Protocol III to the Agreement.

7. The Minister and the chief career public servant in each ministry shall be jointly liable in law for any damage or destruction of any government property, including any record, file or any other document, held by it, for any misrepresentation in the asset inventory filed with the Implementation Monitoring Committee, or for any wasteful use of the ministry's financial resources.

8. The Government shall be responsible for the day-to-day government of Burundi during the interim period. If during that period the Government should, without the approval of the Implementation Monitoring Committee, take any of the actions indicated in subparagraphs (a) - (d) below, such action may subsequently be reviewed by the transitional Government and, if found not to have been in the interests of good governance, summarily cancelled or reversed:

a. Alter the conditions of service or levels of remuneration of public servants;

b. Make any appointment to or promotion within the public administration;

c. Sell State-owned immovable property;

d. Enter into any contract for the supply of goods or services or the construction of any building, or for the erection or maintenance of any Government infrastructure, which will have the effect of incurring financial obligations on the part of the transitional Government. Any such contract concluded without the approval of the Implementation Monitoring Committee may be annulled by the transitional Government.

9. During the interim period there shall be no deployment of the defence force or of any armed wing of a Party outside the framework of Protocol III.

10. No arrest of a returnee or refugee shall be permitted without notification and justification to the Implementation Monitoring Committee or a sub-committee or agency designated by it, and in any event no arrest or charging of a refugee or returnee or holder of political public office for a crime committed for a political purpose prior to the signature of the

For additional analytical, marketing, investment and business opportunities information, please contact
Global Investment & Business Center, USA
(202) 546-2103. Fax: (202) 546-3275. E-mail: rusric@erols.com

Agreement shall be permitted until the installation of the transitional Government.

11. The Implementation Monitoring Committee may request and shall receive from the transitional Government any information relating to governmental activities, any relevant data regarding governance or any information relating to or required for the monitoring, supervision or implementation of the Agreement, including information relating to any international financial assistance.

12. The Implementation Monitoring Committee shall assist in soliciting or obtaining any international or foreign aid or assistance contemplated by the Agreement. It may generally advise any donor and suggest conditionalities in regard to any aid or assistance to be granted to, or agreements to be concluded with, the Government of Burundi. For this purpose it shall be informed of the details of any international agreements to be concluded with, or foreign aid to be donated to, the Burundian Government.

13. The Implementation Monitoring Committee may, at its discretion and for purposes of supervising, monitoring or ensuring the implementation of the Agreement, issue directives to any Party or participating party. All parties shall comply with such directives within the period specified in the directive.

14. In the event that a Party or participating party fails to comply with a directive of the Implementation Monitoring Committee, the Committee may:
    a. Place the party on terms to comply;
    b. Failing compliance with such warning, and after offering the party an opportunity to explain its non-compliance, suspend such party from participating in the transitional arrangements;
    c. Request the appropriate assistance of any international body or State or Party in enforcing compliance.

15. The participating parties shall do all in their power to ensure that their members observe the provisions of the Agreement, including, but not limited to, the prompt full and wide dissemination of the provisions of the Agreement relating to the ceasefire, disarmament, and reporting to quartering locations.

16. The participating Parties shall assist the Implementation Monitoring Committee and the Facilitator in an intensive public campaign to win support for the Agreement and to promote peace and reconciliation.

17. They shall take disciplinary measures, including expulsion, against any member who contrary to the spirit and letter of the Agreement and the pledge annexed hereto commits an act of violence or destroys or damages public or private property.

For additional analytical, marketing, investment and business opportunities information, please contact
Global Investment & Business Center, USA
(202) 546-2103. Fax: (202) 546-3275. E-mail: rusric@erols.com

PROTOCOL III: PEACE AND SECURITY FOR ALL

PREAMBLE

We, the Parties,

Recalling the commitments entered into in the Declaration of 21 June 1998 with a view to resolving the Burundi conflict through peaceful means and putting an end to all forms of violence,

Aware of the necessity to promote lasting peace and having analysed the questions relating to the principles of peace and security for all, to the defence and security forces and to the cessation of hostilities, and the arrangements with a view to achieving a permanent ceasefire,

Have agreed as follows:

CHAPTER I PEACE AND SECURITY FOR ALL

Article 1
Principles of peace and security for all

1. All Burundian citizens have the right to live in peace and security without any discrimination whatsoever.
2. The sovereignty of the people through the Constitution and the laws that stem from it shall be respected by all.
3. The institutions have the primary duty to guarantee:
    a. The security of all citizens;
    b. The protection of the inalienable rights of the human person, starting with the right to life, and the rights embodied inter alia in the Universal Declaration of Human Rights and in the international conventions to which Burundi is a party;
    c. The protection of all the ethnic communities of the population through specific mechanisms for the prevention of coups d'état, segregation and genocide;
    d. Respect for the law and combating of impunity;
    e. Good governance;
    f. Sovereignty of the State and integrity of the national territory.
4. Any foreign intervention other than under international conventions shall be prohibited. All recourse to foreign forces shall be prohibited, except when authorized by the institutions empowered to do so.
5. All Burundian citizens shall be under an obligation to respect the right of their fellow citizens to peace and security, as well as to respect public order.

For additional analytical, marketing, investment and business opportunities information, please contact
Global Investment & Business Center, USA
(202) 546-2103. Fax: (202) 546-3275. E-mail: rusric@erols.com

6. The prerequisites for the establishment and maintenance of peace and security are:
    a. Unity within the defence and security forces;
    b. Political neutrality of the defence and security forces;
    c. The professional, civic and moral qualities of the defence and security forces;
    d. Neutrality and independence of the magistracy;
    e. Control of illegal possession and use of weapons.
7. The use of force as a means of access to and retention of power shall be rejected.
8. The defence and security forces belong to all the people of Burundi. They shall be an instrument for the protection of all the people, and all the people must identify with them.
9. The establishment of militias and terrorist and genocidal organizations, the practice of terrorism and genocide and incitement to those practices shall be prohibited.
10. Political organizations shall promote inclusion; exclusion on ethnic, sexual, regional and religious grounds shall be prohibited.
11. The ideals of peace and national unity shall be promoted and developed within the political parties, and propagation of the ideologies of exclusion, racism and genocide shall be prohibited.
12. The principle of participation of all components of society in the management of all the organs of the State, as well as equality of opportunity for citizens in all sectors of national life, shall be respected.
13. An economic and social policy that ensures the harmonious and balanced development of the people and the nation, as well as a policy of harmonious resolution of social problems, shall be pursued.
14. A culture of peace and tolerance shall be promoted through the development of a sense of patriotism among citizens and of mutual solidarity in the event of a threat, as well as through education and training of all political and technical officials.
15. Provisions for penalizing the violation of these principles shall be adopted.

Article 2
Causes of the violence and insecurity in Burundi

The causes of the violence and security in Burundi are:

The colonial period

1. The breaking apart of the pre-colonial political and administrative equilibrium among the Baganwa, the Batutsi and the Bahuru triggered off by the implementation of the administrative reforms of the 1930s which

For additional analytical, marketing, investment and business opportunities information, please contact
Global Investment & Business Center, USA
(202) 546-2103. Fax: (202) 546-3275. E-mail: rusric@erols.com

resulted in the dismissal from their administrative positions of most of the Hutu chiefs and some of the Tutsi chiefs.

2. A discriminatory system which did not offer equal educational access to all Burundian youths from all ethnic groups.

3. The erosion of some basic traditions, cultural norms and values that had hitherto been the foundations of the unity, solidarity and cohesion of the fabric of Burundian society and of Burundians.

4. The disruption of the traditional socio-political system in effect under the monarchy, which led to erosion of the bonds that provided the foundations of Burundi's political stability.

The post-colonial period

5. Political instability consequent upon the undermining of the legitimacy of the post-colonial institutions, accentuated by:
   a. The poor conception of power; lack of good leadership, lack of respect for the law and demonization of political opponents;
   b. The assassination of great Burundian leaders (Rwagasore, Ngendandumwe, Ndadaye);
   c. Impunity of those committing political crimes and human rights violations and practising regionalism, patronage, cronyism and corruption;
   d. The struggle for influence by the great powers, foreign interference in Burundi's internal affairs and the proliferation of arms in the region;
   e. Failure to satisfy the basic needs of the citizens as a result of economic underdevelopment and lack of a sound economic policy that led to disillusionment and an erosion of support for the political system;
   f. The distortion of Burundi's history;
   g. The ideology and practice of genocide and exclusion.

6. The aftermath of the colonial system, the inadequacy of the basic reforms of the institutional arrangements inherited from colonization for governance, administration and the maintenance of order and security for all.

7. The unbridled struggle for power which, following the principle that "the end justifies the means", resulted in recourse to violence and the deliberate manipulation of ethnic sentiments as legitimate methods of access to and retention of power.

8. Lack of respect by certain political actors for the basic normative rules and principles of good governance, particularly those concerning separation of the legislature, the executive and the judiciary, independence of the magistracy, satisfaction of basic human needs and the maintenance of order and security for all.

For additional analytical, marketing, investment and business opportunities information, please contact
Global Investment & Business Center, USA
(202) 546-2103. Fax: (202) 546-3275. E-mail: rusric@erols.com

9. Lack of respect for the traditions, norms and cardinal principles of the democratic system, including tolerance and respect for the inalienable rights of the human person, especially the right to life.
10. Non-acceptance of peaceful co-existence, diversity and pluralism as guiding principles of life and the basis of national cohesion, unity and solidarity.
11. Lack of appropriate action by the United Nations to rule on the acts of genocide perpetrated in Burundi since independence.

Article 3
Persons responsible for and agents of the insecurity and violence

The following were identified as responsible for and agents of the insecurity and violence:

a. Some foreign countries, foreign organizations, political or otherwise, and certain foreign lobbies;
b. National and foreign individuals and groups, as well as organizations, institutions, parties and movements, which conceived, abetted, condoned, encouraged, incited and practised divisions, violence and violent methods of access to and retention of power;
c. Political, administrative and religious leaders, as well as technical staff, who contributed to perpetrating the genocide;
d. Persons responsible for the violence perpetrated during the crises of 1965-1969, 1972, 1988, 1991 and 1993 to date;
e. The members of the judicial system who have promoted and continue to promote impunity and partiality through corruption, intimidation and manipulation;
f. Those instruments of State power responsible for protecting the population which failed in their mission, particularly those elements of the defence and security forces guilty of excesses and violence against the innocent population;
g. Those elements who practise genocide and their allies.

Article 4
Nature of the insecurity and violence

The violence is political, economic and social in nature and is expressed in genocidal, criminal and terrorist form.

Article 5
Manifestations of the insecurity and violence

The insecurity and violence are manifested in:

For additional analytical, marketing, investment and business opportunities information, please contact
Global Investment & Business Center, USA
(202) 546-2103. Fax: (202) 546-3275. E-mail: rusric@erols.com

a. Civil war; the destruction of public and private property; genocide, massacres, coups d'état, extra-judicial executions, premeditated murders, torture, rape, arbitrary arrests and imprisonment and other inhuman and degrading forms of treatment;
b. Massive forcible displacements of individuals, families and groups who as a result leave their customary places of residence and become refugees outside the country or remain inside the country as displaced and regrouped persons in camps, tents, shacks and other makeshift arrangements;
c. Destruction of national and socio-economic infrastructures, as well as of public and private property.

Article 6
Consequences of the insecurity and violence

The most serious consequences of the insecurity and violence are:

a. Increase in crime, in the number of disabled persons, orphans, widows and widowers, impoverishment of the people, and all kinds of social deviation;
b. Lack of respect for authority and the law giving rise to anarchy, mistrust and lack of civic spirit, which lead to civil unrest and rebellion;
c. The spread of the culture of violence, leading to a general disdain for the sanctity of human life;
d. Arbitrary practices, widespread abuse of power, corruption and the plundering of national resources.

Article 7
Victims of the insecurity and violence

The main victims of the insecurity and violence are:

a. The nation, some political officials, and individuals forced to flee from their original places of residence into exile, settlements and camps;
b. Individuals, groups, and categories of the population, both Hutu and Tutsi, targeted on account of their beliefs or political affiliation and on the basis of their ethnic origin.

Article 8
Protection of the inalienable rights of the human person

It is the duty of the State:

For additional analytical, marketing, investment and business opportunities information, please contact
Global Investment & Business Center, USA
(202) 546-2103. Fax: (202) 546-3275. E-mail: rusric@erols.com

a. To protect the inalienable rights of the human person, starting with the right to life and including the rights to freedom, security, work, education and freedom of expression, and all other rights embodied inter alia in the Universal Declaration of Human Rights and in the international conventions to which Burundi is a party;
b. To prohibit and punish violations of the inalienable rights of the human person;
c. To institute a proactive policy aimed at promoting human rights through education and training of the population, including all political and technical officials.

Article 9
Security-related regional and international issues

The three most pertinent security-related regional and international issues are:

a. The close relationship of Burundi's internal security to security in Great Lakes region and to external factors such as insecurity in the neighbouring countries, hegemonist and/or genocidal ideologies in the Great Lakes region, the arms trade and the presence of mercenaries;
b. The need to create conditions that encourage peaceful co-existence, foster a culture of peace and tolerance and cultivate a hospitable environment that encourages people to remain in their places of residence within their country rather than flee as refugees;
c. The need to promote participation in and respect for the international conventions on refugees.

CHAPTER II THE DEFENCE AND SECURITY FORCES

Article 10
Principles relating to the defence and security forces

1. The defence and security forces shall reflect the firm resolve of Burundians, as individuals and as a nation, to live as equals, in peace and harmony, and to be free from fear.
2. The defence and security forces shall be established in accordance with the Constitution. Apart from the defence and security forces so established, no other armed organization may be created or raised.
3. The defence and security forces shall teach and require their members to abide by the Constitution and the laws in force and by the international conventions and agreements to which Burundi is a party.
4. The maintenance of national security and of national defence shall be subject to Government authority and parliamentary oversight.

For additional analytical, marketing, investment and business opportunities information, please contact
Global Investment & Business Center, USA
(202) 546-2103. Fax: (202) 546-3275. E-mail: rusric@erols.com

5. The defence and security forces shall be accountable for their actions and work in all transparency. Parliamentary committees shall be set up to supervise the work of the defence and security forces in accordance with the legislation in force and the parliamentary rules and regulations.
6. Neither the defence and security forces nor any of their members shall, in the performance of their duties:
   a. Injure the interests of a political party which is legitimate under the Constitution;
   b. Manifest their political preferences;
   c. Favour in any manner the interests of a political party;
   d. Be a member of a political party or an association of a political nature;
   e. Take part in political activities or demonstrations.

Article 11
Principles of organization of the defence and security forces

1. The defence and security forces shall consist of a national defence force, a national police and an intelligence service, all established in conformity with the Constitution.
2. The defence and security forces shall be subordinate to civilian authority in respect for the Constitution, the law and the regulations.
3. The defence and security forces shall be open to all Burundian citizens without discrimination.
4. The defence and security forces shall promote within their services a non-discriminatory, non-ethnicist and non-sexist culture.
5. Organic laws shall determine the creation, organization, training, conditions of service and functioning of the defence and security forces.
6. Within the limits determined by the Constitution and the laws, only the President may authorize the use of armed military force:
   a. In defence of the State;
   b. In the restoration of order and public safety;
   c. In the discharge of international obligations and commitments.
7. When the national defence force is utilized in one of the cases referred to in paragraph 6 above, the President shall officially consult the authorized competent bodies and shall promptly inform the Legislature, in detail, of:
   a. The reason or reasons for the use of the national defence force;
   b. Any location where that force is deployed;
   c. The period for which that force is deployed.
8. If the Legislature is not in session, the President shall convene it in special session within seven days from the use of the national defence force.
9. The defence and security forces shall respect the rights and dignity of their members in the context of the normal constraints of discipline and training.

For additional analytical, marketing, investment and business opportunities information, please contact
Global Investment & Business Center, USA
(202) 546-2103. Fax: (202) 546-3275. E-mail: rusric@erols.com

10. The members of the defence and security forces shall have the right to be informed of the socio-political life of the country and to receive civic education.

Article 12
Missions of the defence and security forces

1. Missions of the national defence force

The missions of the national defence force shall be:

   a. To ensure the integrity of the national territory and the sovereignty of the country;
   b. To combat any armed aggression against the institutions of the Republic;
   c. To intervene exceptionally in the maintenance of public order at the formal request of the authorized civilian authority;
   d. To participate in assistance activities in case of natural disasters;
   e. To contribute to the development of the country through major works, production and training;
   f. To defend the vital points.

2. Missions of the national police

The missions of the national police shall be:

   a. To maintain and restore public order;
   b. To prevent offences provided for by law, investigate and prosecute their perpetrators and make arrests in accordance with the law;
   c. To ensure respect for the laws and other regulations for whose enforcement they are directly responsible;
   d. To ensure the physical protection of persons and their property;
   e. To ensure the protection of infrastructures and public property;
   f. To relieve and assist persons in danger or in distress;
   g. To intervene in case of catastrophe or disaster;
   h. To develop various civil defence scenarios;
   i. To ensure road safety throughout the national territory;
   j. To ensure protection of public gatherings at the request of those involved, on orders from the administrative authorities, or on their own initiative;
   k. To ensure the missions of the judicial and administrative police;
   l. To ensure protection of the courts and tribunals;
   m. To deal with criminal cases of major importance, such as economic crimes and cases attributable to roving delinquents or groups organized at the national or international level;

For additional analytical, marketing, investment and business opportunities information, please contact
Global Investment & Business Center, USA
(202) 546-2103. Fax: (202) 546-3275. E-mail: rusric@erols.com

n. To produce and make use of crime statistics;
o. To deal with the policing of immigration and emigration and the status of aliens;
p. To monitor the movements of aliens throughout the national territory;
q. To keep watch on the land, lake and air borders;
r. To issue travel documents and residence permits;
s. To ensure protection of the institutions.

3. Missions of the intelligence service

The missions of the intelligence service shall be:

a. To seek out, centralize and make use of all information likely to contribute to the protection of the State, its institutions and its interests at the international level, as well as to the prosperity of its economy;
b. To detect as early as possible activities aimed at creating insecurity and violence or at changing the institutions of the State by unlawful means;
c. To detect as early as possible recourse to the manipulation of ethnic or regionalist feelings as means of access to or retention of power;
d. To detect as early as possible any threat to the constitutional order, public safety, territorial integrity or national sovereignty;
e. To detect as early as possible any threat to the country's ecological environment;
f. To detect as early as possible terrorist intrigues, illicit drug trafficking and the formation of criminal organizations;
g. To detect malfunctions and cases of misappropriation of funds within the State services.

Article 13
Structure of the defence and security forces

1. Structure of the national defence force

The transitional Government shall be responsible for deciding upon the structure of the national defence force.

2. Structure of the national police
   a. The national police shall be coordinated within one Ministry, i.e., the one responsible for public security.
   b. Its structure shall be:

For additional analytical, marketing, investment and business opportunities information, please contact
Global Investment & Business Center, USA
(202) 546-2103. Fax: (202) 546-3275. E-mail: rusric@erols.com

i. First level: Since the Ministry is responsible for public security, the head shall be a member of the Government;
ii. Second level: A national police headquarters responsible for coordinating all the police forces. It shall be headed by a director-general with administrative skills and knowledge of police techniques;
iii. Third level: Departments: each department shall represent a specialized area of police work.

This structure is illustrated in Annex II to the Agreement.

3. Structure of the intelligence service

The structure of the intelligence service shall be such as to enable the service, given its special nature, to preserve the secrecy of its operations while allowing for control by the National Assembly, especially with regard to the budget. The intelligence service shall be placed under the responsibility of a member of government.

4. Command of the defence and security forces

Command posts shall be distributed on the basis of competence and merit while ensuring the necessary ethnic balances.

Article 14
Composition of the defence and security forces

1. Composition of the national defence force
   a. There shall be a single defence force composed of all components of the Burundian nation irrespective of ethnic, regional, gender and/or social status.
   b. The national defence force shall include members of the Burundian armed forces and combatants of the political parties and movements in existence at the time of restructuring of the army, as well as other citizens who wish to enlist.
   c. After the signature of the Agreement, the combatants of the political parties and movements, as well as the existing national defence force, shall be placed under the authority of the transitional Government.
   d. A technical committee consisting of representatives of the Burundian armed forces and combatants of the political parties and movements, as well as of an external military advisory and training group, shall be established by decision of the transitional

For additional analytical, marketing, investment and business opportunities information, please contact
Global Investment & Business Center, USA
(202) 546-2103. Fax: (202) 546-3275. E-mail: rusric@erols.com

Government to implement the procedures for the establishment of the national defence force.

e. Members of the Burundian armed forces found guilty of acts of genocide, coups d'état, violation of the Constitution and human rights and war crimes shall be excluded from the national defence force. Combatants of the political parties and movements found guilty of the same offences shall also not be accepted into the national defence force.

f. Recruitment into the national defence force shall be conducted in a transparent manner, individually, voluntarily and on the basis of personal merit, physical fitness, moral and professional qualifications and potential.

g. For a period to be determined by the Senate, not more than 50% of the national defence force shall be drawn from any one ethnic group, in view of the need to achieve ethnic balance and to prevent acts of genocide and coups d'état.

2. Composition of the national police

a. There shall be a single national police composed of all citizens of the Burundian nation wishing to form part of it, irrespective of ethnic, regional, gender and social status.

b. The national police shall include members of the current national police, combatants of the political parties and movements and other citizens who meet the requirements.

c. A technical committee comprising representatives of the existing police force and the political parties and movements and of external advisors and instructors on police issues shall be established by decision of the transitional Government to implement the procedures for the establishment of the national police.

d. All persons, including current members of the police force and combatants of the political parties and movements, found guilty of genocide, the coup d'état of 21 October 199??, human rights violations or war crimes shall be excluded from the national police.

e. Not more than 50% of the members of the national police shall be drawn from any one particular ethnic group, with a view to achieving the necessary balances and preventing acts of genocide or of coup d'état.

3. Composition of the intelligence service

The composition of the intelligence service shall be such as to enable the service, given its special nature, to preserve the secrecy of its operations while allowing for control by the National Assembly.

Article 15
Size of the defence and security forces

For additional analytical, marketing, investment and business opportunities information, please contact
Global Investment & Business Center, USA
(202) 546-2103. Fax: (202) 546-3275. E-mail: rusric@erols.com

1. Size of the national defence force
    a. The following criteria shall be used to determine the strength of the national defence force:
        i.   Potential internal and external threats;
        ii.   The economic and financial resources of the country;
        iii. The budget allocated to the defence and security forces;
        iv.   The defence policy of the country.
    b. The transitional Government, in consultation with the technical committee, shall determine the size of the national defence force.
2. Size of the national police
    a. The following criteria shall be used to determine the strength of the national police:
        i.   Surface area of the country;
        ii.   Population;
        iii. Population density;
        iv.   Urbanization level;
        v.   Economic resources;
        vi.   Crime level;
        vii. Budgetary allocation.
    b. The transitional Government, in consultation with the technical committee, shall determine the size of the national police.
3. Size of the intelligence service

The size of the intelligence service shall be such as to enable the service, given its special nature, to preserve the secrecy of its operations while allowing for control by the National Assembly.

Article 16
Balances within the defence and security forces

1. The following criteria shall be used to determine the imbalances in the defence and security forces:
    a. Political;
    b. Ethnic;
    c. Regional;
    d. Gender.
2. Correction of the imbalances in the defence and security forces shall be approached progressively in the spirit of reconciliation and trust in order to reassure all Burundians.
3. Correction of the imbalances shall be achieved during the transition period through the integration into the current defence and security forces of the combatants of the political parties and movements and through the recruitment of other Burundian citizens.

For additional analytical, marketing, investment and business opportunities information, please contact
Global Investment & Business Center, USA
(202) 546-2103. Fax: (202) 546-3275. E-mail: rusric@erols.com

4. For purposes of rapid reduction of the command-level imbalances, accelerated training of commissioned and non-commissioned officers from among the combatants of the political parties and movements shall be conducted in Burundi and abroad as soon as the transition period commences.

Article 17
Recruitment

1. Recruitment shall be conducted in accordance with the following criteria:
   a. Transparency;
   b. Voluntary service;
   c. Age;
   d. Personal record and level of training;
   e. Medical tests of physical and intellectual aptitude.
2. Recruitment criteria based on educational level shall be determined by the transitional Government.
3. A national commission shall be assigned responsibility for selecting candidates for all levels of the national defence force and national police, taking care to ensure the necessary ethnic balance.

Article 18
Training

1. The defence and security forces shall have technical, moral and civic training. This training shall include the culture of peace, aspects of conduct relating to the democratic multi-party political system, human rights and humanitarian law.
2. Decentralization of the centres for training police constables, rank and file troops and non-commissioned officers shall be undertaken.

Article 19
Organic laws, regulatory texts and disciplinary system

For the defence and security forces, organic laws, regulatory texts and disciplinary rules in conformity with the relevant provisions of the Agreement shall be adopted.

Article 20
Names of the defence and security forces

1. The name of the defence force shall be decided upon by the transitional Government.
2. The name of the police shall be "National Police of Burundi".

For additional analytical, marketing, investment and business opportunities information, please contact
Global Investment & Business Center, USA
(202) 546-2103. Fax: (202) 546-3275. E-mail: rusric@erols.com

3. The name of the intelligence service shall be "General Intelligence Service".

Article 21
Demobilization

1. Demobilization shall begin after the signature of the Agreement in accordance with the implementation timetable (see Annex V).
2. To move from war to peace requires demobilization within the defence and security forces as well as for the combatants of the political parties and movements.
3. Demobilization shall involve both the members of the Burundian armed forces and the combatants of the political parties and movements.
4. Lists of people to be demobilized shall be compiled.
5. Members to be demobilized shall be provided with some form of appropriate identification.
6. Demobilization criteria and a demobilization package shall be drawn up.
7. The categories of people to be demobilized shall be:
   a. Volunteers;
   b. Those members who are handicapped or disabled;
   c. Those who do not meet the age criteria;
   d. Those whose discipline is such that they cannot be retained within the new defence and security forces;
   e. Individuals whose educational level is such that they would not be able to undergo military or police training;
   f. Members of the Burundian armed forces and combatants of the political parties and movements who will be rationalized to yield efficient and affordable defence and security forces.
8. An organ to deal with the socio-professional reintegration of demobilized troops shall be established.
9. A technical committee to work out the programme and modalities of demobilization shall be set up.
10. The international community shall be requested to assist in the process of demobilization.
11. Following the demobilization process, a certificate shall be issued to demobilized troops.
12. Each demobilized person shall receive a demobilization allowance.

Article 22
Military or compulsory civic service

The future institutions of the country shall examine the issue in the light of the needs of the time.

For additional analytical, marketing, investment and business opportunities information, please contact
Global Investment & Business Center, USA
(202) 546-2103. Fax: (202) 546-3275. E-mail: rusric@erols.com

Article 23
National, regional, and international environment

1. Peace in Burundi requires a favourable national, regional and international environment.
2. Burundian politicians shall undertake to respect the political neutrality of the defence and security forces.
3. After the signature of the Agreement, the armed signatories to the Agreement, politicians and political leaders, religious organizations and civil society shall be called upon to address to the Burundian population signals and messages of peace, reconciliation and national unity.
4. National observatories shall be established on genocide, ethnic hegemony and domination, oppression and exclusion, coups d'état, political assassinations, arms trafficking and human rights violations in the Great Lakes region. The establishment of similar observatories at the regional and international levels shall be promoted.
5. The Parties undertake to contribute to the restoration of peace in the Great Lakes region.

Article 24
Security partners

The security partners are:

1. The Government and the defence and security forces;
2. State institutions including local authorities;
3. The population, particularly through their support and cooperation in enforcing the laws;
4. The countries in the region;
5. The international community.

CHAPTER III PERMANENT CEASEFIRE AND CESSATION OF HOSTILITIES

Definitions and general principles

Article 25
Definitions

1. Ceasefire means the cessation of:
   a. All attacks by air, land and lake, as well as all acts of sabotage;
   b. Attempts to occupy new ground positions and movements of troops and resources from one location to another;
   c. All acts of violence against the civilian population — summary executions, torture, harassment, detention and persecution of

For additional analytical, marketing, investment and business opportunities information, please contact
Global Investment & Business Center, USA
(202) 546-2103. Fax: (202) 546-3275. E-mail: rusric@erols.com

civilians on the basis of ethnic origin, religious, beliefs and political affiliations, incitement of ethnic hatred, arming of civilians, use of child soldiers, sexual violence, training of terrorists, genocide and bombing of the civilian population;

    d. Supply of ammunitions and weaponry and other war-related stores to the field;

    e. All hostile propaganda between the Parties, both within and outside the country;

    f. Any other actions that may impede the normal evolution of the ceasefire process.

2. The cessation of hostilities shall involve:

    a. Announcement of a cessation of hostilities 48 hours after the signing of the ceasefire agreement, through command channels and print and electronic media;

    b. Cessation of hostilities shall be regulated and monitored through the committee to follow up, supervise, monitor and implement the Agreement (Implementation Monitoring Committee);

    c. Release of all the political prisoners, closure of all the forced regroupment camps and respect for civil and political rights and freedoms shall take place from the date of signature of the Agreement;

    d. Cessation of hostilities brought about by emergency laws, political imprisonment and arbitrary arrests shall take effect from the date of signature of the Agreement;

    e. Cessation of defamatory, untruthful or ethnicist statements by the media and publications shall take place from the date of signature of the Agreement.

3. The different types of hostilities are:

    a. Political hostilities:

        i. Verbal aggression and denigration;

        ii. Political imprisonment;

        iii. Forced regroupment camps;

        iv. Violation of political rights and freedoms;

    b. Military hostilities:

        i. Armed clashes between the belligerents;

        ii. Infiltration of armed groups from neighbouring countries;

        iii. Attacks on the population by the belligerents.

4. The belligerents are:

    a. The Government forces;

    b. The combatants of the political parties and movements which signed the Declaration of 21 June 1998;

    c. The combatants of political parties and movements operating within the country which did not sign the Declaration of 21 June 1998;

    d. The political and ethnic militias operating within the country.

For additional analytical, marketing, investment and business opportunities information, please contact
Global Investment & Business Center, USA
(202) 546-2103. Fax: (202) 546-3275. E-mail: rusric@erols.com

Article 26
General principles

1. The following principles are agreed upon:
   a. The provisions of article 25.1 (d) above shall not preclude the supply of food, clothing and medical support to forces in the field;
   b. Freedom of movement of persons and goods throughout the country shall be guaranteed;
   c. All persons detained or taken hostage on account of political belief or activities shall be released and given the latitude to relocate to anywhere within the country;
   d. Humanitarian assistance shall be facilitated through humanitarian corridors in order to render assistance to displaced persons, refugees and other sinistrés;
   e. The parties shall establish a Joint Commission for Peace and Security, hereinafter referred to as the Ceasefire Commission, which shall be responsible for peace and security functions and shall work in close conjunction with a peacekeeping force following the entry into force of the Agreement;
   f. The laying of mines of any type shall be prohibited, and all parties shall be required to undertake to mark and signpost any danger areas to be identified to peacekeeping forces;
   g. The forces in areas of direct contact shall proceed to an immediate disengagement;
   h. Illicit trafficking of arms and the infiltration of armed groups shall be controlled with the collaboration of neighbouring countries;
   i. The parties shall undertake to locate, identify, disarm, and assemble all armed groups in the country;
   j. The parties shall ensure that armed groups operating under their command comply with the process;
   k. Mechanisms for dismantling and disarming all militias and disarming civilians holding arms illegally shall be established;
   l. Amnesty shall be granted to all combatants of the political parties and movements for crimes committed as a result of their involvement in the conflict, but not for acts of genocide, crimes against humanity or war crimes, or for their participation in coups d'état.
2. Disengagement
   a. Disengagement shall mean the immediate breaking of contact between the opposing military forces of the Parties to the Agreement at places where they are in direct contact by the effective date and time of the ceasefire.
   b. Immediate disengagement at the initiative of all military units shall be limited to the effective range of all weapons. Disengagement to

For additional analytical, marketing, investment and business opportunities information, please contact
Global Investment & Business Center, USA
(202) 546-2103. Fax: (202) 546-3275. E-mail: rusric@erols.com

put all weapons out of range shall be conducted under the guidance of the Ceasefire Commission established pursuant to article 27 below.

c. Where disengagement by a party is impossible or impractical, the Ceasefire Commission shall find an alternative solution to render the weapons safe.

Article 27
Verification and supervision

1. Ceasefire Commission
   a. The Ceasefire Commission shall consist of representatives of the Government, the combatants of the political parties and movements, the United Nations, the Organization of African Unity and the Regional Peace Initiative for Burundi.
   b. The Ceasefire Commission shall be a decision-making body.
   c. The Ceasefire Commission shall take its decisions by consensus.
   d. The Ceasefire Commission shall be responsible, among other things, for:
      i. Establishing the location of units at the time of the ceasefire;
      ii. Establishing liaison between the parties for the purpose of the ceasefire;
      iii. Finding appropriate solutions in the event of difficulty in disengagement;
      iv. Conducting investigations of any ceasefire violations;
      v. Verifying all information, data and activities relating to military forces of the parties;
      vi. Verifying the disengagement of the military forces of the Parties where they are in direct contact;
      vii. Monitoring the storage of arms, munitions equipment;
      viii. Monitoring the quartering of troops and police;
      ix. Undertaking the disarmament of all illegally armed civilians;
      x. Undertaking mine clearance throughout the country.
   e. The parties undertake to provide the Ceasefire Commission immediately with all relevant information on the organization, equipment and positions of their forces, on the understanding that such information shall be held in strict confidence.
2. Re-deployment of all troops to quartering centres
   a. Following disengagement, all troops shall be re-deployed to quartering locations.
   b. A map identifying the military quartering locations shall be made available to the Implementation Monitoring Committee.

For additional analytical, marketing, investment and business opportunities information, please contact
Global Investment & Business Center, USA
(202) 546-2103. Fax: (202) 546-3275. E-mail: rusric@erols.com

    c. Upon re-deployment, all forces shall provide relevant information to the Ceasefire Commission on troop strength, movements and weapons they hold at each location.

    d. All facilities customarily made available to soldiers, but which cannot be provided at the quartering locations, such as hospitals, logistics units and training facilities, shall be supervised by the Ceasefire Commission.

    e. The Ceasefire Commission shall verify the reported data and information. All forces shall be restricted to the declared and recorded centres and all movements shall be subject to authorization by the Ceasefire Commission. All forces shall remain in the declared and recorded centres until the integration and demobilization process is completed.

    f. Quartering shall be conducted in two stages:
       i. The first stage shall cover the quartering of the current Government's troops in their barracks;
       ii. The second stage shall cover the quartering of the other negotiating armed parties' troops at sites previously identified and prepared.

3. Maintenance of peace and security
    a. In the context of the Agreement, the Ceasefire Commission shall be responsible for the maintenance of peace and security.
    b. Upon the entry into force of the Agreement, each Party shall agree with the Ceasefire Commission appropriate security measures for:
       i. Its leading members;
       ii. The free movement of its members in Burundi;
    c. All embassies of Burundi in neighbouring and other countries providing shelter for Burundian refugees and residents shall provide them with passports, identity papers and any other requisite documents to which all Burundian citizens are entitled;
    d. Entry into Burundi through border posts shall be facilitated for the civilian and combatant members of the political parties and movements.

4. Peace and security functions
    a. The peace and security functions of the Ceasefire Commission shall be:
       i. To guarantee respect by all the parties for the definitive cessation of hostilities;
       ii. To guarantee the peace and security of the people;
       iii. To ensure the search for and recovery of all arms, the neutralization of militias throughout the country and the disarming of the civilian population;
       iv. To ensure the security of institutions and high-ranking political figures;

For additional analytical, marketing, investment and business opportunities information, please contact
Global Investment & Business Center, USA
(202) 546-2103. Fax: (202) 546-3275. E-mail: rusric@erols.com

   v. To ensure the security of senior foreign personnel and experts;

   vi. To ensure the demining of the whole country;

   vii. To ensure the effective quartering of the defence and security forces, arms control, and respect for disciplinary rules within and outside the camps;

   viii. To supervise the operations for resupplying the troops.

  b. The expert functions shall be:

   i. To assign the defence and security forces to their stations;

   ii. To conduct the identification of sites for military camps in military zones located outside the towns;

   iii. To supervise the operation for the demobilization of troops and police not retained within the new defence and security forces.

5. International peacekeeping force

The mandate of the peacekeeping force referred to in article 8 of Protocol V to the Agreement shall be to verify implementation of the provisions contained in this Chapter. In addition to its verification function, the force may be requested by the Ceasefire Commission to provide assistance and support to the implementation process, as appropriate.

Article 28
Ceasefire implementation timetable

The ceasefire implementation timetable shall be determined by the Ceasefire Commission.

PROTOCOL IV: RECONSTRUCTION AND DEVELOPMENT

PREAMBLE

We, the Parties,

Having considered the issues relating to the overall problem of reconstruction and development, including those associated with rehabilitation and resettlement of the refugees and sinistrés, with physical and political reconstruction and with economic and social development,

Having identified the principles, guidelines and activities for the transitional institutions in dealing with these issues,

Having incorporated the essentials of our work, including the analysis of the origin of the specific problems and the principles, guidelines and activities

For additional analytical, marketing, investment and business opportunities information, please contact
Global Investment & Business Center, USA
(202) 546-2103. Fax: (202) 546-3275. E-mail: rusric@erols.com

required to remedy this problem, in a report of Committee IV which serves as a reference document for the present Protocol and is reproduced as Annex IV to the Agreement,

Have agreed:

1. To support the rehabilitation and resettlement of the refugees and sinistrés by complying with the provisions of Chapter I of the present Protocol;
2. To work towards the country's physical and political reconstruction in conformity with the principles and measures set out in Chapter II of the present Protocol;
3. To strive towards the economic and social development of Burundi by following. the guidelines defined in Chapter III of the present Protocol.

CHAPTER I REHABILITATION AND RESETTLEMENT OF REFUGEES AND SINISTRES

Article 1
Definitions

1. For the definition of the term "refugee", reference is made to international conventions, including the 1951 Geneva Convention Relative to the Status of Refugees, the 1966 Protocol Relative to the Status of Refugees and the 1969 Organization of African Unity Convention Governing the Specific Aspects of Refugee Problems in Africa.
2. The term "sinistrés" designates all displaced, regrouped and dispersed persons and returnees.

Article 2
Principles governing return, resettlement and reintegration

1. The Government of Burundi shall encourage the return of refugees and sinistrés and resettle and reintegrate them. It shall seek the support of other countries and international and non-governmental organizations in carrying out this responsibility.
2. It shall respect the following principles:
   a. All Burundian refugees must be able to return to their country;
   b. Refugees no longer in their first country of asylum are entitled to the same treatment as other returning Burundian refugees;
   c. Return must be voluntary and must take place in dignity with guaranteed security, and taking into account the particular vulnerability of women and children;
   d. The reception mechanisms must be put in place in advance of the return;

For additional analytical, marketing, investment and business opportunities information, please contact
Global Investment & Business Center, USA
(202) 546-2103. Fax: (202) 546-3275. E-mail: rusric@erols.com

e. Returnees must have their rights as citizens and their property restored to them in accordance with the laws and regulations in force in Burundi after the entry into force of the Agreement;

f. All sinistrés wishing to do so must be able to return to their homes;

g. Specific conditions must be provided for sinistrés who believe that they can no longer return to their property, so as to enable them to return to normal socio-professional life;

h. In the return of the refugees and the resettlement and reintegration of the returnees and displaced and regrouped persons, the principle of equity, including gender equity, must be strictly applied in order to avoid any measure or treatment that discriminates against or favours any one among these categories.

Article 3
Preparatory activities

The Government shall undertake the following preparatory activities:

a. Establishing and constituting a National Commission for the Rehabilitation of Sinistrés (CNRS), which shall have the mandate of organizing and coordinating, together with international organizations and countries of asylum, the return of refugees and sinistrés, assisting in their resettlement and reintegration, and dealing with all the other issues listed in the report of Committee IV. To this end, it shall draw up a plan of priorities. The members of the CNRS shall be drawn inter alia from the participating parties and the Government of Burundi, and shall elect the Commission's chairperson;

b. Establishing and constituting a Sub-Commission of the CNRS with the specific mandate of dealing with issues related to land as set out in article 8 (j) of the present Protocol;

c. Convening, in collaboration with the countries of asylum and the Office of the United Nations High Commissioner for Refugees, the Tripartite Commissioner, involving in it representatives of the refugees and international observers;

d. Requesting international organizations and the host countries concerned to conduct a gender and ago disaggregated census of the refugees, including the old caseload refugees (1972);

e. Conducting a multi-dimensional census of the sinistrés;

f. Organizing information and awareness campaigns for refugees and sinistrés as well as visits to their places of origin;

g. Undertaking information and awareness campaigns on the mechanisms for peaceful coexistence and return to collines of origin;

h. Setting up reception committees where they do not yet exist. The role of these committees shall be to receive and provide support services for all

For additional analytical, marketing, investment and business opportunities information, please contact
Global Investment & Business Center, USA
(202) 546-2103. Fax: (202) 546-3275. E-mail: rusric@erols.com

the sinistrés returning to their homes, ensure their security and assist them in organizing their socio-economic reintegration.

Article 4
Guidelines governing resettlement and integration

The CNRS shall decide on the activities for the resettlement and integration of refugees and sinistrés in accordance with the priority plan taking into account the availability of resources, in order to achieve the following aims and objectives:

a. To ensure the socio-economic and administrative reintegration of the sinistrés;
b. To give all returning families, including female- and child-headed families, food aid, material support and assistance with health, education, agriculture and reconstruction until they become self-sufficient;
c. To provide communes, villages and collines with assistance in the reconstruction of community infrastructures and with support for income-generating activities, paying special attention to women and enhancing their roles in building and sustaining families and communities;
d. To settle all those who believe that they cannot yet return on sites close to home, in order to enable them to go and till their fields initially and return to their land later on;
e. To encourage, to the extent possible, grouped housing in the reconstruction policy in order to free cultivable land;
f. To ensure equity in the distribution of resources between the ethnic groups on the one hand and the provinces on the other, and to avoid overlap between the various parties involved;
g. To promote the participation of the population in the resettlement activities;
h. To help returnees to recover the property and bank accounts left in Burundi before their exile and whose existence has been duly proven;
i. To offer intensive language courses for returnees to mitigate the language problems;
j. To assist returnees in other areas such as medical services, psycho-social support, social security and retirement, education of children and the equivalency of diplomas awarded outside Burundi.

Article 5
Actions with regard to returnees in their country of asylum

The Government shall undertake the following actions with regard to returnees in their country of asylum:

For additional analytical, marketing, investment and business opportunities information, please contact
Global Investment & Business Center, USA
(202) 546-2103. Fax: (202) 546-3275. E-mail: rusric@erols.com

a. Helping returnees settle their disputes in their country of asylum relating notably to immovable property, bank accounts, social security, etc;

b. In the context of agreements between countries or social security institutions, helping those who were employed in the country of asylum receive social security benefits to which they are entitled in respect of such employment;

c. Studying ways of indemnifying and compensating returnees for property in the country of asylum they are unable to take with them, profit from or sell;

d. Assisting pupils and students in their two final years of study in primary, secondary and higher education wishing to complete their studies in the country of asylum.

Article 6
Other actions

Any other action decided upon by the CNRS in accordance with the priority plan and in the light of available resources may be taken.

Article 7
Access and safety of international personnel

The Government shall allow international organizations and international and local non-governmental organizations unrestricted access to returnees and other sinistrés for purposes of the delivery of humanitarian assistance. It must guarantee the safety of the staff of such organizations and must also facilitate the provision of short-term aid for repatriation, appropriately supervised and without discrimination.

Article 8
Issues relating to land and other property

To resolve all issues relating to land and other property, the following principles and mechanisms shall be applied:

a. Property rights shall be guaranteed for all men, women and children. Compensation which is fair and equitable under the circumstances shall be payable in case of expropriation, which shall be allowed only in the public interest and in accordance with the law, which shall also set out the basis of compensation;

b. All refugees and/or sinistrés must be able to recover their property, especially their land;

c. If recovery proves impossible, everyone with an entitlement must receive fair compensation and/or indemnification;

For additional analytical, marketing, investment and business opportunities information, please contact
Global Investment & Business Center, USA
(202) 546-2103. Fax: (202) 546-3275. E-mail: rusric@erols.com

d. Refugees who do not return may receive a just and equitable indemnification if their land had been expropriated without prior indemnification and in contravention of the principle set out in sub-paragraph (a) of the present article;

e. The policy with respect to distribution of State-owned land shall be reviewed so that priority can be given to the resettlement of sinistrés;

f. An inventory of destroyed urban property shall be drawn up with a view to making it habitable in order to redistribute it or return it as a priority to the original owners;

g. A series of measures shall be taken in order to avoid subsequent disputes over land, including the establishment of a register of rural land, the promulgation of a law on succession and, in the longer term, the conduct of a cadastral survey of rural land;

h. The policy of distribution or allocation of new lands shall take account of the need for environmental protection and management of the country's water system through protection of forests;

i. Burundi's Land Act must be revised in order to adjust it to the current problems with respect to land management;

j. The Sub-Commission on Land established in accordance with article 3 (b) of the present Protocol shall have the specific mandate of:
    i. Examining all cases of land owned by old caseload refugees and state-owned land;
    ii. Examining disputed issues and allegations of abuse in the (re)distribution of land and ruling on each case in accordance with the above principles;

k. The Sub-Commission on Land must, in the performance of its functions, ensure the equity, transparency and good sense of all its decisions. It must always remain aware of the fact that the objective is not only restoration of their property to returnees, but also reconciliation between the groups as well as peace in the country.

Article 9
National Fund for Sinistrés

A National Fund for Sinistrés shall be established, and shall derive its funding from the national budget and from grants by bilateral and multilateral aid agencies or assistance from non-governmental organizations.

Article 10
Vulnerable groups

The Government shall ensure, through special assistance, the protection, rehabilitation and advancement of vulnerable groups, namely child heads of families, orphans, street children, unaccompanied minors, traumatized children,

For additional analytical, marketing, investment and business opportunities information, please contact
Global Investment & Business Center, USA
(202) 546-2103. Fax: (202) 546-3275. E-mail: rusric@erols.com

widows, women heads of families, juvenile delinquents, the physically and mentally disabled, etc.

CHAPTER II PHYSICAL AND POLITICAL RECONSTRUCTION

Article 11
Reconstruction programme

1. The transitional Government shall initiate and finance, with the support of the international community, a programme of physical and political reconstruction that takes a comprehensive approach incorporating rehabilitation, peace-building, promotion of the rights and freedoms of the human person, economic growth and long-term development.
2. The reconstruction programme shall be conducted and carried out in accordance with a realistic timetable that takes account of local capabilities and external inputs. The programme must be designed with a view to equity so that all categories of the population may benefit from it.

Article 12
Physical reconstruction

Physical reconstruction aims at assisting in the return of the refugees and sinistrés, as well as at the rebuilding of destroyed physical property. Physical reconstruction shall be conducted, transparently and equitably, in such a way as to:

a. Take into account both those who are being resettled or reintegrated and the communities receiving them;
b. Contribute to correcting the imbalances relating to public infrastructures, including school infrastructures;
c. Solve the problems relating to the repayment of loans that some Burundians had borrowed from banks and financial institutions for which the object financed has been destroyed;
d. Ensure sound management of rebuilt infrastructures;
e. Make use of human capital as an essential element of reconstruction;
f. Create conditions conducive to reconstruction and the reactivation of production activities;
g. Enhance the intervention capacity of the communes;
h. Draw on national solidarity.

Article 13
Political reconstruction

For additional analytical, marketing, investment and business opportunities information, please contact
Global Investment & Business Center, USA
(202) 546-2103. Fax: (202) 546-3275. E-mail: rusric@erols.com

Physical reconstruction and political reconstruction must be mutually supportive. Political reconstruction is aimed at making national reconciliation and peaceful coexistence possible, and must be directed towards the establishment of the rule of law. In this context, the following programmes and measures shall be undertaken:

a. Launching of a multi-faceted national reconciliation programme;
b. Promotion of the rights and freedoms of the human person;
c. Education of the population in the culture of peace;
d. Initiation of tangible actions for the advancement of women;
e. Reform of the judicial system;
f. Support of democratization, including strengthening of the parliamentary system and support for the political party system;
g. Support for the development and strengthening of civil society;
h. Provision of support for independent media.

CHAPTER III ECONOMIC AND SOCIAL DEVELOPMENT

Article 14
Development programme

The transitional Government shall launch a long-term economic and social development programme. With the support of international agencies, it shall begin work on remedying the economic situation, reversing the trends resulting from the crisis, particularly the intensification of poverty, and taking up the challenges that impede economic development.

Article 15
Principal objectives

The Government shall endeavour to correct the imbalances in distribution of the country's limited resources and to embark on the path of sustainable growth with equity. It shall set itself the following principal objectives:

a. Increasing rural and urban household income;
b. Providing all children with primary and secondary education at least to the age of 16;
c. Reducing the infant mortality rate by at least half;
d. Giving the entire population access to health care;
e. Improving the well-being of the population in all areas.

Article 16
Guidelines governing development

For additional analytical, marketing, investment and business opportunities information, please contact
Global Investment & Business Center, USA
(202) 546-2103. Fax: (202) 546-3275. E-mail: rusric@erols.com

In pursuit of these objectives, the Government shall follow the guidelines set out hereunder on the basis of the measures specified in the report of Committee IV (see Annex IV):

a. Working towards macro-economic and financial stabilization;
b. Attempting to solve the problem of external and domestic public debt;
c. Initiation of structural reforms in the social sectors;
d. Creation of an environment conducive to the expansion of the private sector;
e. Efforts to create new jobs and compliance with the criteria of equity and transparency in employment;
f. Ensuring good governance in the management of public affairs;
g. Rendering operational the Court of Audit established under the provisions of Chapter I of Protocol II to the Agreement;
h. Transformation of the communes into focal points for development and promotion of greater public access to State services by means of a decentralization policy;
i. Promotion of the role of women and youth in development, with the aid of specific measures to benefit them;
j. Initiation of Burundi's integration into the region;
k. Equitable apportionment of the benefits of development.

Article 17
Implementation

1. For the implementation of the reconstruction and development measures, an Inter-Ministerial Reconstruction and Development Unit shall be created to which the Ministries of Planning, Finance and Reintegration shall second personnel. Support for this Unit shall be sought from the World Bank, the United Nations Development Programme, the Office of the United Nations High Commissioner for Refugees, the European Commission and others. It shall have the following mandate:
   a. Preparation, within six weeks of the signing of the peace agreement, of an emergency reconstruction plan that will set the priorities for reconstruction and provide an initial estimate of costs. In preparing this plan, the National Commission for the Rehabilitation of Sinistrés shall be consulted and invited to submit proposals. This emergency plan shall also serve as the basis for discussion at a donor conference;
   b. Subsequently, preparation of a detailed reconstruction plan covering the transition period as set forth in Chapter II of Protocol II to the Agreement;
   c. At the same time, preparation of a medium- and long-term development plan.

For additional analytical, marketing, investment and business opportunities information, please contact
Global Investment & Business Center, USA
(202) 546-2103. Fax: (202) 546-3275. E-mail: rusric@erols.com

2. The three plans shall be submitted to the National Assembly for approval. They will be guided by the measures proposed by Committee IV (see Annex IV, chapters II and III) while adapting the priorities in response to developments in the situation and bearing in mind opportunities for financing.
3. Donors will be involved in the work of the Unit, and may request an international auditing company to monitor all financial operations and accounts that may be established.

PROTOCOL V: GUARANTEES ON IMPLEMENTATION OF THE AGREEMENT

PREAMBLE

We, the Parties,

Aware of the importance of guarantees in any peace process, and particularly in the implementation of peace agreements,

Having learned the lessons from the failure of previous agreements in Burundi,

Desirous that peace and reconciliation should be based on an agreement that is clear, precise, specific, unequivocal, comprehensive and implementable in Burundi in accordance with the implementation timetable contained in Annex V to the Agreement,

Having expressed a solemn commitment to assume joint responsibility for the content of the Agreement,

Concerned also about the negative impact of the conflict on Burundian women and children,

Recognizing the unique potential of women to contribute to the healing, reconstruction and development of Burundian society,

Aware that the Burundian people is the focus and beneficiary of the Agreement concluded in its name,

Confident of the will and ability of Burundians to restore peace and harmony in their country, with the support of the international community,

Resolved to ensure the effective implementation of the Agreement,

Have agreed as follows:

For additional analytical, marketing, investment and business opportunities information, please contact
Global Investment & Business Center, USA
(202) 546-2103. Fax: (202) 546-3275. E-mail: rusric@erols.com

Article 1
Acceptance and support of the Agreement by the Burundian people

All the Parties commit themselves to undertake a broad campaign to inform and sensitize the population about the content, spirit and letter of the Agreement.

Article 2
Transitional institutions

1. The transitional institutions shall be established and operate in accordance with the relevant provisions of Chapter II of Protocol II to the Agreement.
2. The men and women called upon to lead the transition must, at all times, show integrity, determination, patriotism and competence, and devote themselves to the interests of all Burundians without any discrimination. They must take a solemn oath before assuming their duties.
3. The duration of the transition period shall be as specified in article 13 of Protocol II to the Agreement.

Article 3
Implementation Monitoring Committee

A committee to follow up, monitor, supervise and coordinate the implementation of the Agreement, hereinafter referred to as the Implementation Monitoring Committee, shall be established.

1. Role of the Implementation Monitoring Committee

    The functions of the Implementation Monitoring Committee shall be to:

    a. Follow up, monitor, supervise, coordinate and ensure the effective implementation of all the provisions of the Agreement;
    b. Ensure that the implementation timetable is respected;
    c. Ensure the accurate interpretation of the Agreement;
    d. Reconcile points of view;
    e. Arbitrate and rule on any dispute that may arise among the signatories;
    f. Give guidance to and coordinate the activities of all the commissions and sub-commissions set up pursuant to each protocol for the purpose of implementing the Agreement. These commissions and subcommissions shall include the following:
        - The Technical Committee to implement the procedures for the establishment of a national defence force;

For additional analytical, marketing, investment and business opportunities information, please contact
Global Investment & Business Center, USA
(202) 546-2103. Fax: (202) 546-3275. E-mail: rusric@erols.com

- The Technical Committee to implement the procedures for the establishment of the national police;
- The Ceasefire Commission;
- The Reintegration Commission;
- The National Commission for the Rehabilitation of Sinistrés;

g. Assist and support the transitional government in the diplomatic mobilization of the financial, material, technical and human resources required for the implementation of the Agreement;

h. Decide on the admission of new participating parties in accordance with article 14 of Protocol II to the Agreement;

i. Perform any other duty specifically allocated to it by the Agreement.

2. Composition and structure of the Implementation Monitoring Committee

a. The Implementation Monitoring Committee shall have the following composition:
   i. Two representatives of the Parties;
   ii. One representatives of the Government;
   iii. Six Burundians designated for their moral integrity;
   iv. Representatives of:
      - The United Nations;
      - The Organization of African Unity;
      - The regional Peace Initiative on Burundi;

b. The Implementation Monitoring Committee shall be chaired by the representative of the United Nations, who shall act in consultation with the Government, the Organization of African Unity and the Regional Peace Initiative on Burundi;

c. The Implementation Monitoring Committee shall be based in Bujumbura and shall have an Executive Council, to which it may delegate such of its powers as it deems appropriate;

d. There shall be a secretariat to service the Implementation Monitoring Committee and the Executive Council.

3. Functioning and powers of the Implementation Monitoring Committee

a. The Implementation Monitoring Committee shall begin its operations upon the appointment of its chairperson, and its mandate shall end when the Government elected during the transition period takes office. It shall draw up its own rules of procedure and work programme.

b. The Implementation Monitoring Committee shall possess the requisite authority and decision-making powers to perform its functions impartially, neutrally and effectively.

c. Decisions of the Implementation Monitoring Committee shall be taken by the Parties, by consensus or failing that by a **four-fifths** majority.

For additional analytical, marketing, investment and business opportunities information, please contact
Global Investment & Business Center, USA
(202) 546-2103. Fax: (202) 546-3275. E-mail: rusric@erols.com

Article 4
The Facilitator

The Facilitator shall continue in his role as moral guarantor, recourse authority and conciliation agent.

Article 5
Commissions

1. The Implementation Monitoring Committee, in collaboration with the Government, shall establish commissions and sub-commissions responsible for sectoral activities as provided for in paragraph 1 (g) of article 3. Their activities shall be coordinated by the Implementation Monitoring Committee, to which they shall report.
2. The Implementation Monitoring Committee shall, when setting up commissions and subcommissions, specify their composition, functions, structures, location, decision-making process and leadership, as well as the timetable for the completion of their activities.
3. International Judicial Commission of Inquiry
   a. The transitional Government shall address the request referred to in article 6, paragraph 10, of Protocol I to the Agreement to the United Nations Security Council within 30 days from its installation.
   b. International criminal tribunal

      The Government of Burundi shall address the request referred to in article 6, paragraph 11, of Protocol I to the Agreement to the United Nations Security Council within 15 days after publication of the report of the International Judicial Commission of Inquiry.

4. National Truth and Reconciliation Commission

   The transitional Government, in consultation with the Bureau of transitional National Assembly, shall establish the National Truth and Reconciliation Commission pursuant to article 8 of Protocol I to the Agreement not later than six months after taking office. The Commission shall begin work within 15 days after its establishment.

5. Technical Committee to implement the procedures for the establishment of a national defence force
   a. The establishment of the national defence force, its name, its strength, its training, its conditions of service and its functioning shall be as defined in the relevant provisions of Chapter II of Protocol III to the Agreement and in organic laws, regulatory texts

For additional analytical, marketing, investment and business opportunities information, please contact
Global Investment & Business Center, USA
(202) 546-2103. Fax: (202) 546-3275. E-mail: rusric@erols.com

and disciplinary rules adopted pursuant to article 11, paragraph 5, and article 19 of that Protocol.

b. The organic laws, regulatory texts and disciplinary rules referred to above shall be adopted by the appropriate transitional institutions within 30 days from the adoption of the Constitution.

c. The Technical Committee to implement the procedures for the establishment of a national defence force referred to in article 14, paragraph 1 (d) of Protocol III to the Agreement shall be constituted within 15 to 30 days after the adoption of the texts referred to in paragraph (b) above. Its work shall begin within seven days after its constitution, and shall be concluded before the start of the electoral process.

6. Technical Committee to implement the procedures for the establishment of the national police

a. The creation, name, missions, composition, strength, training, conditions of service and functioning of the national police shall be as defined in the relevant provisions of article 14, paragraph 2, article 15, article 17, paragraph 3, and article 20 of Protocol III to the Agreement.

b. The Technical Committee to implement the procedures for the establishment of the national police set up pursuant to the provisions of article 14, paragraph 2 (c) of that Protocol shall be constituted within 15 to 30 days from the date when the transitional Government takes office. Its work shall begin within seven days after its constitution, and shall be concluded before the start of the electoral process.

7. Ceasefire Commission

a. The ceasefire, as defined in article 25 of Protocol III to the Agreement, shall take place on the date of signature of the Agreement.

b. The Ceasefire Commission provided for in article 27, paragraph 1 of Protocol III to the Agreement shall be established by the Implementation Monitoring Committee on the day the Committee starts its activities. It shall begin its work upon the appointment of its chairperson.

c. In conformity with article 27, paragraph 1 of Protocol III, the Ceasefire Commission shall consist of representatives of the Government, the combatants of the political parties and movements, the United Nations, the Organization of African Unity and the Regional Peace Initiative for Burundi.

d. The Ceasefire Commission may establish offices in the military regions of the country, as well as in the quartering locations and at other points as its functions may require.

For additional analytical, marketing, investment and business opportunities information, please contact
Global Investment & Business Center, USA
(202) 546-2103. Fax: (202) 546-3275. E-mail: rusric@erols.com

    e. The functions of the Ceasefire Commission shall be as defined in article 21, article 27, paragraphs 1(d), 2, 3 and 4 and article 28 of Protocol III of the Agreement.

    f. The operations consisting of the ceasefire, disengagement, quartering and demobilization of the forces shall be completed within six months from the commencement of the activities of the Ceasefire Commission.

    g. Deployment and operations of the international peacekeeping force provided for in article 27, paragraph 5 of Protocol III to the Agreement shall commence as soon as possible after the establishment of the Ceasefire Commission. They shall be conducted in coordination and cooperation with the Ceasefire Commission.

    h. In performing their duties, the members of the Ceasefire Commission as well as those of the international peacekeeping and security force shall enjoy complete freedom of movement throughout the territory of Burundi.

    i. The amnesty provided for in article 26(1) of Protocol III to the Agreement shall go into effect on the date of signature of the Agreement.

8. Reintegration Commission

    a. The organ provided for in article 21, paragraph 8 of Protocol III to the Agreement, hereinafter referred to as the Reintegration Commission shall have the role of organizing, supervising, monitoring and ensuring the effective economic and social reintegration of the troops and combatants who, as a result of the demobilization process carried out in conformity with article 21 of Protocol III to the Agreement, have become civilians.

    b. The Reintegration Commission shall consist of representatives of the Government, the United Nations and the Organization of African Unity. It shall be chaired by the Government.

    c. The Reintegration Commission shall commence its activities on the day of its establishment. These activities must be completed before the commencement of the electoral process.

9. National Commission for the Rehabilitation of Sinistrés

The organ provided for in article 3, paragraph (a) of Protocol IV to the Agreement, shall be constituted within 30 days after the signature of the Agreement. It shall begin its work upon the election of its chairperson and shall report to the Implementation Monitoring Committee. It shall be based in Bujumbura. It shall be in place until the end of the transition period.

Article 6
Genocide, war crimes and other crimes against humanity

For additional analytical, marketing, investment and business opportunities information, please contact
Global Investment & Business Center, USA
(202) 546-2103. Fax: (202) 546-3275. E-mail: rusric@erols.com

The Implementation Monitoring Committee shall ensure implementation of the measures specified in Protocol I to the Agreement relating to the prevention. suppression and eradication of acts of genocide, war crimes and other crimes against humanity.

Article 7
Role of the international community

1. The involvement of the international community in the implementation of the Agreement is necessary, both as a moral and diplomatic guarantee and as a provider of technical, material and financial assistance.
2. In this respect, the Burundian Government shall immediately following the signature of the Agreement send formal requests to the countries and organizations agreed upon by the Parties inviting them to participate in and render their financial, technical and material support to the implementation of the Agreement as provided for in the relevant provisions of the present Protocol and of Protocols I, II, III and IV.

Article 8
Peacekeeping

Immediately following the signature of the Agreement, the Burundian Government shall submit to the United Nations a request for an international peacekeeping force in conformity with and for the purposes set forth in article 27, paragraph 5 of Protocol III to the Agreement. Account must be taken of United Nations practice in this respect. This force shall be responsible inter alia for:

a. Ensuring respect for the ceasefire;
b. Supervising integration;
c. Providing technical support for demobilization aid and training;
d. Ensuring protection of the institutions and of any public figure who so wishes;
e. Assisting in the establishment and training of an ethnically balanced special unit for the protection of the institutions.

Article 9
Financial guarantees

Implementation of all the reforms and programmes contained in the Agreement will require financial support from donors. In this context, the Facilitator, in coordination with the Implementation Monitoring Committee and the transitional Government, shall take the necessary steps for a donors' conference to be convened to raise funds for the reconstruction of Burundi.

For additional analytical, marketing, investment and business opportunities information, please contact
Global Investment & Business Center, USA
(202) 546-2103. Fax: (202) 546-3275. E-mail: rusric@erols.com

Article 10
Role of the region

1. The Parties urge the heads of State of the countries of the region to continue to provide their support for the peace process in Burundi.
2. The heads of State of the region shall also constitute guarantors of the Agreement.

For additional analytical, marketing, investment and business opportunities information, please contact
Global Investment & Business Center, USA
(202) 546-2103. Fax: (202) 546-3275. E-mail: rusric@erols.com

STRUCTURE OF THE NATIONAL POLICE OF BURUNDI

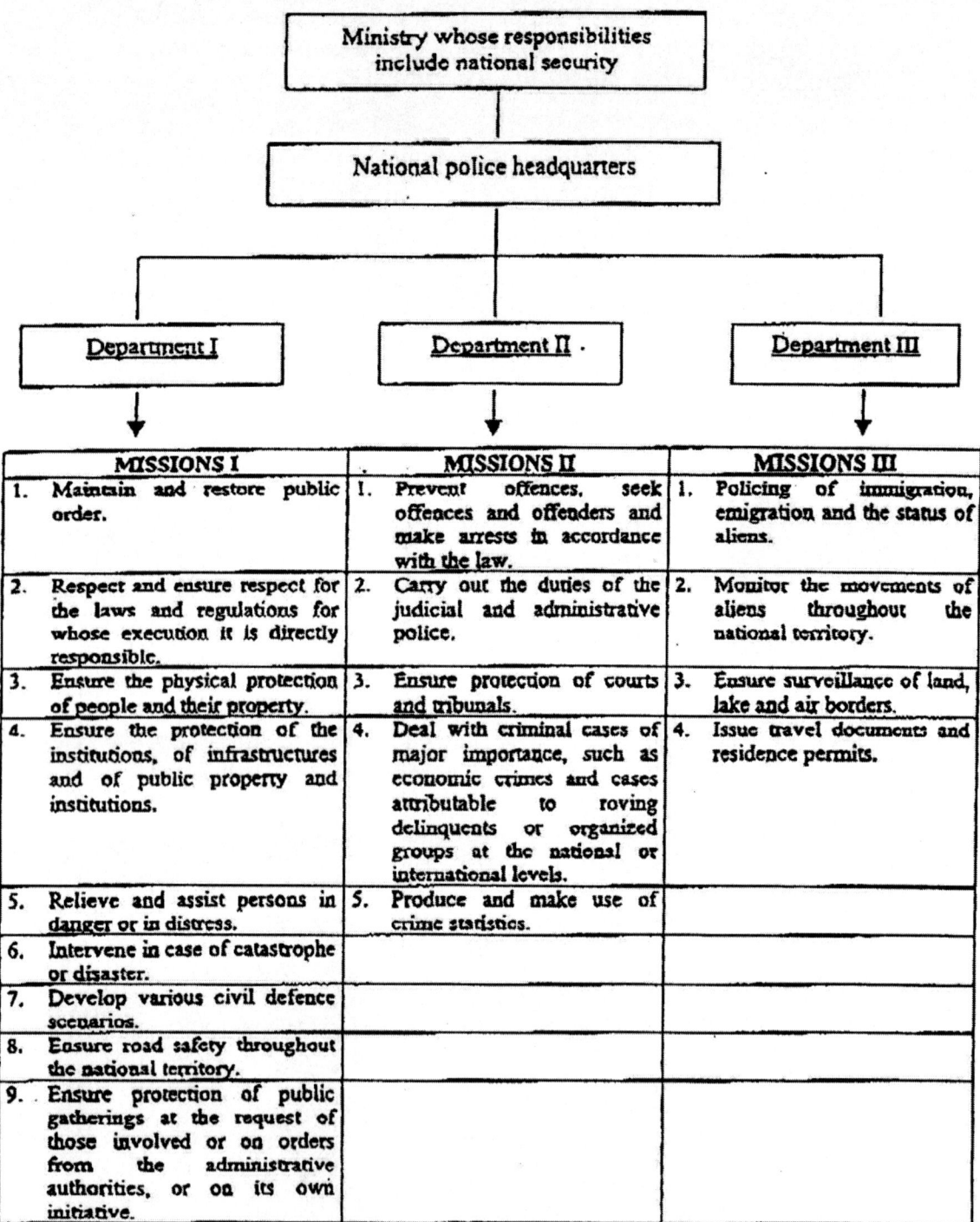

MISSIONS I	MISSIONS II	MISSIONS III
1. Maintain and restore public order.	1. Prevent offences, seek offences and offenders and make arrests in accordance with the law.	1. Policing of immigration, emigration and the status of aliens.
2. Respect and ensure respect for the laws and regulations for whose execution it is directly responsible.	2. Carry out the duties of the judicial and administrative police.	2. Monitor the movements of aliens throughout the national territory.
3. Ensure the physical protection of people and their property.	3. Ensure protection of courts and tribunals.	3. Ensure surveillance of land, lake and air borders.
4. Ensure the protection of the institutions, of infrastructures and of public property and institutions.	4. Deal with criminal cases of major importance, such as economic crimes and cases attributable to roving delinquents or organized groups at the national or international levels.	4. Issue travel documents and residence permits.
5. Relieve and assist persons in danger or in distress.	5. Produce and make use of crime statistics.	
6. Intervene in case of catastrophe or disaster.		
7. Develop various civil defence scenarios.		
8. Ensure road safety throughout the national territory.		
9. Ensure protection of public gatherings at the request of those involved or on orders from the administrative authorities, or on its own initiative.		

IMPLEMENTATION TIMETABLE

For additional analytical, marketing, investment and business opportunities information, please contact
Global Investment & Business Center, USA
(202) 546-2103. Fax: (202) 546-3275. E-mail: rusric@erols.com

ANNEX V

TIMETABLE FOR THE IMPLEMENTATION OF THE AGREEMENT:
PROTOCOLS I, II, III AND IV

SERIAL SEQUENCES	ACTIVITIES	TIMING	EXECUTION	ARTICLES AND PARAGRAPHS
Signing + 30 days	1. First meeting of Implementation Monitoring Committee to decide on Executive Council	Immediately after signature	Facilitator, Parties	
	2. Informal donors meeting on a technical level	15 Sept. 2000 Brussels	European Commission / Facilitation, donors, international community	
	3. Pledge by participating parties	Immediate Within 7 days	Participating parties	Annex I
	4. Establishment of mechanism to investigate the status and release of prisoners	Immediate	Government / National Assembly	
	5. • Current National Assembly to adopt Peace Agreement • Law permitting free political activity • Repeal of repressive legislation	Immediate	National Assembly	Protocol II, art. 22 para. 2(a), (b), (c)

For additional analytical, marketing, investment and business opportunities information, please contact
Global Investment & Business Center, USA
(202) 546-2103. Fax: (202) 546-3275. E-mail: rusric@erols.com

6. Implementation Monitoring Committee set up in Bujumbura	Immediate	Implementation Monitoring Committee / UN / OAU / Facilitator / region	
7. Peace forces to be solicited from UN / OAU / region	Immediate	Current Government / Facilitator / Signatories Implementation Monitoring Committee	
8. Monitoring of current Government activity + IMC to monitor and set up mechanisms to resolve disputes among Parties	Immediate Within 7 days	Implementation Monitoring Committee	
9. Campaign to popularize the Agreement	Immediate	Facilitator, participating parties, Implementation Monitoring Committee	Protocol II, art. 22, para. 16
10. Ceasefire dissemination	Immediate	BDF / Armed groups or interim force	
11. Establishment of reception mechanisms for refugees and sinistrés	Immediate - 30 days	UNHCR, Govt. of Burundi + international organizations	Protocol IV, art. 2, para. 2(d)
12. Creation of National Commission for the Rehabilitation of Sinistrés (CNRS) and National Fund for Sinistrés	Immediate - 30 days	Government / UNHCR / Implementation Monitoring Committee	Protocol IV, art. 3(a) and 9

For additional analytical, marketing, investment and business opportunities information, please contact
Global Investment & Business Center, USA
(202) 546-2103. Fax: (202) 546-3275. E-mail: rusric@erols.com

	13. Other preparatory actions for the settlement and reintegration of refugees and sinistrés	Immediate ongoing	Govt. of Burundi, UNHCR and other international organizations	Protocol IV art. 3 (d) - (h)
	14. Temporary immunity for political offences pending installation of transitional National Assembly	1 - 30 days	Current National Assembly	Protocol II, art. 22, para. 2(c)
30 days to 180 days	15. Convening of Tripartite Commissions	30 days	Governments of Tanzania, Democratic Congo, Rwanda, / Burundian Government / UNHCR	Protocol IV, Art. 3(c).
	16. Government assets register	Within 30 days	Current Government	Protocol II, art. 22, para. 6(b)
	17. Creation of Reconstruction and Development Unit	30-45 days after signing	Technical ministries / donors / IMC, international organizations.	Protocol IV, art. 17, para.1
	18. Arrangements for start of transition in place including reception centres, assembly points security for assembly points.	30 days Continuous	Executive Council of Implementation Monitoring Committee	
	19. Members of the transitional National Assembly to be named	Within 60 days	Participating Parties / Implementation Monitoring Committee	Protocol II, art. 22, para. 3(b)

For additional analytical, marketing, investment and business opportunities information, please contact
Global Investment & Business Center, USA
(202) 546-2103. Fax: (202) 546-3275. E-mail: rusric@erols.com

20. Transitional President to name members of the Cabinet	Within 60 days	Transitional President / Implementation Monitoring Committee	Protocol II, art. 22, para. 4
21. Implementation Monitoring Committee to check if conditions for Transitional National Assembly in place (what additional steps to be taken by Parties / Government / UN)	60 days after signature	Implementation Monitoring Committee	Protocol II, art. 22, para. 5
22. Members of transitional National Assembly and transitional Executive to return to Burundi	60 days	Parties / Implementation Monitoring Committee / Government	
23. Logistics for returning members of the transitional National Assembly and transitional Executive including travel documents	1- 60 days	Implementation Monitoring Committee + Government	Protocol II, art. 22, para. 6(a)
24. Security arrangements for members of the transitional National Assembly / Executive and members of political parties in exile to be sought and installed	Within 60 days	Ceasefire Commission	Protocol III, art. 27, para. 4(a)
25. Preparation of an emergency reconstruction plan	45-60 days after signature	National Assembly / Reconstruction & Development Unit	Protocol IV, art. 17, para. 1(a)

For additional analytical, marketing, investment and business opportunities information, please contact
Global Investment & Business Center, USA
(202) 546-2103. Fax: (202) 546-3275. E-mail: rusric@erols.com

	26. High-level international donors' conference	45-120 days after signature	Facilitator, donors, international organizations, IMC, CNRS, RDU	
	27. Prepare D-Day commitments for disarmament / demobilization / reintegration (personnel register)		BDF / Armed groups / interim force / Ceasefire Commission	
	28. Disarm, assemble and train armed groups	Interim period	Ceasefire Commission	
(Transition) D-Day	29. Confirmation of camps closed or transformed into voluntary villages	D-Day	Transitional Government	
	30. National Assembly disbanded Transitional National Assembly installed	D-Day	Transitional National Assembly / IMC	
	31. Transitional Executive installed - move into premises	D-Day	Transitional Executive / IMC	
	32. Transitional National Assembly meets to elect Bureau	D-Day + 3 days	Transitional National Assembly	
	33. Review the propriety of all contracts, recruitment, during preceding period	Ongoing D-Day	Transitional National Assembly / transitional Government	
	34. Establish Commission on Judicial Reform	D-Day + 30 days	Transitional National Assembly	Protocol II, art. 17, para. 1
	35. Establish Administrative Reform Commission	D-Day + 30 days	Transitional National Assembly	Protocol II, art. 17, para. 1

For additional analytical, marketing, investment and business opportunities information, please contact
Global Investment & Business Center, USA
(202) 546-2103. Fax: (202) 546-3275. E-mail: rusric@erols.com

36. Establish Constitutional Commission	D-Day + 30 days	Transitional National Assembly	Protocol II, art. 15, para. 4
37. Appoint heads of Police, Defence and National Intelligence		Transitional Government	Protocol II, art. 15. para. 18
38. Appoint Provincial Governors	D-Day + 30 days	Transitional Government	Protocol II, art. 15, para. 19(a)
39. Appoint Commune Administrators	D-Day + 30 days	Transitional Government / transitional National Assembly	Protocol II, art. 15, para. 19(c)
40. Appoint Constitutional Court judges	D-Day + 30 days	Transitional President	Protocol II, Art. 15, para. 19(b)
41. Establish Land Sub-Commission (subordinated to CNRS) which will take action on land issues	D-Day + 30 days	CNRS / participating parties / transitional Government	Protocol IV, art. 3(b)
42. Special assistance programmes for vulnerable groups	D-Day + 30 days	Transitional Government + international assistance + CNRS	Protocol IV, Art. 10
43. Prepare detailed plan for physical and political reconstruction for the transition period	D-Day + 30 days	Transitional Nat. Assembly + Reconstruction & Devpt. Unit + transitional Government	Protocol IV, art. 17, para. 1(b)
44. Request UNSC to set up International Judicial Commission of Inquiry	D-Day + 30 days	Transitional Government/UN	Protocol I, Art. 6, para. 10

For additional analytical, marketing, investment and business opportunities information, please contact
Global Investment & Business Center, USA
(202) 546-2103. Fax: (202) 546-3275. E-mail: rusric@erols.com

45. Establish conditions of service and adopt organic laws of New Defence Force	D-Day + 30 days	Transitional National Assembly / transitional Government	Protocol III, Art. 19
46. Establish Commission on prisons, political prisoners, prisoners on death row and working conditions for prison guards	D-Day + 30 days	Transitional Government	Protocol II, Art. 15, para. 20
47. Adopt laws on judicial reform	Ongoing from D-Day	Transitional National Assembly	
48. Review of all judges and solicit international assistance. Appointment of new ones judged	Ongoing from D-Day	Transitional Government	Protocol II, Art. 17, para. 10
49. Review of all existing legislation (amendment or repeal)	Ongoing from D-Day	Transitional National Assembly + transitional Government	
50. Mass campaign on reconciliation	Ongoing from D-Day	Transitional National Assembly / transitional Government / political parties	Protocol I, Art. 6, para. 3 and Protocol IV, art. 13(c)
51. Implement judicial and administrative reforms	Ongoing from D-Day	Transitional Government / transitional National Assembly	Protocol II, art. 17, paras. 1 & 2
52. Adapt Local Government Law	Ongoing from D-Day	Transitional National Assembly	

For additional analytical, marketing, investment and business opportunities information, please contact
Global Investment & Business Center, USA
(202) 546-2103. Fax: (202) 546-3275. E-mail: rusric@erols.com

53. Preparation of a medium and long-term development plan	D-Day + 90 days	Government / Donors / international organizations / transitional Government / international assistance / National Assembly	Protocol IV, art.17, para. (c)
54. Establish the Electoral Commission nominating authority	D-Day + 90 days	Transitional National Assembly / transitional Government	Protocol II, art. 20, para. 3
55. Implement Committee IV proposals on economic development and reconstruction	D-Day + 90 days ongoing	Transitional Government / transitional National Assembly	Protocol IV, arts. 11 - 16
56. Establish Truth & Reconciliation Commission	D-Day + 6 months	Transitional Government / transitional Nat. Assembly	Protocol I, art. 8 Protocol II, art. 5, para. 4
57. Adopt Electoral Law	D-Day + 12 months	Transitional National Assembly	Protocol II Art. 20, para. 5
58. Electoral Commission demarcates collines and zones. Prepare for colline elections	Within 18 months of D-Day	Electoral Commission	
59. Hold local government elections (Colline level)	Within 18 months of D-Day	Electoral Commission	Protocol II, Art. 20, para. 12
60. Hold local government elections (Commune level)	Within 18 months of D-Day	Electoral Commission	

For additional analytical, marketing, investment and business opportunities information, please contact
Global Investment & Business Center, USA
(202) 546-2103. Fax: (202) 546-3275. E-mail: rusric@erols.com

61. Adapt new Commune Administrators	After commune level election	Commune Councils	Protocol II, Art. 20, para. 13(a)
62. Pass Constitutional text	D-Day + 18 months	Transitional National Assembly	
63. Hold referendum on Constitution	Within 24 months of D-Day	Electoral Commission / transitional Government / transitional National Assembly	Protocol II, art. 15, para. 7
64. Certify Constitutional text (or amend and resubmit)	Within 23 months of D-Day	Constitutional Court	Protocol II, art. 20, para. 4(a)-(g)
65. Prepare for election: regulations, establish multi-party committee	Within 30 months of D-Day	Transitional Government / National Assembly / Electoral Commission	
66. Hold elections for the National Assembly	Within 30 months of D-Day	Electoral Commission	Protocol II art. 6, para. 17 & 15
67. Commune Councils to elect Senators. Co-opt Twa to Senate	Within 30 months of D-Day	Electoral Commission and Senate	
68. Merge Burundi Defence Force and armed groups	Transition period	Transitional Government	
69. Demobilize to new strength levels		Ceasefire Commission / transitional Govt.	
70. Confirm new defence force complies with 50/50 rule	After election	Transitional Government	

For additional analytical, marketing, investment and business opportunities information, please contact
Global Investment & Business Center, USA
(202) 546-2103. Fax: (202) 546-3275. E-mail: rusric@erols.com

71. National Assembly (new) and Senate meet to elect new President	

I. SUMMARY OF CONSTITUTIONAL AND TRANSITIONAL PROPOSALS FOR BURUNDI

A. GENERAL REMARKS

1. Background

The proposals contained in Protocol II represent a more complex and interrelated set of propositions than they may appear when considered individually.

With this in mind, the Bureau of the Committee felt that there was a need to provide an outline of this "package" of proposals, if only to illustrate the overall balance the Bureau sought to achieve. It would also serve to illustrate that these proposals emanate from and have been canvassed in over a thousand hours of debate, negotiations and consultations with the parties since April 1999. Furthermore, the proposals themselves are directed at the actual concerns raised by all the parties. It is these concerns rather than the precise proposal formulations that parties have adopted that the Bureau's proposals have been fashioned to address. No party should have expected to have all its proposals incorporated, and certainly not in the identical form in which they were proposed.

The mandate given to Committee II, back in October 1998, was to establish an institutional setting for a future government of Burundi considered as "acceptable to all".

The Committee based its initial agenda on those aspects of the popularly endorsed 1992 Constitution that appeared to be uncontentious, and attempted to set out those that were subject to dispute. Once the parties' responses were obtained on the issues in dispute, the Bureau established a nine-point working agenda for the Committee and duly conducted in the Committee debate lasting over 720 hours. The sessions ended on 15 April 1999.

Thereafter the Bureau established a first draft of a protocol for discussion. The initial draft, like the present protocol, was divided into two chapters. The first chapter dealt with the institutional setting and fundamental values that would have to figure in a definitive constitution to be drafted by the future transitional

For additional analytical, marketing, investment and business opportunities information, please contact
Global Investment & Business Center, USA
(202) 546-2103. Fax: (202) 546-3275. E-mail: rusric@erols.com

National Assembly. The second chapter covered the issues of the transition. Between April 1999 and April 2000 the protocol was updated seven times, in accordance with the debates, which took place either amongst or with clusters, individual parties or regrouped clusters, highlighting the points of disagreement and the options proposed by the groups to resolve them. It was the seventh draft which served as a basis for the final proposal. On the 10% of the text that remained in sharp dispute, the parties concluded that they would not find agreement no matter how much time was allocated for further negotiations. They requested the Bureau to make compromise proposals in regard to these outstanding items. The protocol thus represents both the uncontested text and also those proposals which were themselves fashioned from the options suggested by the parties.

There has been occasional confusion regarding the exact mandate of Committee II. Some have thought that the Committee's task was to write a new constitution for the Republic of Burundi. In fact, our mandate was to establish only such principles as the Burundi believed were necessary for the re-establishment of a democratic system within their country. It is the task of the Barundi to draft their own constitution in due course, to put the flesh on the constitutional skeleton.

B. SUMMARY OF PROPOSALS

1. Electoral system

The "electoral system" does not merely concern the system of voting, but must be understood in the context of the full variety of the institutional and other mechanisms providing for inclusive and multi-ethnic participation in the structures of government and the Senate.

2. Ethnic over-representation

The electoral system set out in the Agreement is premised on the principle of universal suffrage (supported by every one of the parties) with a common voter's roll (supported by at least 12 and possibly more of the parties). The electoral system envisages that voting will be in respect of party lists in a proportional representation system in which the lists are required to reflect a high degree of representation of minorities. A system of multi-ethnic lists was supported principally by the centrist parties, including the Government, and opposed only by a minority of parties which had proposed segregated political structures. Some parties have called for as many as 50% of the members of the National Assembly to come from the approximately 15% of the population made up of minorities. The electoral system as proposed here will yield a National Assembly in which, before co-optation as described below, approximately 38% of the members are from the minorities.

For additional analytical, marketing, investment and business opportunities information, please contact
Global Investment & Business Center, USA
(202) 546-2103. Fax: (202) 546-3275. E-mail: rusric@erols.com

3. Additional co-optation to the National Assembly

The proposals allow for the possibility of additional minority representation in the first elections by a co-optation mechanism which grants enhanced representation for opposition parties by allocating an equal proportion of a further 20 seats to all qualifying parties regardless of their popular support. In effect this would mean that members of minority groups (some 15% of the population including the Batwa) should fill some 40% or more of the seats in the National Assembly. It would also mean enhanced opposition representation in the Assembly, and would partially allay fears of a dominant single party.

4. Ethnically balanced Senate

In addition the proposals envisage a second chamber in which two representatives, one Hutu and one Tutsi, will be indirectly elected from each province. This chamber, the Senate, thus has parity in respect of the ethnic membership of its provincial representatives. The Senate is given important powers to confirm or approve strategic appointments and laws of an important nature. It should be stated that the proposals regarding the establishment, powers and composition of the Senate were strongly supported by many of the parties purporting to represent minority concerns - and strongly opposed by the G-7 group of parties. The electoral college for the Senate is comprised of local-level councils constituted on a non-party basis. It need hardly be repeated that this proposal involves parity of membership between members of ethnic groups that constitute 85% and 13% of the population respectively. They will, however, be popularly elected.

5. Co-optation at the local level

In addition, the proposals provide for indirectly elected commune councils and appointed commune administrators, with a safety mechanism to ensure that minorities are adequately represented on the councils. These elections may not be conducted on a party political basis. Again, these proposals flow directly from concerns raised by groups purporting to represent minority concerns.

6. Multi-ethnic presidency

In addition, the proposals envisage that there will be two vice-presidents, each coming from a different political and ethnic group. These proposals also emanate from parties representing minority concerns.

7. Government of national unity

For additional analytical, marketing, investment and business opportunities
information, please contact
Global Investment & Business Center, USA
(202) 546-2103. Fax: (202) 546-3275. E-mail: rusric@erols.com

In terms of the proposals, opposition parties with more than 5% of the popular vote will be entitled to choose to serve in the cabinet. This proposal ensures an inclusive government and blunts the winner-take-all nature of party politics in Burundi.

8. Indirectly elected President

Although the President will in the longer term be directly elected, to accommodate minority concerns in the short term it is proposed that the President be indirectly elected with a high degree of support in the National Assembly. This proposal is also a response to proposals along such lines by parties purporting to represent minority concerns.

9. High decision-making majorities

In regard to decision-making majorities that are required for important matters and certain appointments, high, and some very high, majorities of support are required in the National Assembly. Again, these proposals emanate from the concerns of parties representing minorities. In particular, many important executive appointments are made subject to Senate and National Assembly approval.

10. Security forces guarantee

So as to provide an overall constitutional and security environment in which anxieties raised by the parties can be accommodated, the proposals include as an element of the constitutional framework a security guarantee on the composition of the armed forces. This guarantee requires that at least 50% of the security forces shall be members of minority ethnic groups.

11. Strong Constitutional Court

In addition, against the opposition of the G-7 group of parties the Constitutional Court has been given full judicial power to enforce the Constitution and to act as its guardian even against the Executive and the Legislature. The ethnically-balanced Senate is to confirm appointments to this and other important courts.

12. Extensive Bill of Rights

In this regard the Constitution also sets out a Bill of Rights and a blueprint for society which were supported by all parties. These provisions provide a broad framework for enforceable individual rights and freedoms and group security. The Bill of Rights itself is a progressive and generous charter of all the most important rights and freedoms.

For additional analytical, marketing, investment and business opportunities information, please contact
Global Investment & Business Center, USA
(202) 546-2103. Fax: (202) 546-3275. E-mail: rusric@erols.com

13. Numerous prohibitions against discrimination, exclusion and ethnic hostility

The proposals include various provisions to prevent the fomenting of ethnic violence, hatred or any form of ethnic discrimination or exclusion. The provisions are strict and are to be found in all parts of the Protocol dealing with political life and public administration. Special provisions exist to ensure the participation of the Twa in the Senate.

14. Promoting interest-based, not group-based, political parties

The proposals thus attempt to marry the need for an overall framework of democratic accountability with a system that caters for the fears of minorities by allowing for their considerable over-representation in the institutions of government. It is a system which would, it is envisaged, minimize the potentially disastrous consequences of the correlation between ethnic boundaries and political party by requiring the parties to present a multi-ethnic façade, and yet ensure that the ethnic minorities are represented not only in the Legislature, but in the Presidency and in the Cabinet. In the longer term all parties have agreed that Burundi is required to develop a political party system founded on the aggregation of political rather than group interests.

15. Physical security and political rights

The proposals have been criticized for not ensuring that the members of the National Assembly coming from minority ethnic groups represent those minority groups only. In other words, as it was explained, under these proposals the "wrong sort of Batutsi" will be elected. Tendencies within minority groups will be represented in accordance with their numerical electoral support only. The proposals do not ensure that those ethnic minority groups whose members are over-represented in the National Assembly and in the Senate will achieve such over-representation through ethnically exclusive mechanisms. This criticism has an element of truth in it. The groups of parties which had argued in favour of segregated representation also demanded that the results of such a segregated system must yield parity of power and representation between the representatives of the Bahutu and Batutsi, including alternating Presidents. This was necessary so as to ensure the physical safety of minority groups. The Bureau would have been quite happy to have made provision for such explicitly ethnically segregated mechanisms of representation had the Barundi as a whole agreed to such a proposal.

Parties in the centre of the spectrum and the parties arguing for an ethnicity blind democracy argued that such a system would be undemocratic, would entrench the legacy or existing pattern of inequality and privilege, would provide for two

For additional analytical, marketing, investment and business opportunities information, please contact
Global Investment & Business Center, USA
(202) 546-2103. Fax: (202) 546-3275. E-mail: rusric@erols.com

classes of citizenship and, more centrally, would constitute a permanent source of resentment and tension between the ethnic groups while frustrating the development of a national identity. Most parties agreed that demands to provide mechanisms, constitutional or otherwise, to reassure minorities and to guarantee physical security were legitimate and warranted. But, they argued, mechanisms guaranteeing a special and privileged hold over political and economic power by the political elite of a relatively small minority could not be the basis for stability. It was, they claimed, itself "unbalanced" and proposed by parties with no record of popular support, at least according to the last election. The same comments were directed to the proposal that sought, on a common voter's roll, to accord a Tutsi vote six times the value of a Hutu vote. In effect, the two proposals constituted different approaches to achieving the same result.

16. Balance

The question has arisen whether the proposals are "balanced". The proposals certainly tilt the democratic framework in favor of Tutsi participation and security. There are indeed cases elsewhere in the world where minorities are accorded special status or additional representation in national political structures, though none to the extent or manner proposed here. It was for this reason that most of the elements of the "package" cited above were opposed by adversary parties, yet ironically it has been the other parties in whose favour the proposals work which have objected to the lack of balance. When questioned informally some of these parties, claimed that such balance could only be achieved by a system that accorded the Tutsi minority (-/+ 13%) parity of power in all institutions with the Hutu majority (-/+ 85%). Whether this proposal would provide "balance" was not for the Bureau to decide. The real question for the Bureau was not whether such a proposal was undemocratic, or even whether there was any precedent elsewhere for such an arrangement. It was whether the Barundi, given the circumstances and history of Burundi, would support it. Despite close interrogation and extensive negotiations, the other parties indicated that they could not.

C. TRANSITIONAL ARRANGEMENTS

The transitional arrangements and the basis for the compromise proposals in regard thereto are fully explained in section II below. It is necessary, however, to draw attention to the matters set out in 22 dealing with the implementation of the Agreement.

These matters were not tabled for discussion in this form, but were included when experts drew attention to the necessity to deal with the period between the signature of the Agreement and the actual installation of the transitional Government. These provisions are not exceptional. Most parties have agreed in

For additional analytical, marketing, investment and business opportunities information, please contact
Global Investment & Business Center, USA
(202) 546-2103. Fax: (202) 546-3275. E-mail: rusric@erols.com

private consultations that measures are necessary to protect the public assets of Burundi during this fluid and volatile period. While some have characterized these provisions as a limitation of Burundi's sovereignty, they are not. They merely limit the freedom of one of the parties, the Government, in respect of its actions which could affect the transition. The concrete measures described are analogous to the restraints on an outgoing administration in an electoral democracy.

What remains unspecified is the exact way in which the Barundi are to agree on determining the identities and political apportionment of the leaders and members of cabinet in the transitional period. This, however, was left as a matter for the Barundi themselves to decide.

There was also an expectation by a few parties that the Bureau would draft a complete transitional Constitution. Its brief, however, was to set out the special arrangements that would apply during the transitional period, and to leave those 1992 constitutional details that are unaffected by these proposals intact. In regard to these arrangements, the Bureau has sought to establish a balance based on three principles: inclusion of all parties; no one group to have a decision-making majority; and restoration, as far as possible, of the members and parties dislocated by the assassination of the elected President and the National Assembly members in 1993. The parties on both sides which have challenged this balance have argued for one or other of these balancing principles to be removed.

D. AMENDMENT OF THE PROPOSALS

Finally, it needs to be emphasized that neither the principles nor the transitional arrangements are rigid or cast in stone. Indeed, the Agreement specifically allows for its amendment after signature if 90% of the transitional National Assembly so agree. This is a more flexible provision than that applied at the Burundi Peace Negotiations.

EXPLANATORY COMMENTARY ON PROTOCOL II

II. COMMENTS ON INDIVIDUAL POINTS IN THE PROPOSALS

Preamble, paragraph 3

The obligations with regard to the transitional institutions are covered both in the present Protocol and in Protocols III dealing with "Peace and Security" and V on the "Guarantees on implementation".

Article 1

For additional analytical, marketing, investment and business opportunities information, please contact
Global Investment & Business Center, USA
(202) 546-2103. Fax: (202) 546-3275. E-mail: rusric@erols.com

The fundamental values are intended to set out that blueprint for society ("projet de société") on which all parties are agreed.

Article 2, paragraph 1

After exhaustive debate, no agreement could be reached on whether the Baganwa are a separate community or a dynastic clan. Nor could agreement be reached as to whether the various groups should be classified as "a community", an "ethnic group", a "people", or a "tribe". While some drew attention to the absence of distinguishing characteristics between these groups or communities (there are no religious, linguistic, colour or reliable physical distinctions), others pointed out that the distinction is nonetheless prominent in the people's consciousness. In the end result, all but one party insisted on "ethnic group" or "community", and the Bureau's proposal leaves a notion of ethnic identity to be recorded without preferring any particular classification. All parties agreed that Burundi is one Nation.

Article 2, paragraph 4

Many parties did not support this provision, but as it is only permissive in nature the Bureau can see no harm in its retention. If anything it underlines that the matter is to be determined by the National Assembly.

Article 2, paragraph 5

The latest submissions have raised for the first time whether French should be a national language. There are reasons to believe that such a proposal may be practical (major juridical instruments, public administration drafts, projects, etc. are often drafted in French). But as this issue was raised only in the final submissions, the Bureau felt that it would be unjustifiable to include this proposal in the provision without a previous discussion on the matter. In any case this provision would not apply during the transition period, and the current provision for the use of language in courts and official documents has been dealt with in Chapter II, under the provisional arrangements.

Article 3

The rights listed here do not constitute an exhaustive list. These rights in approximately the same formulation as here have been included in numerous previous drafts and have never been disputed, save that this text, for completeness, also includes the rights to education and development. The 1992 Constitution already contains an elaboration of these rights, and we have proposed only general formulations; their precise formulation will be the task of those drafting the definitive constitution.

For additional analytical, marketing, investment and business opportunities information, please contact
Global Investment & Business Center, USA
(202) 546-2103. Fax: (202) 546-3275. E-mail: rusric@erols.com

Article 3, paragraph 4, first sentence

Contemporary practice recognizes the need to underline specifically, by reference to the equality of both women and men, that women are covered by the commitment to treat citizens as being equal in worth and dignity. The French translation of "everyone" does not solve the problem.

Article 3, paragraph 6

One of the parties had asked that the Bureau include in this provision a proposal on the abolition of the death penalty. Taking into account the current world-wide trend, the Bureau would be tempted to include such a provision, except that:

1. The Constitution of 1992 does expressly contain it;
2. It may well be included in the right to life, and if there is doubt on this question it should be for parliament or for the courts to decide;
3. It can be dealt with by the transitional National Assembly when it drafts the definitive text of the Constitution;
4. This is a provision that covers the post-transition period and would not have any influence on the transition period.

Article 3, paragraph 20

The last sentence neither adds to nor detracts from the right to strike, because reasonable limitations are possible in accordance with article 3, paragraph 29.

Article 3, paragraph 27

Children in armed conflict were not specifically covered in the discussion in the Committee, but in the light of recent international conventions and the rising concern regarding the plight of children, the Bureau included this provision, in the belief that it would receive the support of all parties.

Article 3, paragraph 29

This formulation accords with current comparative "jurisprudential" approaches to the need to provide for and yet restrain the extent of limitations of and derogations from human rights norms.

Article 4

All provisions of this article have been treated in accordance with the agreement reached between the majority of the parties. The essential provisions in this

For additional analytical, marketing, investment and business opportunities information, please contact
Global Investment & Business Center, USA
(202) 546-2103. Fax: (202) 546-3275. E-mail: rusric@erols.com

article are based on the need for all political parties to co-operate in ensuring that the right to vote can be exercised.

Article 4, paragraph 3

The definition of political parties is not the Bureau's. The latter has respected this phrasing, as it is the product of an agreement reached within the working group made up of the G-7, the G-3, ABASA and INKINZO.

Article 4, paragraph 4

Initially, one party expressed a reservation concerning the requirement that all parties be national in nature, but this reservation was withdrawn during the April 2000 session of Committee II.

Article 5, paragraph 4

The substantive proposals can be found in Chapter II of Protocol II, which provides that some aspects of the electoral process are to govern only the first election, and to lapse thereafter.

Article 5, paragraph 5

One group made a detailed proposal on co-opting mechanisms. To the extent that they are dealt with in this text, certain provisions and particular issues have been taken up in Chapter II of Protocol II.

Article 6, paragraph 2, first sentence

The figure of 100 is possibly large for a country of Burundi's resources, but is warranted on account of the need to provide for greater participation of its citizens in an inclusive political process (see Chapter II of Protocol II, art. 15, para.3).

Article 6, paragraph 3

A party had proposed that laws be actually adopted by way of referendum. The better approach is providing for the Legislature to be bound to pass a law as approved by referendum.

Article 6, paragraph 5

The original proposal was amended to bring the majority required in the National Assembly into line with that required in the 1992 Constitution. It does not seem

For additional analytical, marketing, investment and business opportunities information, please contact
Global Investment & Business Center, USA
(202) 546-2103. Fax: (202) 546-3275. E-mail: rusric@erols.com

appropriate to require the same very high majority in both the Senate and the National Assembly.

Article 6, paragraph 8

The current general trend is for the immunity of members of the Legislature to apply to their political activities, but not necessarily to general criminal affairs or failure to meet civic obligations.

Article 6, paragraph 10

The magnitude and exact modalities of enlarging the transitional National Assembly are specified in Chapter II of Protocol II. Within Committee II various options were discussed for a possible enlarging of the definitive National Assembly, but no agreement was obtained.

Article 6, paragraph 14, first sentence

The Bureau is mindful that some parties on one end of the spectrum reject the notion of a senate, holding that Burundi has no need for a costly second house, that the senate will frustrate the law-making process, and that as an ethnically balanced house it will emphasize ethnic divisions. At the other end of the spectrum a senate is rejected because it is not an effective substitute for intra-community or segregated political representation; "unrepresentative Batutsi" would be elected rather than Batutsi in whom only Batutsi have confidence. In the absence of any common ground between these extremes, the Bureau has opted for a system that relies on:

1. Democratic government;
2. Guaranteed multiethnic representation in the Assembly;
3. A second house with an ethnic balance to provide a confidence-building mechanism;
4. An approach that promotes nation-building rather than ethnic competition. The senate is a mechanism used widely in such circumstances, and can hardly be considered abnormal.

Article 6, end of paragraph 14

The most difficult issue regarding the senate is the method by which the senators are to be elected. As its explicit purpose is to provide a forum for regional concerns within an ethnically balanced framework - and yet the system has no geographically distinct ethnic communities or explicitly segregated ethnic elections, nor any means of ethnic identification or registration - indirect elections appeared to the Bureau the only method possible. Yet the text proposed may still

For additional analytical, marketing, investment and business opportunities information, please contact
Global Investment & Business Center, USA
(202) 546-2103. Fax: (202) 546-3275. E-mail: rusric@erols.com

give rise to objections that the ethnic representatives are really regional representatives, not persons representing an ethnic constituency. However, in the long term this in itself may contribute to overcoming the past divisions. The Electoral College, furthermore, is made up of persons whose concerns will be grass-roots developmental issues.

Article 6, paragraph 16

The powers and functions of the senate have been focused on the questions of particular concern to regions and ethnic communities.

Article 6, paragraph 16(c)

Unlike the President of the Republic, the ombudsperson has a non-party political profile, but a major responsibility for ensuring a proper and clean administration. Accordingly, to perform a watchdog role a very high non-partisan degree of support is indicated.

Article 6, paragraph 17

This cooptation mechanism ensures there is no ethnic exclusion at the level of local government. However, if there is a mono-ethnic character to the community, or where there is an appropriate multiethnic character to the council, this mechanism would not come into play.

Article 7, paragraph 1

No agreement was obtained on the mode of election of the President. The system of politically alternating presidents was considered unworkable, democratically unsustainable or even a source of instability. The proposals made were mutually exclusive:

1. One was that the President of the Republic should be elected by the National Assembly and the Senate;
2. The other was that the President of the Republic should be elected by direct universal suffrage.

Because of the political context within Burundi, the Bureau proposes a compromise by creating an initial exception that would reflect the importance of demonstrably wider support for the first President, and would help to stabilize the political institutions by not holding additional presidential elections at the end of the transition. The proposal of indirect elections for the very first election is premised on the need for more universal support for the first President. It is no less democratic and yields an accountable Executive. There is no evidence to

For additional analytical, marketing, investment and business opportunities information, please contact
Global Investment & Business Center, USA
(202) 546-2103. Fax: (202) 546-3275. E-mail: rusric@erols.com

support the argument that directly elected presidents are less vulnerable to a coup d'état than indirectly elected ones provided both are constitutionally sound and based on free and fair elections, The Bureau would propose that this be a unique case, with subsequent presidents being elected by direct universal suffrage.

Article 7, paragraph 4

Various proposals had been made on the Vice-Presidents. The proposal made by the Bureau is to be seen as a compromise suggestion between what the G-3, G-7 and G-8 had initially proposed. The Bureau believes that this option will function as an additional nation-building mechanism by enlarging the presidency so as to cover a wider political range, and therefore will also be seen as a mechanism that should reassure all citizens of Burundi. This is a mechanism that has been utilized elsewhere in deeply divided societies.

Article 7, paragraph 6, first sentence

There has been no objection to this initial Bureau proposal. This provision promotes the concept of a choice by the parties as to whether they participate in a Government of national unity or not. In deeply divided societies this mechanism is achieving ever wider application (see recently Nigeria, Indonesia, South Africa), as it promotes national acceptance of the Government, and hence stability.

Article 7, paragraph 8

This provision is not to be seen as a form of "vote of no confidence". The question of allowing a vote of no confidence will have to be studied by the Constitutional Commission that will be established by the National Assembly during the transition. The exact nature of the relationship of accountability between the President and the National Assembly will depend on the degree of separation of powers decided upon.

Article 7, paragraph 9

This proposal was made in conformity with the 1992 Constitution, which establishes that "The judicial inquiry may only be directed by a team of at least three magistrates from the general office of the Prosecutor of the Republic" (art. 81. 4).

Article 8, paragraph 1

For additional analytical, marketing, investment and business opportunities information, please contact
Global Investment & Business Center, USA
(202) 546-2103. Fax: (202) 546-3275. E-mail: rusric@erols.com

The governors of the provinces fulfil administrative functions. In such a small country as Burundi, with limited resources, the Bureau felt that to submit the governors' posts to elections - or any other form of choice - would only complicate the electoral system and create certain forms of tension between the central power and the districts. In Protocol II, decentralized power within the districts has been provided for.

Article 9

The reforms of the Judiciary have been extensively discussed within the working group of Committee II on the subject. The Bureau has tried within this article to reflect the very different decisions that were taken or discussed. Many of the proposals made during the debates on the Judiciary were subject to general agreement. With reference to paragraph 6, the term "Supreme Council of the Magistracy" has been replaced, here and elsewhere, by "Judicial Service Commission", which is the translation of "Conseil Supérieur de la Magistrature" recognized by the Council of Europe. This is therefore not a substantive change.

Article 9, paragraph 5

Various new suggestions were made in the final submissions given in by the parties. Nevertheless, the Bureau felt it necessary to reflect the decisions taken by the working group on the Judiciary, and even if important suggestions were offered in the final submissions on such issues as the court system, the composition of the Chambers and the funding of the Courts, the Bureau felt that some of the suggestions departed from what had been discussed and agreed.

Article 9, paragraph 8

The aim of introducing the Ubushingantahe is to afford the national legislature a chance to provide for traditional justice as an institution at local level on matters affecting local communities. This proposal was backed by all parties, even though some parties stressed that the change in the nature of the Ubushingantahe justified their worries as to how this traditional institution would be used.

Article 9, paragraph 9

There was a mistake in the Bureau's initial proposal concerning the nomination of the magistracy. It has been modified to include the task of nominating magistrates in the functions of the Judicial Service Commission.

Article 9, paragraph 12

For additional analytical, marketing, investment and business opportunities information, please contact
Global Investment & Business Center, USA
(202) 546-2103. Fax: (202) 546-3275. E-mail: rusric@erols.com

Widespread practice usually insists that there should be a link between public office bearers and judges; the linkage takes place in the Judicial Service Commission, and permits the other stakeholders to participate in the decision-making. Few, if any systems, allow the Judiciary to be completely insulated from accountability or influence from the people through their elected representatives.

Article 9, paragraph 17

The Bureau considered proposals which downgraded the Constitutional Court to a Council, which may serve to diminish its legal status and reduce accessibility to it by ordinary citizens. However, it was felt that this compact requires the firmest guarantees and, in line with the separation of powers doctrine, an institution of calibre and independence to enforce it. Such an institution would also strengthen the rule of law and a culture of legality.

Article 10

The proposals put forward in this article were subject to only limited debate. In the submissions made by the parties in April, most of the contrary proposals put forward related to the wording or fine details of the provisions in question. The Bureau has therefore taken into account those proposals on the structure or wording of the sentences which did not alter the sense of the provisions. Most of the provisions include the main precepts of good governance.

Article 10, paragraph 10

The principle of an Ombudsperson was agreed upon during the April 2000 session of committee II. During the same session various suggestions such as the creation of an Ombudsperson within the army were discussed, but no decision was taken. Nevertheless, the three-fourths approval of the nomination by the National Assembly and the requirement of the approval of the Senate are proposals put forward by the Bureau. It was felt that the Ombudsperson should possess extraordinary credibility - or legitimacy - to fulfil her/his function, especially if she/he is expected to play a conciliatory role.

Article 11, paragraph 3

The military matters dealt with here have been taken from the reports of the Bureau of Committee III, but here may be subject to arrangements that have emerged from the guarantees consequent upon adopting the electoral system set out herein. The issues referred to in Protocol II, though they deal with military matters agreed in Committee III, remain fundamental constitutional issues. Also, only Committee II can identify the final form of the political institutions which supervise certain military appointments and deployments.

For additional analytical, marketing, investment and business opportunities information, please contact
Global Investment & Business Center, USA
(202) 546-2103. Fax: (202) 546-3275. E-mail: rusric@erols.com

Article 11, paragraph 4(e)

One of the groups proposed that this provision be extended to give jurisdiction to civilian courts over military personnel who have committed offences under the "general" or civilian law. There is some merit in this proposal. However, the Bureau feels that it should include such a provision only in consultation with Committee III.

Article 12, paragraph 2(c)

See the definition given in Protocol IV, article 1.2.

Article 13, paragraph 1, first sentence

There is a need to establish the shortest period possible between the signature of the Agreement and its implementation. At an institutional and political level, the Bureau believes that within a month most of the administrative prerequisites to start the transition period can be met. It is conscious that other factors and imperatives coming from the other committees, especially Committee III, must be taken into account, and the time-frame might be modified, especially if an international military and observer presence is a precondition. If that force is a United Nations force, 6 months is a realistic outer limit.

Article 13, paragraph 1, second sentence

The necessary conditions may include: some of the statutory measures to be adopted; establishing reception arrangements for returnees, refugees and displaced people; providing security for the returning political leaders; establishing reception areas for armed groups; insertion of monitors and peacekeepers; confinement to barracks where appropriate; meeting benchmarks for cessation of hostilities if agreed; establishing the mechanisms to receive arms if agreed upon; providing security for armed groups; establishment of international or national bodies; closure of regroupment camps; release of political prisoners.

Article 14, paragraph 5

This provision is subject to a sunrise provision so that parties which do not yet comply with this requirement can subscribe to the Agreement and participate in its structures, and formally adjust their constitutions and structures later. The political parties must be given the opportunity to fulfil the necessary requirements established in the Protocols to the Agreement. The present situation makes it impracticable for some of the political parties to consult their constituencies and their militants before major decisions can be taken. The Bureau therefore

For additional analytical, marketing, investment and business opportunities information, please contact
Global Investment & Business Center, USA
(202) 546-2103. Fax: (202) 546-3275. E-mail: rusric@erols.com

proposes a suspended period of nine months so as to be able to allow such parties to adapt to the new requirements.

Article 15, paragraph 2, first sentence

The purpose of this provision is to ensure that any matter that has not been foreseen or considered will still be regulated by the law pending the adoption of the relevant laws by the transitional legislature. It does not affect or delay the entry into force of the Agreement, but merely serves to place an obligation on one of the Parties, the effect of which is to incorporate the obligations under the Agreement, which are effective upon its signature, into domestic law. This is a separate issue from the entry into force of the Agreement.

Article 15, paragraph 3

The transitional National Assembly is to be expanded to include the political parties not included therein, while ensuring that there arc balances and that it has a popular character. The Bureau proposes that the starting point be the National Assembly which was disrupted by the assassinations of 1993, the ensuing violence and the coup which later followed it in 1996. To start on another basis would not be consistent with the last indicator of popular sentiment, even though the term of this legislature has now expired. On the other hand, the demands of the transition require, temporarily, an expanded and inclusive legislature. However, the mathematics preclude a simple extension if the resultant Assembly is not to provide for a simple rubber-stamping of a draft text prepared by one of the three clusters. This proposal thus marries three arguments:

1. It must in part reflect the last election (and thus be legitimate);
2. It must include all the parties to the Burundi Peace Negotiations (and thus be inclusive) and
3. It must facilitate true give-and-take in discussions (and thus not allow any one grouping more than two-thirds dominance).

The parties themselves could not agree on these principles, choosing to insist on either the first or only the second, and the Bureau received no assistance in this regard from them.

Article 15, paragraph 3(a)

In the 1993 elections FRODEBU won 65 seats, UPRONA 16, for a total of 81 members. The surviving original members will be offered their seats back even if they now belong to new political parties. If they decline or are nominated to the Executive, or are no longer alive, the political party they belong to, or belonged to

For additional analytical, marketing, investment and business opportunities information, please contact
Global Investment & Business Center, USA
(202) 546-2103. Fax: (202) 546-3275. E-mail: rusric@erols.com

at the time of their death, will elect to fill the seat or allow the current replacement to continue in office.

Article 15, paragraph 3(b)

There are 19 parties to the Burundi Peace Negotiations. Two of them are not political parties (Government/National Assembly). The Bureau assumed that two parties will join the Negotiations as additional members (if not, the figures will change slightly). This leaves 19 political parties in total. Of those 19 political parties, two will not be attributed additional seats (FRODEBU and UPRONA). One party (CNDD) is probably represented by its original members. This leaves 16 political parties to which seats must be attributed: 16 x 3 = 48 new seats. The total adds up to 129 members of the National Assembly (81 + 48 = 129). At the G-7 level, the figures are as follows: (65 FRODEBU) + 7 x 3 = 86 or + 8 x 3 = 89. This gives G-7 **two-thirds** or more. The third principle requires that additional representation be provided for, which demands that we add some 15 members who do not belong to the G-7 parties. The unknown element of this equation remains the two political parties who could join the Burundi Peace Negotiations. It is impossible to know if there are members of the 1993 National Assembly amongst their militants, so the Bureau has calculated as if there were not, though this could be modified at the required moment.

Article 15, paragraph 3(c)

The Bureau considered increasing the number of seats per party to give effect to the principle that no group has more than **two-thirds**. However, it would need 5 or 6 seats per party and a legislature of +/-180 to do this, as parties on both sides would obtain additional representation. By taking the balancing group from sitting civil society members, this provision also reduces the opposition to the transition from the civil society sector within the current National Assembly. This brings the total potential number to 157 and demonstrably balances the political composition of the transitional National Assembly, especially in regard to the decision-making majority required.

Article 15, paragraph 5, third sentence

This provision is necessary to underwrite the principles in Chapter I of Protocol II. Making the draft Constitution subject to judicial scrutiny does not affect the sovereignty of the "people". The Transitional National Assembly is an unelected body. The constitution to be approved by the people will not be adjudicated upon once approved by referendum.

Article 15, paragraph 6

For additional analytical, marketing, investment and business opportunities information, please contact
Global Investment & Business Center, USA
(202) 546-2103. Fax: (202) 546-3275. E-mail: rusric@erols.com

A referendum is necessary because the constitution-making body is not an elected one.

Article 15, paragraph 7

This provision is intended to function as a last-resort measure, to break deadlocks and ensure that the time-frames are complied with.

Article 15, paragraph 13

The exact composition of the transitional Government is to be negotiated between the clusters of political parties at Arusha once the broad framework is agreed on. The G-7 at the Burundi Peace Negotiations consisted CNDD, FRODEBU, FROLINA, PALIPEHUTU, PL, PP and RPB. However, the group is taken here to include, if they eventually participate, the armed groups not at Arusha but which originate from or claim to represent parties in the G-7. In the interests of appropriate appointments on the basis of suitability and competence, the Bureau believes that candidates should come from clusters, not pro rata from 19 parties.

Article 15, paragraph 20

These matters were raised in earlier discussions but did not find expression in the earlier draft protocols. The Bureau believes that all parties welcome such a measure.

Article 16

To prevent disruption, any unforeseen breakdown in law and order, or judicial mismanagement, the Bureau considers it necessary to include the provisions listed in this article. These provisions do not preclude legislative and executive action to remedy the defects of the past or to conduct judicial and administrative reforms, but are rather directed at permitting an ordered reform process without disruption caused by legal challenges, legal vacuums or administrative chaos.

Article 17, paragraph 2(b)

In relation to the judicial sector, reference was made to the need for training colleges for "employees". The Bureau has extended the original formulation to cover all sectors of the judiciary, whether administrative employees, judiciary and prison personnel, lawyers, or prosecutors, as well as judges.

Article 17, paragraph 7

For additional analytical, marketing, investment and business opportunities information, please contact
Global Investment & Business Center, USA
(202) 546-2103. Fax: (202) 546-3275. E-mail: rusric@erols.com

The Bureau felt that there was a need to establish a form of rotation within the Constitutional Court so as to ensure representation of diversity amongst the appointees. This form of rotation enables the composition of the Constitutional Court to change periodically but to retain the necessary continuity by designating half of its membership who will remain members of the Court for six years.

Article 17, paragraph 10

One initial proposal stated "foreign judicial personnel shall be appointed on an exceptional basis to form part of the courts and prosecutors' offices in order to create a climate of confidence between the judicial services and litigants". This provision as formulated here will allow for such appointments, but will not prescribe them unless the availability of persons for appointment has been established and the appointment mechanism agrees thereto.

Article 20, paragraph 3

One of the options proposed was that the Independent National Electoral Commission should be made up of representatives of the political parties, civil society and the State, including the Ministry of the Interior. In accordance with international trends, particularly in conflict-ridden societies, we have opted for a truly independent commission.

Article 20, paragraph 7

The exceptional co-optation mechanism:

1. Ensures additional representation of all parties equally, thus providing for greater balance in debates when one party is overwhelmingly dominant. It does so by distributing the seats equally, by avoiding an arbitrary co-optation process or mechanism, and by confining co-optees to those who appeared on the electoral lists;
2. Is not intended to apply after the first election or if there is a balanced spread of parties;
3. Is warranted, despite its limited distortion of the electoral result, which would not drastically alter the outcome, because of the exceptional degree of conflict and insecurity in Burundi.

Article 20, paragraph 8

The Bureau is mindful that some parties oppose the system of blocked lists with proportional representation. The Bureau seriously considered the many options put before it, as well as some that were not advanced (such as alternative preference voting; simple and multi-member constituencies; open list, preferential

For additional analytical, marketing, investment and business opportunities information, please contact
Global Investment & Business Center, USA
(202) 546-2103. Fax: (202) 546-3275. E-mail: rusric@erols.com

voting). For some, weighting "Tutsi" votes to achieve parity would provide the best system. However, where this type of weighting has worked, e.g. in the United Republic of Tanzania, it has been on the basis of geographical division, and never to the extreme extent proposed here. There was a belief amongst others of the need to conduct elections within the ethnic communities, on the basis of parity of representation between the two main ethnic groups, or using an alternative formula yielding the same result. This system would have been implemented directly or by indirect suffrage from the local level to the summit. However:

1. Such a proposal could find no common ground;
2. The risk exists that such an electoral system would exacerbate ethnic tensions and make the divisions within the ethnic communities rigid;
3. It might thus promote more extreme ethnic problems; and
4. It would be extremely complicated to organize owing to the fact that the communities within Burundi are not geographically separated.

The Bureau has therefore made its current proposal in the belief that an electoral system based on proportional representation with blocked lists together with a series of other mechanisms can guarantee the representation of both major ethnic groups. Nevertheless, a limited co-optation method has been included as a necessary balancing mechanism for the first elections.

Article 20, paragraph 13

Various parties supported the idea of electing the commune administrator. The proposal did not obtain the necessary support of the others, and the Bureau has opted to exclude this possibility, owing to the problems of accountability and control that such a proposal could create:

1. The commune administrator must be attached to a legislative body, to whom he is accountable;
2. In case of corruption or other problems, the legislative body (in this case the commune council) should have the power to suspend him and nominate a replacement.

It is no less democratic for the administrator to be indirectly elected, and furthermore at an initial stage the Bureau is not sure there is a need to overload the electoral system by electing the colline councils, indirectly electing the commune council, and directly electing the commune administrator (to be followed by a referendum, and later national elections). Nevertheless, measures will have to be taken within the organic law on commune administration to protect the administrator's obligations and rights.

For additional analytical, marketing, investment and business opportunities information, please contact
Global Investment & Business Center, USA
(202) 546-2103. Fax: (202) 546-3275. E-mail: rusric@erols.com

For additional analytical, marketing, investment and business opportunities
information, please contact
Global Investment & Business Center, USA
(202) 546-2103. Fax: (202) 546-3275. E-mail: rusric@erols.com

STRATEGIC ECONOMIC AND BUSINESS INFORMATION

US ASSISTANCE TO BURUNDI

FY 1997 Development Fund for Africa: $2,591,186

Burundi, a small central African country of 6.2 million people, is in a political crisis and a state of ethnic civil war. With an annual income per capita of $94 (1994), it is among the world's poorest countries and, after Rwanda, is the most densely populated country in Africa. A military coup attempt by the Tutsi minority in 1993 resulted in the assassination of the newly-elected President in October 1993, and the untimely death of his successor in a suspicious plane crash in April 1994. The coup attempt triggered inter-ethnic massacres, displaced large populations, and threatened the democratically-elected government.

An interim ethnic/political power-sharing agreement, the Convention of Government, was negotiated in October 1994 to stem the escalation of violence and to avoid what some feared might be a repetition of the genocide experienced in April 1994 in Rwanda. Through continued political harassment and assassinations during 1995, the Convention of Government has been eroded in favor of the Tutsi minority, leaving the government largely dysfunctional. Civil disobedience has become endemic in the absence of functioning institutions of law and justice. Burundi represents a potential destabilizing force in the Great Lakes Region (Burundi, Rwanda, Tanzania, Uganda and Zaire), a region already weakened by the 1994 Rwanda genocide and large refugee populations. This sub-region is part of the Greater Horn of Africa Initiative (GHAI) where USAID, the Department of State and African governments have made a joint commitment to engage cooperatively in preventive diplomacy and coordinated assistance in an effort to prevent or mitigate the repetition of costly natural and man-made disasters.

THE DEVELOPMENT CHALLENGE

The population of Burundi is 93% rural, largely employed in the traditional agricultural sector and economically dependent on a functioning subsistence agriculture. Armed political conflict by the military and civilians has created a state of insecurity throughout the country. Cultivation and harvesting processes are regularly interrupted. During 1995, violence in the interior, along with sabotage of electrical power systems, has led to significant losses to production facilities, infrastructure, levels of production and income. Coffee production, the largest export, was down 50% in 1994-95. Employment rates have also fallen by 50%. Many homes have been totally or partially destroyed. Internally displaced

For additional analytical, marketing, investment and business opportunities information, please contact
Global Investment & Business Center, USA
(202) 546-2103. Fax: (202) 546-3275. E-mail: rusric@erols.com

and refugee camps in northern Burundi have resulted in extensive deforestation. Foreign assistance expenditures for non-humanitarian development efforts are down by 80%. In sum, all economic indicators have plummeted.

Social indicators in 1992 ranked Burundi among the least advanced countries, with a life expectancy of 50.2 years, a literacy rate among adults at 32.9%, 102 per 1000 infant mortality, and 31% school attendance. While insecurity has prevented detailed survey-taking, all signs indicate that these conditions have significantly worsened during 1993-95. Eighty percent of the population is now estimated to live below the absolute poverty line. Infant mortality rates are aggravated by spread of diarrheal and respiratory infection. All progress realized in primary health care during 1986-92 has been wiped out. Although many hospitals and rural clinics are still operating, they are grossly under-staffed and under-supplied.

The Human Immunodeficiency Virus/Acquired Immune Deficiency Syndrome (HIV/AIDS) epidemic, exacerbated by continuing disturbances and movements of displaced people and refugees, has registered alarming growth in seroprevalence levels. In some towns and semi-urban areas, the incidence of HIV/AIDS has tripled. The national educational system has been disrupted with a 30% reduction in teachers and destruction of schools. An estimated 535,000 Burundians, mainly women and children affected by violence, have been displaced and are dependent on extended family support or are wandering aimlessly in search of a means to survive. During 1995, 220,000 Rwandan refugees in Burundi have added to this burden.

Prior to the crisis, Burundi was moving forward on economic reforms. With USAID assistance, Burundi had implemented new economic policies which created a legal framework for encouraging private businessdevelopment. USAID was assisting Burundians in modernizing research and methods for small farming systems and in analyzing the difficult land tenure and allocation problems of its over-populated arable land base. In the public sector, with USAID funds, the country had started major reforms to decentralize public health services. USAID was training participants in fields of study critical to the country's future development.

With the progressive intensification of civil war and insecurity since 1993, traditional medium-/long-term development programs have been suspended or stopped by USAID and other donors because of difficulties of implementation and insecurity for personnel. USAID's development assistance resources from conventional assistance projects are being redirected into focussed, shorter-term activities designed to assist the country's transition out of its current crisis. The assistance challenge for USAID has changed its focus from development to relief and rehabilitation for vulnerable populations and victims of war. If current

For additional analytical, marketing, investment and business opportunities information, please contact
Global Investment & Business Center, USA
(202) 546-2103. Fax: (202) 546-3275. E-mail: rusric@erols.com

pacification efforts both within and outside Burundi are successful, USAID will direct assistance back into post-war reconstruction and development.

The development challenge will be to convert the program from almost a pure relief effort toward rehabilitation and lesser dependency of local populations on relief aid. The historic trend of repeated outbreaks of random violence around the country may hinder results by keeping the social and economic situation unstable and therefore making rehabilitation difficult. Although its pre-crisis performance was promising, Burundi is not an early candidate for rapid graduation from traditional development assistance. The country will have much rebuilding to do once such assistance is reinstated under stable social, political, economic and operating conditions. Burundi has no external debts with the United States.

OTHER DONORS

In 1995, the donor community pledged an estimated $155 million to Burundi, including $90 million in development aid and $65 million in humanitarian assistance. The European Union has been the largest donor of development assistance (DA), while the United States has led in commitment of humanitarian assistance. In 1995, the United States was one of the largest bilateral donors ($32 million humanitarian aid, $5 million DA) together with France, Belgium and Germany.

The United Nations has by far the largest active presence with the United Nations Special Representative to the Secretary General (UNSRSG), the United Nations Development Programme (UNDP), the United Nations High Commissioner for Refugees (UNHCR), the United Nations Human Rights Center (UNHRC), and the United Nations Children's Fund (UNICEF). During 1995, all donors have significantly reduced disbursement of development assistance and numbers of associated personnel. Humanitarian assistance continues, but activities have been slowed and jeopardized by harassment of international and non-governmental organizations (NGOs). An air of skepticism or a wait-and-see attitude pervades the assistance community until signs of political reconciliation and concrete evidence of improvements to security become evident.

FY 1997 PROGRAM

The environment of instability and insecurity demands a USAID strategy relevant to the priorities created by the crisis and one that can operate in a manner that does not unduly burden a reduced American presence in the country. It is in the U.S. national interest to lower the relief costs by promoting stability within the Great Lakes Region and ending human rights abuses. USAID will maintain an effective pro-active and re-active assistance presence to support ethnic/political conflict resolution while mitigating acts of social destabilization.

For additional analytical, marketing, investment and business opportunities information, please contact
Global Investment & Business Center, USA
(202) 546-2103. Fax: (202) 546-3275. E-mail: rusric@erols.com

The program will focus on human rights protection, consensus-building and ethnic/political conflict resolution from grassroots groups to significant political players.

AGENCY GOAL: BUILDING DEMOCRACY

Since the assassinations of Burundian leaders in 1993 and 1994, both the government and its institutions have been dissolving under inter-ethnic conflict, civilian and military violence, and mounting mortality rates. In October 1994, the Burundian political protagonists negotiated and signed the Convention of Government to serve as an interim power-sharing arrangement. This arrangement was to permit time for reviewing and developing renewed national consensus on a democratic process and institutions of governance for a multi-ethnic society.

During the past year, the Convention of Government has remained in place. The power-sharing intent of the Convention of Government, however, has been compromised due to ethnic minority dominance of government institutions including the military, and official civilian positions at national and local levels. Political positions have hardened, with moderates and consensus-builders pushed more toward one ethnic extreme or the other.

The USAID strategy works to reconstruct a civil society and to evolve indigenous institutions capable of governing fairly and providing minimal standards of security and services to all citizens. USAID has directly financed program activities and provided indirect support, especially to the Office of the U.N. Special Representative of the Secretary General, for conflict mitigation efforts and consensus-building.

These include such activities as: peace radio programming through independent radio, exchanges with South Africa and other countries to understand conflict resolution models; creation of a national network of women's groups and a women's center in Bujumbura to support a nascent women's peace movement; and publication and distribution of a primer as part of the national education curriculum on how to live in a democracy. USAID has also supported regional mediation initiatives such as The Cairo Summit (November 1995) and subsequent actions to promote reconciliation.

The problems of social and political conflict are severe in Burundi and their resolution will take time. USAID activities, in collaboration with other donor programs, have a moderating influence and are the only hope in of helping Burundi return to peace and stability. USAID proposes continuation of these and similar activities, including strengthening local grassroots organizations in mediation, and providing supplemental support to the United Nations

For additional analytical, marketing, investment and business opportunities information, please contact
Global Investment & Business Center, USA
(202) 546-2103. Fax: (202) 546-3275. E-mail: rusric@erols.com

Commission of Inquiry, as necessary, to take the initial steps necessary toward ending the pervasive sense of impunity.

In addition to Democracy and Governance, Burundi will benefit from $85,612 worth of Africa Regionally-funded environmental activities.

☐ Strategic Objective 1: Promote Dialogue, Reconciliation and Stability within a Framework
of Democratic Institutions

BURUNDI FY 1997 PROGRAM SUMMARY

	Encouraging Broad-based Economic Growth	Stabilizing World Population Growth & Protecting Human Health	Protecting the Environment	Building Democracy	Providing Humanitarian Assistance	TOTALS
USAID Strategic Objectives						
1. Promote Dialogue, Reconciliation and Stability within a Framework of Democratic Institutions - Dev. Fund for Africa			85,612	2,505,574		2,591,186
Totals - Dev. Fund for Africa			85,612	2,505,574		2,591,186

Mission Director: Keith Brown

SELECTED PROJECTS

PROMOTE DIALOGUE, RECONCILIATION AND STABILITY WITHIN A FRAMEWORK OF DEMOCRATIC INSTITUTIONS, 695-S001

For additional analytical, marketing, investment and business opportunities information, please contact
Global Investment & Business Center, USA
(202) 546-2103. Fax: (202) 546-3275. E-mail: rusric@erols.com

STATUS: Continuing
PROPOSED OBLIGATION AND FUNDING SOURCE: FY 1997: $2,591,186
DFA
INITIAL OBLIGATION: FY 1995; **ESTIMATED COMPLETION DATE**: FY 2002

Purpose: To reconstruct a civil society based on respect for human rights and property; to support national reconciliation, peaceful conflict resolution, and restoration of stability; and to assist evolution of indigenous, culturally understandable and acceptable institutions capable of fair governance in a democratic context.

Background: Since the assassination of the country's first democratically-elected president in October 1993, the Government of Burundi and its institutions have become dysfunctional and largely unrepresentative as the country has descended into increasingly violent inter-ethnic (Tutsi and Hutu) and inter-clan conflict. Burundian protagonists negotiated an interim Convention of Government in October 1994 to stem the escalation of violence but its ethnic power-sharing basis has been eroded in favor of the minority. Much of the predominately rural society has been disrupted, with ethnic fears, suspicions and hatreds deepened by acts of civil war. In the early months of 1996, in conditions of a weakened economy and a population tired of conflict, the frequency and level of violence may be moderating. However, little political reconciliation and no real consensus-building have occurred among the inter-ethnic political protagonists orchestrating the current crisis.

USAID Role and Achievements to Date: In the field of democracy and governance (DG), USAID, through the National Democratic Institute, assisted Burundi, as did other donors, during 1991-93 to mount the first democratic elections and to strengthen democratically-oriented institutions of governance. With the onset of political crisis and civil violence in late 1993, these positive results have largely been lost. USAID redirected program efforts in 1993 to mitigate the potential destructiveness of the crisis. DG activities were re-geared toward bringing opposing sides together, promoting non-violent solutions to resolve political conflict, developing popular understanding of basic democratic principles and evolving indigenous institutions of governance capable of governing fairly and equitably and ending the current state of criminal impunity.

USAID funded a democracy primer for primary and secondary schools, and launched an independent radio production studio for reconciliation. USAID also supported the United Nations Special Representative of the Secretary General (UNSRSG) to mount a major international seminar of political principals from which sprung the agreement to negotiate an interim Convention of Government, financed through the UNSRSG a national multi-media campaign for peace, and

For additional analytical, marketing, investment and business opportunities information, please contact
Global Investment & Business Center, USA
(202) 546-2103. Fax: (202) 546-3275. E-mail: rusric@erols.com

mobilized a movement for reconciliation and redevelopment among women leaders and local non-governmental organizations (NGOs).

USAID also provided, through the UNSRSG, support to the work of the International Commission of Inquiry to bring putsch leaders from 1993 to justice; and support for the Cairo Summit which gathered key political leaders of the Great Lakes Region to negotiate strategies for resolving intra-regional civic violence and problems such as refugee populations destabilizing the region. Currently, USAID implements two activities under this strategic objective, one for DG activities and the other a human resources development activity which focuses on training in DG fields, but also serves as a cross-cutting resource supportive of other elements of the USAID/ Burundi program.

Description: USAID concentrates its DG efforts in five fields: (1) promoting conflict resolution and reconciliation of Burundian society and political leadership, in particular the activities of the Commission of Inquiry and regional African-led peace initiatives; (2) rebuilding popularly sustainable institutions of fair governance; (3) creating responsible and open print and broadcast media; (4) broadening school curricula and teaching to include lessons in respect for human and property rights, DG principles and institutions andcivic responsibility; and (5) developing a civic infrastructure and leadership potential for social responsibility through local NGOs, social and church organizations with emphasis on women's and youth activities.

Host Country and Other Donors: Most other donors have contributed to the democratic governance effort through the United Nations system, especially through UNSRSG and the United Nations Children's Fund (UNICEF); the European Commission has funded an independent "peace" radio initiative; there is broad bilateral support for a women's peace movement involving those who are largely victims rather than participants in the civil war but also key to restoring the social and economic viability of the rural society. Withholding of traditional development assistance budgets and withdrawal of technical personnel by most donors including the Bretton Woods institutions has heightened pressure for progress on DG matters.

Beneficiaries: Target groups for DG activities include government and elected officials and political leaders, military, radio and print journalists, leaders and members of women's and youth groups, local NGOs evolving civic roles in social and economic rehabilitation, teachers and school children, and the radio-listening public.

Principal Contractors, Grantees or Agencies: U.S. private voluntary organizations including Search for Common Ground, National Democratic Institute, AFRICARE; international non-governmental institutions such as

For additional analytical, marketing, investment and business opportunities information, please contact
Global Investment & Business Center, USA
(202) 546-2103. Fax: (202) 546-3275. E-mail: rusric@erols.com

International Alert; multilateral partners such as the UNSRSG and United Nations Children's Fund; and local NGOs.

Major Results Indicators:
Baseline Target
Independent, open media with Non-existent 80 broadcast journalists/editors trained. (1997)
professional standards of (1996) 4 independent FM radio licenses approved objectivity, impartiality, and and frequencies assigned. (1997)
balanced treatment of subjects. 100% increase in balanced radio programming and coverage, and absence of "hate radio." (1997)
Civil society re-assembled. Largely 50 communities and NGOs involved in national Local communities and absent dialogue on power-sharing. 60 new local NGOs indigenous organizations (1996) supported in management, program development. functional in civic, social and (1997) development activities.

Multi-ethnic women's peace and reconciliation movement with productive activities in 14-16 provinces. (1997) Local participation and group Largely 50% increase in local mixed ethnic NGOs, involved in organizing by private members absent reconciliation, economic reconstruction and in mixed of society to improve social (1996) collaboration among NGOs, joint actions and resource and economic conditions. utilization (1997) 20 magistrates, judges and lawyers in long-term training for greater ethnic balance and competence. (1997)
Human rights violations Violations Joint initiatives between ITEKA and SONERA, diminished.

Establishment continue separate and opposing mono-ethnic human rights of professional justice (1996) associations. (1997) system, civilian protection Constructive results realized by judicial reform process forces, separate from the initiated by Commission of Inquiry to address impunity army with non-military (1997) objectives. Humane Options for pursuing higher education by those conditions in prisons. excluded from national institutions of higher learning. (1997)

For additional analytical, marketing, investment and business opportunities
information, please contact
Global Investment & Business Center, USA
(202) 546-2103. Fax: (202) 546-3275. E-mail: rusric@erols.com

ECONOMY & ECONOMIC DEVELOPMENT

EXTERNAL TRADE

There is a persistent trade deficit owing to depressed world coffee prices. However, Burundi may benefit from a global coffee retention plan which began in early 2001. Implemented under the auspices of the Association of Coffee Producing Countries (ACPC), it involves a 20 per cent production holdback by ACPC members to boost prices in a market depressed by a supply glut. Although Burundi is not a full member of the ACPC, it is like to gain from an expected rise in world prices.

Economic sanctions were imposed by seven African nations in 1996 in protest at the violence used by President Buyoya's Tutsi army. Landlocked, reliant on imports of fuel and exports of coffee and tea for foreign exchange, the blockade hit the economy hard. The sanctions were lifted in January 1999.

EXPORTS

Principal exports are coffee (normally 75 per cent of total), manufactures, tea (5 per cent), cotton fabrics (3 per cent).

Main destinations: Germany (typically 26 per cent of total), Belgium/Luxembourg (11 per cent), Switzerland (5 per cent), Tanzania (5 per cent).

IMPORTS

Principal imports are machinery and equipment (normally 18 per cent of total), petroleum products (15 per cent), food (10 per cent).
Main sources: Belgium/Luxembourg (typically 17 per cent of total), France (12 per cent), Japan (9 per cent), Germany (7 per cent).

Burundi's communal and political conflicts are closely linked to its economic inadequacies. As one of the ten poorest nations in the world, Burundi is designated by the UN as a Least Developed Country (LDC). In societies of scarcity such as Burundi and Rwanda, the government is the repository of wealth, privilege, and power. In Burundi, therefore, Tutsis believe that if they lose control of the government, they will lose economic security as well. Despite the persistence of genocide and politicide in Burundi, it has nevertheless been one of largest recipients of international development aid, and has scrupulously implemented austerity measures favored by aid providers. Because of the close relationship between the lenders and the regime, some observers have charged that the international financial community looks favorably upon Tutsi-domination and is loath to highlight the issue of genocide.

For additional analytical, marketing, investment and business opportunities information, please contact
Global Investment & Business Center, USA
(202) 546-2103. Fax: (202) 546-3275. E-mail: rusric@erols.com

According to World Bank data, 95 percent of the population are subsistence farmers who may grow small amounts of cash crops (especially coffee) to generate a meager income. At the time of the 1988 massacres, Burundi was in the midst of a World Bank supported effort to move away from a subsistence economy by boosting private investment and diversifying exports. These reforms have not significantly affected the economy, and yearly income stands at $210 per person. The country remains heavily dependent on foreign aid, as it always has been. In fact, Burundi has been extraordinarily successful in raising foreign assistance, sometimes receiving more money than it has asked for. As with neighboring Rwanda, population density and growth (3.06 percent per year) remain major problems. In fact, in a 1990 report by the Population Crisis Committee (Washington, DC) on the challenge to democracy caused by population growth, Burundi was cited as one of the most unstable countries in the world due to its population problems. In Burundi, both Catholicism and traditional religions have encouraged large families.

ECONOMIC SITUATION[1]

BACKGROUND

Following an improvement that started in mid-1998, Burundi's security situation worsened in the last quarter of 1999, as rebel skirmishes multiplied. The Arusha peace negotiations between the warring parties resumed in mid-January 2000, with Mr. Mandela's appointment as mediator following Mr. Nyerere's death.

Burundi faces a very difficult situation, with steadily falling world prices for coffee (Burundi's main source of foreign exchange). It is estimated that in 1999 real GDP contracted by about 1 percent, owing to the reduced supply of inputs resulting from a dearth of foreign exchange and the adverse impact of a drought and population displacement on agricultural activity. On average, inflation fell to an annual rate of 3.5 percent in 1999 from 12.5 percent in 1998, but a sharp acceleration took place in the second half of the year.

As a result of a weak revenue performance without a corresponding adjustment in expenditure, the fiscal primary balance (defined narrowly as the difference between government revenue and noninterest outlays, excluding foreign-financed investment), on a commitment basis, switched from a surplus of 0.8 percent of GDP in 1998 to a deficit estimated at 0.4 percent in 1999. As foreign financing is estimated to have turned into a net outflow of almost 1 percent of GDP, the financing requirements of the government were met largely by an accumulation of external arrears and domestic bank borrowing.

---

[1] The International Monetary Fund Report

For additional analytical, marketing, investment and business opportunities information, please contact
Global Investment & Business Center, USA
(202) 546-2103. Fax: (202) 546-3275. E-mail: rusric@erols.com

The persistent decline in foreign exchange reserves and the further accumulation of external arrears, estimated at US$84.0 at end-1999, reflected the continued large deterioration in the terms of trade, the absence of corrective measures, and minimal international assistance. The reduction in imports, associated with the rationing of foreign exchange, translated into a narrowing in the trade and external account deficits. By end-1999, Burundi's gross official reserves had fallen to some US$49.6 million, reducing the import coverage from seven months of imports at end-1998 to about four months at end-1999.

Despite a depreciation of the Burundi franc by about 24 percent in domestic currency terms during the year, the differential between the official exchange rate administered by the central bank and the parallel market rate increased to 85 percent in 1999. In November, the authorities introduced a second official market for foreign exchange with a freely determined rate, allowed residents to hold foreign exchange deposits, and legalized foreign exchange bureaus.

EXECUTIVE BOARD ASSESSMENT

Executive Directors expressed concern about the severe impact on economic development of the drawn-out civil conflict and the flaring up of rebel violence at the end of 1999. They noted in particular the devastation of the economic and social infrastructure, massive displacement of people, and impact on the poor. Directors expressed hope that the Arusha peace talks will rapidly reach a lasting solution for the restoration of social peace and political stability.

Directors noted the deterioration in Burundi's macroeconomic and financial situation during 1999 - in particular, the contraction of GDP, the resurgence of strong inflationary pressures, a weakening of the fiscal accounts, and the severe deterioration of the foreign exchange position. They recognized that the major economic adjustments that are needed would have to await the re-establishment of peace and the resumption of international assistance. However, Directors urged the authorities to begin implementing appropriately strong measures without delay to restore macroeconomic stability, especially in the areas of fiscal, monetary, and exchange rate policies.

Directors were of the view that, despite some improvement over 1999, the fiscal deficit under the budget for 2000 was not compatible with the need to reduce inflation and conserve the country's scarce foreign reserves. Accordingly, they strongly encouraged the authorities to curtail the wage bill increase, control strictly other expenditures, adjusting them promptly in case of a revenue shortfall, and improve budget management to introduce more efficiency and transparency. In this connection,

For additional analytical, marketing, investment and business opportunities information, please contact
Global Investment & Business Center, USA
(202) 546-2103. Fax: (202) 546-3275. E-mail: rusric@erols.com

Directors noted the desirability of switching expenditure from the military to the social sectors when the security situation improves. Directors commended the authorities for the courageous actions taken in January to raise retail prices for petroleum products and to increase government revenue. They also stressed the need to reinforce these actions by eliminating customs exemptions and strengthening customs and tax administration.

Directors urged the authorities to strengthen monetary policy and regain control of broad money through the discontinuation of the unlimited refinancing policy, a substantial increase in the refinancing rate, and strict enforcement of reserve requirements for commercial banks. They also stressed the need for tightening supervision of the financial sector and enforcing observance of prudential ratios and provisioning requirements.

Directors noted that, despite regular adjustments during the year, the official exchange rate did not appropriately reflect inflation differentials with Burundi's partner countries and changes in the terms of trade. They observed that the current exchange rate policy had resulted in a major loss in Burundi's competitiveness, adversely affected economic activity, and led to an ever-increasing gap with the parallel market rate. Directors noted with concern the introduction of the second official foreign exchange market, which gives rise to a multiple currency practice, and encouraged the authorities to remove this practice soon by consolidating the two official markets into a single auction system.

Noting the lack of progress on structural reforms, Directors recommended that priority be given to the liberalization of the coffee sector, which could help provide opportunities for growth and poverty reduction in the agricultural sector. Priority should also be given to the rationalization of public enterprise management, which would improve the sector's financial situation and free public resources.

Directors expressed concern about the weaknesses of the statistical database, which limited the ability of both the authorities and the Fund to evaluate economic development and formulate appropriate policies. They called on the authorities to strengthen efforts to collect essential economic and financial statistics and to ensure their consistency, particularly regarding the national accounts, the balance of payments, and external debt. Directors noted that these efforts could be supported by technical assistance, including from the Fund.

Directors encouraged the authorities to work closely with Fund staff to prepare the basis for emergency post-conflict assistance and the resumption of financial support from donors, and some Directors noted that this could pave the way for possible additional support under the Poverty Reduction and Growth Facility.

For additional analytical, marketing, investment and business opportunities information, please contact
Global Investment & Business Center, USA
(202) 546-2103. Fax: (202) 546-3275. E-mail: rusric@erols.com

BURUNDI: SELECTED ECONOMIC AND FINANCIAL INDICATORS, 1995-99

	1995	1996	1997	1998	1999
	(Annual percentage change)				
Domestic economy					
GDP at constant market prices	-7.3	-8.4	0.4	4.8	-1.0
Consumer prices (period average)	19.4	26.4	31.1	12.5	3.5
	(In millions of U.S. dollars) 1/				
External economy					
Exports, f.o.b.	112.9	40.5	87.4	64.0	56.4
Imports, f.o.b.	-175.5	-100.0	-96.1	-123.5	-93.5
Current account	-4.3	-39.2	-1.7	-59.6	-21.2
(in percent of GDP)	-0.4	-4.4	-0.2	-6.7	-3.1
Overall balance	1.1	-86.7	-34.8	-55.8	-26.9
Gross official reserves	215.3	144.7	117.3	70.5	49.6
(in months of imports, c.i.f.)	21.0	14.2	9.0	7.2	4.4
Change in real effective exchange rate					
(in percent) 2/	5.6	2.5	18.9	-10.6	-14.9
	(In percent of GDP) 1/				
Financial variables					
Revenue and grants	21.3	17.8	16.8	18.2	19.1
Total expenditure and net lending	25.9	27.5	22.2	23.4	25.1
Primary fiscal balance 3/	-0.4	-3.4	-3.5	0.8	-0.4
Overall fiscal balance (excluding grants)	-8.2	-11.9	-8.4	-6.2	-7.2
Change in broad money (in percent)	5.8	14.5	10.4	0.0	42.2
Interest rate (in percent) 4/	9.5	9.1	9.3	9.6	10.3

Sources: Burundi authorities; and IMF staff estimates.
1/ Unless otherwise indicated.
2/ Bilateral trade-weighted period averages; a negative sign signifies a depreciation.
3/ On a commitment basis and excluding grants.
4/ Twelve-month deposit rate.

ECONOMIC PROFILE

AGRICULTURE

The agriculture sector is the mainstay of the economy. It typically employs around 90 per cent of the population and contributes around 50 per cent of GDP. However, the civil war, pressures on land and ecological damage have caused a 25 per cent contraction of the subsistence economy in recent years. Although

For additional analytical, marketing, investment and business opportunities information, please contact
Global Investment & Business Center, USA
(202) 546-2103. Fax: (202) 546-3275. E-mail: rusric@erols.com

Burundi is potentially self-sufficient in food, large numbers of internally displaced people rely on food parcels given by humanitarian organisations.

Most land under cultivation is devoted to subsistence crops - mainly cassava, bananas, sweet potatoes, pulses, maize and sorghum.

Cattle rearing is also an important source of food, as is fishing on Lake Tanganyika.

The main cash crop is coffee, which accounts for up to three-quarters of the country's exports. More than 90 per cent of coffee production is arabica, which is being encouraged with higher producer prices. Other cash crops include tea, cotton, palm oil and tobacco.

INDUSTRY AND MANUFACTURING

The industrial sector, which is based on import substitution, typically accounts for between 15-20 per cent of national output. Production is based almost entirely in Bujumbura and includes beer, soft drinks, cigarettes, glass, textiles, insecticides, cement, oxygen and coffee processing. Civil war has discouraged foreign investment and high import costs have hampered development of industrial capital.

MINING

Gold mining resumed in 1984.
Tungsten is also mined.
Substantial nickel reserves (up to 5 per cent of world total) have been found, but low world prices and an inadequate infrastructure mean extraction is not economically viable.
Deposits of vanadium and uranium are being surveyed.
Phosphates and limestone are used for cement production.

HYDROCARBONS

Reliance on imported petroleum. Petroleum reserves have been located under the Ruzizi Plain and under Lake Tanganyika. A pipeline to the Tanzanian coast is under consideration.

ENERGY

Wood is the main source of energy, providing 95 per cent of the subsistence sector needs.

For additional analytical, marketing, investment and business opportunities
information, please contact
Global Investment & Business Center, USA
(202) 546-2103. Fax: (202) 546-3275. E-mail: rusric@erols.com

Burundi has three power stations.
Large peat deposits are also being developed.

AFRICA'S COFFEE GROWING AREAS

About 25 million people worldwide are employed in coffee industry, most of them in Third World countries, which grow, harvest, and process the beans prior to their shipment to the United States and Europe. Many of these countries offer dry or unwashed coffee beans, which provide a full-mouth feel and a wilder flavor because they are dried out in the air in the sun and barely processed more. Washed beans go through many steps, with the end result being a bean that is as clean as it is pretty, and coffee vendors frequently take further steps to pick out deformities and broken beans so that what is left is "perfect. One of the most famous brands of coffee beans is Arabica.

One can have a poor-tasting Arabica and one can have a nice-looking, good-tasting Robusta, but the industry's standard is definitely for washed Arabicas of exceptional flavor. The work entailed to achieve this is considerable, which accounts for the price difference and definitely shows in the cup. Because so many Third World countries, the source of most coffees, have declared independence from their colonial parents, names change. This can be confusing. For example, Zaire was once the Belgian Congo and rests just east of a country named Congo; they both produce coffee, but Zaire is a premier producer.

COFFEE IN AFRICA

For centuries, coffee was a staple in African cultures which cultivated it not as a beverage, but as a solid food. The Africans would combine the beans with animal fat and chew them like nuts, enjoying their concentrated sweet taste. They often made thick flatcakes of pulverized coffee beans mixed with dried fruit and salted butter. The African explorer, John Speke, wrote of discovering natives around Lake Victoria offering coffee in soup, but it is primarily as a "chew" that coffee is most likely to be found. The Somalis, for example, eat roasted and ground coffee solids mixed with toasted grains, and their craftsmen are famous for their specially created wooden mortars used for grinding up the coffee beans. The dried ripe skins of unprocessed coffee beans are sold as chews at native markets. Somalis and Ethiopians brew them into a beverage that tastes, some say, like straw.

Ugandans are particularly well known for their special woven baskets they make exclusively for these chews. Ugandans also mix green beans with sweet grasses and various spices, dry them, and then wrap them in grass packets to be hung in their homes as both decoration and talisman. Among the many African countries that grow coffee are Zaire, Sierra Leone, Uganda, Ghana, Burundi, Nigeria,

For additional analytical, marketing, investment and business opportunities information, please contact
Global Investment & Business Center, USA
(202) 546-2103. Fax: (202) 546-3275. E-mail: rusric@erols.com

Rwanda, Angola, Congo, the Ivory Coast, and, most importantly. This "Switzerland" of Africa is the most notable coffee growing country on the continent, and one of the seven most important coffee countries in the world today. Because the land never experiences frost, the beans are highly acidic, heavily aromatic, and particularly sought after for blending with beans from other countries. Kenya has some 300,000 plantations and exports nearly its entire crop. The larger bean, named Kenya AA, is exceptional and added to espresso blends, provides a lovely aromatic kick. Although coffee is not used as a beverage in most African countries, its marketability is well understood and it produces a substantial cash crop. As for their beverage of choice, most drink tea.

BURUNDI

This east central African country produces about 34,000 tons each year of high grade Arabica beans that brew a cup with a big body, high acidity and rich taste. Good alone and excellent in a blend.

CAMEROON

This republic in West Africa produces 85,000 tons of coffee, but only a limited crop of Arabicas, which are indeed sweet and mellow a nice find for a change of taste. Their peaberry (small) and elephant (giant) Arabica beans provide a sweet drinking cup.

IVORY COAST

Robustas are the beans here, and France gets most of them, although some U.S. instant coffee blenders have used them. A very distant cousin of the more famous and better African beans, it is grown on smallholdings in southern and central parts of the country. Coffee yield per year tops 250,000 tons, the greatest of any African country.

ETHIOPIA

Ethiopia produces primarily Arabica coffee (some 225,000 tons) from wild trees in the provinces of Djimmah, Sidamo, Lekempti and Salo in the west and Southwest. Ethiopia is believed to be one of the two birthplaces of the coffee bean (the other more established source being Yemen). Addis Ababa, its capital is the chief interior coffee market. The primary names for Ethiopian coffee beans are Abyssinian, Djimmahand Harar that is also known as Harrar and Harari. Harar is the most noted coffee of Ethiopia grown in plantations near the ancient capital of Harar, which is both a city and province in the country. Coffee now known as Harar used to be sold as either long berry Mocha or Abyssinian long berry and is usually exported through Djibouti or Aden. These coffees are

For additional analytical, marketing, investment and business opportunities information, please contact
Global Investment & Business Center, USA
(202) 546-2103. Fax: (202) 546-3275. E-mail: rusric@erols.com

described by connoisseurs as winery or fruity. The beans except for those in Sidamo are generally dry-processed. The coffee of Ethiopia, one of the countries where coffee is a native plant, faded in popularity for a while.

KENYA

One of the world's best, this is another example of a "winey" bean, with a full-bodied, acidic taste that has a distinct tang. Although coffee is indigenous to the African continent, coffee in Kenya came from the Isle of Bourbon (Reunion) with the Roman Catholic missionaries as late as 1893. Kenya is considered the Switzerland of East Africa for its fine quality and tremendous export of nearly 1.5 to 2 million bags a year (about 225,000 tons) of beans grown on about 300,000 plantations. Grown at high elevations (5,000 feet), these carefully washed Arabicas are consistently great; the ones with a blackberry overtone are even greater. The designations of AA and AAA and, sometimes, AA are more marketing than cup quality, but basically indicate larger size. I think they make a good espresso and certainly an exceptional stand-alone cup. Ironically, Kenyans drink their other famous crop, tea, and sell their entire coffee crop.

TANZANIA

The Tanzania is most often a peaberry bean, smaller and rounder than most coffee beans, which are double beans to each cherry and flat. This one is sharp with a winey acidity yet very rich in flavour. Similar to Kenyan coffee but thinner, Arabica coffee from this East African country is sometimes still referred to by its former country name, Tanganyika. The finest is the Kibo Chagga, cultivated by the Chagga tribe in the upper slopes of Mount Kilimanjaro. Moshior Arusha, named for shipping ports, are other Tanzania coffees.

ZAIRE

The Republic of Zaire has been known by not one but two previous names: the Belgian Congo and the Democratic Republic of the Congo. Like the rose by any other name, Zaire coffee beans are high-grade unwashed Arabicas with high acidity, rich flavor, and very good body. The two best coffees are from Kivu and Itur, and, because they grow so near the Rwanda-Burundi border, they are similar to those Arabica beans; they make good blenders. Only about 10 percent of their very plentiful yearly crop of 98,000 or more tons per year are exported. Alas, Belgium (no hard feelings apparently), Italy, France, and Switzerland get the bulk of Zaire's beans.

EXTERNAL TRADE EVOLUTION 1990 - 1999

IMPORTS

For additional analytical, marketing, investment and business opportunities information, please contact
Global Investment & Business Center, USA
(202) 546-2103. Fax: (202) 546-3275. E-mail: rusric@erols.com

- 189 -

EU imports in mio euro	1990	1991	1992	1993	1994	1995	1996	1997	1998	1999
Agricultural products (chapter 01-24)	39,8	41,4	41,5	46,3	49,0	87,2	36,2	47,9	49,3	31,3
TOTAL imports	74,1	70,7	73,5	86,6	73,0	144,5	58,8	48,6	60,2	40,7

% of TOTAL imports	1990	1991	1992	1993	1994	1995	1996	1997	1998	1999
Agricultural products	54%	59%	57%	53%	67%	60%	62%	99%	82%	77%

index 1990 = 100	1990	1991	1992	1993	1994	1995	1996	1997	1998	1999
Agricultural products	100	104	104	104	123	219	91	120	124	79
TOTAL imports	100	95	99	117	99	195	79	66	81	55

EXPORTS

EU exports in mio euro	1990	1991	1992	1993	1994	1995	1996	1997	1998	1999
Agricultural products (chapter 01-24)	8,7	6,1	6,8	8,7	12,6	9,1	8,6	8,3	7,5	4,2
TOTAL exports	89,5	84,3	76,3	74,7	75,3	78,0	52,4	41,1	60,1	37,8

% of TOTAL exports	1990	1991	1992	1993	1994	1995	1996	1997	1998	1999
Agricultural products	10%	7%	9%	12%	17%	12%	16%	20%	13%	11%

index 1990 = 100	1990	1991	1992	1993	1994	1995	1996	1997	1998	1999
Agricultural products	100	70	79	79	145	105	99	96	87	48
TOTAL exports	100	94	85	85	84	87	59	46	67	42

BALANCE

Balance in mio	1990	1991	1992	1993	1994	1995	1996	1997	1998	1999
TOTAL trade balance	15,4	13,6	2,7	-11,9	2,3	-66,5	-6,3	-7,5	0,0	-2,9
Exports/Imports ratio	121%	119%	104%	86%	103%	54%	89%	85%	100%	93%

For additional analytical, marketing, investment and business opportunities
information, please contact
Global Investment & Business Center, USA
(202) 546-2103. Fax: (202) 546-3275. E-mail: rusric@erols.com

DEMOCRACY AND HUMAN RIGHTS IN BURUNDI[2]

Burundi is ruled by an authoritarian military regime led by self-proclaimed interim President Pierre Buyoya, who was brought to power in a bloodless coup by the largely ethnic Tutsi armed forces in 1996 and who abrogated the Constitution. In 1998 the Buyoya regime reached a political agreement with the opposition-dominated National Assembly, which adopted a Transitional Constitutional Act and a transitional political platform. The agreement brought the predominantly ethnic Hutu opposition party FRODEBU into the Cabinet. Buyoya holds power in conjunction with a political power structure dominated by members of the Tutsi ethnic group. Political parties operate under significant restraints. Since 1993 the country has suffered from a civil war with thousands of civilian deaths and mass internal displacement. The judiciary is controlled by the ethnic Tutsi minority and is not impartial.

The security forces are controlled by the Tutsi minority and consist of the army and the gendarmerie under the Ministry of Defense, the judicial police under the Ministry of Justice, and the intelligence service under the presidency. Security forces committed numerous serious human rights abuses.

The country is poor and densely populated, with 92 percent of the population dependent on subsistence agriculture. Many internally displaced citizens have been unable to grow food and depend largely on international humanitarian assistance. Per capita income is less than $200 per year. The civil war has caused severe economic disruption, especially to the small modern sector of the economy, which is based mainly on the export of coffee, tea, and cotton. The Government has announced that it plans to privatize publicly owned enterprises, but efforts to carry out such a transformation are lagging. Other governments in the region that had imposed economic sanctions on the country lifted them in January.

The Government's human rights record remained poor. Citizens do not have the right to change their government. Security forces continued to commit numerous extrajudicial killings. The armed forces killed armed rebels and unarmed civilians, including women, children, and the elderly. Rebel attacks on the military often were followed by army reprisals against civilians suspected of cooperating with the insurgents. Despite Buyoya's stated commitment to end abuses by the military, his Government was unable or unwilling to do so, and perpetrators were not punished. Impunity for those who commit serious human rights violations, and the continuing lack of accountability for those who committed past abuses, remained key factors in the country's continuing instability. There were credible

---

[2] Bureau of Democracy, Human Rights, and Labor U.S. Department of State

For additional analytical, marketing, investment and business opportunities information, please contact
Global Investment & Business Center, USA
(202) 546-2103. Fax: (202) 546-3275. E-mail: rusric@erols.com

reports of disappearances and the security forces continued to torture and otherwise mistreat persons. Prison conditions were life threatening. Arbitrary arrest and detention, and lengthy pretrial detention, are problems, and there were reports of incommunicado detention. The court system suffers from a lengthy case backlog.

The dysfunctional justice system was unable to resolve pressing issues of detention and impunity because of its lack of independence, its inefficiency and administrative disruption, and the partiality of Tutsi officials. Authorities infringe on citizens' privacy rights. The Government controls the media and restricts freedom of speech and of the press. It restricts freedom of assembly and does not permit political demonstrations. The Government restricts freedom of association and movement. At the end of the year, the army forcibly relocated an estimated 330,000 Hutus in an effort to stop rebel attacks on the nearby capital, Bujumbura.

The armed forces sometimes limited access to certain areas by human rights observers, citing dangerous security conditions. Violence and discrimination against women continued to be problems. The Government is unable to protect the rights of children or prevent discrimination against the disabled.

The indigenous Twa (Pygmy) people remain marginalized economically, socially, and politically. Incidents of ethnically motivated destruction and killing occurred throughout the country. State discrimination against Hutus is widespread. Soldiers required internally displaced persons to perform forced labor. Child labor is a problem.

Rebel Hutu militias also continued to commit many serious abuses, including repeated killings of unarmed civilians, and requiring civilians to perform forced labor.

RESPECT FOR HUMAN RIGHTS

RESPECT FOR THE INTEGRITY OF THE PERSON

A. POLITICAL AND OTHER EXTRAJUDICIAL KILLING

Security forces committed numerous extrajudicial killings. On January 4, soldiers killed more than 55 civilians in Mubone, Kabezi commune, Bujumbura Rural province, according to international human rights observers. The Government promised to investigate; however, any findings were not made public. It is not known if those responsible were punished.

For additional analytical, marketing, investment and business opportunities information, please contact
Global Investment & Business Center, USA
(202) 546-2103. Fax: (202) 546-3275. E-mail: rusric@erols.com

On May 26, soldiers killed 11 Hutu civilians, including women and children, most of whom lived in the household of a man suspected of participating in the 1993 killing of Tutsis, according to an international human rights observer.

On July 19, soldiers killed 30 civilians in Kanyosha commune, Bujumbura Rural province, according to international observers.

On August 11, the army shot and killed an estimated 50 civilians in Kanyosha commune, Bujumbura Rural province, according to international human rights observers. On August 12, the army used grenades and machine guns to kill an unknown number of civilians in Ruziba, Bujumbura Rural province, observers reported. The army suspected the civilians of collaborating with rebels. International observers were prevented from investigating because of security forces' claims that the areas were unsafe. The Government promised to investigate; however, its findings were not made public.

On October 9, a soldier shot and killed six persons, including three children and two women, at the Ruyaga regroupment site in Bujumbura Rural province where they had been moved forcibly, according to the authorities. Seven others were injured. The soldier was detained immediately although his name was not released publicly, authorities said.

There were reports that soldiers shot and killed some persons who tried to leave "regroupment sites" to which Hutus were forcibly relocated starting in September (see Sections 1.f. and 2.d.).

Deaths in prisons continued due to disease and malnutrition (see Section 1.c.).

Amnesty International (AI) estimates that 200,000 persons were killed in ethnic violence between October 1993 and the end of 1998. No credible countrywide casualty figures were available for 1999. Throughout the year, the Government and security forces frequently prevented journalists and human rights observers from going to areas where casualties occurred, making it difficult to gather information about the perpetrators and the victims. AI reported that the army and rebel groups killed 600 civilians between November 1998 and March 1999 in Bujumbura Rural province alone. Based on media and other reports, much of the extrajudicial killing and destruction during the year was concentrated in the province around the capital and in the southern and eastern provinces.

Accurate information about landmines is hard to obtain. However, the armed forces apparently use mines to prevent rebels from accessing territory, and rebel groups use landmines as tools of terror. Landmine-related civilian injuries and deaths were reported, particularly in provinces along the southern border with Tanzania.

For additional analytical, marketing, investment and business opportunities information, please contact
Global Investment & Business Center, USA
(202) 546-2103. Fax: (202) 546-3275. E-mail: rusric@erols.com

A domestic human rights organization reported that 51 persons were sentenced to death in the regular criminal courts during the first 10 months of the year. A death sentence handed down by a military court was carried out in July, and legal irregularities in the case prompted protests by AI. On July 28, Corporal Bonaventure Ndikumana was sentenced to death for deliberately killing an officer. Ndikumana was executed the next day without being allowed to file an appeal of his conviction as required by law, according to the authorities and AI. No executions were carried out in 1998. In 1997, after a 15-year period with no executions, the State executed 6 of 38 civilians sentenced to death for the first time since 1982.

In May the media reported the surprise announcement of a judgment in the trial of the 1993 assassination of President Melchior Ndadaye. The Supreme Court sentenced five members of the army to death and 23 others to prison. Another 38 persons were acquitted, 10 cases were sent back for further review, and 5 cases were dropped because the suspects had died. No high-ranking army officers were convicted, although charges were brought originally against many past and present senior army members. The new Attorney General, who is a Hutu, announced that the case would be reopened.

In January rebels killed 178 civilians in Makamba province, according to the media. The civilians were killed either by rebels or were caught in a crossfire between the rebels and the army, according to reports.

On August 28, Hutu rebels killed 39 persons in Bujumbura, most of them Tutsi civilians according to the authorities. Victims were shot or burned. The authorities permitted rapid access to the scenes of the attacks.

On October 12, unknown attackers killed two U.N. foreign staff members and seven others during a U.N. humanitarian assessment mission to Rutana province. Officials said that rebels carried out the attack, possibly to halt humanitarian aid. The Government called on Tanzania to arrest the perpetrators, who it said fled to Tanzania after the attack. Rebels accused the armed forces of committing these killings. In response to this attack, the U.N. halted most of its field operations indefinitely. A grenade attack in Bujumbura's central market in November killed 5 persons and injured 14 others.

There are no definitive statistics available on how many civilians were killed by Hutu rebels; the Government stated that killings by rebels represent the majority of civilian casualties. Rebels reportedly often kill civilians for suspected collaboration with the regime and for their refusal to pay "taxes" to rebels. Hutu rebels ambushed minibuses carrying civilians on national highways, robbing and killing the occupants.

For additional analytical, marketing, investment and business opportunities information, please contact
Global Investment & Business Center, USA
(202) 546-2103. Fax: (202) 546-3275. E-mail: rusric@erols.com

Three persons accused of the 1995 killings of Italian religious workers were not tried. The Government did not identify or bring to justice the persons responsible for the June 1996 killing in Cibitoke province of three foreign employees of the International Committee of the Red Cross.

B. Disappearance

Human rights groups reported that abductions and disappearances occurred during the year, but no credible overall figures were available. AI reported on October 5 that it had credible reports of the disappearance of three persons believed to have been arrested by soldiers in September. According to AI, at least one of the men was believed to have been executed and secretly buried. The media carried brief reports of kidnapings of civilians by Hutu rebels.

C. Torture and Other Cruel, Inhuman, or Degrading Treatment or Punishment

The Transitional Constitution Act prohibits these abuses; however, members of the security forces continued to torture and otherwise abuse persons. In one such case, AI reported that members of the security forces were believed to have withheld food from detainees and beaten one of them severely. There were no know prosecutions of members of the security forces for these abuses.

At the end of the year, signs emerged of renewed government support for policing of the capital and countryside by armed civilians, which raised fears of the return of militias created in 1995 to destabilize the then Hutu-led government.

Conditions in state-run prisons were life threatening and are characterized by severe overcrowding and inadequate hygiene, clothing, medical care, food, and water. A total of about 10,000 inmates are housed in facilities built to accommodate a maximum of 3,600 persons. Prisoners rely on family members to provide an adequate diet, and officials say that prisoners suffer from digestive illness, dysentery, and malaria. Poor prison conditions contributed to deaths of prisoners from disease and malnutrition. In April AI reported that a 12-year-old boy, improperly charged in connection with 1993 killings, had been abused sexually by male inmates at Bujumbura's central prison.

U.N. human rights monitors were permitted to visit prisons.

D. Arbitrary Arrest, Detention, or Exile

The law prohibits arbitrary arrest, detention, and exile; however, security forces arbitrarily arrested and detained persons. Limits on the length of pretrial detention were not respected. Presiding magistrates are authorized to issue

For additional analytical, marketing, investment and business opportunities information, please contact
Global Investment & Business Center, USA
(202) 546-2103. Fax: (202) 546-3275. E-mail: rusric@erols.com

arrest warrants. Police and gendarmes can make arrests without a warrant, but are required to submit a written report to a magistrate within 48 hours. A magistrate can order the release of suspects or confirm charges and continue detention, initially for 15 days, then subsequently for periods of 30 days, as necessary to prepare the case for trial.

The law requires arrest warrants. The police are required to follow the same procedures as magistrates; however, the police have detained suspects for extended periods without announcing charges, certifying the cases, or forwarding them to the Ministry of Justice as required. There were numerous instances of arbitrary arrest. Bail was permitted in some cases. Human rights organizations reported that incommunicado detention exists, although it is prohibited by law.

The disruption of the political process and the general insecurity severely impeded the judicial process. In mid 1999, an estimated 7,500 pretrial detainees constituted 78 percent of the total prison population. About 750 of an estimated 9,500 detainees reportedly were released in 1999, but these reports could not be confirmed.

The Government has not used forced exile as a means of political control. However, many persons remained in voluntary exile in Belgium, Kenya, Tanzania, Zaire, and elsewhere. Some senior authorities maintain their families outside the country. A number of officials of the government of deposed president Sylvestre Ntibantunganya, who fled the country in 1996, have not yet returned.

E. DENIAL OF FAIR PUBLIC TRIAL

The Transitional Constitutional Act provides for an independent judiciary; however, in practice the judiciary is not independent and is dominated by ethnic Tutsis. An international human rights organization estimated in 1998 that ethnic Hutus accounted for only 5 percent of the country's judges and lawyers, although they constitute an estimated 85 percent of the population. Most citizens assume that the courts promote the interests of the dominant Tutsi minority; members of the Hutu majority believe that the judicial system is biased against them.

The judicial system is divided into civil and criminal courts with the Supreme Court at the apex. The armed forces have a separate judicial system, and there is a labor court.

Citizens generally did not have regular access to civilian and military court proceedings. Defendants in theory are presumed innocent and have the right to appeal; however, in practice some lawyers say that the structure of the court system inappropriately limits the possibility of appeals for those accused of the

For additional analytical, marketing, investment and business opportunities information, please contact
Global Investment & Business Center, USA
(202) 546-2103. Fax: (202) 546-3275. E-mail: rusric@erols.com

most serious crimes. While defendants have a right to counsel and to defend themselves, in practice few have legal representation. The civil court system functions, but the lack of a well-trained and adequately funded judiciary constrains expeditious proceedings. Many citizens have lost confidence in the system's ability to provide even basic protection. The majority of persons arrested on criminal charges since October 1993 remain in pretrial custody.

In July the National Assembly passed a new criminal code, which was scheduled to take effect in January 2000, and in theory provides protections for suspects' rights to a lawyer before official charges are filed and during pretrial investigations.

There are some clearly identifiable political prisoners. Charges against defendants convicted for nonpolitical crimes sometimes are politically motivated.

F. ARBITRARY INTERFERENCE WITH PRIVACY, FAMILY, HOME, OR CORRESPONDENCE

The Transitional Constitutional Act provides for the right to privacy, but the authorities reportedly do not respect the law requiring search warrants. Security forces are widely believed to monitor telephones regularly.

Beginning in September, following rebel attacks on the mainly Tutsi-inhabited capital (see Section 1.a.), the Government forcibly relocated an estimated 330,000 mainly Hutu inhabitants of Bujumbura Rural province to "regroupment sites" where security forces could more readily monitor and control their movements. Inhabitants were moved to sites with inadequate sanitation and insufficient access to water, food, shelter, and medicine. The Government's stated rationale for these forced relocations was to protect the relocated persons from rebel attacks.

RESPECT FOR CIVIL LIBERTIES

A. FREEDOM OF SPEECH AND PRESS

The Transitional Constitutional Act does not impose restrictions on the media; however, the Government restricts freedom of speech and of the press. A press law requires that newspaper articles undergo review by a government censor 4 days before publication, and the Government controls the media and harasses and detains journalists.

The regime controls much of the news, since it owns the only regularly published newspaper and the major radio and television stations. The government-owned Le Renouveau is published 3 times a week. Other newspapers, including at least one opposition newspaper, appear irregularly. Political tracts circulate, and two

For additional analytical, marketing, investment and business opportunities information, please contact
Global Investment & Business Center, USA
(202) 546-2103. Fax: (202) 546-3275. E-mail: rusric@erols.com

private faxed newsheets are published almost daily. These represent a variety of political viewpoints. In June the National Communications Council suspended the activities of the FRODEBU opposition political party's newspaper, L'Aube de la Democratie. In October the Council temporarily suspended the newspaper, La Verite.

Security forces and the regime harass journalists, questioning or detaining them or having their property searched and seized. In June the editors of two private faxed newsheets were detained for brief periods for failing to send advance copies of their dispatches to government agencies, even though the advance review law applies only to daily newspapers. In September the Defense Minister publicly compared some journalists to rebels and indicated that they should be treated as such. When journalists protested what they described as a death threat, the Minister explained that he meant only to criticize unprofessional journalists.

The government-owned radio broadcasts in the Kirundi language, French, and Swahili and offers limited English programming. The private radio station, Umwizero, is financed by international donors and broadcasts in French and Kirundi. Listeners also can receive transmissions of the British Broadcasting Corporation, the Voice of America, and Radio France Internationale. A clandestine radio station operated by Hutu rebels once broadcast briefly from the Democratic Republic of Congo.

No laws or regulations limit academic freedom, and no persons at the University of Burundi were persecuted for what they published or said. However, the state university remains primarily ethnic Tutsi. Tensions occasionally flare between Hutu and Tutsi students on campus, where politically and ethnically motivated killings occurred in 1995 and 1996.

B. FREEDOM OF PEACEFUL ASSEMBLY AND ASSOCIATION

The Government restricts freedom of assembly. The Transitional Constitutional Act permits political demonstrations, but in practice none have been allowed by the Government.

The Government restricts freedom of association and has arrested members of organizations and political parties.

The Transitional Constitutional Act permits political parties to operate; however,the regime places restrictions on groups critical of its policies.

C. FREEDOM OF RELIGION

For additional analytical, marketing, investment and business opportunities information, please contact
Global Investment & Business Center, USA
(202) 546-2103. Fax: (202) 546-3275. E-mail: rusric@erols.com

The transitional Constitutional Act provides for freedom of religion, and the Government respects this right in practice. There is no state religion, and the Government does not restrict freedom of worship.

D. FREEDOM OF MOVEMENT WITHIN THE COUNTRY, FOREIGN TRAVEL, IMMIGRATION, AND REPATRIATION

The Transitional Constitutional Act provides for these rights; however, the Government restricts this right in practice. Beginning in September the regime forcibly relocated an estimated 330,000 Hutus from Bujumbura Rural province. Residents of parts of Bujumbura Rural more heavily populated by Tutsis were not subject to relocation. The relocated population, at "regroupment sites," some of which were remote, at times lacked access to food, safe drinking water, shelter, basic sanitation, and health care. Authorities said that they were relocating the population to protect it from rebels, but there were credible reports that the displacements also were used to remove rebels from the relocated population and to impede civilian assistance to rebels. Persons who tried to leave the sites, allegedly to search for food and water, reportedly were shot, sometimes fatally, by soldiers.

At year's end, about 550,000 other citizens remained in internally displaced persons (IDP's) camps created in 1993-94 throughout the country. With the recently relocated persons, a total of 13 percent of the population live in 360 sites, according to an international relief organization. Inhabitants of these sites raised some of their own food with the permission of the armed forces. Soldiers guarding these camps provide a measure of protection to camp inhabitants; however, they sometimes commit human rights abuses against them.

Camp inhabitants often are required to perform labor for the soldiers without compensation (see Section 6.c.).

Civilians who remain outside the sites reportedly have been killed by Hutu rebels for allegedly collaborating with authorities and by the armed forces on suspicion of collaborating with the rebels.

The authorities occasionally restricted foreign travel for political reasons in the past; there was one such case in 1999. In August an official from the FRODEBU wing of the party, which is critical of the regime, was prevented temporarily from leaving the country for consultations related to the peace talks in Arusha. Authorities cited legal, not political, reasons.

The majority of citizens could travel legally in and out of the country.

For additional analytical, marketing, investment and business opportunities information, please contact
Global Investment & Business Center, USA
(202) 546-2103. Fax: (202) 546-3275. E-mail: rusric@erols.com

Travel within the country is possible but could be hazardous in areas of rebel activity, particularly in parts of Bujumbura Rural, Bururi, Rutana, and Makamba provinces.

The armed forces sometimes denied access to certain areas to human rights observers, citing dangerous security conditions (see Section 4).

The U.N. High Commissioner for Refugees (UNHCR) reported that as of the end of September, about 11,000 Burundian refugees were repatriated in the course of the year from Rwanda, Tanzania, the Democratic Republic of Congo, and other countries. During the same period, an estimated 25,000 Burundians fled Burundi to Tanzania, according to the UNHCR. Approximately 296,000 Burundian refugees, most of them Hutu, remain in Angola, Cameroon, the Republic of the Congo, the Democratic Republic of Congo, Kenya, Malawi, Rwanda, Tanzania, and Zambia. Some of these persons fled as early as 1972, and many fled following the assassination of former president Ndadaye in October 1993.

The Government has granted first asylum in recent years.

Approximately 325 citizens of the Democratic Republic of Congo live in Burundi, many of whom claim asylum. Rwandan refugees who fled the 1994 ethnic massacres in Rwanda departed the country by 1997. Another 200,000 Rwandans who came in earlier waves of refugees, some as early as 1959, are not registered officially with the UNHCR and are integrated into Burundian society.

There were no reports of the forced return of persons to a country where they feared persecution.

RESPECT FOR POLITICAL RIGHTS: THE RIGHT OF CITIZENS TO CHANGE THEIR GOVERNMENT

Citizens do not have the right to change their government. The Transitional Constitutional Act makes no provision for elections. The 1992 Constitution and 1994 Convention of Government were suspended by the Buyoya military regime that assumed power on July 25, 1996, in a bloodless coup. On that date, the regime dissolved the National Assembly and banned political parties. About 3 weeks later, Buyoya announced the restoration of the National Assembly and political parties with certain restrictions. The National Assembly is dominated by the opposition party, FRODEBU, which draws the majority of its membership from the Hutu ethnic group.

For additional analytical, marketing, investment and business opportunities information, please contact
Global Investment & Business Center, USA
(202) 546-2103. Fax: (202) 546-3275. E-mail: rusric@erols.com

In April 1998, multiparty peace talks began in Arusha, Tanzania, and Burundi's regime subsequently launched an internal peace process. On June 4, 1998, the National Assembly and the Government entered into a partnership agreement. The National Assembly adopted a Transitional Constitutional Act and a Transitional Political Platform. The act changed the structure of government by eliminating the post of prime minister, creating two vice presidents, removing the National Assembly Speaker from the line of presidential succession, and enlarging the National Assembly. The act placed no time limits on the President's or the National Assembly's term of office. By year's end, no such limits had been enacted, and no future presidential or national assembly elections had been scheduled.

The Transitional Political Platform endorses in general terms the restoration of democracy and correction of the ethnic imbalance within the army and the judicial system. It calls for the creation of an international tribunal to try crimes of genocide. No such tribunal had been created by year's end.

On June 12, 1998, a new Government was announced in which the First Vice President and 10 of the 22 cabinet ministers are members of FRODEBU. The Cabinet includes 12 Hutus, including the Minister of External Relations. Progovernment ethnic Tutsi members hold the key Ministries of Defense, Interior, Justice, and Finance.

Under the 1992 Constitution, deposed President Ntibantunganya would have remained in office until 1998. The last elections to fill the Assembly took place in June 1993. The Transitional Constitutional Act stipulates that the National Assembly shall consist of 121 parliamentarians: those elected in 1993 who sat in the previous National Assembly, plus 40 new members--28 members of civil society appointed by the President and one representative each (selected by their respective parties) from all 12 officially recognized political parties not previously represented. Not all of those elected in 1993 are alive or in the country, and the vacant seats were filled by substitutes from the same political party as the original parliamentarian. Tutsi supporters of the Government filled many of the 40 new seats.

POLITICAL PARTIES OPERATE UNDER SIGNIFICANT CONSTRAINTS.

The National Assembly has nominal budgetary oversight, but the Council of Ministers legally can enact a budget if the National Assembly fails to do so. The Transitional Constitutional Act gives the President the authority to declare a state of emergency by decree after consulting with the National Assembly Speaker, the National Security Council, and the Constitutional Court.

For additional analytical, marketing, investment and business opportunities information, please contact
Global Investment & Business Center, USA
(202) 546-2103. Fax: (202) 546-3275. E-mail: rusric@erols.com

No legal restrictions hinder the participation of women or indigenous people in elections or politics; however women and the ethnic Twa (Pygmies) are underrepresented in government and politics. Of the 22 cabinet seats, 1 is filled by a woman, who serves as the Minister of Women, Welfare, and Social Affairs. (In the previous government women held 2 of the 24 cabinet seats.) In 1993 women were elected to 9 of 81 seats in the National Assembly. One of these nine women was killed in Cibitoke province in 1995. The expansion of the National Assembly and the filling of vacant seats has brought the total of female parliamentarians to 16. One of the nine members of the Supreme Court is a woman as are three of the seven Constitutional Court members, including its president. About 1 percent of the population is Twa, but there are no Twa in the Cabinet. One Twa is an appointed member of the National Assembly (also see Section 5).

GOVERNMENTAL ATTITUDE REGARDING INTERNATIONAL AND NONGOVERNMENTAL INVESTIGATION OF ALLEGED VIOLATIONS OF HUMAN RIGHTS

Domestic human rights groups received varying degrees of cooperation from government ministries. The local human rights group, Iteka, continued to operate and publish a newsletter. Amnesty International representatives and the U.N. Special Rapporteur for Human Rights visited the country during the year. The U.N. High Commissioner for Human Rights maintains an office in the country, but reduced its observer staff in October due to poor security conditions (see Section 1.a.).

Real and claimed insecurity in rural areas was cited by the regime in denying access to some areas of the country to journalists, international relief workers, and human rights observers. Army elements in the field frequently denied access to human rights observers when the army was accused of human rights violations. For example, human rights observers were denied full access to areas in Bujumbura Rural province, where the army is believed to have killed more than 50 civilians on August 10, 11, and 12 (see Section 1.a.).

DISCRIMINATION BASED ON SEX, RELIGION, DISABILITY, LANGUAGE, OR SOCIAL STATUS

The Transitional Constitutional Act provides equal status and protection for all citizens, without distinction based on sex, origin, ethnicity, religion, or opinion. However, the Government failed to implement effectively the act's provisions. Hutus continue to perceive, correctly, that the Tutsi-dominated government and army discriminate against them. The question of exclusion was a central question at the peace talks in Arusha.

For additional analytical, marketing, investment and business opportunities information, please contact
Global Investment & Business Center, USA
(202) 546-2103. Fax: (202) 546-3275. E-mail: rusric@erols.com

WOMEN

Violence against women occurred, but its extent is undocumented. Wives have the right to charge their husbands with physical abuse, but they rarely do so. Police normally do not intervene in domestic disputes, and the media rarely report incidents of violence against women. No known court cases dealt with the abuse of women.

Women face legal and societal discrimination. Explicitly discriminatory inheritance laws and discriminatory credit practices continued. By law, women must receive the same pay as men for the same work, but in practice they do not. Women are far less likely to hold mid-level or high-level positions. In rural areas, women traditionally perform hard farm work, marry and have children at an early age, and have fewer opportunities for education than men.

CHILDREN

The law provides for children's health and welfare, but the Government cannot adequately satisfy the needs of children and, in particular, of the large population of orphans resulting from the violence since 1993. Many of the victims in the civil war are children. The Government provides elementary education at nominal cost through grade six. About 44 percent of children are enrolled in primary school. The Government provides subsidized health care.

PEOPLE WITH DISABILITIES

The Government has not enacted legislation or otherwise mandated access to buildings or government services for persons with disabilities. There are few job opportunities for the physically disabled in Burundi, where most jobs involve significant manual labor.

INDIGENOUS PEOPLE

The Twa (Pygmies), who are believed to be the country's earliest human inhabitants, now make up only about 1 percent of the population, and generally remain economically, socially, and politically marginalized. Most Twa live in isolation, uneducated, and without access to government services, including health care. One Twa was appointed to the National Assembly, but the Twa are underrepresented in the political process.

NATIONAL/RACIAL/ETHNIC MINORITIES

The principal national problem continued to be ethnic conflict between the majority Hutus and the minority Tutsis. Burundi's civil conflict stems from more

For additional analytical, marketing, investment and business opportunities information, please contact
Global Investment & Business Center, USA
(202) 546-2103. Fax: (202) 546-3275. E-mail: rusric@erols.com

than three decades of violence and systematic discrimination, which compounds the fears by both sides of genocide and exclusion. Tutsis claim to have been the targets of a genocide carried out in 1993 by Hutus angered over the assassination of democratically elected Hutu president Ndadaye. The Tutsis historically have held power, and they dominate educated society and control the security forces. In 1996 a coup deposed president Ntibantunganya, a Hutu, and replaced him with Major Pierre Buyoya, a Tutsi.

The Transitional Constitutional Act provides equal status and protection for all citizens, without distinction based on sex, origin, ethnicity, religion, or opinion. However, the Government failed to implement effectively the act's provisions. The Tutsi-dominated government and army discriminate against Hutus. State discrimination against Hutus, who constitute an estimated 85 percent of the population, affects every facet of society, but most strikingly higher education and certain branches of the Government such as the armed services and the judicial system. The President and the Tutsi-dominated army retain their dominance in decision making and have not initiated genuine power sharing.

WORKER RIGHTS

A. THE RIGHT OF ASSOCIATION

The Labor Code protects the rights of workers to form unions, although the army, gendarmerie, and foreigners working in the public sector are prohibited from union participation. Most union workers are urban civil servants.

According to the Confederation of Free Unions of Burundi (CSB), an umbrella trade union, 60 percent of the 80,000 formal private sector employees are unionized. All employees in the public sector, except those prohibited by law, are unionized.

Since gaining independence from the Government in 1992, the CSB has been dependent financially on a system of checkoffs, as are local unions. In 1995 a rival umbrella trade union, the Confederation of Burundi Unions (COSEBU) was founded. Both COSEBU and the CSB represented labor in collective bargaining negotiations in cooperation with individual labor unions during the year.

Tutsis dominate the formal sector of the economy and the unions.

The Labor Code permits the formation of additional unions or confederations outside the CSB. When settling disputes in which more than one labor union is represented, the law stipulates that the Minister of Labor must choose the union representing the greatest number of workers to participate in the negotiations.

For additional analytical, marketing, investment and business opportunities information, please contact
Global Investment & Business Center, USA
(202) 546-2103. Fax: (202) 546-3275. E-mail: rusric@erols.com

The Labor Code provides workers with a restricted right to strike. The restrictions on the right to strike and to lock out include: All other peaceful means of resolution must be exhausted prior to the strike action; negotiations must continue during the action, mediated by a mutually agreed upon party or by the Government; and 6 days' notice must be given. The law prohibits retribution against workers participating in a legal strike, and this provision is respected. Strikes by telecommunications and social security workers took place without government intervention.

Unions are able to affiliate with international organizations.

B. THE RIGHT TO ORGANIZE AND BARGAIN COLLECTIVELY

The Labor Code recognizes the right to collective bargaining, formerly acknowledged only by ordinance. Since most workers are civil servants, government entities are involved in almost every phase of labor negotiations.

Public sector wages are set in fixed scales in individual contracts and are not affected by collective bargaining. In the private sector, wage scales also exist, but individual contract negotiation is possible.

The Labor Code gives the Labor Court jurisdiction over all labor dispute cases, including those involving public employees. Negotiations are conducted largely under the supervision of the tripartite National Labor Council, the Government's highest consultative authority on labor issues. The Council represents government, labor, and management and is presided over and regulated by the Minister of Labor.

The Labor Code prohibits employers from firing or otherwise discriminating against a worker because of union affiliation or activity. This right is upheld in practice.

There are no functioning export processing zones.

C. PROHIBITION OF FORCED OR COMPULSORY LABOR

The law prohibits the performance of forced or compulsory labor by adults or children; however, soldiers guarding internally displaced persons sites often require inhabitants to cook, fetch water, chop wood, and perform other chores without compensation. The rebels also require peasants to perform uncompensated labor, including the transport of supplies and weapons. Apart from these situations, forced labor is not known to occur. There were no reports of forced child labor.

For additional analytical, marketing, investment and business opportunities information, please contact
Global Investment & Business Center, USA
(202) 546-2103. Fax: (202) 546-3275. E-mail: rusric@erols.com

D. STATUS OF CHILD LABOR PRACTICES AND MINIMUM AGE FOR EMPLOYMENT

The Labor Code states that children under the age of 16 cannot be employed by "an enterprise" even as apprentices, although it also states that they may undertake occasional work that does not damage their health or interfere with their schooling. In practice, children under age 16 in rural areas do heavy manual labor during the daytime in the school year.

The minimum age for military service is 18, but there are believed to be some children below that age in the army.

Children are prohibited legally from working at night, although many do so in the informal sector. Most of the population lives by subsistence agriculture, and children are obliged by custom and economic necessity to participate in subsistence agriculture, family-based enterprises, and the informal sector. The law prohibits forced and bonded labor by children, and the Government enforces this prohibition effectively (see Section 6.c.).

E. ACCEPTABLE CONDITIONS OF WORK

The formal minimum wage for unskilled workers is $0.27 (160 francs) per day in the cities of Bujumbura and Gitega, and $0.23 (140 francs) in the rest of the country, with a graduated scale for greater skill levels. This amount does not allow a worker and family to maintain a decent standard of living, and most families rely on second incomes and subsistence agriculture to supplement their earnings. A 1997 survey of day labor wage rates in nine provinces by an international organization revealed that actual wages ranged upward from the equivalent of $0.30 per day.

Unionized employees, particularly in urban areas, generally earn significantly more than the minimum wage. Public sector wages are set by agreement between the government and either the CSB or COSEBU. The Labor Code stipulates an 8-hour workday and a 40-hour workweek, except in cases where workers are involved in activities related to national security. Supplements must be paid for overtime. Foreign workers are protected by law and are not subject to discrimination.

The Labor Code establishes health and safety standards that require an employer to provide a safe workplace and assigns enforcement responsibility to the Minister of Labor. However, the Ministry does not enforce the code effectively. Health and safety articles in the Labor Code do not address directly workers' rights to remove themselves from dangerous tasks.

For additional analytical, marketing, investment and business opportunities information, please contact
Global Investment & Business Center, USA
(202) 546-2103. Fax: (202) 546-3275. E-mail: rusric@erols.com

F. TRAFFICKING IN PERSONS

No law was known specifically to prohibit trafficking in persons, although abduction and imposition of involuntary servitude have been serious crimes since the colonial era. There were no reports of trafficking in persons during the year.

For additional analytical, marketing, investment and business opportunities
information, please contact
Global Investment & Business Center, USA
(202) 546-2103. Fax: (202) 546-3275. E-mail: rusric@erols.com

ETHNIC CONFLICTS IN BURUNDI AND NEIGBORING COUNTRIES

HUTU AND TUTSI IN BURUNDI

REGIONAL CONTEXT: THE TUTSI AND THE HUTU, BROTHERS IN BLOOD

Genocide has been usefully described as "the promotion, execution and/or implied consent of sustained policies by governing elites or their agents - or in the case of civil war either of the contending authorities - that result in the deaths of a substantial portion of a communal and/or politicized communal group." Under this as well as other definitions of the term, there can be no question that in 1994 the Tutsis of Rwanda have been the target of a campaign of genocide waged by the government of Juvenal Habyarimana and allied elements within the Hutu community.

INSEPARABLE CONFLICTS IN RWANDA AND BURUNDI

In the second half of the twentieth century, Rwanda and Burundi have shared a history of communal conflict which has resulted in death and internal and external refugee flows on a massive scale. It is therefore impossible to understand the history or current conditions of one country without reference to its neighbor. Hence, for a more comprehensive appreciation, researchers making use of this Burundi file should also examine Minorities at Risk project materials on Rwanda.

In attempting to make sense of the deadly dynamic of communal conflicts which have periodically been visited upon Rwanda and Burundi, it must first be stated that in this story there are no universal angels or universal villains. Rwanda and Burundi share many characteristics such as size, geography, language, culture, economy, and historical experience. Almost eerily, both have a similar population of communal groups, which can be very roughly broken down as 85 percent Hutu, 14 percent Tutsi, and 1 percent Twa. Politically, since regaining independence from European colonizers in the early 1960s, Rwanda has been controlled by the majority Hutus, while in Burundi Tutsis have maintained their status as a dominant minority. Tragically, genocide has been a chosen instrument for Hutu elites in Rwanda and Tutsi elites in Burundi in their struggle to monopolize state power and the numerous benefits which flow therefrom.

While the primary blame for genocide in Rwanda must rest with Hutu elites and in Burundi with Tutsi elites, it must be noted that the targeted communities in the respective countries have harbored their share of radicals who have called for

For additional analytical, marketing, investment and business opportunities information, please contact
Global Investment & Business Center, USA
(202) 546-2103. Fax: (202) 546-3275. E-mail: rusric@erols.com

retribution in kind. Hence, Tutsi extremists in (or from) Rwanda and Hutu extremists in (or from) Burundi cannot be absolved of responsibility for perpetuating a climate of fear in which genocide has occurred. On the other hand, elite circles in both Rwanda and Burundi have featured moderates who have championed genuine national reconciliation and non-group based politics. Many of these moderates have found themselves targeted for extermination in the various episodes of genocide along with the persecuted communal group.

Hutu leaders in Rwanda and Tutsi leaders in Burundi, both at the national as well as local level, have skillfully exploited inter-group tensions and violence in the neighboring state in order to justify their methods of political monopoly (dictatorship), physical exclusion (provoking refugee flows), and physical elimination (genocide). Ambitious politicians in both countries have employed an effective nightmare vision which runs something like this: "Look across the border and see what will happen to us (Hutus in Rwanda, Tutsis in Burundi) if we lose power and they take over."

On the level of official dogma, it has generally been the case in both Rwanda and Burundi that problems of inter-group conflict simply do not exist, except where they are artificially invented by radical dissidents or foreign (often meaning missionary) subversives. Hence, while the state is officially said to engage in no form of group exclusion, regime opponents are routinely labelled as "tribal terrorists" and blamed for provoking what are described as spontaneous violent outbursts against their kindred. For their part, leaders have traditionally issued bromidic statements about the essential need for "national unity" and undertaken cosmetic reforms with little or no genuine commitment to fundamental reconciliation.

While twentieth century history and current events suggest little ground for optimism for reconciling Hutu-Tutsi differences in Rwanda and Burundi, there is reason to believe that the rivers of blood which have flowed can be checked. In pre-colonial times, the political structures and culture of Rwanda and Burundi seem to have successfully managed and mitigated Tutsi-Hutu schisms, at least to the point that massacres were not commonplace. Over the hundreds of years that their histories have been joined, Hutus and Tutsis have shared lifestyles and intermarried to the point that at present visual identification is, in most cases, problematic. If one accepts the argument of most analysts that the conflict in both countries in not tribal or ethnic in nature but essentially political and economic (that is, the Hutu-Tutsi distinction is one of class), then rational solutions reached by bold leadership are always possible.

Indeed, in 1988, in the wake of renewed massacres, President Buyoya of Burundi (a Tutsi) began a genuine effort to bring his country's contending communities together. This reform initiative resulted in a democratic election in

For additional analytical, marketing, investment and business opportunities information, please contact
Global Investment & Business Center, USA
(202) 546-2103. Fax: (202) 546-3275. E-mail: rusric@erols.com

June 1993 in which a Hutu, Ndadaye, took power. Although the process of democratization in Burundi is far from complete, one measure of its effectiveness may be the fact that after the dual assassination of presidents Habyarimana and Ntaryamira in April 1994, Rwanda rapidly descended into genocide while Burundi remained relatively stable, although by no means free of Hutu-Tutsi violence.

DIVISIONS AMONG TUTSI

Although the Tutsi-Hutu schism forms the major dilemma of twentieth century Burundi history, it would be too simplistic not to acknowledge that other divisions exist in society. Since the early 1960s, the Tutsi-Hima, a powerful clan, have tended to dominate not only Hutus but also other Tutsis. Tutsi-Himas are traditionally associated with the south of Burundi, as this is the region they inhabited when they migrated to the country in the 14th to the 18th centuries. Interestingly, the Hima were a low status group in pre-colonial Burundi. After independence, the Hima were great rivals with the Tutsi-Abanyaruguru. In 1971, for example, a number of Tutsi-Abanyaruguru officials were arrested and charged with plotting to overthrow the government. It was in this period (1970-71) that President Micombero (a Hima) was attempting to purge Abanyaruguru from his government. As a consequence, the threat of civil war between Tutsis arose. The next year, however, a major episode of genocide occurred, suggesting that an ethnic opponent (the Hutu) was used by Tutsi leaders to rally and unite their people. In addition to internal Tutsi divisions, the Hutu community is by no means monolithic, and has varying geographic and social affiliations.

DISCRIMINATION AGAINST HUTUS

Despite the existence of intra-group divisions, a fundamental fact of life in Burundi has been discrimination against Hutus by Tutsis, occasionally exploding into large-scale massacres. As Lemarchand has observed: "Ethnic supremacy lies at the very heart of the 1972 and 1988 crises." Before reforms were begun in the late 1980s, and even to some extent afterwards, the government's conduct suggested that, while officially maintaining that Burundi had no ethnic problems, the practice of discriminating against Hutus was considered a key ingredient in the regime's survival. Like aspiring politicians in Rwanda, Tutsi elites in Burundi have skillfully employed an "us versus them" ideology to legitimize their power. This theory comports with the argument of many observers that at the root of the ethnic conflict is a political leadership ambitious to mobilize support by means of manufactured tribal hatreds. Interestingly, the success of government propagandizing on the nature of ethnic strife, which emphasizes "foreign subversion" aspects, has often received much play in the international media.

Tutsis discrimination against Hutus was most keenly felt in two ways: denial of educational opportunities, which meant that most government positions (which

For additional analytical, marketing, investment and business opportunities information, please contact
Global Investment & Business Center, USA
(202) 546-2103. Fax: (202) 546-3275. E-mail: rusric@erols.com

required education and other skills) were filled by Tutsis; and, by means of a strange 'girth by height' requirement, blockage of Hutu entry into the armed forces. Thus, Tutsis were insured domination of both the government apparatus and the means of coercion. The extent to which the army was associated with Tutsis is demonstrated by the fact that during ethnic violence Tutsis often fled to military camps for protection, while Hutus ran from them. Even as late as March 1994, the army refused to furnish a breakdown of its troops and claimed that in ongoing ethnic clashes the military was remaining neutral. Despite this official military position, it is obvious to all observers that Burundi will see no peace if the security forces are not restructured, subordinated to civilian institutions, and recruited in a way that more accurately represents the ethnic composition of the country.

POLITICAL MOBILIZATION ALONG ETHNIC LINES

The development of inter-group relations under the Belgian administration virtually ensured that as attempts were made to democratize the country, political mobilization would occur along ethnic lines. Burundi's rulers, until the 1990s, consistently refused to implement a multiparty political system on the grounds that every ethnic group would have its own party, fragmenting the country. Indeed, the constitution enacted in March of 1992 specifically banned single-ethnicity parties. The ethnic dimension of politics remains an explosive issue. For example, in June 1993, following Ndadaye's (a Hutu) win of the presidency (with 71 percent of the vote, mostly from Hutus), Tutsi students and civil servants demonstrated in Bujumura, the capital, to protest the "ethnic sentiments" of the vote.

HUTU RADICALISM

While Tutsi elites hold primary responsibility for the mass killings which have taken place in Burundi since independence, it must be remembered that the Hutu community has harbored a dangerous radical element dedicated to provoking conflict. Particularly pernicious has been the role played by the radical Party for the Liberation of the Hutu People (Palipehutu), which was founded in the 1980s. Typical Palipehutu tactics were demonstrated in November 1991, when the group launched attacks in northern towns in the hope of provoking a general Hutu uprising (300 Tutsi civilians were left dead and 1,000 Hutus were killed by the army). In April 1992, Palipehutu rebels invaded Cibitoke province from their sanctuaries in Rwanda. In response, the government initiated a large-scale anti-rebel offensive. Small-scale incursions have also been made into Burundi by Hutu exiles operating out of Tanzania.

In April 1994, following the assassination of (Hutu) President Ntaryamira, media reports cited the existence of an apparently newly formed Hutu "Armee

For additional analytical, marketing, investment and business opportunities information, please contact
Global Investment & Business Center, USA
(202) 546-2103. Fax: (202) 546-3275. E-mail: rusric@erols.com

Populaire" (People's Army) operating in the Kamenge region north of the capital. In many cases, the sinister strategy of Hutu extremists has been to target Tutsi civilians with the knowledge that the Tutsi security forces will respond with massive attacks on Hutu civilians, thus provoking a cycle of violence.

THE WEST AND INTERNATIONAL ORGANIZATIONS

For decades it has been obvious that Burundi has been a potential locale for genocide. Indeed in 1972 and 1988 mass murder occurred while the international community watched but did little to stop the killings. As Minority Rights Group observed in 1982: "The apparent indifference of the international community, especially that of Western governments, may be explained by a deeply-rooted and guilt-based fear of censuring the conduct of nations in the developing world. This is no less the case today. The virtual absence of international protest at the time surely encouraged the government to pursue its discriminatory policies. While the official version [of 1972] is barely plausible to impartial observers, Burundi's bilateral and multilateral relations have not been affected." While international protests in 1988 were more numerous (particularly by the US Congress), a coordinated effort was not undertaken under international auspices to alleviate Burundi's ethnic divide.

Belgium and France have played a similar role in Burundi as they have in Rwanda. After independence, the armed forces relied heavily on Belgium for advisors and equipment. To its credit, Belgium did terminate its security cooperation pact with Burundi after 1972, but the French stepped in and provided military assistance during and after the killings of that year. As of 1987, France and Burundi still maintained a military training agreement, and it was only in 1993 that France offered to help reform the armed forces.

During the killings of 1988, the State Department departed from its previous statements blaming both sides for killing civilians, and specifically charged the army with initiating large scale killings. Later, the US House of Representatives voted 415-0 for a non-binding resolution condemning ethnic violence in Burundi and urging the government to step up efforts at achieving national reconciliation. More importantly was a threatened cut-off of American aid. This action by the Congress, combined with considerable State Department pressure, apparently helped convince President Buyoya that an investigation was needed of his country's ethnic problems.

While individual nations have generally remained passive in reacting to developments in Burundi, so too has the United Nations. There were no UN sanctions or investigations of the 1988 massacres. After massacres began again in October 1993, the UN refused to send peacekeepers to the country (in the Security Council, the US argued against such a mission, fearing it would be an

For additional analytical, marketing, investment and business opportunities information, please contact
Global Investment & Business Center, USA
(202) 546-2103. Fax: (202) 546-3275. E-mail: rusric@erols.com

open-ended commitment with no definite plan for withdrawal). If the UN response to Burundi's conflicts has been inadequate, then the Organization of African Unity (OAU) played its traditional low key role as well. Prevented by its charter from interfering in the internal affairs if member states, the OAU has never inserted itself successfully into an internal conflict. As an organization, the OAU is officially designated as a collective of heads of government, and hence has traditionally supported the party in power. In fact, the OAU supported Burundi after the 1972 killings and after the initial massacres of 1988. Although in 1993 and 1994 the OAU debated peacekeeping forces for both Rwanda and Burundi (a small contingent was deployed in Rwanda and later withdrawn), in February 1994 the OAU set aside plans for a peacekeeping force for Burundi.

COMMUNAL CONFLICT IN BURUNDI, 1988-94

Perhaps the central event which defines relations between Hutus and Tutsis in Burundi is the genocide of 1972, which still resonates in the national consciousness. Tutsi intellectuals see Burundi's genocide of 1972 as the natural consequence of a Hutu conspiracy to exterminate all Tutsi. Mirroring this attitude, Hutu activists advance the concept of grand Tutsi strategy stemming from 1972 to eliminate Hutus, the so called "Simbananiye plan" (named after a notorious Tutsi hardliner). Unlike 1972, however, Burundi's communal conflict of the last six years has not been nearly so deliberate. Twenty-two years ago, Hutu elements did indeed attempt to overthrow the state, which provoked a massive retaliation by Tutsi authorities directed by the highest echelons of government. In the 1988 massacres, in contrast, the violence was more indiscriminant and localized. In 1988, Hutus in various communities assaulted local officials, which prompted Tutsi to massacre civilians in response. One theory of the violence has it that the massacres may have resulted from a government crackdown on coffee smuggling in the north, which Hutus misinterpreted as the opening phase of ethnic slaughter.

Another qualitative difference in Burundi's most recent phase of violence (1988-94) is that it has taken place in a context of reforms of the political system. In the late 1980s, there was great discord among ruling elites after Buyoya seized power in military coup in September 1987 and initiated a "liberalization" program. Buyoya's reforms, although they were limited and cautious, raised the ire of Tutsi harlinders at the same time that they lifted Hutu expectations to new heights. Similarly, in 1993 President Ndadaye (a Hutu) undertook to transform the country's political structures by naming a female Tutsi Prime Minister and opening the government to all groups.

Although genocide has not occurred in Rwanda since 1988, the potential for such an episode remains extreme. In 1990, communal violence led to 3,000 deaths, with 50,000 refugees fleeing into Rwanda. The next year, in November,

For additional analytical, marketing, investment and business opportunities information, please contact
Global Investment & Business Center, USA
(202) 546-2103. Fax: (202) 546-3275. E-mail: rusric@erols.com

simultaneous attacks by Palipehutu rebels in Cibitoke and Kaynaza provinces resulted in 3,000 deaths and 50,000 refugees into Rwanda and Zaire. In May 1992, the government put down a coup attempt by rebellious soldiers. Later, in a reshuffling of the government Hutus received 60 percent of cabinet positions. Most threatening of all, in October 1993 disaffected military forces revolted, resulting in the death of President Ndadaye (a Hutu). Clashes between Hutus and Tutsi, including Tutsi-dominated military units, began.

Three waves of killings were reported in October 1993: Tutsi soldiers against Hutu civilians, Hutus against Tutsi, and Tutsi against Hutu. Both Hutu and Tutsi's engaged in the massacre of innocent civilians with an estimated number of deaths of 150,000 plus an additional 800,000 to one million refugees fleeing into Rwanda, Tanzania, Zaire. 100,000 were internally displaced. The coup received widespread condemnation and quickly collapsed. Loyal military officers urged civilians to resume control. A period of extreme unease with isolated killings continued to prevail until April 6, 1994, when Presidents Ntaryamira of Burundi and Habyarimana of Rwanda (both Hutus) were killed when the airplane they were aboard was shot down by a rocket near Kigali, capital of Rwanda. While genocide occurred in Rwanda, only sporadic violence transpired in Burundi.

ATTEMPTS TO RECONCILE THE REGIME AND ITS OPPONENTS

Reform efforts before 1988 usually consisted of hollow appeals for unity with little or no substantive follow through. An exception occurred in 1977, when President Bagaza's land reforms ended the system of Tutsi feudal landlords. Nevertheless, urgently needed modifications in the political system have typically been thwarted by Tutsi fears that, if they give up their hold on power, a process will be initiated under which they will be physically exterminated by vengeful Hutus. Yet President Buyoya sought to transform the system in a lasting manner by with the following measures: giving an equal number of cabinet positions to Hutus and Tutsis; recruiting more Hutus into the civil service; naming a Hutu Prime Minister; establishing a national commission to study ethnic violence (described as a commission on "national unity", the euphemism for problems of ethnicity); repealing anti-Catholic Church policies; and in a symbolic gesture, recruiting Hutus into the President's personal guard. Despite Buyoya's apparently genuine efforts, local Tutsi administrators continued their repressive and discriminatory activities against Hutus.

Buyoya encouraged additional measures to bring his country's contending communal and political factions together. In February 1991, a "National Unity Charter" was endorsed by 89.1% of voters. The Charter called for ending military rule, restoring the constitution, and ensuring harmony between Hutu and Tutsi. One month later, a National Unity Code was issued which pledged equal rights

For additional analytical, marketing, investment and business opportunities information, please contact
Global Investment & Business Center, USA
(202) 546-2103. Fax: (202) 546-3275. E-mail: rusric@erols.com

for Hutus, Tutsis, and Twas and condemned political violence. The Code was prepared by a committee of national reconciliation composed of politicians, church figures, and regular citizens. The next year, in March, a new constitution was adopted which vested executive power in a directly-elected president who serves for 5 years. Ethnically-based political movements were banned under this constitution, hence parties had to pledge support for the concept of "national unity," recruit membership from every province, and reflect the ethnic diversity of Burundi. With the new constitution in place, the framework for elections was set, and they were held in June 1993.

For the first time in the country's history, Burundians exercised their right to change government by democratic means in a free and fair election. Ndadaye, a Hutu, won the presidency. The surprise with which many ruling Tutsi greeted Ndadaye victory suggests that many of them believed their own propaganda that Burundi had not ethnic fault lines. In order to reassure nervous Tutsis, the new President quickly named one of their number as Prime Minister. In addition, 9 out of 23 cabinet seats were reserved for Tutsis. Ndadaye was assassinated in October 1993, an act which inevitably led to widespread strife. On 13 January 1994 the Catholic Church, often divided along ethnic lines during violence, brokered a constitutional settlement between competing factions.

WHY GENOCIDE IN RWANDA AND NOT IN BURUNDI?

A key question given the parallels between Rwanda and Burundi is why, after the assassination of the Presidents in April 1994, Rwanda rapidly sank into genocide while Burundi remained relatively stable. Several theories can be advanced. First, since the late 1980s a process of democratization has existed in Burundi, although it is far from complete. For example, there were widespread killings in Burundi following the November assassination of the first Hutu President. However, the degree to which these were coordinated or spontaneous is not clear, and it may be that important elements of the armed forces in Burundi were not willing to engage in genocide. Unlike the Tutsi regime in Burundi, Habyarimana only engaged in a showcase form of liberalization to buy off opponents and placate foreign observers.

Another possible explanation for the explosion in Rwanda and the relative calm of Burundi (to date) may be that the example of the former inhibited the latter. There is evidence to support this argument. For example, a recent attempt by elements of the Burundi military to stage a coup were decisively rebuffed by a majority of the troops, who may have feared a spiral of violence in its wake.

The best explanation for the difference between the two countries is probably that the Rwandan genocide was the result of an organized conspiracy. After the death of the President, roadblocks were quickly established by Hutu militias, the

For additional analytical, marketing, investment and business opportunities information, please contact
Global Investment & Business Center, USA
(202) 546-2103. Fax: (202) 546-3275. E-mail: rusric@erols.com

Presidential Guard went on search and destroy operations in the capital based on prepared "hit lists" (the Prime Minister was killed and three Cabinet members were arrested). A radical Hutu radio (known as "Mille Collines", or "a thousand hills") incited ethnic slaughter (in these broadcasts, Tutsi were described as "foreigners" from Ethiopia, and Hutus were urged to throw Tutsi in Rivers so that they would float back to their true home). In addition, simultaneous outbreaks of violence were reported throughout the country, which indicated that a coordinated scheme was in place. Appropriately, Alison des Forges has called Rwanda a "highly centralized execution of genocide."

The destabilizing potential of spillover effects from Rwanda remains extreme in Burundi. In 1993, Burundi hosted almost 300,000 refugees from Rwanda. One month after the assassination of the Presidents, the press reported that there were 100,000 Rwandan refugees in Burundi, with 27,000 in the Myanga province alone. Ominously, there were stories in March 1994 that Rwandan Tutsi refugees were assisting the Burundi army (composed of Tutsis) to commit killings in the capital.

RISK ASSESSMENT

Before it is possible to be reasonably optimistic about Burundi's future, the central role played by ethnicity must be acknowledged before meaningful reforms can proceed. Under various Tutsi regimes, official ideology dictated that there were no internal divisions in society, except when invented by subversives. Interestingly, when Hutus took power in 1993, they were obliged to downplay Hutu-Tutsi differences and emphasize national unity for fear of provoking a Tutsi reaction. In this climate, sustainable solutions for Burundi are burdened with risks. Intermarriage and geographic mingling render proposals to partition the country between the communal groups highly problematic. Proportional representation in the political system will not be accepted by Tutsi since it would automatically lead to Hutu domination, which they equate with Tutsi extermination. For these reasons, a "trend toward ethnic depolarization" predicted by Lemarchand in 1992 does not seem likely to occur in the near future.

In 1994-1995, Burundi did not explode into civil war or large-scale ethnic slaughter as did neighboring Rwanda. However, conditions in the country point to a genocide in the making: a post-colonial history of bitter ethnic rivalry, violence, and genocide; military and security forces under the control of one group (the Tutsi); repeated political crises over the composition of the government; a constant cycle of murders and revenge-killings; and the existence of extremist Hutu and Tutsi militias. Although the democratic order which brought President Melchior Ndadaye (a Hutu) to power in June 1993 survived his assassination in

For additional analytical, marketing, investment and business opportunities information, please contact
Global Investment & Business Center, USA
(202) 546-2103. Fax: (202) 546-3275. E-mail: rusric@erols.com

October of the same year, this victory was tenuous at best. Despite limited efforts at amelioration, the vicious ethnic divide remains unsolved. The basic political dilemma of Burundi is that democracy inevitably leads to Hutu ascendancy commensurate with their numerical superiority, even while the mechanisms of coercion, particularly the military, remain solidly within the Tutsi sphere of competence. As a US State Department report concluded: "Burundi's fundamental problem continues to be ethnic conflict between majority Hutus, who gained political power only with the election of Ndadaye, and minority Tutsis, who have historically held power and still control the military and dominate educated society. De facto ethnic discrimination against Hutus - 85 percent of the population - colors every facet of society and institutions, including the military and the judicial establishment..."

Following Ndadaye's death (10/93) and the concomitant political turmoil, security conditions precluded a new presidential election. Instead, prolonged negotiations resulted in a power-sharing agreement (1/94) between the Hutu dominated FRODEBU (Front for Democracy in Burundi, legalized in 1992) and the Tutsi dominated UPRONA (Party for Unity and Progress in Burundi, the former ruling group). Under the accord, Hutu Cyprien Ntaryamira became President, but substantial concessions were made for UPRONA representation at the highest levels of government. Following the assassination of Ntaryamira along with Rwanda's president Habyarimana (4/94), Burundi again experienced a volatile political vacuum. A new round of lengthy talks resulted in the appointment (9/94) of Hutu Sylvestre Ntibantuganya as president. Ntibanyuganya was overthrown by former military president Buyoya in June 1996, and fighting between the government and Hutu rebel groups have been on the rise since.

Officially, the Army high command (virtually all Tutsi) has pledged its loyalty to the democratic process and has remained neutral in power-sharing negotiations. In practice, the armed forces constitute the striking force of the Tutsi elite, furnishing that group with political leverage they cannot achieve at the polls. Although desperately needed reform initiatives have been announced for the army, notably an effort to recruit Hutus as Non-Commissioned Officers, it is safe to estimate that in 1994-1995 the army remained approximately 95 percent Tutsi at all ranks. While definite information is lacking, it seems clear that elements of the Tutsi military have collaborated with Tutsi extremists by offering encouragement, information, and arms. Similarly, the US State Department reported that a faction within Burundi's civilian intelligence service was furnishing similar aid to Hutu extremists. Thus, due to both inability and complicity, the authorities have not prevented gross human rights violations by security, military, and militia forces.

Throughout 1994-1995, and again in 1997-98, stories of killings and small-scale massacres have been routine, sometimes appearing on a daily basis. Through

For additional analytical, marketing, investment and business opportunities information, please contact
Global Investment & Business Center, USA
(202) 546-2103. Fax: (202) 546-3275. E-mail: rusric@erols.com

the second half of 1995, news services reported small-scale massacres (with both Tutsis and Hutus as perpetrators), particularly in the environs of Bujumbura, the capital. The level of violence was reflected in a December 1995 report by the medical charity Doctors Without Frontiers which stated that hundreds of people were dying each month in ethnic clashes, with women and children constituting forty percent of the casualties. In addition to random acts of violence, there is some evidence of a more systematic pattern of murders. For example, in August 1995 a high ranking Hutu politician alleged that Tutsi extremists were instituting a coordinated plan to assassinate Hutu officials at the provincial and local levels. Since the June 1996 coup, civilians have died by the thousands in fighting-some as a direct target of government or militia troops. Splits within the Hutu rebel groups have also led to an increase in fighting and in attacks against innocent civilians. Since the end of 1996, the government has adopted a policy of moving villagers into armed protective camps. It is estimated that 350,000 people were living in these camps during 1997. Hutu rebels accuse the government of commiting gross human rights violations in the camps, but independent reports of conditions within the camps are not available.

Chillingly, as in Rwanda, certain Burundi media are explicitly dedicated to inciting vicious ethnic hatred. Such parallels and spillover effects between Rwanda and Burundi are always apparent. For example, currently there are credible reports of collaboration between extremist Hutus of Burundi and Rwanda to destabilize their respective governments. A large number of Rwandan Hutus, many of them members of military and militia units loyal to the former Hutu regime, remain in exile in Burundi and Zaire and are eager to participate in such operations.

One measure of upheaval in Burundi resides with refugee figures: in late 1994 the US Committee for Refugees estimated that there were 400,000 internally displaced people, while 180,000 persons had fled to Zaire and a further 150,000 to Tanzania. Repatriations from these countries began in 1994, and at the end of 1997, it was estimated that over 200,000 refugees remained internally displaced within Burundi, and 260,000 continue to live in Tanzania and Democratic Republic of Congo (former-Zaire).

In the current super-heated political atmosphere of Burundi and the concentration of government attention on fighting rebel groups, the proper investigation and prosecution of perpetrators of the violence is nearly impossible. Hence, murderers operate with impunity and a cycle of revenge-justice prevails. Furthermore, even if the government functioned normally, the theoretically independent judiciary is dominated by Tutsis. The courts, therefore, can hardly claim disinterest in the ethnically-driven crimes which nominally fall under their purview.

For additional analytical, marketing, investment and business opportunities
information, please contact
Global Investment & Business Center, USA
(202) 546-2103. Fax: (202) 546-3275. E-mail: rusric@erols.com

After the 1996 coup, FRODEBU split into two factions: one faction pledged to negotiate with the new government for peace while the other faction, vowed to continue armed resistance to the military ruler. Throughout the second half of 1996, 1997, and into the first half of 1998, fighting continued throughout the country making some areas inaccessible. Thousands were reportedly killed in November-December 1996 when fighting heated up, and reports continued to come in of violence, killings and fleeing. The army adopted a policy of forced relocation of Hutus in late 1996 which led to increased deaths from both the conflict and disease.

Though the government and CNDD have been involved in peace talks since December 1996, agreement on any issues is difficult to establish. It is estimated that 200,000 or more people have been killed in violence in the country since 1993. The most recent attempts at peace negotiations began in ernest in June 1998, but it is unlikely they succeed in ending the conflict, especially since both the opposition and government have internal splits that are based in the issue of negotiations themselves (i.e. some factions oppose peace negotiations altogether).

For additional analytical, marketing, investment and business opportunities information, please contact
Global Investment & Business Center, USA
(202) 546-2103. Fax: (202) 546-3275. E-mail: rusric@erols.com

BURUNDIAN REFUGEES IN TANZANIA: THE KEY FACTOR TO THE BURUNDI PEACE PROCESS

There has been a considerable Burundian refugee population, almost entirely Hutu, in countries neighboring Burundi, and especially Tanzania, since the 1972 mass slaughter of Hutus when 300,000 are reported to have fled. Several smaller periodic outflows of refugees, in 1965, 1969, 1988 and 1991, augmented the 1972 caseload numbers. Though roughly 40,000 refugees repatriated to Burundi in anticipation of the 1993 elections, nearly 240,000 stayed behind. There was another mass exodus of over 400,000 Hutu refugees following the October 1993 crisis. While a large number of refugees subsequently returned, a steady outflow of refugees predominantly from the south continues up to the present day. The refugees are now about 470 000 in Tanzania, which represent more than 7 % of the Burundi population.

Since June 1998, the parties to the Burundi conflict have started peace talks in Arusha under the auspices of former Tanzanian President Julius K. Nyerere. One of the negotiating committees in the talks, Committee IV on Reconstruction and Development, was specifically tasked to find a solution to the refugee plight and allow them to return safely to Burundi and to be restored in their citizen rights. Both the Facilitator, the late Julius Nyerere, and the chair of the Committee IV have visited the camps and supported their participation in the talks. Following those visits, a delegation from the camps attended the June session of the talks.

Prospects for a solution to the plight of the refugees are closely linked to a political settlement in Burundi and now the resolution of the 1998-99 DRC war. The Burundian refugee camps in Tanzania are stigmatised for being highly militarised and for harbouring rebel movements, including CNDD, Palipehutu, and Frolina. This accusation is partly a result of a well waged propaganda campaign by the Buyoya government in Burundi, which claims that Tanzania is not a neutral host for the Arusha peace process; partly a result of Tanzania's own duplicitous policies - Burundi has, since last year, become more insecure with a series of attacks partly staged from Tanzania unleashing new rounds of violence in Southern Burundi between the army and the rebel groups and new influxes of population into Tanzania; and partly a result of the humanitarian community's own chequered past in the region, particularly its experience of the Rwandan refugee camps in Zaire between 1994 and 1996, which included perpetrators of the genocide.

Refugees themselves are also exposed to a situation of high tension and insecurity at the border between the two countries and as a result of the cross-lake military activity due to the Congo war. The FDD rebels have been fighting on Kabila's side since the war broke out in August 1998. With the Agreement for a

For additional analytical, marketing, investment and business opportunities information, please contact
Global Investment & Business Center, USA
(202) 546-2103. Fax: (202) 546-3275. E-mail: rusric@erols.com

Cease-fire in the DRC - which includes a commitment to disarm armed groups, including the Burundian rebels, it is feared that a lot of the rebels have returned to Tanzania from the DRC.

REFUGEE FLOWS INTO TANZANIA

THE 1972 CASELOAD

The 1972 caseload of Burundian refugees fled predominantly to Tanzania, Rwanda and eastern Zaire. In Tanzania, the bulk of the 1972 refugees settled among the local population or in refugee camps that later became permanent settlements in three zones in the Tabora region. In these settlements, Burundian families were each given five hectares of land, became self-reliant cultivators, and enhanced the productivity of the region, which in turn benefited the host population. In Rwanda, however, the Burundian refugees found little land and few opportunities and faced substantial hardship following the 1990 invasion of Rwanda by the Rwandan Patriotic Front (RPF). In Zaire, refugees found greater opportunities and some became rich from the trade in palm oil, ivory, gold and diamonds.

The old caseload refugee population in Tanzania spawned the first organized Hutu armed groups, Palipehutu and Frolina, which launched cross-border incursions against Burundi beginning in the 1980s. Palipehutu branched out to attract a small number of followers in Rwanda and Burundi as well. Frolina drew its support from both refugee and local populations originating almost exclusively from southern Burundi. Both groups recruited from refugee camps and settlements, and carried out active training and small-scale cross-border attacks from the bush not far from their Tanzanian encampments.

In anticipation of the 1993 democratic transition, relief and development agencies sponsored a large, voluntary repatriation of refugees to Burundi, even though many of those who returned had no clear title to land. Some members of Palipehutu and Frolina refused to return to their homeland during these repatriation operations. Instead, they whipped up fears and spread propaganda to enliven the refugees' suspicions of both the UNHCR repatriation program, and the trustworthiness of the Burundian government. However, others returned and participated in the presidential campaign as FRODEBU militants. FRODEBU was officialised in 1992, when multipartism was introduced, but Palipehutu remained clandestine. The assassination of Melchior Ndadaye, the first democratically elected Hutu president on 21 October 1993 triggered massive massacres of Tutsis, soon followed by a violent repression of the army on the Hutus. The presidential campaign had been ethnicised by both sides, and Palipehutu members were later accused of mobilising the Hutus on racist themes.

For additional analytical, marketing, investment and business opportunities
information, please contact
Global Investment & Business Center, USA
(202) 546-2103. Fax: (202) 546-3275. E-mail: rusric@erols.com

THE CONSEQUENCES OF THE 1993 CRISIS IN BURUNDI

As a result of the October 1993 crisis, hundreds of thousands of Hutu refugees, fearing reprisals from the Burundian military fled again for their lives into neighboring countries. Many of the refugees from the previous 1972 caseload, especially those who had lost relatives, bitterly complained that they were duped by the international community into believing that it had been safe for them to return to Burundi. Furthermore, the mass exodus far exceeded the capacity of existing relief operations to respond, leading to mortality rates more than twice the number considered "acceptable" for complex emergencies. This scenario enabled both Palipehutu and Frolina to once again draw considerable support from the refugee population in western Tanzania.

In early 1994, following a lull in the violence, large numbers of refugees in Tanzania who had fled in 1993 began to return out of concern that they would lose their harvests or their land. However, civil war intensified at the end of 1994, and there was an additional outflow of refugees into Tanzania resulting from ongoing violence and instability in the northern provinces of Burundi.

FROM RWANDA TO ZAIRE: THE REFUGEE CAMPS AS A BASE FOR THE HUTU INSURGENCY

Some Burundian refugees who fled to Rwanda following the 1993 October crisis are known to have participated in the 1994 Rwandan genocide in areas near their settlements. These "refugees" were forced to flee again during the mass exodus of Rwandan Hutus into eastern Zaire in the aftermath of the genocide. Some of those refugees have already returned to Burundi. Most preferred to stay in eastern Zaire and were organized into approximately 11 camps along an 80-kilometer stretch of South Kivu on the Burundian border. Others lived in and around the towns of Bukavu and Uvira. Some of these refugees lived among five camps where Rwandan refugees were also living. In these mixed camps, Burundians and Rwandans forged a military alliance, which later became a major source of instability for both countries.

A growing Burundian insurgency operating from the refugee camps in eastern Zaire gained international notoriety for its ongoing military co-operation with the Rwandan génocidaires. During the early period of their exile in eastern Zaire, the Burundians depended on members of the former ex-FAR and allied Interahamwe militias for arms, training, logistical support and joint military operations. Together, these rebel allies organized a military campaign with the intention of creating a Hutu zone inside northern Burundi from where they could launch their respective guerrilla campaigns. With the growth of the CNDD/FDD (Centre for the Defence of Democracy with its armed wing, the Forces for the Defence of Democracy created in September 1994) movement out of eastern Zaire, the

For additional analytical, marketing, investment and business opportunities information, please contact
Global Investment & Business Center, USA
(202) 546-2103. Fax: (202) 546-3275. E-mail: rusric@erols.com

Burundians eventually attracted their own political and military backers and established separate arms and logistical pipelines.

When Buyoya took power for the second time in Burundi in a 1996 coup, Burundian and Rwandan Hutu rebel insurgency operations launched from eastern Zaire were in full gear. Sporadic attacks, in the south by Frolina and in the north by Palipehutu, and regular ambushes and military operations by the FDD had destabilised 13 out of the 15 provinces. Both Frolina and Palipehutu splinter groups operated from small bases within Tanzania, in the Kigoma and Ngara districts respectively.

The autumn 1996 launch of the ADFL rebellion in eastern Zaire squashed the Hutu rebellion for a time. In late September 1996, the refugee and Hutu insurgency camps in South Kivu were attacked by the combined force of the Rwandan, Burundian and Ugandan armies and the ostensibly Banyamulenge-led ADFL rebels. The Burundian refugees and rebels were the first victims. As a result, the Burundian exiled population in Zaire was dispersed. Many refugees were forced back into Burundi where they were killed by the Burundian army. It was some time before the rebels were able to re-establish themselves in neighboring countries, such as Tanzania and, to a far lesser degree Zaire, and regroup for their military effort.

TANZANIA'S RESPONSE TO REFUGEE CRISIS

The spillover of the Rwandan, Burundian and Zairian conflicts into western Tanzania increased tensions within Tanzania as well. Tanzanian authorities faced domestic pressure to address the instability, crime and environmental degradation caused by the immense refugee populations.

THE EXPULSION OF RWANDAN REFUGEES FROM TANZANIA IN 1996

Tanzania unfairly came under international scrutiny for allowing the Rwandan génocidaires to use its territory as a base for launching renewed attacks against Rwanda. Tanzania loathed being perceived as harboring génocidaires and international fugitives. The Rwandan refugees also embarrassed Tanzania with their political agitation in the camps. Despite persistent lobbying efforts, it was some time before Tanzania was granted funding and logistical support from the donor community to deploy police to monitor security in the Rwandan refugee camps. By late 1996, international opprobrium and donor fatigue over assistance to the Rwandan refugees had grown to an unmanageable point. Tanzania felt pressure to collude with the Rwandan government in forcibly expelling over 250,000 Rwandan refugees in December 1996, some of whom had lived in Tanzania since the 1960s.

For additional analytical, marketing, investment and business opportunities information, please contact
Global Investment & Business Center, USA
(202) 546-2103. Fax: (202) 546-3275. E-mail: rusric@erols.com

Tanzania's reputation as one of the most generous asylum countries was severely tarnished by the expulsion of Rwandan refugees in December 1996, following the closing of its border in March 1995 to Burundian and Rwandan refugees fleeing Burundi in clear violation of the 1951 UN Refugee Convention. In its defence, Tanzania claimed that its resources had been over-stretched and insecurity on its western frontier had become untenable.

Shortly thereafter in May, Tanzania deployed troops to its border with Burundi, citing concern over Burundian troop pursuits of refugees, and insecurity resulting from refugee influxes. By July, both Tanzania and Burundi had deployed significant numbers of troops along their mutual border. During this period, only handfuls of Burundians managed to cross into Tanzania and those caught were sometimes forcibly repatriated. UNHCR and NGOs providing relief assistance in western Tanzania were barred from certain border areas. By 1996, Tanzania claimed to be in a military state of high alert. The military build-up on Tanzania's western border still remains in effect.

TANZANIA'S ATTITUDE TOWARDS BURUNDIAN REFUGEES

Tanzania's view of the Burundian refugees and rebellion was different from its view of the Rwandan refugees. Following the 1996 Buyoya coup, Tanzania shifted towards increased sympathy for the Burundian rebellion out of a sense of growing solidarity, and an intention to bring the Buyoya regime to its knees. At that point, Julius Nyerere took the lead to impose sanctions on the Buyoya regime.

Initially, Tanzanian officials welcomed the newly arriving, beleaguered Hutu refugees and rebels. However, not long after their arrival, Tanzanians were heard chastising themselves for having "mistakenly" failed the Hutu rebellion in the past. Still influenced by their former panafricanist perspective, Tanzanian authorities likened the Hutu rebellion to the South African "liberation" movement against the former apartheid regime. Officials stated that the Hutus should have received robust Tanzanian backing similar to what was given to the southern African liberation movements and Museveni's forces in their overthrow of Uganda's previous brutal regime.

The association between Tanzanian and Burundian armed groups dates back to the period after 1972 when Burundians began to settle in western Tanzania. A certain number of exiles even served in the Tanzanian People's Defence Forces. Others who had previously served in the Burundian army established their own armed groups and orchestrated small scale rebel attacks from Tanzanian soil. Both Palipehutu and Frolina forces have maintained bases in Tanzania since the early 1980's. Although Tanzanian authorities intermittently jailed rebel leaders or clamped down on their militant activities, for the most part they looked the other way. The Burundian Hutus spoke the same language and shared ethnic and

For additional analytical, marketing, investment and business opportunities information, please contact
Global Investment & Business Center, USA
(202) 546-2103. Fax: (202) 546-3275. E-mail: rusric@erols.com

family ties with Tanzanians on the other side of border, and the Hutu cause was often sympathetically viewed as "just". Solidarity with the Hutu cause grew immensely after the October 1993 crisis. Burundian rebels received limited military assistance and political support even while Tanzania denied asylum to new hordes of Burundian refugees.

THE 1997 ROUND-UPS OF BURUNDIAN REFUGEES AS A RESPONSE TO INTERNATIONAL CRITICISM

As long as the Rwandan refugees remained in Tanzania, the Tanzanian government was accused of allowing the camps to be used for the shelter, recruitment and launching of cross-border attacks by genocidal groups. Tanzanians rightly argued that the accusations were unfair since the humanitarian community was equally at fault and since Tanzania itself was destabilised by these militant activities. However once the Rwandans were expelled, Tanzania came under further scrutiny for similar activities in the remaining Burundian refugee camps. After the forced expulsion of Burundian refugees from eastern Zaire, and the onset of the ADFL rebellion in 1996, vast numbers fled anew to western Tanzania. Among the civilians were a large number of Burundian rebels who later used Tanzania as a base to regroup and mobilise their insurgency.

At the height of its frustration with the international community over criticism, initiated by the Burundian government, that it was hosting the Burundian rebellion, the Tanzanians launched a massive "round-up" of most Burundians living outside of refugee camps or settlements. The round up included Burundians that had lived independently in Tanzania since the 1960s, as well as the 1972 caseload. Many of these Burundians had settled in villages, married local Tanzanians and integrated effectively into the local society. Local Tanzanians, many with shared ethnic or family relations, depended on Burundian labor, initiative and skills. The Burundians had helped local economies grow, eking out marketable crops from previously unproductive and disused land. During the round-ups, many of these Burundians were forced from their homes, separated from spouses and family, and often not even give the opportunity to collect their belongings. Adding further to the resentment, Burundians who could afford to pay bribes to local authorities or police were sometimes released. Only recently has the Tanzanian government begun to acknowledge the protests of the old caseload refugees about their unexpected forced encampment.

Burundian refugees began to fear the capriciousness of the Tanzanian authorities. Refugees often expressed their concern and confusion to ICG representatives over the round-ups: "The government put us in the camps. We don't know why they put us in the camps." Some Burundian refugees speculated that the Burundian government had paid the Tanzanians off, particularly as many Tanzanian officials were subsequently transferred. With the Rwandan example

For additional analytical, marketing, investment and business opportunities information, please contact
Global Investment & Business Center, USA
(202) 546-2103. Fax: (202) 546-3275. E-mail: rusric@erols.com

on their minds, many refugees hold the view that Tanzania might at any time forcibly repatriate them back to Burundi. The round-ups further instilled within the refugees a will to reclaim or fight for their own homeland. It is unclear whether Tanzania intended the round ups to further militarise the exiled Burundian population.

THE REFUGEE SITUATION

CURRENT FLOWS AND CONDITION OF REFUGEES INTO WESTERN TANZANIA

Refugee flows into the Kigoma region of western Tanzania are sorely under-reported by sources other than UNHCR and IRIN. Travel to and around the camps is difficult. Very few foreign journalists travel to western Tanzania, and the Tanzanian journalists that come out from Dar Es Salaam are less focused on the refugee issue.

UNHCR estimates that a total of 288,000 Burundian refugees are currently residing in neighboring countries . The vast majority totaling 266,000, are in western Tanzania. Refugees in Kigoma district number 158,000, while the total in Ngara is 110,000. In 1998, it was estimated that a total of 12,817 refugees returned to Burundi from Tanzania, of which 2,276 participated in UNHCR organized returns.

Refugees from Burundi continue to flee into western Tanzania, mainly driven by fighting in the southern Burundian provinces of Rumonge, Nyanza Lac, Bururi, and Makamba as well as Bujumbura Rural. All Burundians fleeing their homeland immediately receive prima facie refugee status with minimal screening for personal data and reasons for flight. Some exiles from the south are rebels or displaced persons from other provinces ranging as far as Bubanza. Because there is a repatriation program from western Tanzania, mainly back to the two key provinces of Ruyigi and Cankuzo, some outside observers assume that there has been no overall increase in refugees. Other factors contributing to the confusion of refugee flows are: the flight of Congolese refugees into northern Burundi from the war in the DRC, and the return of Burundian refugees from the DRC after the outbreak of hostilities in August 1998.

The majority of refugees who fled Burundi in the first half of 1998 were reported to be men. These male refugees told UNHCR that they were fleeing because they had become targets and that they had left women and children behind. During the second half of the year, more families began to arrive as the military intensified attacks on villages. Most refugees are now reported to be children. While ICG was in the region in the autumn of 1998, refugees were reported to be arriving at twice the normal weekly rate, which humanitarians workers considered a rather "big influx." As a result of recent fighting and regroupment policy of the

For additional analytical, marketing, investment and business opportunities information, please contact
Global Investment & Business Center, USA
(202) 546-2103. Fax: (202) 546-3275. E-mail: rusric@erols.com

government of Burundi, the influx of refugees has increased in October and November 1999.

ICG visited all of the Kigoma transit sites and interviewed many refugees. Several way stations were near the border area close to Kasulu and were difficult to access by road. At these sites, the refugees were first cared for by religious charities until they could be attended to by UNHCR staff. The Kibondo station was close to the border and well attended to by humanitarian staff, especially since there was an active repatriation program underway. The most troubling way station was a collection point, which refugees reached by boat, but which was inaccessible to UNHCR and other humanitarian organizations (except for the local Caritas agency). This was the main entry point for those fleeing southern Burundi, including most of the young men. These refugees were fed limited rations by a local Caritas parish, and were transported by boat to Kiberizi only when their numbers reached a critical mass. Medical staff expressed grave concerns that starving and injured refugees had to "first manage the trek, then the transit."

The outlying stations are problematic since most of the refugees arrive in bad physical condition. For several months, the humanitarian staff repeated that refugees arrive in conditions more destitute than they had seen before. They are severely malnourished; many face acute starvation. It is apparent that refugees are hiding in the bush for long periods of time before making their way into Tanzania. Some refugees stay hidden until they think either the military or fighting has moved on; some do not know a way out and wait for safe escort; some await rebels to escort them around land mines and booby traps; and still others hide from the rebels. Some refugees believe that they are being prevented from leaving, though the causes for this were difficult to ascertain.

Refugees are arriving with numerous mine and other conflict-related wounds. Humanitarian staff report receiving large numbers of seriously injured refugees who "first spent some time in the bush with their fresh injuries before reaching us. Most of the injured are young males between 16-30 years of age. Some with only mild war injuries are able to reach the camps before being hospitalized. The seriously injured arrive with complicated bone injuries due to bullets and land mines. The gunshot wounds treated by one doctor were most often in the stomach and chest. Medical staff reports that one out of ten of the war injured are landmine victims. Those with machete wounds rarely survive the arduous journey out of Burundi. As one doctor remarked, "we don't get many machete wounds because they can't make it here alive. They either die from the injury or are more easily finished off."

The refugees, local population and humanitarian staff all expressed grave concern over land mines. One group of refugees encountered land mines while

For additional analytical, marketing, investment and business opportunities information, please contact
Global Investment & Business Center, USA
(202) 546-2103. Fax: (202) 546-3275. E-mail: rusric@erols.com

fleeing towards a way station south of Kasulu. Tanzanians who cross into Burundi to do business have been injured or killed by mines. Based on his experience, a security officer reported that "there are mines planted by the Burundian military all over the border area." Many in peril of starvation and additional attacks remain hidden in Burundi waiting for rebels to show them a way out around the mines.

Refugees are fleeing Burundi for a host of reasons. Some refugees in the north and centre of the country, particularly from Gitega and Ruyigi, are trying to escape forced participation in joint civilian military patrols; these refugees are fearful of summary execution by the military, and attacks by rebels who disapprove of the patrols or ambushes on the front line. People from Kayanza said that they fled after their entire villages were destroyed. Other refugees say they fled from internally displaced camps where they were starving

Those in the south fled fighting between the military and rebels or from fear of reprisals by the military. Refugees from Makamba were reportedly told by both sides of the conflict to leave their villages and flee to Tanzania. Refugees from the south reported that "much of Makamba had been wiped out." Many young men felt that they were not safe from either side. Some said they had followed Burundian government orders to save their lives and were then targeted by rebels for collaboration. Most young men interviewed said they were fleeing round-ups by the military of Hutu men in villages. They said these round-ups resulted in either execution or imprisonment (and torture). One group of refugees described their ordeal; "They take some of the young boys in round-ups and then burn and bomb [using grenades] others. Whole villages are being burned. The young men are dealt with separately." One humanitarian security officer claimed that based on his experiences with the fleeing refugees there was a "clear sign that genocide" was being committed in southern Burundi.

Others have told ICG that they were forced to flee by the rebels, and that they were used as human shields by the rebels on their way to the Tanzanian border. The refugees fleeing from the South come in two waves. Many arrive quickly after fresh fighting. The rest stayed hidden in the bush until they could find a safe escort out of the country.

More recently, refugees claim to flee Burundi for three reasons: they are afraid of regroupment camps; they see the army distributing weapons to the Tutsi population; and they flee forced enrolment of young men by Hutu rebellion.

REPATRIATION OF THE REFUGEES

On the basis of a Tripartite Agreement between UNHCR, Burundi and Tanzania, signed on 12 March 1998, UNHCR is facilitating voluntary repatriation from the Kibondo district in Tanzania to Ruyigi inside Burundi. The program is in response

For additional analytical, marketing, investment and business opportunities
information, please contact
Global Investment & Business Center, USA
(202) 546-2103. Fax: (202) 546-3275. E-mail: rusric@erols.com

to refugees who have expressed a desire to be repatriated, as well as UNHCR's positive security assessment and absence of regroupment camps in homeland provinces. There is no such facilitation from Ngara, which is close enough to the border for spontaneous repatriation, or Kasulu district because the provinces of origin are too insecure. 23,000 were repatriated to Burundi during 1998 and a further 4,978 were repatriated between January and April 1999.

The UN Secretary General has used the dialogue over humanitarian needs to manage the continuing tensions between Burundi and Tanzania. In 1998 and in 1999, Madame Ogata traveled to the region to hear the perspectives of both governments and to visit refugee sites. The Burundian government was successful in presenting its views on the militarization of the camps. The Burundians wanted UNHCR to move from simply facilitating to actually promoting repatriation, but UNHCR remained committed to working out modalities only for "spontaneous" repatriation. The Burundian government sought permission for regular, official visits to Tanzania. It also called on UNHCR to conduct organized information visits to Burundi by the refugees in the camps. Neither idea received warm support from Tanzania. To push its point, the Burundian government also asked UNHCR and the Tanzanian government to halt the actions of "intimidators" who then agreed were impeding repatriation. While the meeting addressed but did not resolve all sensitive issues, it produced the added benefit of building confidence and opening better lines of communication between the two countries. It also established blueprints for an organized repatriation program. A second tripartite meeting was scheduled for December 1998 to discuss the practical issues of refugee return. It was cancelled by the Tanzanian government after Bujumbura sent an official note to the Tanzanian government protesting against cross border infiltration. No meeting has been rescheduled yet.

The Kibondo camp staff report that the numbers of "recycled" refugees has dropped since UNHCR organized voluntary repatriation began earlier in 1998. New arrivals to Kibondo must first stop at transit stations for registration, so fewer have tried to cheat their way back into camps. Most of the recyclers from Kibondo have returned because they found their local collines too dangerous or difficult, particularly if their houses had been destroyed, their land seized, or if they had been accused of colluding with the rebels. As of August 1998, UNHCR noticed that it was getting a small number of returnees from the organized repatriation. One humanitarian worker stated that "as soon as we get 300 new arrivals, we send 300 back. They should be talking to each other."

In the first four months of the organized repatriation, mainly women and children returned. Adult men were returning spontaneously on their own, but after the Burundian authorities called for this to cease, more men joined the formal, arranged repatriation.

For additional analytical, marketing, investment and business opportunities information, please contact
Global Investment & Business Center, USA
(202) 546-2103. Fax: (202) 546-3275. E-mail: rusric@erols.com

ARE THE CAMPS IN WESTERN TANZANIA MILITARISED?

Western Tanzania is the central, external base of the Hutu rebellion against the Buyoya regime. As a result of the escalating regional conflict in August 1998, FDD rebel forces quickly moved to the DRC to support the Kabila government against the Congolese rebels backed by Rwanda, Uganda and Burundi. Since the Agreement for a Cease-fire in the DRC was signed in Lusaka in July 1999, a good number of FDD fighters have gone back to Tanzania and the level of military activity there has increased again. While bases in the interior of Burundi remain critical, Western Tanzania is a focal point for key activities of the rebellion including: military mobilisation, recruitment, training, fund-raising, political strategizing, communications, arms trafficking, resource distribution, medical treatment, naval operations and the launching of cross-border attacks, all of which ICG analysts observed. A few of these activities occur in refugee camps sheltering the Burundians, however, most of the more militant activities occur outside the domain of the camps. Given the large number of Burundian refugees in western Tanzania, it can be expected that such activities would take place. For the most part, these Burundians aspire to return to their homeland and reclaim their rights, and, if necessary are ready to use force to achieve these goals. Many see the rebellion as the only defense for those left behind. Others say they have little to lose and may as well die fighting inside Burundi.

It is not difficult to meet with many of the rebel leaders and their troops outside of the refugee camps in western Tanzania. Meetings within the refugee camps were more difficult to arrange given the policies of the Tanzanian Ministry of Home Affairs (MHA) and the proclivities of the camp management staff. Much of the rebel leadership operated outside of the camps where they were able to move about freely, albeit often secretly. According to various rebel factions, the Tanzanian government will not let them carry out military activities openly. In fact, if they are caught they either pay fines or bribes, or are sent to prison, though they claim that recently none have received sentences. The rebels claim they have adapted to Tanzanian politics and operate "quietly" in a "non-visible" way.

OVERVIEW OF THE KIGOMA CAMPS

Currently, UNHCR oversees Burundian refugee camps in the Ngara and Kigoma sub-regions of western Tanzania. Camps in the Kigoma sub-region are located in proximity of the towns of Kigoma, Kasulu and Kibondo. At the time of research, there were six UNHCR way stations for the Kigoma district at Kagunga, Biharu, Manyovu, Kiberizi I, Kiberizi II and Mabamba. The camps in the Kigoma district include: Mtabila I and II, Moyovosi, Nyarugusu, Mkugwa, Nduta, Kanembwe, Mtendeli.

For additional analytical, marketing, investment and business opportunities information, please contact
Global Investment & Business Center, USA
(202) 546-2103. Fax: (202) 546-3275. E-mail: rusric@erols.com

In short, the camps are organized into blocks, streets and plots. In an effort to avoid the pitfalls of the Rwandan camps, the Burundian refugees are not organized according to their communes of origin. New arrivals are assigned to the next available plot, and family reunification is not initiated until after a refugee is screened and settled. Block and street leaders are chosen in yearly elections organized by UNHCR and the Tanzanian MHA. The block leaders are the standard interlocutors between the refugee community and outsiders. The majority of camp leaders are middle-aged men, but some are women and older men. A group mentality pervades the meetings of the block leaders, some of whom become agitated over outsiders seeking individual appointments or meetings. The considerable level of distrust among various political factions within the refugee camps manifests itself in exchanges between block leaders. Refugee leaders are also organized into security committees, which establish patrols and work to maintain a semblance of order. The "camp leaders" are a mixed lot; some are educated, organized and effective, and others are not. Differences in leadership qualities became apparent during UNHCR registration process in August 1998, when some successfully organized their constituents for the procedure, and others failed.

CAMP MANAGEMENT UNDER UNHCR AND MHA

In general, the Kigoma refugee camps are highly organized and well managed by UNHCR and Ministry of Home Affairs authorities. Staff from UNHCR and MHA attempt to make the camps as successful and comfortable as possible, promoting the welfare of the refugees through women's co-operatives, education programs (although one major complaint of the refugees is that they are not permitted secondary education), horticultural training and community services and other projects. Kigoma is a fairly isolated region with few amenities, an environment that camp staff endure with notable resilience. In contrast, the donor community's frugality and poor resource management has led to unnecessarily high mortality rates in the camps. For example, the inadequate funding of water treatment and malarial eradication programs caused numerous, preventable deaths. Another serious problem has been the overwhelming employment of local Tanzanians on the staffs of UNHCR and NGO implementing partners, at the insistence of the Tanzanian government. The Tanzanian staff are inclined to carry out the agenda of the Tanzanian government, which may not necessarily be aligned with UNHCR. Local staff is also over eager to protect their government, particularly where it concerns issues of security, political expression and militarization.

CAMP SECURITY: THE ROLE OF TANZANIAN POLICE

Both MHA staff and Tanzanian police may live in, or adjacent to, the refugee camps. UNHCR and NGO staff typically reside at considerable distance from the

For additional analytical, marketing, investment and business opportunities
information, please contact
Global Investment & Business Center, USA
(202) 546-2103. Fax: (202) 546-3275. E-mail: rusric@erols.com

camps and must commute using poor roads. Refugees can apply for permits to travel out of the camps for specified periods of time. Otherwise, they are expected to remain within a certain radius of the camp borders. Camp management staff, NGOs and organized refugee committees try to monitor infringements on this policy in an effort to curtail environmental destruction, crime, unruliness, and feuds with local villagers. Within the camps, refugee leaders, assisted by Tanzanian police posted in the camps, often handle domestic disputes and violence. The camps are basically stable, though several human rights and humanitarian agencies have expressed concern over the high level of sexual and gender violence in the camps.

In early August 1998, a contingent of security police mandated by a new UNHCR package deal with the Tanzanians was deployed to the refugee camps in western Tanzania. The security package includes financial incentives and other materials such as tents, vehicles and communications equipment. The Tanzanian camp police live in compounds in the refugee camps and work in conjunction with the Tanzanian district and regional police offices. The new police contingents are tasked with enforcing law and order and maintaining the civilian nature of the camps.

The agreement was called for specifically to counter criticisms that the UN had not been doing enough to secure the civilian nature of the refugee camps. However, the police may be creating a false sense of security. It is not in a strong position to curtail insurgency or criminal activities by refugees who reside outside of the camps, or leave the camps in order to carry them out. The police presence may in fact obscure the fact that the camps provide a base for preparing military excursions.

The police assigned to the camps have a mixed record. For the most part, the policemen are seen as fair, and refugees feel adequately comfortable co-operating with them on matters of justice. There are however considerable complaints that the police steal, bribe and even aggrandize charges against uncooperative refugees. Similar complaints against the police exist within the general Tanzanian population as well. There have been a few cases reported in which police have been bribed to endorse accusations by refugees who falsely accuse their political rivals. At the Kiberizi transit site, ICG observed how the police denied humanitarian workers access to newly arriving refugees so that the police could loot the meagre possessions of the refugees.

THE POLITICAL AND MILITARY NATURE OF THE KIGOMA CAMPS

Like most other refugee camps around the world, the Burundian camps in Tanzania are highly politicized. The Burundian refugees have fled for their lives from a devastating conflict; many have lost relatives, friends, homes and their

For additional analytical, marketing, investment and business opportunities information, please contact
Global Investment & Business Center, USA
(202) 546-2103. Fax: (202) 546-3275. E-mail: rusric@erols.com

possessions. The exile from Burundi, the experience of being a foreigner, and the unpleasant conditions of the refugee camps all serve to nurture their political views. The refugees consist of a cross-section of the wider Burundi population: cultivators, laborers, school teachers, college faculty, lawyers, businessmen and even former politicians and government officials.

Although UNHCR has not adequately collected data on the demographics and origins of the various waves of caseloads, certain trends and patterns can be deduced. For example, the caseload coming from Uvira after the AFDL operation is said to contain a majority of young, militant men. At the time of research, the camps which fall under the most suspicion for sheltering members of armed groups were Mtabila I and II, Moyovosi and Nduta. These camps are said to contain scores of young men, Uvira caseload refugees, refugees forced into camps during the 1997 round-ups and recent arrivals from southern Burundi - all of whom are said to be more volatile.

The Kigoma district camps are situated close to the border area where most of the current military action is taking place in southern Burundi, and all experience heavy traffic in and out of their parameters. Most of the refugees detained for security violations and military activities have come from these particular camps. Other than Nduta, the Kibondo area camps are generally more quiet even though they are receiving increasing numbers of new caseload refugees. The Ngara camps were fairly unstable until 1996. Today a few of the Ngara camps are used by more militant Hutu rebels.

Since 1993, various waves of refugees have brought political changes to the Kigoma area camps. While the region has been traditionally fertile for Palipehutu and Frolina, the CNDD/FDD has come to the fore in the Kigoma region particularly since the 1996 arrival of rebels from their disbanded bases in eastern Zaire. Most of the refugee camps are dominated by one particular group, but they still share turf with representatives and constituencies from the others. There is also considerable internal movement between the different camps. Within the camps, veteran leaders from Palipehutu and Frolina have been forced to share ground with newly emerging ones. At present, CNDD/FDD are known "to be ruling" the majority of newer caseload camps.

The real political authorities in the camp however are not readily apparent; they tend to hide behind the screen of the ostensible "camp" or "zone leaders". In part, this is done to satisfy the Tanzanian authorities and staff managing the camps, who deny any political expression in the camps, even if it is unlikely to lead to violence. The Tanzanian approach has led to various political groups scrambling for ad hoc and murky ways to communicate with foreign observers, diplomats, expatriate staff and NGOs. The prohibition of any form of political activity or identification has created a false environment in the camp.

For additional analytical, marketing, investment and business opportunities
information, please contact
Global Investment & Business Center, USA
(202) 546-2103. Fax: (202) 546-3275. E-mail: rusric@erols.com

MAINTAINING CIVIL ORDER

UNHCR, and to a much lesser extent its implementing partners, have a two fold approach. UNHCR exercises a soft approach for political leaders who make themselves known privately in order to engage with UNHCR. The hard approach is reserved for political and military leaders who do not come forward; if they are caught, they may be turned over to local authorities. The effect of this policy has been to drive the military leaders, a secretive group anyway, further underground. The confusion is compounded by outsiders' attempts to distinguish the political representatives from the military ones. Although formally one may speak of the political and military wings of the various armed parties, in reality, the divisions do not always exist, and there is considerable overlap between the two structures.

UNHCR, MHA, and camp managers are not fully aware of what takes place in the camps both because the camps are quite large and because field officers rarely stay overnight in them. Most camps are several hours from staff residential compounds. Few confidence-building measures are undertaken to engage the refugees in dialogue concerning their political interests. Instead, the priority has been to use iron fist tactics to maintain the civilian nature of the camps. The Tanzanian authorities are summoned if there is any detection of physical conditioning or maneuvers that could be interpreted as military training or for violent incidents of political in fighting. Those overseeing the camps are on constant lookout for activities, which could qualify as fund-raising, taxation, mobilization and recruitment. Accusations of subversive activities have been leveled by one political group at another, and it has been difficult for authorities to determine whether accusations are legitimate or engineered to discredit rivals. Within the past two years (1996-1998), serious security incidents qualifying as military activities numbered less than half a dozen.

Generally, the camps remain "calm and quiet" for long periods of time, and subversive activities are not visible. There have been a few exceptional incidents and heightened periods of tension around key external events. For example, camp witnesses claim that before the January 1998 attack on the airport in Bujumbura, there was a noticeable increase in organized refugee meetings and what appeared to be recruitment activities. In another case, witnesses claim that additional meetings took place and political tension pervaded the camps before the Arusha meetings in June and July 1998. Camp staff report that various groups appeared to be jockeying for stronger positions within the camps in the periods just before and after the Arusha meetings.

In August 1998, ICG observed the mobilization of nearly two thousand refugees for transit from Kigoma to the DRC for military operations (which went largely undetected by humanitarian workers, who attributed camp disappearances to the

For additional analytical, marketing, investment and business opportunities information, please contact
Global Investment & Business Center, USA
(202) 546-2103. Fax: (202) 546-3275. E-mail: rusric@erols.com

problem of recycling). Most camp staff report that the camps have been easy to calm down even after noticeable subversive activities. As one camp manager explained, "the MHA call a meeting, a few people are arrested and the police use intimidation to quiet would-be agitators."

While there has been the occasional confiscation of handguns, locally made guns, bullets and a few rounds of ammunition ? most used for common crimes ? weapons are not generally seen in the camps. Only a few celebrated security incidents have taken place inside the camps. For example, in January 1998 training of Frolina was reported in Nduta camp by a rival political group. In two other instances in 1997 and 1998, men were caught, none with weapons, leaving the perimeters of Moyovosi camp for military training or operations. The men were arrested and went through judicial proceedings. Those who confessed to be combatants were sent to "special" camps, either at Kigowa in the Tabora region or Mwisa in Kagera. The Tanzanian authorities are loathe to create an additional site for "combatants" and prefer instead to send them to "special" camps. The others who did not declare their status as combatants were given suspended sentences for being "illegally in the country" and were then sent back to the refugee camps. The key message was that self-professed or "confirmed" combatants would not be accepted into the regular refugee camps; harsher punishment was unlikely, although small numbers of refugees have served time in the Kigoma prison. In late 1998, a few trucks full of young men were intercepted by the police. The refugees were sentenced for leaving the camps illegally.

THE ISSUE OF POLITICAL EXPRESSION OF THE REFUGEES

It is clear that MHA and Tanzanian camp managers are keen to suppress all forms of political activity. However, the issue of the politicisation of the camps should not be confused with the issue of the civilian nature of the camps. Many policymakers and NGOs have equated politicisation with militarisation. They have therefore been adverse to allowing various forms of political expression within the refugee camps. In fact, many have advocated against any form of political mobilisation. While political agitation may lead to insecurity, the consequences of prohibiting political activities must also be taken into account.

The stifling of political expression could be considered a violation of the rights of the refugees. In any case, it has had the consequence of de-legitimising political activity in the eyes of the refugees and precludes them from playing a productive role in the political resolution of the Burundian conflict. It has also pushed their political activities further underground; meanwhile, hard-liners continue to gain influence. To loosen the grip of the extremist political and military leaders, the international community must present the refugees with alternatives. Promoting peaceful participatory activities such as political training and preparing the

For additional analytical, marketing, investment and business opportunities information, please contact
Global Investment & Business Center, USA
(202) 546-2103. Fax: (202) 546-3275. E-mail: rusric@erols.com

refugees for a future role in the political process could serve as moderating influences and encouraging the development of a healthy civil society. Programs which promote constructive dialogue concerning relevant socio-political issues could be useful. Some of these activities are being offered as "peace" activities by UNICEF or community services, but there is a need to move beyond these lofty kinds of education to more practical endeavors.

It is difficult to have fruitful discussions with Tanzanian authorities, refugee camp managers and staff on these issues, because they invariably deny that any political activities exist in the camp. Publicly, they claim that any form of political activity would automatically lead to instability in the camps. Privately, some admit to other motives. For one, the Tanzanian government does not want anything to interfere with Nyerere's orchestration of the political dynamics of Arusha. Secondly, some say that Tanzania's hard-line approach towards the refugees is in response to unfair criticism by the international community and attacks on Tanzanian sovereignty. Others sincerely believe that if Tanzania permits political activities in the camps, then "the Buyoya people will infiltrate the camps and stir up trouble, throw a grenade or two, in order to claim that there is in-fighting among the political parties. This has happened before." Humanitarian staff reported a few cases where Burundian and Congolese government infiltrators were caught in the Kigoma refugee camps. Humanitarian groups also question how the Burundian government was able to compile information on UNHCR on precise activities allegedly taking place in the camps. In one instance, a document was found which contained a hit-list of refugees. The refugees and local population allege that repressive policies are also due to ethnic Tutsi influence in the Tanzanian power structures. It is difficult to assess whether Tanzania's policy is a matter of control or prudence. In either case, there is a large number of local Tanzanian staff who ensure that their government's policies are carried out.

In fact most refugees should be given some credit for their civil behaviour in the camps, particularly in contrast to the Rwandan refugees and historical examples of camps in eastern Zaire. The international community has a tendency to keep fighting its last battle, in this case, the militarisation of the refugee camps in eastern Zaire. There were ubiquitous complaints from humanitarian workers on the ground that international donors and diplomats visit the camps exclusively to look for military activities. One expatriate relief worker with long experience in the area said: "Many of these refugees are just simple farming people, peasants. Yet diplomats keep coming here asking questions about militarisation. We don't see the training in the camps that they fear. They should be looking instead at the huge forest and savannah areas outside of the camps. If they really wanted to, they could fly surveillance planes to see. We wanted to show them the conditions of the roads, the camps and talk to them of food needs. But they came only focused on the militarisation of the camps."

For additional analytical, marketing, investment and business opportunities information, please contact
Global Investment & Business Center, USA
(202) 546-2103. Fax: (202) 546-3275. E-mail: rusric@erols.com

The political leaders of the refugees admit that they themselves have learned lessons from their own past experiences. Those from the Uvira refugee caseload (which includes members of both the FDD and Palipehutu) are particularly conscious of maintaining a different standard in the Tanzanian camps. They recognize that the warlord quality of leadership and political in-fighting that predominated in the Uvira camps resulted in both loss of life and their own failure to attain their political goals. Some have subsequently modified their behavior in an effort to be taken seriously as political players. This is one positive effect that Nyerere and the Tanzanian government's political support of the rebellion have had. The rebel leaders are actually learning to be more astute political players and to understand that their goals are more likely to be achieved if they participate in a political process.

The political and military leaders within the camps keep a low profile. With the exception of visible military activity around the time of the Arusha meetings, camp leaders tend to engage in more militant activities outside the camp so as not to attract unfavorable attention to their refugee communities. In general, the worst forms of political infighting have been avoided. Afraid of being expelled from Tanzania in the same way as the Rwandan refugees, Burundian refugees tread more lightly. The rebel groups are also cautious for practical reasons; they realize that it is easier for them to gain access to money, food, shelter, medicines and other material needs from the camp if the refugee population is not attracting scrutiny.

INFORMATION FLOWS IN THE CAMPS

One of the key problems facing refugees in the western Tanzania camps is that they have little access to outside information on events in their homeland, the region and, more significantly, the Arusha peace process. The Burundian refugees constantly complain about the dearth of objective media coverage of current events and general educational information. Many refugees ask why they are not provided programming similar to what they received in the eastern Zaire camps on Radio Agatashya. Now some projects of radio stations or programming have been proposed for western Tanzania.

When ICG visited the camps, the refugees refused to engage in dialogue without first being provided with information on Arusha, the nature of political affairs affecting their country and even the situation in particular communes in Burundi. Despite being refugees for many years, few had an understanding of the functions of the UN or the international community beyond the provision of basic refugee needs. Much of their frustration with the humanitarian operations could be countered by furnishing them with adequate information.

For additional analytical, marketing, investment and business opportunities information, please contact
Global Investment & Business Center, USA
(202) 546-2103. Fax: (202) 546-3275. E-mail: rusric@erols.com

More importantly, if refugees had access to news and feature programs, they would undoubtedly feel more included in the Arusha process as well as broader political developments in their country and the region. Reliable, relevant information could also mitigate the consequences of hard-line propaganda spread throughout the camps. Countering "hate media" is a rallying cry for many policy-makers focused on the Great Lakes region, yet the opportunity to provide alternatives for the refugee populations in western Tanzania is being overlooked.

THE DISCUSSION ABOUT THEIR PARTICIPATION IN THE ARUSHA PEACE TALKS

Some of the refugees have been directly involved in political affairs in the past, others currently are engaged in camp leadership issues, and some have been participating in the Arusha process since June 1998 albeit as an open secret. Delegations from the armed groups came directly from the camps. However, the camp authorities claimed not to have been consulted and complained that Nyerere bypassed both UNHCR and MHA officials by not informing them about his decision to permit key political and military leaders from the camps to attend the peace talks.

However, there is a strong sentiment among the refugees that they are being denied participation and are being fed false information on Arusha, the Tripartite refugee agreement, the situation in their own country, and other issues. Refugees are also concerned that the Tanzanian authorities are sending mixed signals, allowing some refugees to leave the camps and participate at Arusha clandestinely.

Because they will play a critical role in any peace and transition process, the refugees feel that they should be incorporated into the Arusha process. Exclusion from Arusha hardens their perspective towards the peace process and increases their distrust of the Tanzanian authorities and the international community. And it is quite clear that the refugees will gravitate towards more militant options as long as their political and participatory needs are not being met.

At the time of research, UNHCR's sub-regional Kigoma office was interested in facilitating refugee participation in both the Arusha process and in broader political discussion. The office recognizes that the voice of refugees in western Tanzania should be heard at the international and regional level.

Within UNHCR as a whole, there were mixed sentiments regarding refugee participation at Arusha and in general political affairs. UN staffs in Burundi seemed to reject the idea. Local staff, as well as officials familiar with the Great Lakes, were divided on the subject. Some advocated that the refugees should be entitled to express their views and have a voice at Arusha as long as their

For additional analytical, marketing, investment and business opportunities information, please contact
Global Investment & Business Center, USA
(202) 546-2103. Fax: (202) 546-3275. E-mail: rusric@erols.com

involvement was limited to specific, apolitical refugee needs and not rooted in political party agendas. In this capacity, the refugees could participate as cross-party representatives of civil society. Others advocate that the refugees should not only be permitted to partake in political activities, but should be afforded political representation at Arusha.

Some refugee leaders, who had already been approached, rejected the notion that they should lay aside their political mantle in order to participate in an apolitical framework. This view was strongly held by the leaders of the armed groups who already have representation at Arusha. The more experienced leaders assert that the resolution of the Burundian conflict will require army reform. This is a politicised issue of prime concern to the refugee population and their leaders, and they realize that solutions to political problems will require them to bolster their military efforts.

Following the March session of the Arusha peace talks, Nyerere visited the camps and made a statement in favour of refugee participation in the talks, and more specifically in Committee IV on Reconstruction and Development that deals with the issue of refugee return and rehabilitation. A delegation of refugees attended the June 1999 committee session of the talks and came up with a statement asking for a transition government; an international post-Arusha peacekeeping force; the reform of the army; the trial of the 1993 putschists, the liberation of political prisoners; and the military intervention of Tanzania if necessary. The refugees also asked that reconstruction aid should only resume after the peace agreement is signed in Arusha, and that the Tripartite meeting be postponed until then. In the mean time, the delegation asked for the refugees to be given refugee status, land, and primary and secondary education in the camps.

Although this statement was very politicised, it can be expected that the participation of the refugees at Arusha had beneficial effects: refugees attending Arusha were able to bring first-hand information back to the camps; a renewed relationship between refugee populations and a wider variety of political actors was created.

THE REBELLION IN WESTERN TANZANIA

MILITARY ACTIVITY OUTSIDE THE REFUGEE CAMPS

The Burundi rebellion's military activities in western Tanzania generally take place outside of the camps. The rebellion's political leaders claim that Tanzania forbids them to conduct military activities overtly. However, they also claim that Tanzania has provided instructions for maintaining discrete military operations. It is apparent that some rebel leaders in the Kigoma district move with ease through the main towns, some are recognized and even well known. Others tread

For additional analytical, marketing, investment and business opportunities information, please contact
Global Investment & Business Center, USA
(202) 546-2103. Fax: (202) 546-3275. E-mail: rusric@erols.com

more carefully and are sometimes afraid to be seen conversing in public. Some rebel leaders have jobs in western Tanzania. While the executive committees for most of the major rebel armed groups reside in western Tanzania, all have key representation in Dar Es Salaam. The town of Kigoma has become a central hub for the rebel movement. Here rebels often feel relaxed and circulate freely among the local population, but refuse to see the press.

In the Tabora region settlement camps, rebel leaders operate with less scrutiny. One rebel leader returned to the settlements after Arusha and was granted permission by the Tanzanian authorities to hold a meeting on the peace talks and to prepare videotape for the exiled community overseas. At one point, the Tanzanian government pressed UNHCR to provide police to the old settlements as part of the security package deal. UNHCR rejected this request because it has not been responsible for the camps since it handed them over to the local authorities in 1985. As in the refugee camps, the Tanzanians creatively search for ways to hold the UN responsible for activities undertaken by the armed parties in the region.

THE REBELLION'S RESOURCES

The Burundian rebels easily recruit from among the vast pool of disgruntled and bored male refugees in western Tanzania. Some new recruits do not relish the idea of going into battle or of risking their lives by crossing back into Burundi; they plead not to be enlisted, but are short of alternatives. The rebellion claims their movement has grown since Arusha began. Following the inclusion of armed groups at the talks, new supporters have joined the rebellion.

Competing rebel groups travel, often to the same camps, to find recruits, even funding basic supplies such as food, blankets and medicines. All of the rebel groups complain of the lack of funding, arms and other resources necessary to carry out a sustained military campaign in Burundi.

The main complaint of the rebels is the lack of international support. As one rebel leader said: "we don't have anyone to support us the way the Banyamulenge are supported by Rwanda and Uganda, or Kabila is supported by Zimbabwe and Cuba. We don't have enough weapons." When the Congo war started, the Burundian rebel leaders were distressed that Tutsi solidarity in the region would increase, and that their chances for a successful military campaign would be limited. However, after Kabila recruited and mobilized the Burundian rebellion from Tanzania to join his operations in the DRC, their enthusiasm soared. Tanzania became the hub of the movement to join Kabila's forces in the DRC. The FDD rebels in particular have received training and equipment from Kabila and Zimbabwe since the war started. After the signing of the Lusaka agreement, most came back to Burundi and Tanzania. However, they seem to be still quietly supported by Kabila and Zimbabwe; some are kept on stand by since the signing

For additional analytical, marketing, investment and business opportunities information, please contact
Global Investment & Business Center, USA
(202) 546-2103. Fax: (202) 546-3275. E-mail: rusric@erols.com

of the Lusaka agreement; others have been encouraged to go back to Burundi and to step up their attacks in order to keep the Burundi army busy at home and to force it to repatriate some of the troops stationed on the Congolese side of Lake Tanganyka.

BURUNDI-TANZANIA; AN UNEASY RELATIONSHIP

TANZANIA'S SECURITY CONCERNS

To the dismay of the Tanzanians, the Burundian conflict has a nasty habit of spilling over onto its soil. Tanzania's security has been affected in a number of ways. Over the past few years, Tanzania has greatly expanded its military operations at its borders to protect the country's territorial integrity and to defend its population against Burundian soldiers crossing the border in hot pursuit of Hutu rebels and refugees. Tanzania recognizes that many civilians living on both sides of the Tanzanian/Burundi divide are not necessarily conscious of the official borders; some have inter-married and many families are intermingled. They plant crops on both sides of the border and travel back and forth to conduct small-scale business unaware of economic sanctions in place at the time. In the face of Burundi's military actions, Tanzania claimed to care for the security needs of its people and refugees.

Since the Burundian army has created a 5 kilometer buffer zone on its side of the border, local inhabitants who cross over to attend their crops have become targets of military gunfire. One international dispute arose when a Tanzanian woman crossed into Burundi to care for her crops and was shot trying to flee. Both governments claimed that the woman had died on their respective sides of the border, and each had maps to prove it. The Tanzanian Ministry of Defence launched an internal investigation and undertook surveys, which concluded that the woman was killed on the Burundian side. In another incident in July 1998, Tanzanians were killed and injured after crossing into Burundi to conduct small business. Many local people and refugees have been victims of mines and booby traps planted by the Burundian Armed Forces on the Burundian side of the border. The Tanzanian authorities and humanitarian community have had to develop a medical program to deal with the injured. Often, when explosions and gunfire are heard going off in Burundi near the border, local residents fear that they are meant to be the targets. Some residents complained that "gunfire and bombs are hitting too close".

Tanzania has emphasised that its military forces in the border region are also there to protect the Burundian refugee population. In the company of a high-level UNHCR delegation, a senior Tanzanian official told the refugees that Tanzania would protect them. Some refugees interpreted the speech as a sign that they shared a "common enemy".

For additional analytical, marketing, investment and business opportunities information, please contact
Global Investment & Business Center, USA
(202) 546-2103. Fax: (202) 546-3275. E-mail: rusric@erols.com

Tanzania continues to suffer from instability in its western region caused by the large refugee community. When food supplies in the camps are inadequate, refugees have leave the camp to forage for food. This leads to increasing criminality, pillaging, crop raiding and violence against locals. The Rwandan refugee population also continues to be a problem. Some Rwandan refugees refused to depart and others returned following their massive, forced repatriation. Those in camps in the Kigoma sub-region have not been officially classified as "refugees", but rather as "asylum seekers" who are awaiting the results of screening processes. (The screening was completed in October 1998). The presence of these refugees among the Burundians is a cause of concern. Some of the Burundian refugees fear the Rwandans; others are susceptible to the hard-line views and violence that the Rwandans espouse.

Kigoma is a key storage and transit point for Tanzanian, local and foreign arms traffickers and smugglers plying their trade on Lake Tanganyika. Locally based operations have links in the region to southern Africa, Zambia, eastern DRC and Burundi and outside links to China, Oman, Dubai, United Arab Emirates, India and Pakistan. A few smugglers have continued their operations to, from, and through Burundi even when sanctions existed; though they bitterly complain of being forced to suspend most of their business activities. Others have become suppliers to the Burundian rebellion based in western Tanzania, Zambia, southern Burundi and eastern DRC. Many of them are at least locally known. The Burundian rebellion has profited from the smuggling network out of Kigoma, and depends on logistical and military supplies from this pipeline. Though they are furthering the ends of the armed parties to the conflict in Burundi, the smugglers operate with impunity. Tanzanians are bribed to look the other way or otherwise benefit from being involved.

The DRC conflict also has a major destabilising impact on western Tanzania. Extensive recruitment and mobilisation of both Burundians and Congolese by Kabila's officials has taken place in Kigoma. The mobilisation was directed from the Congolese consulate in Kigoma, and was supervised by a former Burundian diplomat. Large numbers of men left their refugee camps and the surrounding environs, and were loaded onto boats for transport to eastern DRC near Kalemie. Most of the recruits did not have previous military training. Some expressed regret at having to go but claimed to have no other option. Even injured refugees, some recovering in a hospital ward, were persuaded to go to the front. Some local Kigoma residents, disturbed by the military undertaking, took several recruiters to the local police who subsequently released them. Local police officials denied the Congo war recruitment operation, though some facilitated the undertaking.

In October - November 1999, the government of Tanzania has shown new concern about the situation in the Kigoma region. The Deputy Minister of Home

For additional analytical, marketing, investment and business opportunities information, please contact
Global Investment & Business Center, USA
(202) 546-2103. Fax: (202) 546-3275. E-mail: rusric@erols.com

Affairs visited the area in November and decided that movements of refugees outside of the camps should be restricted. For long, Kigoma has been out of the political mainstream and is distrusted in the ruling party's national arena. Since the parliamentary representative for Kigoma town does not belong to the ruling party, his views do not sufficiently resonate at the national level. Outside of western Tanzania, various Tanzanian politicians have alternatively belittled the refugee presence or criticised it to suit their political objectives. With the presidential elections in June 2000, the Tanzanian authorities want to restrict refugees' movements out of the camps to prevent them from voting. A fear persists that refugees could swell the ranks of the local constituencies with whom they have family and ethnic or cultural ties, and out-vote the governing party in the region.

TANZANIA'S AMBIGUOUS ROLE IN THE BURUNDI PEACE PROCESS

Tanzania feels that it has not received the credit it deserves from the international and donor community for its moderating influence in the Burundian crisis. First, having been viewed as a model "asylum" country, Tanzania is harshly criticized for its support of the Burundian rebellion, and the assumed military nature of the refugee camps within the country's borders. Tanzania feels that it has become the "scapegoat" for a refugee crisis, which the Burundian government and security forces should take responsibility for having created it in the first place.

National and local Tanzanian authorities complain that top UNHCR officials and important members of the NGO community have been convinced by the Burundian government's public relations campaign that Tanzania is a major part of Burundi's problem. Mortified by its own failings in eastern Zaire, the humanitarian community fears being accused of repeating its mistakes in Tanzania now; Burundian officials have taken advantage of these feelings of guilt. Tanzanians say that instead of pointing the finger at them, the international community should acknowledge its own failure to take important political and security actions at the level of the UN Security Council which could have prevented or alleviated the humanitarian crisis.

Second, they feel insulted that the efforts of Mwalimu Nyerere, who led the peace process from March 1996 until October 1999, are not recognized as genuine. Allegations abound that Nyerere was biased towards the Hutu because the Tanzanian government allowed rebels to operate from the refugee camps on the country's western border and because most Hutu leaders of the opposition went to exile in Dar Es Salaam.

Tanzania's impartiality in the peace negotiations has been however continuously questioned by the Burundian government as well as by the diplomatic community. While the international community has funded the Arusha process

For additional analytical, marketing, investment and business opportunities information, please contact
Global Investment & Business Center, USA
(202) 546-2103. Fax: (202) 546-3275. E-mail: rusric@erols.com

and the Mwalimu Nyerere Foundation since June 1998, more and more voices have drawn attention to the fact that political support, if not military, to one side of the conflict was compromising the neutrality of Nyerere's mediation's. The Burundian government has successfully attracted international condemnation of Tanzania's support for the rebels, both in and outside of the refugee camps. A proposal for an OAU fact-finding mission to investigate refugee militarisation in Tanzania was flatly rejected by the Tanzanian government, which claimed the focus should instead be on Burundi. In its defence, Tanzania has written to the UN Security Council to draw attention to Burundian military build-up, and offensives taking place on the Burundian side of the border.

Most recently, on 12 November 1999, the Security Council issued a press release on the Burundi situation calling on the States of the region to ensure the neutrality and civilian character of the refugee camps and to prevent the use of their territory by armed insurgents. That press release can be interpreted as a clear signal that Tanzania should do more to control the Kigoma region's security.

THE MILITARY OPTION AGAINST THE BUYOYA REGIME

One of the reasons why Tanzania's neutrality is questioned is that, during certain periods within the past few years, Tanzania felt that it had at least the silent approval of relevant regional and international governments to pursue a military campaign against Burundi, though it never had ample resources to do so. The height of Tanzania's enthusiasm for a military confrontation with Burundi came in the spring of 1996. At that time, Tanzania was playing a lead role in the preparation of a multinational force to stabilize Burundi. But, after the Buyoya coup in July 1996 and after foreign backers pulled the plug, Tanzania became embittered by the loss of energy and resources expended on the effort. Very recently, the Ministry of Defense asked the Tanzanian government for a substantial troop reduction in the west due to the coastlines of the deployment and waning military objectives.

For most of the second half of the 1990s, Tanzania has been prepared to exercise military options to force change in Burundi. Tanzania has consulted regional and other foreign allies, increased its resources and manpower on the border, and tolerated the Burundian rebellion's activities on its territory. The local humanitarian community is aware of Tanzania's military build-up but has been confused about Tanzania's motives. Humanitarian agencies have been denied access to border and other areas by Tanzanian authorities. As one official remarked, "For us, one of the key issues in the region is denial of access. There are certain no-go areas in western Tanzania." Regular border monitoring of the region by humanitarian agencies is not permitted.

For additional analytical, marketing, investment and business opportunities information, please contact
Global Investment & Business Center, USA
(202) 546-2103. Fax: (202) 546-3275. E-mail: rusric@erols.com

Publicly, Tanzania keeps its distance from the armed parties. While Tanzania has provided support to the rebellion in many ways - freedom of movement, political activity outside of the camps, political support, resources and military training - the support has always been circumscribed. Tanzania wants to keep Burundi destabilised by supporting the rebellion, but for the time being has otherwise reduced its military ambitions towards Burundi.

However, Nyerere's death on 14 October could have a very negative impact at this stage of the process. President Mkapa, Minister Kikwete, or the Tanzanian chief of staff have been threatening the Burundi government to give massive support to the rebellion if negotiations were not moving. This line is supported by a number of pro-Hutu lobbies in Tanzania. The common view is that if Tanzania's ambition for the rebels was stronger, there would be a marked improvement in the rebellion's performance. Nyerere had a moderating effect on those lobbies and wanted to give a chance to the negotiations in Arusha. With the upcoming elections, it is not sure that the new Tanzanian leadership's attitude will be non-violent. If the Burundi negotiation process doesn't quickly produce results, Tanzania can argue that it is time again for a military intervention in Burundi.

GROWING TENSION BETWEEN BURUNDI AND TANZANIA

After numerous claims of aggression by rebels from the Tanzania territory and counterclaims from Tanzanians, the two Ministers of Defence have met on 12 August to discuss border security. The discussion focused on the general causes of insecurity as well as on the particular incidents that happened on the border. The meeting ended with proposals to improve co-operation on security at the border.

However, Burundi has recently again accused Tanzania of allowing refugee camps on its soil to be used as bases for ethnic Hutu rebels. Both countries accused each other of lax security along their border. The Burundi government says Tanzania is not doing enough to police the camps. It also claims that the rebels who killed two UN workers in Rutana in October 1999 had crossed over from Tanzania. In a letter to the Security Council, Tanzania denied any responsibility for the attack. The Foreign Minister Jakaya Kikwete said in an interview: "If they have a problem in their country, there is no use trying to find a scapegoat...It's outrageous. The government of Burundi cannot in any way exonerate itself from its primary responsibility of providing security for United Nations personnel as well as its own citizens," the foreign ministry said in a statement."

The growing animosity over the camps issue has also been fed by rumours that the Burundi army is planning to attack the camps in Tanzania. Hutu rebels claim Burundi and Rwanda have deployed thousands of soldiers near the border to prepare for an assault on the refugee camps around the Tanzanian town of

For additional analytical, marketing, investment and business opportunities information, please contact
Global Investment & Business Center, USA
(202) 546-2103. Fax: (202) 546-3275. E-mail: rusric@erols.com

Kigoma, as they did in 1996 on the Zaire camps. Tanzania's Minister said reports of a possible attack on the camps in Tanzania were just rumours put around by the rebels, but added: "In situations like these it's very easy to find yourself being drawn into other people's problems". With the present influx of refugees (about 5000 in the first two weeks of November 1999), the likelihood of incidents at the border is increasing. Although at this point, it would be disastrous for Burundi to fight a war against Tanzania, the possibility of an incident triggering a war can not be ruled out.

THE MANDELA EFFECT: PROSPECTS FOR PEACE IN BURUNDI

Involved in a civil war since the assassination in 1993 of Melchior Ndadaye, the first elected president, Burundi is now at a crossroads. Since 1998 the government of Major Pierre Buyoya (who returned to power in July 1996) has been engaged in a negotiation process with FRODEBU, winner of the 1993 elections, as well as with most of the Burundian political groups. This process, which began under the auspices of Julius Nyerere, has been in the hands of Nelson Mandela since December 1999. It finally seems to be on the point of reaching a peace agreement sponsored by the region and the international community: the most optimistic are talking of the agreement being signed within the next few months.

After three and a half years of isolation for the country as a result of regional sanctions and the suspension of international development co-operation, Mandela has breathed new life into the Arusha process and has put Burundi back on the international agenda. His appointment was a victory for the Burundian government, which has concentrated its diplomatic efforts since Nyerere's death in releasing the negotiation process from the grip of the region, particularly that of Tanzania, which it accuses of bias. The government has criticised the Facilitation team for the methodology applied in the Arusha process, especially its formation of negotiation groups on an ethnic basis, faillure to take internal dialogue efforts into account and, above all, refusal to allow "dissident" armed bands, the Jean-Bosco Ndayikengurukiye branch of the FDD and the Cossan Kabura wing of the FNL, to participate in the negotiations.

Mandela's first priority is to terminate the Arusha process as quickly as possible. In order to do this, he proposes to conclude work in four committees (nature of the conflict; democracy and good governance; peace and security; reconstruction and development) and work directly on a draft agreement. By his unaccommodating approach to the conflict and his reminder to the Burundian political class that they must show a sense of responsibility, he has provoked a healthy debate on questions related to an amnesty for those guilty of war crimes and crimes against humanity, the integration of rebel forces into the army, power sharing and the transition. He has also put pressure on the government to

For additional analytical, marketing, investment and business opportunities
information, please contact
Global Investment & Business Center, USA
(202) 546-2103. Fax: (202) 546-3275. E-mail: rusric@erols.com

dismantle the regroupment camps in rural Bujumbura, and to allow the political parties to become active and permit freedom of the press.

His hope for concluding the Arusha process rapidly is founded on the significant progress made since June 1998. Violently rejected by Tutsi public opinion in 1996, the idea of negotiating with the Hutu rebels is now more widely accepted. The great majority of Burundians, tired of the war and of their politicians, do not want to move backwards and lose what has been gained over 22 months of discussion in Arusha. As for the government, it is confronted with huge social and economic difficulties. It is losing more and more credibility and is strongly rejected by both Tutsi and Hutu public opinion. In addition, the work in committees has produced encouraging results. The debate on the stakes of change and the modernisation of the state and of Burundian society has largely taken place. The participants have agreed on the setting up of an international commission of enquiry into the massacres that have taken place since independence, especially those of the Hutu elite in 1972 and of Tutsi in 1993, and a national committee of truth and reconciliation. Agreement has also been reached on the reform of the institutions and the principle that elections will be organised, the reform of the army, a repatriation programme for refugees and economic reconstruction. Finally and above all, Mandela has succeeded in obtaining a promise from the FDD and the FNL that they will participate at the next session of Committee III, planned for the end of April.

Nevertheless, with the tempting prospect of rapidly concluding an agreement, it must not be forgotten that the greatest challenge is not the signing of the document, but its implementation, nor that none of the major political compromises expected is yet on the table. In the first place, despite the agreement in principle of all the rebel factions to participate in the Arusha process, a permanent ceasefire has not been agreed. The rebels' entry into the process at this advanced stage in the negotiations is accompanied by the risk that what has been achieved so far will be thrown back into question and give rise to new divisions or new alliances. In addition, the Burundian conflict cannot be isolated from that of the DRC, which is on an almost continental dimension; nor can the application of the future Arusha accords from that of the Lusaka accords. The tactical alliances between Kabila, the ex-FAR, the Mai-Mai and the FDD on the one hand, and the Burundian Armed Forces and the Rwandan Patriotic Army on the other, as well as Kabila's strategy of bringing the war to the borders of "aggressor" countries, have raised the stakes in the violence on Burundian territory. It is now essential that the Burundian rebels are integrated into a strictly Burundian political process to avoid the risk of their being marginalised definitively by the Lusaka agreement, which already classifies them as "negative forces". And even if a ceasefire is signed between the belligerents, the regional instability leaves open the possibility that the two Burundian parties may challenge the agreement and resort to the war option.

For additional analytical, marketing, investment and business opportunities information, please contact
Global Investment & Business Center, USA
(202) 546-2103. Fax: (202) 546-3275. E-mail: rusric@erols.com

In the second place, acknowledgement of the genocide and the amnesty is an issue that still arouses impassioned reactions as the victims and survivors of 1993 confuse the amnesty with the notion of impunity. As a prerequisite to the signing of an agreement at Arusha, certain Tutsi radicals, who have always been against negotiating with the "génocidaires", want to see the 1993 genocide acknowledged as such. They are even threatening to take up arms if their demand is not taken into account. As regards the Tutsi politicians participating at Arusha - who have recognised the crimes committed on both sides and the necessity of enquiries - they are using the reappearance of the genocide issue at this advanced stage of the process as a tactic to block the negotiations.

Finally, talks about who will lead the transition, and hence the compensation for the other pretenders to power, have not yet taken place. In saying openly that the present regime must consider giving up power, Mandela has launched the debate on the transition and obliged President Buyoya to put aside his reservations and carry out a campaign in the region and among western diplomats to explain the need for a "realistic" solution that would ensure a degree of continuity and stability. It might be assumed that the intransigence shown by some on the genocide issue is in large part related to the debate on the choice of a leader for the transition. As the end approaches, and after much opportunistic positioning dictated by the perception that the next government will be decided in Arusha, the parties are finally grouping into two camps: those for Buyoya and those against.

The stakes in this debate need to be set out clearly. It is undeniable that the ultimate objective of the negotiations is that the present oligarchy cedes power now or later and accepts the principle of an electoral process and a changeover of political power between parties. The real question is to know when and how, for it is absolutely essential to avoid a new wave of violence in the country. Enough blood has already been spilled on both sides and the fears are real. Yet the Burundian political actors still hesitate today between the benefits of violence and those of peace, between the continuity of a system or its rupture, between their individual interests and the interests of society

It is essential that the Arusha process should succeed if the violence is to end and if all Burundians are to be allowed to play an active part in the construction of a new, free and responsible society. Success is also required in order to complete and reinforce the Lusaka agreement and to save the credibility of the idea of negotiations as a mechanism for resolving conflicts in a region in which the logic of weapons and intolerance has dominated for decades.

INTRODUCTION

For additional analytical, marketing, investment and business opportunities information, please contact
Global Investment & Business Center, USA
(202) 546-2103. Fax: (202) 546-3275. E-mail: rusric@erols.com

In the seven years since Burundi's first elected President, Melchoir Ndadaye, was assasinated, triggering the start of a long and vicious civil war, Burundi has known virtually every kind of formula for dialogue and political compromise - from failed democracy to a failed power-sharing agreement, from the 1996 coup and the "Partnership for Peace" government to the Arusha talks. Since June 1998, the warring parties have been engaged in a negotiation process - initially under the auspices of former Tanzanian President Julius Nyerere and, since December 1999, former South African President Nelson Mandela. Mandela's appointment has given a new dynamism and visibility to the peace process. For the first time, a peace agreement, sponsored by the region and the international community, may be within reach. Optimists are speaking of an agreement in June.

But a number of factors could delay an agreement; or, in the event that an agreement is reached, jeopardise its implementation. The main stumbling blocks are: the difficulty in getting all those involved in the conflict to sign a ceasefire, failure to implement the Lusaka agreement in the Democratic Republic of Congo (DRC), arguments over references to past genocide, army reforms and the leadership of the transition government.

The aim of this report is to make a detailed evaluation of the results of the Arusha peace talks and the challenges that have to be met if conditions for a lasting peace are to be created in Burundi.

THE ARUSHA PROCESS: POINT OF NO RETURN?

Since the launch of the regional initiative on Burundi in November 1995, there have been ten summits of regional heads of state, including five since the beginning of the Arusha negotiations in 1998.

Between June 1998 and January 2000, the different parties to Arusha have met thirteen times: in June, July, October and December 1998, in January, March, May, July, September and November 1999, and in January, February and March 2000. On 21 June 1998, the participants signed a ceasefire declaration, which was immediately denounced by one of the rebel factions. In July 1998, they agreed on the procedural rules for the negotiations; in October 1998, they set up various committees. These comprise Committee I on the nature of the conflict; Committee II on democracy and good governance; Committee III on the security forces; and Committee IV on reconstruction and development. In February 2000, they approved the creation of Committee V on the guarantees for the agreement.

Since the last plenary meeting under Nyerere's presidency in January 1999, the committees have met in session eight times. There have been two consultations between the six so called "key players" - Front for Democracy in Burundi

For additional analytical, marketing, investment and business opportunities information, please contact
Global Investment & Business Center, USA
(202) 546-2103. Fax: (202) 546-3275. E-mail: rusric@erols.com

(FRODEBU), National Union for Progress (UPRONA), National Council for the Defence of Democracy (CNDD), Party for National Recovery (PARENA), the government and the National Assembly. The first took place in Dar es Salaam in September 1999, the second in January 2000. An additional consultation, among the heads of delegations, took place in March 2000, at which the Facilitation team distributed four "protocol projects", a compilation of the debates held in each committee.

STATE OF THE DISCUSSIONS

COMMITTEE I ON THE NATURE OF THE CONFLICT

Dealing with the question of the nature of the conflict and of the genocide, the participants reviewed the tragic periods of Burundi's history since independence: 1965, 1969, 1972, 1988, 1991 and 1993 up to today. They covered the definition of genocide and crimes against humanity, their deep-rooted causes, the way they are commited and the ideology behind them, the role of the political class and the national institutions, and the regional and international context of the killings.

The participants moved imperceptibly from expressing their positions to revealing their interpretations of the history of their country. For example, it became clear during the debates on the nature of the conflict that the political conscience of each party was formed around different traumatic periods.

According to Mathias Hitimana of the Party for the Reconcilliation of the People (PRP), the overthrow of the monarchy in November 1966 was the beginning of the destruction of the Burundian nation. When the king was killed a few years later, in 1972, "someone hitherto sacred was killed, and if a king can be killed, then what is the value of a peasant's life?"

For the Tutsi parties, the 1993 massacres confirmed the influence of "the genocide ideology" in Rwanda on the Hutus of Burundi. This was encouraged by the Belgian colonising power and sadly illustrated by the 1959 "social revolution" and the Rwandan genocide in 1994. According to the Tutsis, the existence of this extremist ideology justified a strong military regime dominated by the Tutsi.

For the Hutus, the political conscience of their parties was conceived out of the massacres of their leaders in 1965 and then of their elite in 1972. They saw the state as an instrument of their oppression and of the confiscation of privileges by a minority. They rejected the argument that the Rwandan social revolution influenced Burundi's Hutus, pointing out that in September 1961 the majority of Hutu voted for UPRONA, the nationalist party led by Prince Rwagasore.

For additional analytical, marketing, investment and business opportunities information, please contact
Global Investment & Business Center, USA
(202) 546-2103. Fax: (202) 546-3275. E-mail: rusric@erols.com

The various parties were unable to agree on a common view of history during their debates and it was clear that reconciling different perceptions could not become an object of negotiations. But at the last Dar es Salaam consultation in January 2000, consensus was reached on several important points including on the principle of an international judicial commission of inquiry. Its mission would be "to enquire into and establish the facts, to qualify them, to establish responsibilities, then to submit its report to the Security Council."

However, the parties remain at odds over its "judicial" character - its authority to compel witnesses to supply all the elements necessary for its investigation, and its mandate to indict. From the outset, UPRONA has refused to agree that the commission would be judicial and called for the immediate adoption of a national law on genocide, which would allow the state to prosecute and judge those responsible even before the agreement is concluded.

But FRODEBU wants the work of an eventual international tribunal to begin only once a political agreement has been signed. It suggests that a law on genocide should be discussed during the transition period.

UPRONA has also called for the commission's work to make use of the United Nations August 1996 international commission of enquiry into the circumstances of the 1993 coup, which concluded in its final report that there had been "acts of genocide" against the Tutsis. In that perspective, UPRONA criticizes the formulation of the Project for Protocol I of Committee I "in case the report (of the future international judiciary commission of enquiry) concludes that there were acts that can be qualified as genocide". UPRONA's fear is that the 1993 genocide will not be recognized.

For its part, FRODEBU wants the commission to examine the massacres that have taken place since independence and contests the validity of the 1996 UN report's conclusions, quoting the cover letter from the President of the Security Council to the UN Secretary-General. This letter stated that "the commission of enquiry was unable to work freely and its members worked in extremely difficult conditions." FRODEBU is also calling for other reports to be included in the terms of reference of the future commission of enquiry; for example, the Whitaker report, which established that a "cold-blooded genocide" was committed against the Hutu in 1972.

The negotiators also agreed on the setting up of a national truth and reconciliation commission to look into crimes since independence, to arbitrate and "to propose pertinent measures likely to promote reconciliation and pardon" and to clarify historical events. This committee would be composed of members of parliament, civil society, political parties and women's and church-related associations.

For additional analytical, marketing, investment and business opportunities information, please contact
Global Investment & Business Center, USA
(202) 546-2103. Fax: (202) 546-3275. E-mail: rusric@erols.com

The most controversial question concerns the amnesty, which was raised by Nelson Mandela in his first speech during the session in Arusha in January 2000. This arouses a great deal of passion because most Burundians confuse this issue with the notion of impunity. For the majority of Tutsis, amnesty is perceived as impunity for the génocidaires (those responsible for the genocide) of 1993. In contrast, Hutu leaders highlight the fact that many of their numbers have already been assassinated or imprisoned, or have gone into exile since 1993. They consider that an amnesty is of more interest to the Tutsis, who have been in power for 35 years, than the Hutus, who have only had access to government for three years (1993-96).

In reality a fair number of the negotiators and their supporters have good reason for concern about any eventual legal proceedings and could profit from this amnesty. These range from the perpetrators of the 1972 massacres against the Hutus, the officers and civilians presumed to be behind the assassination of President Ndadaye, the organisers of the villes mortes (city-wide strikes) to the members of the rebel movements, and the organisers of the 1993 massacres.

Consequently, those who are negotiating for themselves also have the power to block the negotiations, if their interests are not preserved. Thus, we find ourselves facing a delicate debate between the need to satisfy the demands of the powerful for impunity and the preservation of the idea of justice called for by both Hutu and Tutsi victims. In order to maintain the support of their constituencies, none of the parties can allow itself to show favour for an immediate and total amnesty. All of them are bound to argue that all crimes of genocide and crimes against humanity should be excluded from the amnesty law.

COMMITTEE II ON DEMOCRACY AND GOOD GOVERNANCE

Committee II deals with the institutions, the electoral system, the functioning of political parties and the transition (program, institutions and duration). At the last session on 10 April 2000, the discussions covered a number of issues:

The electoral system: Although there is consensus on the principle of elections, there are profound differences over how they should be carried out and over the timetable, (though it is generally accepted that a general election cannot be held very soon). But the crucial differences are on how the elections should be held. The predominantly Hutu parties want to keep the one-person/one-vote system, while the mainly Tutsi parties favor an indirect electoral system. PARENA and the PRP propose adopting the Belgian system of community voting. This view, which implies that the Tutsis and the Hutus would organize democratic elections within their respective groups, corresponds to the vision of "two peoples, one nation" system developed by the mainly Tutsi-dominated parties.

For additional analytical, marketing, investment and business opportunities information, please contact
Global Investment & Business Center, USA
(202) 546-2103. Fax: (202) 546-3275. E-mail: rusric@erols.com

The Agreement Protocol of Committee II proposes that communal, legislative and presidential elections should be held within 36 months following the beginning of the period of transition. In the countryside, the heads of the collines (hills) would be elected by universal suffrage and would constitute an assembly together with the Bashingantahe. This assembly would elect a "council of the collines", which would in turn appoint a communal administrator. At the level of legislative elections, the Protocol proposes an electoral system on the basis of "blocked lists with proportional representation". UPRONA proposes that only 80 per cent of the deputies would be elected directly. PARENA and FRODEBU support setting up a co-option mechanism "to correct the imperfections of the elections". At the level of presidential elections, FRODEBU wants to keep the majority vote system, while the government wants the president to be elected by at least two-thirds of the National Assembly. The Protocol Project of Committee II has to date kept both options.

The political parties: FRODEBU hopes to see the parties continue to be a part of the political scene, while the government and UPRONA want to see their influence decline. According to the latter, the political parties are responsible for the ethnic polarization of Burundian society. The compromise now emerging is for the law covering political parties to be discussed during the transition. The Protocol proposes that "the parties commit themselves in writing to fight against any political ideology aiming to encourage hate or discrimination… No party will be admitted to participate in the transition arrangements if it does not respect the commitments made…"

The institutions: The government proposes to create a Senate as a way of channeling and containing people's ambition or ability to create problems within an institutional framework, while also giving status to former dignitaries. In addition, the institutionalization of a right of veto for the minority could provide reassurance and act as a counterweight to a mainly Hutu National Assembly. But FRODEBU and the CNDD do not agree on the creation of a Senate, arguing that this would be an anomalous grouping intended to guarantee immunity for some and to diminish the power of the Assembly by a right of veto. FRODEBU and PARENA propose a High Council of State charged with "following through on the implementation of the peace agreement and interpreting the terms of the agreement in the event of dispute between signatories, and with former presidents of the Republic automatically appointed members". On the other hand, all the parties are in agreement on the reform of the judiciary system, particularly the modernization of laws and the correction of ethnic imbalances within the magistracy.

The Transition: This constitutes a major obstacle to the process and is at the center of debates. All parties agree on the responsibilities of the transitional government, but not on who is capable of leading it. The Protocol Project

For additional analytical, marketing, investment and business opportunities information, please contact
Global Investment & Business Center, USA
(202) 546-2103. Fax: (202) 546-3275. E-mail: rusric@erols.com

proposes that: "during the period of transition a widely representative government of national unity should be constituted, comprising representatives of the different parties in proportions agreed in Arusha."

This government would have a president and a vice-president, a transitional legislature and a transitional executive. At the beginning of the negotiations, the period of transition proposed by the different parties varied from six months to ten years. Today it varies between two and three years. This period should allow for the adoption of a constitution, the creation of a constitutional court, an electoral law, reform of the justice system and the administration, and finally, the implementation of the agreement. The Project already outlines the founding principles that the constitutional court must establish, for example that "the armed forces cannot be composed of more than 51 per cent of any ethnic group whatsoever."

On the question of a choice of leader for the transition, the positions and approaches remain opposed and inflexible. The government expressed clearly in September 1999 that "a government in place does not negotiate its own departure", and President Buyoya hopes that this question will be resolved by the mediator. FRODEBU hopes that the people who will lead the transition, the presidents of the Republic, the National Assembly and the Senate, will be approved at Arusha, and is presently seeking to create a public anti-Buyoya consensus by mobilizing the most parties possible in Arusha. This central question cannot be answered in Committee II. It must be resolved within another framework. The next session, at which the rebels are supposed to participate, will be a major test. In fact, the stance taken by the rebel movements on this issue could tip the balance either way. The continuation of the peace process will depend on this question being resolved.

COMMITTEE III ON PEACE AND SECURITY

Committee III deals with the reform of the defense and security bodies (the size of the army, demobilization, recruitment and the future of the rebels), the end of hostilities and a permanent ceasefire. The parties agree on the principles governing the armed forces: political neutrality and no discrimination in recruitment, as well as on separate missions for the army, police and secret services.

The parties have not reached any agreement on the size of the armed forces. On the question of its composition, the Facilitation team has proposed that "the National Defence Forces will have members of the present defense force as a base, along with members of the armed political groups". It also proposed "that members of the present National Defense Forces recognized as guilty of acts of genocide, violations of the constitution or of human rights, as well as of war

For additional analytical, marketing, investment and business opportunities information, please contact
Global Investment & Business Center, USA
(202) 546-2103. Fax: (202) 546-3275. E-mail: rusric@erols.com

crimes, will be excluded from the new army. The armed political groups recognized as guilty of crimes of the same nature will also not be accepted." Another major divergence concerns the gendarmerie: the government wants to keep the gendarmerie within the army, while FRODEBU wants to detach it from the military body. FRODEBU has counted on the gendarmerie since 1993. Composed of soldiers from the north and center of Burundi, it could act as a counterbalance to the army, which is recruited mainly from the south.

Questions concerning the end of hostilities, a permanent ceasefire and the demobilization of the armed groups could not be dealt with, partly because of a lack of time, but above also because the armed groups have not yet participated in the talks. The dissident Forces for the Defence of Democracy (FDD) and Cossan's National Liberation Forces (FNL) are supposed to join the debate at the Committee III session that was scheduled to begin on 24 April 2000. The Facilitation team proposes the creation of a sub-committee for Committee III to tackle the chapter on the cessation of hostilities. It would comprise the government and representatives of the armed groups, presided over by a South African.

COMMITTEE IV ON RECONSTRUCTION AND DEVELOPMENT

Committee IV has dealt with three chapters: the rehabilitation and reinstallation of the refugees and internally displaced, reconstruction, and economic and social development. It has practically finished its work, with the exception of a few questions dealing with the recovery of property by refugees and the displaced, and the social and professional reintegration of demobilized soldiers and rebels.

It has established that 345,000 refugees have crossed into Tanzania, Rwanda, Kenya, the DRC, Zambia, Angola, DRC-Brazzaville, Malawi and Cameroon since 1993. Around 200,000 have been living in Tanzania since 1972. The total number of internally displaced people is 808,000, of whom 44 per cent are in rural Bujumbura. Committee IV estimates that 650,000 of these will want to return home. It recommends that the UNHCR undertake a census among the refugees aimed at "noting the wishes and grievances of these refugees concerning the recovery of their lands or alternative measures". It also recommends that the national commission for the rehabilitation of the victims of war - to be created on the conclusion of the agreement - carry out a similar census with the same objectives.

The committee suggests that information sessions to raise awareness of the peace agreement should be organized, as well as visits to places of origin before any definitive return home. The participants agree on a series of measures aimed at repatriation, but not on the modalities and conditions regarding compensation for lost properties.

For additional analytical, marketing, investment and business opportunities
information, please contact
Global Investment & Business Center, USA
(202) 546-2103. Fax: (202) 546-3275. E-mail: rusric@erols.com

As regards land, Committee IV established a principle that "each refugee/internal victim must be able to recover his/her goods. If recovery should prove impossible, each must receive a fair compensation and/or indemnity ". A national fund should be set up for victims. A calendar still has to be established for the return of the refugees, but this depends on the calendar for the transition itself, which is to be decided in Committee II.

As regards reconstruction, Committee IV estimated that between 150,000 and 200,000 houses will have to be rebuilt, along with at least fifteen per cent of hydraulic structures, a dozen hospitals and 120 schools. It established a series of measures for political reconstruction: a program of national reconciliation, the promotion of human rights, education on peace, the role of women, reform of the judiciary, aid for democratization and for parliament, promotion of civil society and the media, and support for political parties.

Regarding development, Committee IV proposes an economic reform plan, aimed particularly at reforming and privatizing public enterprises, the reform of the coffee sector, reform in the education sector, and regional decentralization and integration. An emergency reconstruction plan must be drawn up within six weeks of the agreement, followed by a more in-depth plan for the transition period, which should be worked out with the help of the World Bank, UNDP and the European Union. It concluded that a minimum of 80,000 jobs would have to be created to meet the employment needs of the demobilized, the repatriated and civil servants (unemployed after the reform of the administration). Committee IV estimated that 60,000 soldiers would be demobilized at a cost at $US 50 to 100 million, which would include a transitional salary and training for former soldiers. Discussions on demobilization will have to wait for the conclusion of work in Committee III.

COMMITTEE V ON GUARANTEES FOR THE IMPLEMENTATION OF THE AGREEMENT

Mandela immediately wanted to make the question of the guarantees a priority and put it on the agenda for the February 2000 session. In Nyerere's view, there was no use in setting up this committee before the agreement was signed. Accordingly, no steps have yet been taken with the UN and the Organization for African Unity (OAU).

Mandela was appointed President of this Committee at the February session. The Facilitation team hoped that the Tanzanian judge, Mark Bomani, responsible for the Burundi Peace Negotiations (BPN), would be elected Vice-President, but his candidacy was unanimously rejected by the predominantly Tutsi parties. It was finally decided that the presidents of the other committees would elect the vice-president.

For additional analytical, marketing, investment and business opportunities information, please contact
Global Investment & Business Center, USA
(202) 546-2103. Fax: (202) 546-3275. E-mail: rusric@erols.com

Committee V must consider the monitoring mechanisms to be included in the agreement; the calendar to be implemented; the sanctions to be applied in case the agreement is not respected and the eventual use of force; as well as the funding for the measures contained in the agreement. It must also consider demobilization, the return of refugees, and the different commissions that will have to be set up, as well as reconstruction and economic redistribution. This is considered essential for ensuring that the benefits of the peace are visible to the combatants and to the population. The committee must also examine guarantees of security for all and particularly for those returning from exile; respect for human rights and mechanisms for dealing with a possible abuse of power by the transition government.

The initial debate on the guarantees for implementation has not yet taken place, but some proposals are beginning to appear. The seven Hutu parties grouped with G7 are hoping for a regional intervention (South Africa, Uganda, Tanzania and Kenya), and an international force to protect institutions and state dignitaries. FRODEBU/PARENA are proposing that 2,000 men should be sent to protect new and former state officers, as well as an international peacekeeping force. The government would prefer that international observers are sent, and a national committee established to follow up on the agreement. The army, supported by most of the Tutsi parties, categorically rejects any form of foreign military intervention.

AN EVALUATION OF THE ACHIEVEMENTS

The general political debate on policy questions came to a virtual close in June 1998 with the participants reaching a consensus on a certain number of principles. These include the need to hold enquiries into the massacres, the principle of elections and the institution of a state of law, the integration of rebel forces and reform of the army, the return of the refugees and development centered on social justice. Committees I and IV have almost finished their work; Committees II and III was supposed to meet once again in April 2000.

Arusha has been a real learning experience for all those participating in the talks. The negotiators have been obliged to revise their definition of genocide according to the 1948 Convention, to learn what a demobilization program implies and, within the framework of Committee II, to reflect on electoral systems and institutions, etc. In short, the Arusha process has brought about a kind of "technical catching up" for all the participants who have benefited from the expertise of the Committee presidents. There were very wide gaps between the participants in terms of knowledge and technical competence; some already had experience of managing a state, while the experience of others was purely militant. By going into the details of each subject, important issues such as genocide were demystified making demagogy and propaganda less possible.

For additional analytical, marketing, investment and business opportunities information, please contact
Global Investment & Business Center, USA
(202) 546-2103. Fax: (202) 546-3275. E-mail: rusric@erols.com

Arusha also made it possible for those outside the country to confront their points of view with those from inside. But especially, it obliged all the participants to continue dialogue in the committees and to develop a mutual acceptance of each other's demands to have the right to participate in discussions on the future of the country.

Little by little, the discussions made it possible to pick out what was negotiable and what was not, at least in the first phase of negotiations. For the government, everything is negotiable except the immediate departure of Buyoya; for the CNDD, everything is negotiable except the fusion of the armies and a return to the constitutional legality of 1993; for PARENA, everything is negotiable except the continued presence of Buyoya.

However, none of the sensitive questions has been seriously dealt with and consequently none of the major political compromises required has been made. The debate has advanced on what is at stake, but a concrete program, and guarantees of physical, political and economic security for everyone still remain to be negotiated, and the individuals to personify these still have to be chosen. The obstacles that remain over the questions of genocide, the transition, army reform and the ceasefire must find a more suitable and discreet framework than the Committees in order to be resolved.

For additional analytical, marketing, investment and business opportunities information, please contact
Global Investment & Business Center, USA
(202) 546-2103. Fax: (202) 546-3275. E-mail: rusric@erols.com

SUCCESSES AND FAILURES OF THE NYERERE APPROACH:

EIGHTEEN-PARTY NEGOTIATIONS

The logic of inclusive participation in the Arusha process springs from the regional summit of 25 June 1996, which advocated the inclusion in the talks of the twelve partners to the Convention of government, from which the CNDD was excluded. That summit was convened after the failure of the Mwanza I and II negotiations (22 March-2 April 1996) between UPRONA and FRODEBU.

The same 12 political parties saw their hour of glory pass with Buyoya's coup d'état on 25 July 1996. Buyoya suspended them immediately, regarding them as nuisances and divisive, and knowing the circumstances behind their birth in 1992 during the introduction of a multi-party system. The state financial support made available at that time led to the spawning of many political groups. Only three of these parties came forward for the 1993 presidential elections (UPRONA, FRODEBU, PRP) the others existed mainly through the Convention of government.

In his first speech on 25 July 1996, Buyoya indicated his real interlocutor by affirming that he was ready to negotiate with the CNDD. Negotiations then took place in Rome under the auspices of the Community of Sant'Egidio (between 1996 and 1997). But the region had decided otherwise on the fate of the political parties. Faithful to the conclusions of the Arusha summit of 25 June 1996, the heads of state imposed sanctions on the "putschist" government on 31 July and defined conditions for their suspension. These were to be: the re-establishment of the political parties, the restoration of the constitution and the government's commitment to the negotiation process. In September 1997 two more conditions were added, the lifting of the ban on the movement of former Presidents Bagaza, Ntibantunganya and Ngendakumana (National Assembly), and the dismantling of regroupment camps.

When the discussions began in Arusha in June 1998, 18 political parties were invited - including CNDD, Parti pour la Libération du Peuple Hutu (PALIPEHUTU), Front pour la Libération Nationale (FROLINA) and PARENA, which were not in the Convention. Then arose the well-known problems with regard to methodology that fuelled so much discussion and criticism of the Facilitation team, as much by Burundians as by the international observers and institutional donors. It should be stressed that these criticisms, which were largely well founded, were also widely used to delay the debates, particularly by the government delegation and UPRONA.

For additional analytical, marketing, investment and business opportunities information, please contact
Global Investment & Business Center, USA
(202) 546-2103. Fax: (202) 546-3275. E-mail: rusric@erols.com

Since the beginning, Arusha has been a huge media show, where the participants meet journalists, special envoys and diplomats, all impatient to be briefed on the latest developments.

It was certainly necessary to involve all the parties in one way or another to avoid the formation of a common front opposed to negotiations. It would in fact be simplistic to think that the "small" political parties have nothing to do with the violence and have no place in Arusha. A large number of the mainly Tutsi parties, especially PARENA, Rally for Democracy and Economic and Social Development (RADDES), PRP and INKINZO, have contributed to the finances of the Tutsi militias, and to the ville morte actions during the 1994-96 period, which the army largely tolerated, if not actively encouraged, at the time. However, some parties are economic-political enterprises, sometimes mounted by a single family with the sole aim of maneuvering one of its members into position to take up a post as secretary of state or ambassador".

Arusha offered these parties a stage, a per diem (around $US 150 per day) and, as a result, a temporary life insurance. There were three major consequences. First of all, serious eighteen-party negotiations were shown to be impossible. The Facilitation team was often overtaken by the maneuvering of one or other party, sometimes giving the impression of discovering the Burundian problem rather than resolving it, and had obvious language difficulties (the Burundians speak Kirundi and French while the majority of the Facilitation team speak Swahili and English).

Next, such a public environment is not conducive to flexibility with regard to position taking. On the contrary, each attempt at a mini-compromise must be made openly in the face of public opinion in Bujumbura and of party militants, often before being able to offer any guarantee from the other side.

Finally, a mechanism such as this, which gives everyone a right to speak and a right of veto, does not encourage negotiations to take place on fundamental interests, but rather on the basis of power-sharing between elite groups. Observing the positioning and re-positioning maneuvers of the politicians involved since June 1998, it becomes clear that many of them expected power to be distributed at Arusha.

In an attempt to remedy these problems of methodology and "in order to facilitate the progress of the negotiations", the Facilitation team suggested setting up negotiation groups within each Committee. The idea came from Committee II, which sought to facilitate the discussion on the electoral system by separating supporters of direct elections and those of indirect elections into distinct groups. In fact, since March 1999 the government had been working on a project for Burundian society, centered on a long transition that would guarantee Buyoya's

For additional analytical, marketing, investment and business opportunities information, please contact
Global Investment & Business Center, USA
(202) 546-2103. Fax: (202) 546-3275. E-mail: rusric@erols.com

presence for a few years. Scared of being taken by surprise, the group of "Forces for Democratic Change" (FRODEBU, CNDD, the Liberal Party (PL), the People's Party (PP), the Rally for the People of Burundi (RPB), FROLINA and PALIPEHUTU), soon to become known as G7 (the group of seven), then decided to meet in Moshi in Tanzania. "Mwalimu Nyerere's positive response to G7's request to go to Moshi for talks before the last session of Arusha IV was based on this thinking. For the same reason, the members of G8 (the eight-party group composed of PARENA, PRP, the Burundian-African Alliance for Salvation (ABASA), the National Alliance for Law and Economic Development (ANADDE), the Alliance of the Valliant (AV-INTWARI), INKINZO, the Independent Workers' Party (PIT) and the Party for Social Democracy (PSD) remained in Arusha to harmonize their position."

But the setting up of these blocs was immediately contested by the government as a move seeking to promote ethnic identities and giving a platform to the extremists. G7 defined itself as the group defending the principle of one-person/one-vote, but was in fact a Hutu bloc. G8 was promoting the interests of the minority, the genocide argument and the issue of guarantees and included only Tutsi-dominated parties. Meanwhile, G3 (the government, the National Assembly and UPRONA) claimed to unite both Hutus and Tutsis, UPRONA and part of FRODEBU in its policy of partnership and national unity. And suddenly, FRODEBU had one foot in the partnership and one in G7. Thus it was in the same bloc as the armed bands, while maintaining links with the government without officially denouncing violence.

With the suspension of sanctions in January 1999, the government believed that it could win a respite. But the creation of the blocs in May 1999 led to a balance of force that was unfavorable to the government and revived the hostility between it and the Facilitation team. As a senior Burundian civil servant put it: "Nyerere tricked us…" The Facilitation team wanted to encourage an anti-Buyoya consensus by maneuvering to put the government in the minority (G7 + G8 = G15). The government and its delegation to the talks always feared that it would not pass the test of a vote if Arusha resorted to this method to choose a transition government.

The tension between the Facilitation team and the government rose to such a level that the process was almost definitively blocked. At the closing plenary session in July 1999, the Facilitator and the Minister for the Peace Process had an intense disagreement over the issue of the participation of the armed factions. Immediately afterwards Nyerere fell gravely ill and the opportunity for improving his relations with the Burundi government was lost. In an attempt to save the process, a new methodology was established with consultations between key players in Dar es Salaam in September. While this led to a certain relaxation in the atmosphere between these six negotiators, it nonetheless created another

For additional analytical, marketing, investment and business opportunities information, please contact
Global Investment & Business Center, USA
(202) 546-2103. Fax: (202) 546-3275. E-mail: rusric@erols.com

type of conflict between the six principal parties and the twelve "small parties", scandalized at the prospect of being marginalized.

COMPETITION BETWEEN THE INTERNAL AND EXTERNAL PROCESSES

The disagreement between the government and the Facilitator was not only a question of methodology. It was based on a misunderstanding from the start.

Between the beginning of his mediation attempt in March 1996 and the putsch in July 1996, Nyerere consulted Buyoya regularly and set up a technical committee charged with examining the request presented by the Ntibantunganya government at the time of the deployment of a military regional assistance force. When the July coup was announced, Nyerere felt betrayed and accused Buyoya of seizing power to avoid regional intervention.

For the countries of the region, sanctions were "the only viable alternative to remaining passive or intervening militarily - an option envisaged in some circles, but which the Security Council was not prepared to accept... The countries of the region did not have the necessary resources to support an intervention without the backing of the major powers through a Security Council resolution." In reality, regional policy since 1996 has essentially been to pressure and weaken the Buyoya government. The first tool was sanctions: "If these sanctions brought the different components of civil society affected by the sanctions to increase their pressure on the government, this could only meet the expectations of the region's heads of state."

It has also been a policy to brandish the threat of military intervention, or even the threat of a coup d'état sponsored by the region. Neither Nyerere, nor Uganda nor Rwanda has concealed that they have attempted to "recruit" candidates to succeed Buyoya. By this policy of pressure, the region was giving de facto political support to the opposition in exile and trying to change the balance of power between the military regime and its opposition by direct intervention in Burundian politics.

From then on relations between Nyerere and the Buyoya government became a test of strength. Each wished to dictate the terms and conditions of the negotiations according to their respective views of the perceived or real balance of power in Burundi.

This distrust was particularly evident in the various manipulations around the partnership that the government of Burundi concluded with the National Assembly. This was presented as a power-sharing formula legitimizing the regime in place. As the partnership was conceived, the regime counted on it serving as the foundation of the Arusha negotiations. In fact, the partnership was

For additional analytical, marketing, investment and business opportunities information, please contact
Global Investment & Business Center, USA
(202) 546-2103. Fax: (202) 546-3275. E-mail: rusric@erols.com

the result of an internal negotiation, without any intermediary, between the government and a good number of FRODEBU leaders, including the President of the Assembly, the Secretary-General of the party and other important party leaders. The government counted on the fact that the internal wing of FRODEBU would be capable of convincing the politicians outside the country to accept the partnership as the result of real negotiations. Arusha was to serve to persuade those from outside, the politicians in exile as well as the rebels, to adhere to this agreement.

Nyerere and Museveni fought the partnership from the outset. They saw it as a delaying tactic by the government, and did their best to circumvent the negotiations before they were due to begin on 21 June 1999. They were also determined to put pressure on the President of the Assembly until the last moment to ensure that the new constitutional act of transition remained unsigned.

This policy of applying pressure succeeded to a certain degree since the Arusha process finally took first place over the internal process. But it failed to make Buyoya leave and almost definitively blocked the talks. It gave the government the impression that not only did the mediation process take Hutu interests alone into account, but that it was ready to offer them a solution on a silver platter. All the efforts that the government deployed to win over the Hutu seemed to be thwarted by the promises of support given to the external FRODEBU wing by the mediation process and by the illusion of power which that gave them. The more the government felt itself to be in a hostile environment, the more it maneuvered to win time and blocked any possibility of real political compromise.

It was certainly unrealistic on the part of the government to believe that those working together in the partnership could simultaneously sit on both sides of the negotiating table. Irrespective of the Facilitation team's offer of support to FRODEBU, it was inevitable that the FRODEBU members of the partnership would be torn between solidarity with their party, which was putting all its bets on Arusha, and their role within the state, which called for a degree of unity with the military regime.

THE FAILURE OF THE CEASEFIRE

The inability to resolve the problem of violence was the third source of dispute and the main failing of Arusha as conceived by Nyerere. There are two reasons for this. First, the distrust between the government and the Facilitation team led to the question of violence being manipulated by the various parties, each trying to keep a margin for maneuver. Second, those who control the violence on each side have not been brought face to face and their interests have not been seriously negotiated.

For additional analytical, marketing, investment and business opportunities information, please contact
Global Investment & Business Center, USA
(202) 546-2103. Fax: (202) 546-3275. E-mail: rusric@erols.com

At the first session in June 1998, the ceasefire was the priority. But scarcely had the parties signed it on 21 June 1998 when it was immediately denounced by the armed branch of the CNDD, the FDD, which declared that they did not recognize Nyangoma's authority over their movement. Since then the ceasefire issue has been off the agenda and the question of the FDD's participation has not been resolved.

To the great indignation of the government, Nyerere first refused to invite this "dissident" group on the principle that he could not accept internal party "coups" unless the rules of procedure governing the negotiations were revised. Authorising a dissident group's participation would mean opening the talks to all candidates and risk encouraging party divisions. In addition, Nyangoma threatened to withdraw from Arusha if Jean Bosco Ndayikengurukiye, the FDD leader, were invited.

On the insistence of the Burundian government and international observers, Nyerere finally proposed four formulas in December 1998 as preludes to the participation of the dissident FDD members. Either the two factions should become reconciled; or Jean Bosco should summon an FDD Assembly according to correct form and legalise the rejection of Nyangoma; or he should create a new movement; or the FDD should participate in the government delegation.

This last option was a way for Nyerere to disguise a denunciation of the supposed collusion between the government and the Jean Bosco FDD. Nyerere suspected that the government was seeking to short-circuit the political negotiations by signing a ceasefire under its own conditions. It is true that the government had discreetly tried to contact Bosco several times since December 1998 through the intermediary of his brother, Augustin Nzojibwami, one of the architects of the partnership and head of the internal wing of FRODEBU, and through the help of some South African NGOs. It had been insisting since July 1998 on the presence of all the armed factions at Arusha.

In this context of mutual distrust, the FDD leadership was also reluctant to rejoin Arusha, fearing that Nyerere would force them to reconcile with Nyangoma and come to the negotiations as a negligible force. Nyerere then accused them of holding the negotiations hostage and proposed continuing the process without them. His idea was to reach a multi-party political agreement that would remove the reason for the FDD to continue fighting. Tanzania would have acted as guarantor of the agreement and would have committed itself to marginalizing those who refused to give up their arms. When the agreement for a ceasefire in the DRC was signed in July 1999, Nyerere believed that the fate of the FDD, described as "negative forces to be disarmed" by this agreement, was resolved and that the process would go forward without them.

For additional analytical, marketing, investment and business opportunities information, please contact
Global Investment & Business Center, USA
(202) 546-2103. Fax: (202) 546-3275. E-mail: rusric@erols.com

Although some of the Facilitator's arguments on these points were well founded, the failure to include the armed factions in the negotiations constitutes a fundamental flaw in the Arusha process. By relegating the issue of violence to second place and not removing the ambiguity over the nebulous question of the rebellion, he confirmed the government's suspicions about the bad faith of the Facilitation team, as well as Tanzania's duplicity with regard to the peace process.

For the Burundian government, the Facilitator was seeking to utilize the two means of applying pressure available to him: sanctions and the violence. After the suspension of sanctions due to international pressure, he wanted to keep the violence as a potential means of pressure. In addition, Tanzania has always made it known that it had not ruled out one day providing massive support to the rebellion. Nyerere himself said to some members of the government delegation in July: "I do not have experience in negotiations. My experience is in support for liberation movements."

But an agreement signed without the rebels could not work for several reasons. First, concluding an agreement that would not stop the war immediately would bring no guarantee for a future end to the war. It was unrealistic to think that an agreement that included the government (and thus the army), but less than half the rebel movement would force the two parties to abandon violence. Most peace accords considered as "unfinished business" or as injuring one of the two parties have little chance of holding.

The regional context could fuel many opportunities for external support and the resumption of the war for one or other party. Secondly, leaving the rebel movements out of the process would provide a possible way out for FRODEBU, which could try to "exit" from the agreement or to denounce it if the rebellion gained strength in the future. Finally, there is little chance that even FRODEBU would accept the separation of the military and political aspects because effective government requires control of the armed forces.

In any case it is almost impossible to negotiate an agreement and encourage the parties to the conflict to build a common future when emotions are raised by the daily acts of war committed by both sides. Experience shows that in a context of violence, the Hutus and Tutsis automatically return to extreme ethnic positions.

THE ATTITUDE OF THE INTERNATIONAL COMMUNITY AND HOW THE PEACE PROCESS HAS BECOME PERSONALIZED

Since March 1996 the international community and the region's heads of state had placed all their hopes in Julius Nyerere's leadership. They had a vision of making Burundi an experimental laboratory for African solutions to African

For additional analytical, marketing, investment and business opportunities information, please contact
Global Investment & Business Center, USA
(202) 546-2103. Fax: (202) 546-3275. E-mail: rusric@erols.com

problems in the Great Lakes region. However, much criticism has been laid against the Arusha process by international observers and donors. This criticism contributed towards the suspension of sanctions in January 1999. But at Nyerere's request, donors maintained a de facto embargo on development aid. The official policy at a meeting on Burundi held in New York the same month remained, "don't upset Mwalimu".

It could be said that just as the Facilitation team was dependent on international finance for the Arusha process, so the international community became dependent on the "Nyerere aura" and the theory of "African solutions to African problems", and more concerned about maintaining a framework for negotiations than about their effectiveness. The Burundi Peace Negotiations (BPN) team, composed of former members of Nyerere's government, reinforced this personalization of the process. At the beginning of the process, the BPN team strongly interfered in the committees and in the organization of the debates, but this interference has been much reduced since January 1999.

Only four days after Nyerere's death on 14 October last year, the special envoys of the international community met in New York to discuss the future of the Arusha process. Following this meeting on 18 October, the UN Secretary-General sent a report to the Security Council recommending assistance in identifying a new mediator as quickly as possible. It also called for the continued involvement of the region, and more specifically Tanzania, in the process. The special envoys traveled through the region, trying to promote the ideal profile of a mediator, but they were politely told that the Burundian process was the region's own affair. The Americans nonetheless pushed hard to have Mandela accepted as mediator by the region.

THE NOMINATION OF MANDELA: A TURNING POINT IN THE PEACE PROCESS

The eighth Great Lakes regional summit on Burundi on 1 December 99 nominated Nelson Mandela as the new Facilitator of the Burundian process. The following were present at the summit: Presidents Daniel arap Moi of Kenya, Benjamin Mkapa of Tanzania, Yoweri Museveni of Uganda and Thabo Mbeki of South Africa, as well as the Prime minister of Ethiopia, Meles Zenawi, the Rwandan Prime Minister, Pierre-Célestin Rwigema, the Secretary-General of the OAU, Salim Ahmed Salim, a representative of President Bouteflika of Algeria and the Foreign Minister of Zambia. The DRC and Zimbabwe declined the invitation.

In their final communiqué, the heads of state condemned the "indiscriminate" violence against civilians and called on the new Facilitator to give priority to the question of a ceasefire. They recognized that the negotiations had "reached an advanced stage" and decided that the process would continue in Arusha with the

For additional analytical, marketing, investment and business opportunities
information, please contact
Global Investment & Business Center, USA
(202) 546-2103. Fax: (202) 546-3275. E-mail: rusric@erols.com

existing infrastructure, i.e. with the Facilitation team set up by Nyerere. The heads of state repeated that there was no alternative to a negotiated solution, but insisted on negotiations being concluded as rapidly as possible. Finally, they called on the government to dismantle the regroupment camps immediately.

REGIONAL INTERESTS

The nomination of Mandela, and the consequent involvement of South Africa, marks the first challenge to the region's hold over the Burundian peace process since March 1996. This "sub-region" is an interesting entity to observe. Nyerere gave it content by taking on the leadership of the Burundian process in March 1996 and imposing sanctions in July 1996. The "sub-region" then comprised Tanzania, Uganda, Rwanda, the former Zaire, Ethiopia, Zambia, and Cameroon and Zimbabwe, which successively held the presidency of the Organization for African Unity (OAU) at that time. It is by the way quite ironic to note that the countries initially invited to build a regional consensus on Burundi find themselves in opposing camps in the present conflict in the DRC today.

However, most of these countries very quickly denounced the embargo on Burundi, and it became clear that only Tanzania and Uganda held a firm anti-Buyoya line -- despite the fact that businessmen from these two countries were among the embargo's first violators. The embargo was finally suspended in January 1999 under international pressure. After Nyerere's death it was Museveni, President of the Great Lakes initiative on Burundi who found himself in charge of continuing the regional process.

After 1996, Nyerere and Museveni had been counting on making Burundi a test of political co-operation for the East African Community, which was finally resurrected on 30 November 1999. The center of gravity in the Burundi initiative naturally leans towards this grouping, which has had even greater legitimacy for imposing conditions since Burundi asked to become a member in January 1999.

The countries of the sub-region share a common vision for analysing the Burundi problem. Almost all of them trained in the "Dar es Salaam school" and particularly agree on the fact that the Burundian government, the only remaining regime in the region to evolve from a classic military dictatorship inherited from independence, must be overthrown. But they differ on the credibility of the liberation movements "available" in Burundi. For Tanzania, the Hutu armed movements born out of the refugee camps on its territory since 1972 have legitimacy as liberation movements against the repressive Tutsi-minority government. For Uganda and Rwanda, these armed movements are ideologically too close of those who committed the genocide in Rwanda in 1994.

For additional analytical, marketing, investment and business opportunities
information, please contact
Global Investment & Business Center, USA
(202) 546-2103. Fax: (202) 546-3275. E-mail: rusric@erols.com

But President Museveni cannot pardon Buyoya for having introduced democracy too early into the region (in 1993) and for later returning to power by force (in 1996). He seeks to identify and promote a new generation of politicians, particularly Hutu liberals, and to marginalize the extremists. In a speech at the December summit, he condemned the violence against civilians by both parties: "There is a more important question: who should be the target of armed struggles? What kind of liberation movement targets non-combatants? I also hear the argument that the Burundi army targets civilians. This is not correct."

It seems that the choice of a new Facilitator was a controversial one and that several countries were reluctant to see South Africa mixed up in the mediation process. In the first place, Tanzania did not wish to have its unique role of regional leadership removed from it. This was a question of prestige, of continuing Mwalimu's work, of "liberating" Burundi, one of the only African countries still under a regime inherited from the days of de-colonization. As interference in the internal affairs of neighbors seems to be the rule for the region, Tanzania, which has remained neutral in the anti-Kabila war, has to prove that it is still influential. President Mkapa has clearly stated that Tanzania does not wish to take responsibility for the failure of the process, despite accusations that it has destabilised Burundi, but is anxious to have a share of the glory if it should succeed: "We do not insist that Arusha or Tanzania remains the venue. We also do not insist on certain roles for any Tanzanian or for Tanzania as a whole. For we do not want Tanzania to be the scapegoat for procrastination in the negotiations… [but] I say if we follow diligently on the trail blazed by Mwalimu, working with those who have participated so far in the peace talks, we will… move forward much faster."

For the Ugandan President, keeping control of the Burundian peace process is also a way of establishing the region's authority and his own stature after Nyerere's death. He made this quite clear in his speech to the summit: "Finally, let me stress the fact that this is a regional initiative that is of crucial significance to the future of the region. If we can pull it through, we shall increase confidence in ourselves to solve our own problems without the help of outsiders.

For this Ugandan-Tanzanian co-operation to function, Museveni, so often accused of wanting to build a "Hima empire", must support Tanzania in its mediation efforts and provide reassurance of its neutrality with regard to the Tutsis of Burundi. Accordingly, he convened a summit between Presidents Mkapa and Buyoya in January 2000 to try to improve relations between Tanzania and Burundi. He also invited President Buyoya to Kampala on 10 March 2000 to discuss the evolution in the negotiations, particularly the reform of the army and the issue of the transition. He recently gave Tanzania proof of his impartiality by blocking arms destined for Burundi which were transiting through Uganda. This consignment, originally ordered from China during Buyoya's first presidential

For additional analytical, marketing, investment and business opportunities information, please contact
Global Investment & Business Center, USA
(202) 546-2103. Fax: (202) 546-3275. E-mail: rusric@erols.com

term, was blocked the first time round in Dar es Salaam for several months and then returned to China. After ordering new arms in China, Buyoya sought reassurance from Museveni at the Algiers summit in July 1999 that this consignment could pass through Uganda from Mombasa. But once the consignment arrived at the Kenya-Uganda border, the information was leaked to the Tanzanians who immediately asked for it not to be allowed through.

In reality, it is important for Museveni to keep watch over relations between Rwanda and Burundi, which he interprets as a rapprochement. Since the tensions between the two factions of the Congolese Rally for Democracy (RCD) and the battle of Kisangani between the Rwandan Patriotic Army (RPA) and the Ugandan People's Defence Forece (UPDF) in August 1998, Museveni has been keeping a close eye on Rwanda's alliances. He suspects the country of using Burundian weaponry since he withdrew Ugandan heavy equipment from Goma in the wake of Wamba dia Wamba's departure for Kisangani in April 1999. It will be recalled that the Ugandan press had accused the Burundians of taking part in the battle of Kisangani on the Rwandan side.

Because of this, Museveni was a little reluctant to see South Africa take a more active role in Burundi. In fact, his perception of Thabo Mbeki's government's inclination towards Rwanda in the argument over the RCD leadership raised fears of the emergence of a Rwanda-South Africa-Burundi triangle. Kenya also has doubts about the arrival in the region of the economic power of South Africa - always on the look-out for markets and outlets for its industry.

For Rwanda, the priority is to have Burundi as a stable ally, with a government sharing the same regional security objectives. While war continues to rage in the DRC, a coalition government that would give the Hutus controlling power as the result of the negotiations would constitute an obstacle to the regional war against the Hutu extremists fighting with Kabila. In addition, the Ugandan-Tanzanian exclusive handhold on the Burundian process is of concern to the Kigali government, given the tensions with Uganda since the Kisangani fighting, and with Tanzania, suspected of sympathising with the Burundian and maybe even Rwandan non-génocidaire Hutu opposition.

For these reasons Rwanda has supported the involvement of South Africa in the Burundi peace talks as a counterweight to the region, perfectly aware that the results of the Burundian negotiations will constitute a precedent. Rwanda, which did not hesitate to show its displeasure at the successive reports concerning its admission into the new East African Community, sent only its prime minister to the summit of heads of state on 1 December, thereby revealing its clear distrust of the regional initiative on Burundi.

For additional analytical, marketing, investment and business opportunities information, please contact
Global Investment & Business Center, USA
(202) 546-2103. Fax: (202) 546-3275. E-mail: rusric@erols.com

The evening before, and even on the morning of the 1 December summit, the presidents in attendance complained of the fact that Museveni, who as President of the regional initiative was supposed to consult them, had not informed them that Mandela was a candidate for the Burundian mediation process. In fact, Uganda and Tanzania wanted to promote Ketumile Masire, the former President of Botswana. The formula found to keep the Tanzanians associated with the process was to appoint Joseph Warioba, formerly Prime Minister of Tanzania and member of Nyerere's mediation team, as a deputy to Masire.

Mandela had also been approached with regard to the inter-Congolese dialogue in the DRC foreseen under the Lusaka agreement. However, as Kabila had rejected this proposal ten days before the summit on Burundi, there was a considerable chance that Masire would be the only candidate for the DRC to be proposed by the OAU. It remained only to nominate either Warioba or Mandela for Burundi.

SOUTH AFRICA'S INTERESTS

 The South African government pushed Mandela into accepting the mediation role. The presence of Thabo Mbeki in person at the summits of 1 December 1999 and 22 February 2000 is an indication of this. Using Burundi as a test case, the government is seeking to promote South African diplomacy and its agenda of an African renaissance, a main priority of its foreign policy. It has defined this in the following terms: "As a movement we will also do whatever we can to contribute to the termination of other violent conflicts that are taking place on our continent, fully cognisant of the importance of saving African lives and the creation of conditions of stability, without which no development is possible." Thabo Mbeki had scarcely returned to South Africa when he stated that Mandela's nomination was an indication of confidence in South Africa's capacity to assist in the settlement of regional conflicts, that his government would "do everything" to assist Mandela and that he had already assigned several of his senior officials to the Burundian process.

The main question mark concerns the way in which the partnership between South Africa and Tanzania is going to operate. The two countries have everything to gain from a fruitful co-operation. Through Nyerere's fight against apartheid, they already have a very strong historic link and the South African economic breakthrough in Tanzania reinforces their interdependence. In addition, Thabo Mbeki has announced his intention of building stronger economic and political relations with Tanzania. A South African analyst quoted by Reuters explains: "Thabo Mbeki has evolved a strategy that involves working with countries such as Nigeria in West Africa and Tanzania in East Africa".

For additional analytical, marketing, investment and business opportunities information, please contact
Global Investment & Business Center, USA
(202) 546-2103. Fax: (202) 546-3275. E-mail: rusric@erols.com

Mandela's role in Burundi will give the South African government an entry into the conflicts in the DRC and in Rwanda. Already involved in diplomatic efforts to convince the two branches of the RCD to sign the Lusaka agreement, South Africa has shown that it has a degree of influence over Rwanda. Aware that the minority/majority relationship in Rwanda and Burundi is an essential element of the destabilisation in the Great Lakes, the government of Thabo Mbeki is counting on using this influence in the medium term to stabilise the two political regimes and find economic partners in Central Africa. From this perspective, an attempt at establishing contact between Thabo Mbeki and Kabila was observed in March 2000.

At first, South Africa's involvement did not reassure the Hutu opposition in general and met resistance from the CNDD, which made known its view that South Africa was not neutral before and after the summit in December. It denounced both the sale of South African arms to Burundi and to Rwanda and the contacts made between the Burundian government and the dissident FDD on its territory. The Union for National Liberation (ULINA) also expressed its disapproval. None of the three rebel leaders were present at the summit to demonstrate their opposition. But for the CNDD it is vital to continue to involve Tanzania, which sees its priority objective as a return to majority rule and which has the necessary means to impose this. Indeed, if the objective of the new mediator is only to make peace in Burundi, there is a risk that the agreement reached will not impose the immediate return to the results of the 1993 elections. Ironically, despite the insistence of the Buyoya government of promoting Mandela as the best mediator for Burundi, some Tutsis fear that Mandela will see the Burundi problem only through the South African prism and want to apply the model of majority rule to Burundi.

THE INTERESTS OF THE BURUNDIAN GOVERNMENT

Mandela's nomination was a diplomatic victory for the Burundian government, which had directed its diplomacy towards this objective since Nyerere's death. Burundian delegations toured the region and Europe, lobbying for Mandela, "period".

The contacts between the two countries date from the time of the regional embargo when part of Burundi's exports and imports passed through South Africa, often via Lake Tanganyika and the port of Mpulungu in Zambia. The first contact between Buyoya and Mbeki took place when Mbeki was inaugurated as President in June 1999, and was followed by Buyoya's visit to South Africa in September. Since then, several Burundian delegations have visited the country and the South African government has sent political advisers to Burundi to evaluate the situation.

For additional analytical, marketing, investment and business opportunities
information, please contact
Global Investment & Business Center, USA
(202) 546-2103. Fax: (202) 546-3275. E-mail: rusric@erols.com

The Burundian government has a number of reasons for involving South Africa. Above all, there is the matter of creating a counterweight in the region. First, because the regional mediation effort was perceived as hostile to its interests and it hoped for a more attentive attitude towards the fate of the Tutsi minority. Secondly, because of the Burundians' concern that the war in the DRC could spill over the border - and especially over Kabila's and Zimbabwe's support for the FDD and Tanzania's support for the rebellion. Consequently, they were counting on South Africa to put pressure both on Zimbabwe to end support for the FDD and on Tanzania to ensure better control of its territory and common borders with Burundi. One of the government's primary concerns was that Tanzania would expel Burundian refugees from the Kigoma region (around 300,000), which would serve as a cover for FDD infiltration into the southern provinces of Burundi, giving the rebel movement the chance to occupy some territory. The regional role and South Africa's power of coercion would therefore be a guarantee against this type of strategy. As one government representative put it, "for us, the guarantee of the agreement is that Tanzania doesn't interfere."

After the death of Nyerere, the Burundian government effectively lost the guarantee of Tanzanian moderation. Nyerere wanted to give the negotiations a chance and moderated the desire of certain pro-Hutu lobbies in the army, in parliament and in the business community, all of whom would have preferred a violent solution in Burundi by giving massive support to the Burundian rebel movements. There are still some supporters of an intervention in Burundi, who see this as following the model of the Tanzanian intervention in Uganda in the eighties. Among them are Jakwaya Kikwete, the Minister of Foreign Affairs, John Malecela, President of the CCM, the party in power for 30 years, and the Tanzanian Chief of Staff. They are all known for their hard line towards Buyoya's regime. This position is accentuated by the fact that refugees are continuing to flow into Tanzania. The possibility of the already very high tension between the two countries degenerating into conflict as the result of border incidents cannot be ruled out.

South Africa also has the capacity to assist Burundi economically. South African companies already own big chunks of the economies of Uganda, Rwanda and Tanzania. The creation of a link between the two countries is a first step towards opening Burundian markets to South African products and making the country more independent of international development co-operation. The visit by the South African Minister of Foreign Affairs Nkosazana Zuma to Burundi at the beginning of March was partly linked to the establishment of bilateral co-operation between South Africa and Burundi.

THE MANDELA APPROACH: AN AGREEMENT IN JUNE?

For additional analytical, marketing, investment and business opportunities information, please contact
Global Investment & Business Center, USA
(202) 546-2103. Fax: (202) 546-3275. E-mail: rusric@erols.com

Mandela's approach has breathed new life into the inter-Burundian talks. His first priority is to conclude the Arusha process, which has already gone on for too long, as quickly as possible. He speaks of an agreement by June 2000 and has presented institutional donors with a request for financing a single session of the talks. Mandela and his team are also reflecting on measures for judicial proceedings against non-participants and on securing guarantees for the implementation of the agreement. This pressure is making the price of exclusion from the process very much higher. At the same time it is sending out a warning to each participant of being identified as responsible for the failure and and thus ending up a major loser from the process.

To reach this objective, the mediator has decided on a change of method. He proposes terminating the work in committee and working directly on a draft agreement, which was distributed on 27 March 2000 during the meeting of heads of delegations. He has warned all the participants that they have three weeks to make amendments and recommendations. But he also gave a warning that "some of these amendments and comments will be included in the proposals on merit, but there are many that will not be accepted."

The first characteristic of the Mandela approach is the internationalization of the Burundian problem. By inviting all the presidents of the region, and the major powers: President Bill Clinton and ministers from France (Charles Josselin), Britain (Peter Hain) and Belgium (Louis Michel), he is raising the visibility of the process considerably. In doing so, he also exposes the responsibilities of the international community and invites them to speak with a single voice. He began his mediation effort in New York where he reminded the Security Council that: "the failure of those responsible to provide conditions of security and social development to the people of Burundi does not represent some errant occurrence on the periphery. This hits at the heart of our common human obligation".

His video-conference meeting with Bill Clinton showed everyone that his efforts have the full support of the United States. President Clinton said: "America cares about the peace process... I call on the rebels to stop hostilities... This will be a long and difficult journey, but I am with you." Another summit took place at the end of March with Presidents Obasanjo and Gaddafi. By creating an international unanimity around the process, he is also preventing the Burundians from playing off some international players against others.

The involvement of donors and the simultaneous use of the carrot and stick policy represent a major change from the isolation resulting from the sanctions and the total suspension of development aid since 1996. All countries present at the February summit pledged support to Burundi: "The US will help create economic conditions for the agreement to work." "Belgium is determined to plead

For additional analytical, marketing, investment and business opportunities information, please contact
Global Investment & Business Center, USA
(202) 546-2103. Fax: (202) 546-3275. E-mail: rusric@erols.com

for Burundi's case within the European Union if the regroupment camps are dismantled… to give legal and economic assistance in the demobilization and re-integration of the combatants." "France is prepared to assist Burundi to get out of its state of economic suffocation… and particularly in the domain of reconciliation, the re-integration of the rebels, the changes in the institutions and the electoral system… France will participate in the Committee on the guarantees for the implementation of the agreement when the mediator wishes it to do so." "The UK will be ready to support Burundi when there is peace."

The international community is thus supporting Mandela and seems to be insisting on a successful and quick conclusion to the Burundian process. A change can be observed in international thinking on Burundi since Nyerere's death. The Americans, who had blocked an emergency loan from the World Bank, pushed for the organization of a Security Council meeting that produced a resolution calling for development aid to be resumed in November 1999. They also pressed for South Africa's involvement, providing an opportunity for South African diplomacy to prove itself in Burundi, while keeping in mind a possible role in the DRC. As far as international diplomacy is concerned, any agreement on Burundi should be complementary to the Lusaka agreement and constitute a model for the region.

However, to the extent that the Lusaka accords are not yet being implemented, Burundi continues to resist a rapid conclusion in Arusha. As President Joachim Chissano of Mozambique said, "in the Great Lakes everything is linked, but it cannot be expected that there are simultaneous agreements in all the countries of the region. The process has to be continued." This approach is, however, focusing more on the process itself than on its outcome. It must be doubted whether little Burundi can meet the challenge of reaching peace in a region in which all internal conflicts are exported to the DRC.

The second characteristic of Mandela's approach is to exercise continuous pressure on the political players. In his first contacts with the Burundians, he called on the political class to assume a sense of its responsibilities. In front of the region's heads of state, he stated: "There is a wide-spelled assumption that the problem with Burundi is the absence of leaders who are capable of bringing peace. But innocent civilians are being slaughtered now. There is a serious obligation for each and every leader here to recognize the importance of compromise… By delaying the conclusion of an agreement, you suggest that you don't care about people dying inside Burundi."

Mandela also mentioned the issue of a lack of funds restricting the process: "If you have no sense of urgency, why should we ask for more money?" He particularly stressed the role of the actual President, the President of the Assembly and former Presidents Bagaza and Ntibantunganya: "I expect them to

For additional analytical, marketing, investment and business opportunities information, please contact
Global Investment & Business Center, USA
(202) 546-2103. Fax: (202) 546-3275. E-mail: rusric@erols.com

lead the compromise proposal." He also emphasised the responsibilities of the nine party heads in exile, warning them that too great an intransigence on their part would make the population inside Burundi believe that they are no longer in touch with the country.

Among other themes of his speech were the dismantling of the regroupment camps, which he described as "not fit for any human beings to live in", the release of political prisoners - "a situation that is totally unacceptable, especially to a person like myself who has spent 27 years in jail," - and the lifting of press censorship.

The former South African President surprised everybody by being extremely firm on the ethnic issue and more specifically the domination of the Tutsi minority. He explained to several delegations that apartheid, black or white, had to be fought and advised Buyoya to leave power in time. He adopted a very direct style with all the participants, which came as a real culture shock to Burundians used to allusions and meanings only half-expressed. It was an approach that evoked memories of his negotiations with Frederick De Klerk, the former white South African President. Speaking of the Tutsis, he said on several occasions that "as long as the minority dominates politically, economically and militarily, there can be no peace… You are discrediting yourself if you deny the obvious…" But he also told the participants: "You must accommodate the majority, but if the minority feels the agreement will threaten their existence, they will not co-operate". Referring to the rebels, he said: "They are too weak to tackle military installations. They vent their anger against civilians. They cannot be said to be freedom fighters, they are barbarians, terrorists."

The pressure is particularly strong on President Buyoya, whom Mandela has advised to leave power. During the February summit, Mandela referred to presidents who left power at the height of their glory: himself, Ketumile Masire and Julius Nyerere.

This message was reiterated by Nigeria's President Obasanjo during the March summit: "To speak clearly, as long as the military is in power, society loses the vital habit of thinking creatively and democratically and of resolving its problems in the same spirit. Then comes the day when the military leaves power, for it invariably have to do so, and society has to start again from zero to imbibe democracy."

This pressure has two objectives. First, it obliges President Buyoya to come to Arusha himself to defend his position (in other words, to campaign and negotiate for his retention of his power). Up till now the President's attitude has always been in effect to withdraw from the process and "to leave the Burundians to negotiate, including over who should lead the transition." Secondly, Mandela's

For additional analytical, marketing, investment and business opportunities information, please contact
Global Investment & Business Center, USA
(202) 546-2103. Fax: (202) 546-3275. E-mail: rusric@erols.com

strategy is to provoke a public debate on the other eventual candidates for the transition and to show that this debate ties in with the county's interests and not only those of its elite groups. No matter who the candidate is for the transition, what counts for Mandela is reaching a consensus among the negotiators.

This direct approach by the former South African President has provoked a positive debate, but it has aroused fears at the same time. Some say that the time has come to destroy the myths and ethnic taboos, that it is necessary to see if the participants are serious and that it will probably be impossible to reach an agreement without pressure.

Others emphasize that under such international pressure and in the face of the mediator's insistence on concluding the process rapidly, no participant will take the risk of refusing to sign the peace agreement, but that many questions remain in suspense. First of all, the Burundians perceive that the Facilitation team is stressing an early success for the process to the detriment of the content of the compromises reached. None of the major questions has been resolved: the amnesty, the integration of the rebels into the army and the transition. Committees II and III have not finished their work and the rebels have neither yet participated in the debate nor given their recommendations. Finally, it seems that there was a misunderstanding between the Facilitation team and the Burundians on the agreement project distributed in March 2000.

This is certainly not the "compromise proposal" that Mandela announced in his speech and on which he asked the delegations to work, but rather a synthesis of the discussions in each committee. Yet the Burundians, who are supposed to provide their comments shortly, do not seem to have been warned that this is a synthesis of the debates and not the final document, which is still being prepared. This misunderstanding arises partly from the fact that the mediator, whose time is very occupied, is only in Arusha for the opening of sessions and not for the continuation of their work. This comes under the responsibility of the Facilitation team, in which most of the predominantly-Tutsi parties have no confidence.

Each time Mandela speaks a little too directly, these parties blame it on "bad briefings" by the Tanzanian Facilitation team. In March, Mandela expected the Burundians to sign a statement on the progress made and to ensure the participation of the armed groups, but some Burundians claimed that the Facilitation team was opposed to this.

The controversy over Mandela's visit to Burundi is another example of the tension. After announcing that his first priority was to go to Burundi in December, Mandela had to withdraw his promise, after pressure from several parties who considered such a visit would "legitimise" the government in place. Subsequently, Mandela promised to go to Burundi to talk with the Burundian

For additional analytical, marketing, investment and business opportunities information, please contact
Global Investment & Business Center, USA
(202) 546-2103. Fax: (202) 546-3275. E-mail: rusric@erols.com

military, of which a delegation had visited him in South Africa. But the government considered this insufficient, holding that Mandela must listen and speak to all Burundians who will, after all, be the ultimate guarantors of the process being implemented.

Finally, Mandela's desire for a public debate on the future leader of the transition risks giving the impression to Buyoya and his supporters that a consensus is being sought against him and against the Tutsis. Buyoya's supporters fear that he is going to lose face, as a result of which the process will be blocked again. Criticising the Tutsis when they are the ones who have to concede everything could prove counter-effective.

This stance on the Tutsi minority has put the government, which had itself pleaded for Mandela to accept the mediation role, in a very embarrassing position with regard to its political base. Coming back from the February 2000 summit in Arusha, President Buyoya has himself been obliged to say that the Facilitator seems to have "a simplistic view of the Burundian problem." Ten days after the summit, Mandela announced at Abuja that he was not sure of seeing the process through to its conclusion and that he would perhaps hand over to someone younger. This announcement could also be interpreted as an attempt to put pressure on the players in the negotiations.

The third characteristic of the Mandela approach is the inclusion of the armed factions. The great success of the process up to now is to have apparently succeeded in getting the dissident FDD leader, Jean Bosco Ndayikengurukiye, and Cossan Kabura of the FNL to participate. A meeting took place on 20 March 2000 between the FDD leader and Mandela and resulted in a declaration of principle by Jean Bosco of the FDD's willingness to participate in the negotiations in Arusha, but with "preliminary" conditions that were "not open to discussion". He called for the release of political prisoners and Hutus held in the "Nazi-style" regroupment camps. "Nothing can happen as long as the regrouped people are not released and allowed to return home. Nothing is possible as long as people who voted in favor of democracy are in jails. We shall go to Arusha when those things have been done." A meeting was also held between Mandela and Cossan Kabura a few days later.

Mandela made it clear to Nyangoma during the January session that the dissident FDD faction had to be brought into the process. The South Africans had tried to meet the FDD and FNL leaders before the Arusha summit in February, but without success. The FNL delegation was prevented from traveling by the Tanzanian authorities on grounds that it did not have the official documents (passports and official invitation for South Africa). As for the FDD delegation, it claimed to have a transport problem. A plane was then sent to them from South Africa, but they did not turn up at the airport. Some Burundians then made the

For additional analytical, marketing, investment and business opportunities information, please contact
Global Investment & Business Center, USA
(202) 546-2103. Fax: (202) 546-3275. E-mail: rusric@erols.com

point that referring to the rebels as "terrorists" and "barbarians" was not the best way for Mandela to get them to come and talk in Arusha.

The arrival of the FDD is probably partly due to the diplomatic efforts of Thabo Mbeki, who went to Zimbabwe in mid-March and sent his Ministers of Defence and Foreign Affairs to Lumumbashi a few days later and was even scheduled to meet Kabila. The challenge of getting the FDD to participate in the negotiations is greater than it appears. The FDD have in fact become a regional problem and are the hostages of Kabila and his allies, who have armed them and use them in the war in the DRC. There is little chance that Kabila will allow the FDD to quit his defense force definitively while the war is resuming against Rwanda, Burundi and Uganda.

In any case, until recently the FDD were waiting for the outcome of the war in the DRC and the Lusaka agreement before getting involved in Arusha. If the Lusaka accords are not implemented, they avoid being disarmed as "negative forces" and can hold the Burundian peace process hostage. The question is whether Mandela will be able to convince them both of the immediate benefits of Arusha and to abandon a war that is not their own. But Mandela does not have influence over Kabila - it will be recalled that his mediation between Kabila and Mobutu during the first war in ex-Zaire was a failure - and little influence over Mugabe, who sees him as his main rival.

Faced with this problem, the idea of signing the Arusha agreement without the FDD has again been raised, either involving them later or neutralizing them by a regional coalition that would bring them under the Lusaka accords. Both Nyerere and Museveni defended this position, which also appeals to a number of the international and regional players. The government of Burundi is opposed, however, to the marginalization of those with a role in the violence and is concerned by the fact that there is a risk of having part of the armed factions included in the agreement and another part remaining outside. By "de-politicising" them and making them outcasts, there is every chance of creating a situation similar to that of the Rwandan Interahamwe, which nobody now knows how to resolve.

The entry of the rebels at this stage of the process, although necessary, risks complicating the process for two reasons. The first is the possible rivalry between opposition Hutu politicians and armed Hutu rebels claiming to be the government's interlocutors on the army question. The army issue is the most difficult part of the negotiations for it constitutes the key element of power. This is why the integration of the rebels is at the heart of Hutu claims and Tutsi resistance. As far as FRODEBU is concerned, the military authority should be put at the service of the civil authority and army interference in politics should be avoided. FRODEBU wants negotiations on the integration of the rebels to fall

For additional analytical, marketing, investment and business opportunities information, please contact
Global Investment & Business Center, USA
(202) 546-2103. Fax: (202) 546-3275. E-mail: rusric@erols.com

under a global political agreement, only allowing the rebels to be associated at the "technical level". In reality, FRODEBU fears seeing the limelight stolen by those with the power to end the war and seeing what has been gained over the past 22 months again put in question. The FDD soldiers and civilians are likely to want to negotiate this integration in line with their own interests while setting their own conditions.

The government is proposing "open social and professional integration, including into the army", for the rebels. In fact, the regime is playing several cards at once. First it insisted on the inclusion of the rebels in the negotiations, with several ideas in mind - first of all to identify them, their leaders and their structures, before drawing up a detailed integration plan. Then, to establish a special contact with them in order to isolate the political parties. Finally, to fuel the competition between FRODEBU and the rebel factions, and between the factions themselves.

If a ceasefire is reached, it is probable that when the moment comes the government will insist on army missions "to protect the people" and ensure territorial security. It will be remembered that, when the ceasefire was signed on 21 June 1998, the head of the government delegation expressed reservations, explaining that the "national army was not a party to the conflict" and that "it should continue to maintain order".

Finally, the military power is playing its cards so as to disqualify the enemy. Military personnel are often heard to say that they agree with the proposed fusion - but with whom? At the last consultation in Dar es Salaam, UPRONA took a position that led to the debate taking a step backwards. In a document presented to Committee III, it explained that the future composition of the army "must take into account the genocide element." The idea is that the rebels must first be demobilized and disarmed, and then those with a clean sheet can be recruited. In other words, the army will act as if it were the victor when setting conditions. This position is based on the Lusaka accords, which classify the FDD as "negative forces" to be disarmed, and on proofs of collaboration between the FDD and ex-FAR "génocidaires". It can also be foreseen that when the discussion on integration becomes serious, a problem will arise over the several thousand Hutu already in the army (estimated at between 30 per cent and 35 per cent). These were trained to the same standards as their Tutsi colleagues who would not wish to cede their place and their income to the rebels. Should Mandela's proposal for an army 50 per cent Hutu (and not rebels) and 50 per cent Tutsi be applied, this problem will inevitably arise.

THE CHALLENGES TO THE PEACE PROCESS

THE VIOLENCE

For additional analytical, marketing, investment and business opportunities information, please contact
Global Investment & Business Center, USA
(202) 546-2103. Fax: (202) 546-3275. E-mail: rusric@erols.com

The resurgence of the violence since June, and even more since last September, reflects the rising stakes in the negotiation process. This violence can be explained by several internal and regional factors.

THE STRUCTURE OF THE REBELLION

The rebellion is loosely knit and fluid: it has no front and no firm control of territory; it is a mobile guerrilla movement. Nor does it have a common leadership and its political heads cannot prove that they represent the leaders in the field. With one branch in Dar es Salaam, one branch in Kigoma, one branch in Lumumbashi and one branch in Burundi, they have no common representation.

The rebel movement comprises several groups. The FNL, the armed wing of the Party for the Liberation of the Hutu People (PALIPEHUTU) has been split into two factions since 1992, one branch led by Etienne Karatasi and the other by Cossan Kabura. The CNDD-FDD is also divided into two branches led respectively by Léonard Nyangoma and Jean-Bosco Ndayikengurukiye since May 1998. And then there is Joseph Karumba's FROLINA, which has had its bases in Kigoma in Tanzania since the eighties. It should be pointed out that almost all the leaders of the rebellion come from Bururi.

These different movements operate out of Burundi, Tanzania and the DRC. The FNL is fighting mainly in rural Bujumbura and in the north of Burundi, and the FDD and FROLINA mainly in the south of the country. The dissident FDD led by Jean Bosco operates within the DRC/Zimbabwean force on the banks of Lake Tanganyika and in Kivu. The FNL-Karatasi is commanded by Thomas Bagwihigire, the FNL-Cossan by Nestor Nizigama, the FDD-Jean Bosco by Prime Ngowenubusa and the FDD-Nyangoma by Antoine Mbawa.

Numbering around 1,000, the FNL-Cossan is composed of elite troops, most of them Adventists. Coming mainly from the north and north-west of Burundi, they are PALIPEHUTU and take great pride in having been the first to take up arms in the Burundian Hutu armed struggle. The FNL includes many former Burundian refugees in Rwanda, trained by the ex-FAR under Habyarimana's regime, and some Rwandan ex-FAR. There is talk of a group of ex-FAR instructors trained by the French GIGN in Rwanda prior to 1994 and whose mission is to train, if not to command recent operations in rural Bujumbura. The FNL-Karatasi are around 450 and allied with the Mai Mai in the eastern DRC.

Today, taking both branches together, the FDD consists of 10,000 to 16,000 combatants. Shortly after the events at Kamenge in 1994 and the formation of the CNDD, the FNL entered into competition with the FDD. Trained at the beginning by FNL commanders, the FDD quickly overtook them in regard to resources. This competition was illustrated by the fighting between the FNL and

For additional analytical, marketing, investment and business opportunities
information, please contact
Global Investment & Business Center, USA
(202) 546-2103. Fax: (202) 546-3275. E-mail: rusric@erols.com

FDD in Cibitoke and Bubanza in 1997, and still more recently in June 1999, when the FNL accused the FDD of stealing the glory in the combats against the Burundian army in rural Bujumbura, Cibitoke, Bubanza and Ruyigi.

PSYCHOLOGICAL WARFARE AND MOUNTING STAKES

A large part of the FDD fighting in the DRC has returned to Burundi since June to reinforce its military positions and raise the stakes at the Arusha process with regard to the violence. All the Burundian rebel movements, FDD-Jean Bosco and FDD-Nyangoma, FNL and FROLINA, have launched recent recruitment drives in Burundi and in the refugee camps in Tanzania. The use of the language of violence could be interpreted first of all as a response to the government's blocking of negotiations around June-July, and as a form of pressure; but it is more likely a tactical move in the light of the approaching conclusion of an agreement. As far as the rebels are concerned, they have to take a position of force before negotiating and are consequently recruiting the maximum number of combatants before negotiating their integration into the army.

This opportunity has been given to them by Kabila's strategy of bringing the war back to the east of the DRC. It is certain that the rebel groups have been reinforced by their military alliances in the DRC, although it is difficult to assess how much equipment they have received. The guerrilla movement has also been retrained and reorganised by the Zimbabweans and the Angolans.

There have been infiltrations from Tanzania for several months and these provoked fighting first in the province of Makamba (in the south of Burundi) in the second half of 1999, then towards Rutana (in the south-east) and Ruyigi (in the east). There is talk of an infiltration into these provinces by several thousand rebels. A general movement of armed bands has been observed for some weeks towards the centre of the country (Gitega), towards the forest of Kibira (in the north) and towards the north-east (Cankuzo). After a month of doubtful calm in Makamba, intense fighting has broken out again. Frequent movements have recently been observed from Kigoma to Ubwari peninsula, then to Rumonge in Burundi. The rebels are practising a scorched earth policy on a large scale, setting fire to houses and forcing the population to leave, even pushing it into exile in Tanzania.

The rebels' tactics have also changed towards psychological warfare: attacks on the capital in September and military positions with the aim of creating a siege mentality among the inhabitants of Bujumbura. For example, they indicated that on returning from Dar es Salaam and Arusha in September 1999 there would be attacks on Bujumbura for two weeks.

For additional analytical, marketing, investment and business opportunities information, please contact
Global Investment & Business Center, USA
(202) 546-2103. Fax: (202) 546-3275. E-mail: rusric@erols.com

This strategy could be linked to the assassination of two members of the United Nations and seven Burundians on 19 October 1999 in Muziye, Rutana, which led the UN to decree a phase four situation (last phase before the total evacuation of its personnel). It has not yet been clearly established who was responsible for these killings despite enquiries by the government, which accused rebels based in Tanzania. It is true that PALIPEHUTU published a communiqué in June suggesting that foreigners should leave the country because of the imminence of their planned attack on Bujumbura. However, some continue to see the hand of the army, which could have used the assassinations to discredit the rebels. This argument is limited to the extent that the government was the first to suffer from phase four, which led to the departure of a considerable number of NGOs and the freezing of many projects, thus reducing the currency reserves and jobs from which the government and Burundians were able to profit. Consequently the government lost credibility with regard to its international partners and the Burundians themselves. The following text of a tract distributed in the market is an indication of people's anger:

"The UN has lost two agents ...
They have been assassinated.
Whose fault is this?
And the thousands of other deaths, whose fault are they? We don't know…
To further assist this country that no longer knows which saint it should dedicate itself to, the UN has decided not to assist any further."

No matter who was responsible, this incident led to a meeting on humanitarian law with representatives of the rebel movements and army, organized by the Center Henri Dunant in Geneva from 2 to 4 February 2000. This meeting, presided over by Amadou Toumani Touré, the former President of Mali, enabled a message to be passed to the belligerents, stating that international humanitarian aid was conditional on respect for the law and the security of international personnel. Moreover, this initiative made it possible to raise awareness of the benefits of applying a minimal code of conduct and, indirectly, of the credit that the Burundian participants might draw from it for the inter-Burundian negotiations. But the positive effect of the meeting was dimished by the fact that some armed factions felt that they were represented inadequately.

Do the Rebels want to Negotiate?

Under strong pressure from the region and all the Burundian parties, the head of the FDD finally met Mandela. But he laid down preliminary conditions for his participation in the Arusha talks: the dismantling of the regroupment camps and the release of political prisoners.

For additional analytical, marketing, investment and business opportunities information, please contact
Global Investment & Business Center, USA
(202) 546-2103. Fax: (202) 546-3275. E-mail: rusric@erols.com

These conditions had already been laid down during the last attempted meeting between the FDD and the government in November 1999. This meeting followed an expression of willingness by the FDD to negotiate with the Burundian government directly. However, each attempted meeting failed as the delegations previously sent by Bosco did not have a mandate to negotiate, did not formulate their demands clearly or laid down impossible conditions. These included proposals for putting in place a new constitution, the release of 10,000 "political prisoners", the government's withdrawal from Arusha, the dismantling of the regroupment camps, and the arrest of those responsible for the 1993 coup. But this time there was a clear feeling that the FDD's position was more flexible, first because the number of conditions was reduced, then because the head of the FDD declared that a political agreement was the priority and that "military reforms will come later." This was a marked change in tone compared with the usual rebel demands for immediate changes in the composition of the "mono-ethnic 'putschist' army". It was also to be expected that Bosco would enter the process by taking an extreme position, given his exclusion up to now.

Major Buyoya, voluntarily or involuntarily, met the wishes of the head of the FDD by saying at a press conference on 22 February 2000 in Arusha: "Much criticism has been made against us with regard to regroupment. We accept these criticisms and agree to dismantle the camps. But I can assure you that if the rebels come to the negotiating table, tomorrow there will no longer be any camps." This affirmation was not entirely credible, given that it is difficult for the army to accept dismantling the camps without a ceasefire in place, but it showed that there is at least some room for negotiations.

The FDD's participation in the Arusha process risks, however, creating problems with Nyangoma. The latter has always said that he was leaving the door open for reconciliation with Bosco, but has threatened to quit Arusha if Bosco is independently associated with the CNDD and has always treated Bosco's faction as "dissident". The assassination of his brother and family in Kasulu (Tanzania) in February 2000, for which he holds Jean Bosco's people responsible, risks compromising the reconciliation between the two factions.

The first dissent between Nyangoma and Jean Bosco came after the attack on Bujumbura airport on 1 January 1998. The rebels had decided to intensify their attacks to force the government to capitulate or to negotiate. Responsibility for finding a sponsor, collecting funds and purchasing arms to that end was given to the director of Nyangoma's cabinet, a certain William. But no purchase was made for several months. Jean Bosco went to find Nyangoma and William in Dar es Salaam, but he could not explain the failure. As Nyangoma refused to punish William, Jean Bosco took command of the movement with the support of a committee of officers (Ngowenubusa, Rajabu, Laurent Ngurube and others) and put him in prison.

For additional analytical, marketing, investment and business opportunities information, please contact
Global Investment & Business Center, USA
(202) 546-2103. Fax: (202) 546-3275. E-mail: rusric@erols.com

Nyangoma and the CNDD had by then already lost two major supporters: first Mobutu, who allowed him to operate out of Zaire, and then the networks of Zairean finance that backed his activities between 1994 and 1996. The first DRC war in 1996-97 destroyed the rebels' military bases in Eastern Zaire and dispersed the movement over several countries: Zaire, Zambia, Burundi, Tanzania and Kenya. But after the AFDL operations there still remained some pockets of FDD in South Kivu, aided by the Mai-Mai and armed with weapons recovered from fleeing Zairean soldiers. In order to weaken them and to avoid bases being reformed in the east of the DRC, Rwanda and Burundi threatened reprisals against these movements' local allies.

Towards the beginning of 1998 this support effectively ceased. In any case, Nyangoma was not in Kabila's good books: when the AFDL began its operations in October 1996 in Kivu, Kabila had approached Nyangoma to ask him to keep clear, but Nyangoma refused and fought against the AFDL alongside the FAZ. His attempts to mollify Kabila during the second DRC war seemed to have failed (he was in Kinshasa in January 1999).

At the political level, Nyangoma's credibility diminished with his failed attempt to take the place of Jean Minani at the head of FRODEBU in 1997; in December 1997 the party congress opted to keep Minani. This plan, which aimed at unifying the political branch of FRODEBU with the armed rebel branch, was backed by Tanzania, which supported the formation of a Hutu bloc against the Burundian government, then suffering sanctions. Tanzania had promised Nyangoma support if the negotiations did not take off. But the leadership competition between Nyangoma and Minani, reinforced by regionalist divisions in the movement, made this strategy difficult. It seems that Tanzania even considered for a short time supporting Jean Bosco rather than Nyangoma if the Arusha talks did not begin in June 1998.

Since the start of the Arusha talks, Nyangoma has sought to gain time and to reconstitute his movement, for example by negotiating a military co-operation agreement with Zimbabwe that would include training, the supply of equipment, and financial and diplomatic assistance. Nostalgic for the Rome process, which established him as Buyoya's only interlocutor in 1996-97, he initially criticised Arusha. But by taking a prominent role with G7 and keeping himself out of the war in DRC, the balance of power was turning in his favour. As soon as the Lusaka agreement was signed, he wrote to the mediator, Frederick Chiluba, to impress on him that the "legitimate" FDD were not to be registered among the "negative forces" and therefore disarmed under the terms of the agreement. He has already progressively reintegrated some of the men that Jean Bosco put in prison, including Mbawa, his chief of staff, and most of the movement's officers and politicians from Bururi. If the agreement had been signed without the dissident branch of the FDD, he would have had a chance to appear as winning

For additional analytical, marketing, investment and business opportunities information, please contact
Global Investment & Business Center, USA
(202) 546-2103. Fax: (202) 546-3275. E-mail: rusric@erols.com

out in the negotiations and would have gained the support of those among Bosco's fighters who disagreed with the latter's wait-and-see policy in regard to the negotiations.

After Nyangoma's departure the Jean Bosco FDD vacillated between the different offers of support without any clear policy. Around July 1998, and thus just after the beginning of the Arusha talks, Bosco was approached by radical anti-Buyoya Tutsis seeking to create a Hutu-Tutsi military movement marginalising Nyangoma and was even offered a stay in Dar es Salaam, apparently without the knowledge of his own officers. Convinced of the plan, which promised him regional support, Jean Bosco eliminated or imprisoned those opposed to this strategy. He also chased Nyangoma out of his house in Dar es Salaam. Nyangoma made a complaint to the Tanzanian authorities, who arrested some of Jean Bosco's bodyguards and expelled the head of the FDD from the country. In this way Bosco discredited himself in the eyes of Tanzania and Nyerere. Shortly after these incidents, the war in DRC broke out and the FDD immediately left to assist Kabila, with the aim of re-equipping and reinforcing their own movement.

The rifts within the FDD pose a problem for their participation in Arusha. As in most of the Burundian parties, there is a regionalist split, which Bosco has vainly tried to counter: Officers from the south are now deserting and rejoining Nyangoma. Another major point of tension is between the FDD civilians and FDD soldiers over strategy in the DRC war and at the Arusha negotiations. The movement's politicians have long wanted to participate in Arusha, as they se clearly that there is a risk of ending up major losers. Meanwhile, the military are seeking to gain time, evidently waiting for an outcome to the war in the DRC before deciding on a strategy for the negotiations. Now that the principle of FDD participation is accepted, the politicians are even more concerned about becoming marginalized. If the rebels are to be associated with the Arusha process to negotiate on strictly military questions, the ceasefire and their integration into the army, what place will the politicians have? This concern makes possible either rivalry or alliances between FRODEBU and FDD politicians.

The rebels, FNL and FDD in particular, are surprised at suddenly being contacted, even courted by all the players in the process. They consider that they owe them nothing, given that these same politicians rarely helped them in their struggle. Some among them are aware that the rebels must constitute a united front, so that their divisions cannot be exploited by the participants in the negotiations. But at this advanced stage of the talks, nobody, including FRODEBU, has an interest in the rebels forming such a strong and united bloc, which would dictate conditions to the political actors. In this context, it seems that there have recently been moves towards a coordinated approach to the

For additional analytical, marketing, investment and business opportunities information, please contact
Global Investment & Business Center, USA
(202) 546-2103. Fax: (202) 546-3275. E-mail: rusric@erols.com

negotiations by the staff headquarters of the various rebel movements, in Kigoma in November-December and in Lumumbashi in February. The idea behind these meetings was to set up a co-ordination committee and to express their views on the prerequisites of a ceasefire, on the future of the rebellion and on the reform of the army, but no conclusion has been officially presented.

THE REGIONAL DIMENSION OF THE CONFLICT

Since the Lusaka accords were signed in July 1999, the FDD, which fought on Kabila's side, have returned in large numbers to Burundi and Tanzania. Local press reports and testimonies from the population indicate that there have been new infiltrations from Tanzania into the province of Rutana since last August. It seems that Kabila has asked the Zimbabweans and the Angolans to continue to support the FDD within the framework of his new, post-Lusaka strategy. This strategy has one objective: as fighting was prohibited by the ceasefire agreement in the DRC, "the war must be brought back where it came from", in the words of Abdoulaye Yérodia, the DRC minister of foreign affairs. This means re-exporting the violence towards the eastern DRC, onto the borders with Rwanda, Burundi and Uganda. In Kivu this means encouraging the Mai-Mai movements to rebel against the presence of foreign troops there; in Rwanda, Burundi and Uganda it means supporting the rebel movements against the governments.

This strategy is aimed at destabilizing Rwanda through Burundi. As Burundi is officially at war, weakened economically, politically and diplomatically, it is much easier to destabilize than Rwanda. For Kabila, the benefits of this displacement of the war are evident. He is forcing the Burundian army to withdraw from the southern front on the edge of Lake Tanganyika on the DRC side, which increases the isolation and vulnerability of the Rwandan army. Within this framework it seems that some Zimbabwean commandos have penetrated Kigoma and helped the FDD to cross Lake Tanganyika from the DRC to Tanzania. Some elements of the Zimbabwean army even penetrated the foothills of rural Bujumbura, which overlook the town, in September to evaluate the possibilities for attacking the capital. Reports that the Zimbabweans have trained the FDD in guerrilla techniques recently came out in the Zimbabwean press. President Buyoya went to Kampala and Kigali in September 99 to alert and consult his neighbors on the possibility of the war moving from the DRC into Burundian territory.

The second war in the DRC has strengthened the tactical alliances between the different Rwandan and Burundian Hutu rebel movements and the Mai-Mai popular resistance movements in Kivu. The presence of Burundian Hutus alongside the Interahamwe and ex-FAR has been signaled many times. There was an influx of Rwandan and Burundian Hutu fighters near Kigoma from July 1999, and in Gisenyi on 24 December 1999 during an attack on a re-installation

For additional analytical, marketing, investment and business opportunities information, please contact
Global Investment & Business Center, USA
(202) 546-2103. Fax: (202) 546-3275. E-mail: rusric@erols.com

site, and in Uvira during clashes with the Banyamulenge, and in February 2000 on Burundian territory. The ex-FAR and Interahamwe have also gone to reinforce the Angolan army fighting against UNITA. Eight prisoners taken by the Burundian army confirmed that Rwandan and Burundian Hutu rebels collaborated in the attack on the airport in January 1998.

The ex-FAR and Interahamwe, who passed through Burundian territory as they moved back to the border with Rwanda and into Kivu, have benefited from "the invitation to tender" provided by the violence in Burundi. The Burundian army has been denouncing their presence for a long time, but has never been able to produce proof. Although there have been many accounts by witnesses who confirmed hearing the assailants talking or singing in Kinyarwanda, this could be explained by the fact that a good number of former Burundian refugees who had lived in Rwanda since 1972 were among the rebel fighters, particularly the FNL. These Burundians received assistance from Habyarimana's government and often trained with the FAR.

However, it seems that this alliance between Rwandan and Burundian rebels has been more fragile since the beginning of the year. Fighting between Hutu factions took place in Burundi in February and in Kivu in April 2000. There are several versions of the clashes between the FNL and ex-FAR, a combination of which might complete the puzzle: 1) The FNL wanted to distance itself from the ex-FAR and boost its image at this stage of the peace talks; 2) the FAR accused the Burundians of wanting to be part of the Arusha peace process and of betraying their military co-operation agreement, requiring them first "to liberate Burundi, then Rwanda"; 3) the ex-FAR within the FNL decided to return to Rwanda, invited by Kagame to reintegrate the RPA and the FNL refused to allow this; 4) the Rwandan Hutus, seeing that the outcome of the war in Burundi was doubtful, decided to return to fight in DRC with their arms and equipment, and the FNL killed them to prevent them from leaving; 5) Ex-FAR instructors wanted to take command of operations in rural Bujumbura and the FNL commanders refused; 6) the FNL were infiltrated early this year by 400 ex-FAR who pretended to have come from the DRC, but who were sent by the RPA in agreement with the Burundi military to destabilise the movement from within. According to this final theory, the plan was for the newcomers to start a fight to eliminate as many FNL as possible and to show evidence of collaboration between the FNL and the "génocidaires". But the infiltrators were discovered and almost 200 were killed.

Since the resurgence of violence in Burundi in June 1999, Rwanda has been following the security situation very closely. The massive influx of Interahamwe and ex-FAR, perceived as reinforcements, to Kigoma since July could presage an attack on Burundi. The two countries suspect that Tanzania, irritated on the one hand by the Burundian government's blocking of the Arusha process, and on the other hand by the RCD-Goma's refusal to accept Wamba dia Wamba in

For additional analytical, marketing, investment and business opportunities
information, please contact
Global Investment & Business Center, USA
(202) 546-2103. Fax: (202) 546-3275. E-mail: rusric@erols.com

Lusaka, was envisaging support for the two Hutu rebel movements. The rapprochement between Burundi and Rwanda dates from the suspension of sanctions, but particularly from the visit of Pasteur Bizimungu on 15-17 April 1999. It also coincides with the work of the Joint Rwanda-Burundi Commission on 26 July, which dealt with co-operation in commercial, scientific and judiciary exchanges, agricultural and animal rearing. On security, consultations are held regularly between the military, but also at the level of the higher authorities.

Thus President Buyoya went to Rwanda in September to discuss the possible spread of the war in the DRC to Burundi, and Vice-President Kagame met President Buyoya in the north of Burundi in December 1999. Some joint operations have taken place on the border between Burundi and Rwanda, but these are not new; they have been going on since 1995. A Rwandan security observatory post has been set up on their common frontiers, intended to keep a watch on the movements of Hutu rebels coming from Tanzania and South Kivu. The transport of strategic material and supplies for the two armies deployed in DRC, even for war booty, passes through the port of Bujumbura.

This rapprochement is also motivated by a change in regional alliances. Since the Kisangani clash between the RPA and the UPDF, which exposed their different agendas for the DRC war, Rwanda can no longer rely completely on its Ugandan ally. Realism has won out over the distrust that characterises the relationship between the Burundian and Rwandan armies. Contrary to the ethnic propaganda and the simplifications often made by the international community, the two armies have different histories and approaches and confront each other with arrogance. One is a classic African government army that has supported a military government for 30 years, while the other is the outcome of a guerrilla movement formed in the "school of Dar es Salaam". Burundian distrust of the Rwandans was reinforced by Rwanda's support for the regional policy of sanctions.

THE TEMPTATION OF WAR TO THE BURUNDIAN ARMY

Since Buyoya took power in July 1996, the army has been given huge resources "to terminate" the war. Its numbers have passed from 17,000 to around 50,000 and big investments have been made in equipment. Over 50 per cent of the national budget goes towards military expenditure, which has dramatic consequences in such a poor country. By taking back power and giving the military every means to carry out the war, Buyoya clearly wished to be in a powerful position and able to impose the conditions of the Tutsi minority and of the minority in power on his adversaries during future negotiations.

The war option is encouraged today by the second war in the DRC, but also by the raised stakes that the violence offers with regard to the peace process.

For additional analytical, marketing, investment and business opportunities information, please contact
Global Investment & Business Center, USA
(202) 546-2103. Fax: (202) 546-3275. E-mail: rusric@erols.com

The Burundian government was very reluctant to participate actively in the regional anti-Kabila operation launched in August 1998. Kabila had been the first to denounce the sanctions and allow the use of his territory to circumvent them. This good relationship between the Buyoya and Kabila regimes could have led to the neutralization of the FDD in Kivu if necessary. Aware of the direct contacts between the two governments, the Rwandans carefully avoided informing the Burundians of the organisational details of the war. However, they did give them information about the training provided by Kabila to the FDD and the ex-FAR. When Commandant Gakunzi, a Munyamulenge officer with the AFDL, found himself besieged by the FDD in the Rusizi plain in Kivu on 2 August 1998, he called on the Burundians for reinforcements. The Burundians, caught off guard, sent only ammunition. It was only two weeks later that Buyoya decided to send troops to the DRC, under pressure from the Burundian and Rwandan armies.

Since then, the Burundian government's official line on intervention in the DRC has never changed: "We do not have territory to claim, nor men to put in Kinshasa, nor riches to loot, we are only there to ensure the security of the frontiers and to guarantee the route to the lake." The deployment of a few thousand men is effectively limited to the edge of the lake and on the Zambian border (Pepa, Pweto) at the edge of South Kivu, assuring a control function over the rebels' rear bases. Moreover, Burundi only signed the Lusaka agreement as an observer.

But as Kabila is now preparing an offensive in the east of the DRC and arming the Mai-Mai, the ex-FAR and the FDD, the Burundi military has more and more reason to be in DRC. On the one hand, stability in the DRC is becoming a prerequisite for a ceasefire and the signature of the Arusha agreement. Even if a mandated rebel delegation signs this agreement, there is chance that the instability in the eastern DRC could spill over into Burundi again. The Burundian government fears that the Burundian armed factions will not feel constrained by the agreement and that the Rwandan rebels continue to constitute a threat anyway. It feels supported in this position by its alliance with Rwanda, which shows the example of exporting the conflict outside the country.

In this context of regional warfare, and faced with an upsurge in violence since June 1998, some military and civilian voices have been calling for the preparation of an offensive against the refugee camps in Tanzania, which they accuse of serving as a sanctuary for the rebels. The Burundian army drew up a plan of attack modeled on Rwanda's assault on the camps in Goma in 1996. However, this was rapidly suppressed by the voices of reason in the government and by the Rwandan government, which found the plan much too risky. First of all, Burundi does not have the financial means to support a war with a large country like Tanzania, especially when many of its troops are in the DRC and there is a civil war raging in Burundi itself. Secondly, Burundi has been a victim of regional

For additional analytical, marketing, investment and business opportunities information, please contact
Global Investment & Business Center, USA
(202) 546-2103. Fax: (202) 546-3275. E-mail: rusric@erols.com

hostility since 1996 and could not win a diplomatic battle against Tanzania, which is sheltering 400,000 Burundian refugees and provides a base in Arusha for the talks on Burundi. Finally, Tanzania serves as the sole route for fuel and coffee (the route to Mombasa is much more expensive because of the taxes imposed by the Kenyan government).

The imminent end to the talks and the resumption of the war led the rebels and the Burundian army to seek a definitive advantage on the ground. The resumption of military operations took place between the end of last August and the beginning of this year, more or less benefiting from the period of wavering between the illness and death of Mwalimu and the start of Mandela's role as mediator. The recent operations launched by the army in rural Bujumbura, Rutana and Ruyigi clearly showed a desire to inflict a major defeat on the rebels before having to negotiate with them. This strategy has several advantages: to weaken the adversary and reduce the number of potential rebel candidates to be integrated into the Burundian army (BAF) in the future and to win a degree of popularity among the Tutsis assuming the role of protector. It would also unite the army around the priority of warfare and turn it away from thoughts of a coup. And finally, it would put the army in the position of victor and thus enable it to dictate conditions to the rebels.

With this in view, the February battle between the FNL and the Interahamwe is a godsend for the Burundian army. After being accused of lying about the Rwandan presence on its territory, the Burundian army had a perfect opportunity to weaken the cohesion of the rebellion and to discredit it for its alliances with those recognized as "génocidaires".

THE REGROUPMENT POLICY IN RURAL BUJUMBURA

Starting at the beginning of September 1999, population regroupment was a response to insecurity in the capital. Regroupment was discussed between the President and the army, and the President and his political partners, for several months, especially when the attacks began on the capital. The final decision was taken under military pressure and Bujumbura's Tutsi population after the attack on the upper/middle-class district of Mutanga Nord on 17 September 1999. The principle motive was to avoid panic in the capital and the organization of spontaneous self-defense groups or the resurgence of militias, which would inevitably have begun killing Hutus. Knowing from experience the chaos created by the Tutsi militias in 1995-96 (which led to the fall of the Ntibantunganya government), the Buyoya government tracked them down and kept a very close watch on their leaders to avoid any excesses. But in the Tutsi districts it was rumoured that the President was refusing to distribute weapons for them to defend themselves and that he was going to let the Tutsis be massacred. The credibility and the authority of the state were at stake and the President chose to

For additional analytical, marketing, investment and business opportunities information, please contact
Global Investment & Business Center, USA
(202) 546-2103. Fax: (202) 546-3275. E-mail: rusric@erols.com

respond to the imperatives of security in his own community despite the predictable international reactions.

The regroupment of more than 300,000 people posed enormous problems. First, the very mountainous geography of rural Bujumbura makes it difficult to organize sites and humanitarian assistance. More than half of the 40 sites are situated upon hillsides and are inaccessible to humanitarian organizations, as there are no roads. In many places there is no water. Despite the setting up of a special committee presided over by the Minister of Labor and comprising the governor, the Minister of Health and provincial representatives, the humanitarian result has been catastrophic. Poor co-ordination among humanitarian organisations prevented them from responding to the needs of those in the camps. The medical relief agancy Médecins Sans Frontières withdrew from the camps because the population was suffering from overcrowding, violence and malnutrition, and "the conditions of regroupment are far from meeting the essential minimum. In this context our interventions have little impact for improving the state of these people." In addition, the experience of the camps in 1997 shows that regroupment has long-term consequences. In the provinces "regrouped" in 1997 (Karuzi and Kayanza), a much higher rate of malnutrition and epidemics can be observed as well as a demographic decrease in the active male population; it is supposed that they have rejoined the rebels or have been targeted for reprisals by the army.

From a military point of view, regroupment, which is accompanied by "cleaning up" operations in the hills, using troops brought back from the DRC, had immediate effects on security in the capital. But there are fears that in the medium term the policy will be counter-productive.

First of all, forcing such disastrous conditions onto the population without adequate care or sufficient food is the best way of ensuring that young Hutu men respond to propaganda and rebel recruitment drives, especially as soldiers looted a large number of deserted houses. From the point of view of military intelligence, little seems to have been done to monitor the rebel infiltrations into the camps. Witness accounts from those regrouped indicate that the armed bands intend to blow up the camps and raise panic among the occupants. A fire in one of the camps, which killed several people, is suspected of being started deliberately. Such incidents aim at creating panic among the soldiers and pushing them into criminal acts. A young soldier fired on the population after a crowd panicked and killed six people. A large number of soldiers seem to leave the sites at night to return to Bujumbura, leaving the field clear for rebel attacks.

Finally, regroupment has an economic impact. The inhabitants of Bujumbura, whose food supplies usually come from the surrounding countryside, are

For additional analytical, marketing, investment and business opportunities information, please contact
Global Investment & Business Center, USA
(202) 546-2103. Fax: (202) 546-3275. E-mail: rusric@erols.com

experiencing shortages as the peasants no longer have regular access to the fields.

Moreover, the return of security to Bujumbura since the end of the year has been interpreted in several different ways. It could be due to the regroupment, but other indications are that in fact there were few military operations in rural Bujumbura and that the rebels are living in the houses of the regrouped. The calm could also result from the dissension between the rebel FNL and ex-FAR, which have prevented co-ordinated attacks on the capital. Another version claims that some Hutu leaders have been threatened with death by the military if the rebels attacked the capital again, and that the message was passed on to the rebellion by the same Hutu leaders.

External pressure to close the camps was unanimous and effective. It was exerted by the Security Council (resolution of 12 November 1999), the European Union (statement, dated 8 October 1999), the U.S. government (statement by James Rubin, U.S. State Department spokesman, dated 4 October 1999), Pope Jean-Paul II (statement dated 3 November 1999), Nelson Mandela (who summoned Buyoya to discuss this matter on 17 February 2000) and FRODEBU. The combined pressure finally led Burundi's Minister of Foreign Affairs to announce in New York on 19 January 2000 the dismantling of ten camps. But the army accuses the government of giving in to this pressure when it believed that tangible results were being produced.

An Army Tired of War?

The resurgence of violence and the response given to it has revealed a certain amount of dysfunction within the army. As a Tutsi inhabitant of Bujumbura put it: "There are not many Tutsi who still believe that this army is protecting us!" Such comments are motivated by a number of observations. The former Minister of Defense, Alfred Nkunrunziza has made several bellicose statements, affirming that "the rebels have been pushed 50 km from the city" and "there are no more of them in the city." But these were refuted by the attacks on the city the next day (at Mutanga Nord on 17 September 1999) and in the weeks that followed. The military response during these attacks was not always effective. It should be emphasised that if this situation has only become apparent of late in Bujumbura, there has been a lack of military effectiveness in Makamba province for several months. There are several possible explanations. There may be a problem in anticipating attacks and thus a lack of information on rebel movements. There could also be a problem in allocating resources (part of the army is in the DRC) or in commanding and transmitting orders. Another two options are a laisser-faire attitude due to the lack of motivation, or deliberate attempts to sabotage state authority. In fact the answer is a combination of all these factors.

For additional analytical, marketing, investment and business opportunities information, please contact
Global Investment & Business Center, USA
(202) 546-2103. Fax: (202) 546-3275. E-mail: rusric@erols.com

The soldiers are suffering to a considerable degree from war fatigue. The army has seen its numbers and resources triple over seven years, but without succeeding in defeating the enemy. It has lost some of its determination, is accustomed to the status quo and has learned not to risk its soldiers' lives uselessly. Many officers are now resigned to thinking that they cannot carry off a military victory. In regions like Makamba where the war is continuing, the soldiers and the rebels, experiencing the same living conditions in the field, are developing a certain respect for each other, even a degree of solidarity in some cases. This sometimes takes the form of sharing a beer, food or the spoils of war. In other regions Tutsi traders ensure the city is kept supplied by paying taxes at points controlled by the rebels. Witness accounts indicate that these contacts are becoming increasingly frequent, showing that the negotiations and the political propaganda are falling behind the reality of the field.

At the same time, there are questions about the high command. This army, whose senior command is almost exclusively from Bujuri, has been directly associated with the government for 30 years and thus, de facto, with the management of economic affairs. Many young soldiers complain that their commanders have become "establishment figures" with a upper/middle-class outlook and a civil servant's mentality, more concerned with their material comfort than with the war, and that all the best officers have been marginalized. The accompanying regionalism and social injustice are making a large number of soldiers extremely critical of their superiors. They assert that officers from Bururi get home every evening, but send the "Third Worlders" (from Central and North Burundi) to die on the battlefield.

Buyoya has himself had several meetings with soldiers accused of laisser-faire and he replaced a part of the hierarchy in July. It is possible that these changes took place after the revelation of a coup plot. Around July, when the security situation was deteriorating and negotiations were completely blocked in Arusha, several names were circulating in Bujumbura in connection with such plots. Whether or not the plots existed, the change in the military hierarchy has given the President a few months' respite. In any case, the command structure now seems to be more efficient.

The nomination of Colonel Cyrille Ndayirukiye as Minister of Defense reflects an effort to change the army's image and ensure its cohesion at the command level in a period in which final defeat has to be inflicted on the rebels and the army must be prepared for reforms. A career soldier from Mwaro region, Colonel Cyrille is respected for his military achievements in Northern Burundi in 1997.

But there is a basic contradiction between the revival of the war - and the re-motivation of the troops that implies - and the negotiation process, a contradiction that is not tenable in the long term. The soldiers can be convinced to believe in

For additional analytical, marketing, investment and business opportunities
information, please contact
Global Investment & Business Center, USA
(202) 546-2103. Fax: (202) 546-3275. E-mail: rusric@erols.com

the negotiations and make more efforts to protect the population, but if they see no concrete results after a while, the process will lose its credibility. It is also difficult to get the soldiers to understand the political games and the procrastination associated with the process and encourage them to remain patient.

For additional analytical, marketing, investment and business opportunities information, please contact
Global Investment & Business Center, USA
(202) 546-2103. Fax: (202) 546-3275. E-mail: rusric@erols.com

TRAVEL TO BURUNDI

US STATE DEPARTMENT RECOMMENDATIONS

WARNING (Issued on January 20, 2000): The Department of State warns U.S. citizens to defer travel to Burundi due to the uncertain security situation within Burundi and the surrounding Great Lakes Region. Burundi has been involved in a civil war since 1993. Fighting can be intense and has increasingly involved attacks on the capital, Bujumbura. On October 12, 1999, two expatriate employees of United Nations organizations were shot execution-style during an ambush in Muzye, Rutana Province. On November 23, a hand grenade was thrown into the central market in downtown Bujumbura, killing five and injuring 14 others. Extremist groups are active throughout the Great Lakes Region, and some have committed or threatened violence against U.S. citizens and interests. One such extremist group that operates out of northeastern Democratic Republic of the Congo (DROC) specifically targeted and killed U.S. citizens in March 1999 in southwestern Uganda.

The U.S. Embassy operates with a reduced staff and restricts U.S. Government personnel from traveling outside Bujumbura, the capital, due to unpredictable incidents of violence throughout Burundi. U.S. Government personnel may only travel to areas in Bujumbura deemed safe by the U.S. Regional Security Officer. In addition, family members are prohibited from accompanying U.S. Government employees assigned to Burundi.

U.S. citizens in Burundi should establish and maintain contact with the U.S. Embassy and consider their own personal security in determining whether to remain in the country.

COUNTRY DESCRIPTION: Burundi is a small, inland African nation currently undergoing a period of instability following the assassination of Burundi's first democratically-elected president in 1993. Facilities for tourism, particularly outside the capital of Bujumbura, are limited.

ENTRY REQUIREMENTS: A passport, visa, and evidence of immunization against yellow fever and meningococcal meningitis are required. Only those travelers resident in countries where there is no Burundian Embassy are eligible for entry stamps, without a visa, at the airport upon arrival. These entry stamps are not a substitute for a visa, which must be obtained from the Burundi Immigration Service within 24 hours of arrival. Travelers without a visa are not permitted to leave the country. Travelers should obtain the latest information and details from the Embassy of the Republic of Burundi, Suite 212, 2233 Wisconsin Avenue, N.W., Washington, D.C. 20007; tel. (202) 342-2574 or the Permanent Mission of Burundi to the United Nations in New York, tel. (212) 687-1180.

For additional analytical, marketing, investment and business opportunities information, please contact
Global Investment & Business Center, USA
(202) 546-2103. Fax: (202) 546-3275. E-mail: rusric@erols.com

Overseas inquiries may be made at the nearest Burundian embassy or consulate.

Travelers who wish to travel to the Democratic Republic of the Congo (DROC) with visas and/or entry/exit stamps from Burundi, Rwanda or Uganda may experience difficulties at DROC airports or other ports of entry. Some travelers with those visas or exit/entry stamps have been detained for questioning in DROC.

SAFETY/SECURITY: As a result of the ongoing conflict between government and rebel forces in Burundi, the U.S. Embassy has restricted U.S. Government personnel from flying in or out of Bujumbura during the hours of darkness.

In light of continuing ethnic and political tensions, all areas of Burundi are potentially unstable. Fighting between rebel forces and the Burundian military continues to be a problem in the interior and in the outskirts of the capital. The outlying suburbs of Bujumbura were attacked by Burundian rebels regularly between August and November 1999, and rebels continue to operate in the province surrounding the capital. Local authorities cannot guarantee safety. The U.S. Embassy emphasizes the importance of remaining vigilant and respecting any curfews in effect. Given the ongoing insecurity, travelers should check with the U.S. Embassy in Bujumbura before traveling out of the capital.

One of the many rebel factions in the Great Lakes Region has committed and continues to threaten violence against American citizens and interests. This faction was responsible for the March 1999 kidnapping and murder of several Western tourists in Uganda. On October 12, 1999, two expatriates and seven others were killed during a United Nations mission in Muzye, Rutana Province, Burundi. On November 23, 1999, a hand grenade was thrown into the central market in downtown Bujumbura, killing five and injuring 14 others. A Hutu rebel faction was responsible for the kidnapping of four foreign nationals in August 1998 in the DROC. Hutu rebel factions are known to operate in northeastern DROC and the surrounding areas, including sections of Burundi, Uganda, Rwanda and Tanzania.

CRIME INFORMATION: Street crime in Bujumbura poses a high risk for visitors. Crime includes muggings, purse-snatching, pickpocketing, burglary, and auto break-ins. Criminals operate individually or in small groups. There have been reports of muggings of persons jogging or walking alone in all sections of Bujumbura, especially on public roads bordering Lake Tanganyika.

The loss or theft abroad of a U.S. passport should be reported immediately to local police and to the nearest U.S. embassy or consulate. The pamphlets A Safe Trip Abroad and Tips for Travelers to Sub-Saharan Africa provide useful

For additional analytical, marketing, investment and business opportunities information, please contact
Global Investment & Business Center, USA
(202) 546-2103. Fax: (202) 546-3275. E-mail: rusric@erols.com

information on protecting personal security while traveling abroad and on travel in the region in general. Both are available from the Superintendent of Documents, U.S. Government Printing Office, Washington, D.C. 20402, via the Internet at http://www.access.gpo.gov/su_docs, or via the Bureau of Consular Affairs home page at http://travel.state.gov.

MEDICAL FACILITIES: Medical facilities are limited in Burundi. Serious medical problems requiring hospitalization and/or medical evacuation to the United States can cost thousands of dollars or more. Doctors and hospitals often expect immediate cash payment for health care services.

MEDICAL INSURANCE: U.S. medical insurance is not always valid outside the United States. U.S. Medicare and Medicaid programs do not provide payment for medical services outside the United States. Uninsured travelers who require medical care overseas may face extreme difficulties. Please check with your own insurance company to confirm whether your policy applies overseas, including provision for medical evacuation. Please ascertain whether payment will be made to the overseas hospital or doctor or whether you will be reimbursed later for expenses that you incur. Some insurance policies also include coverage for psychiatric treatment and for disposition of remains in the event of death. Useful information on medical emergencies abroad, including overseas insurance programs, is provided in the Department of State, Bureau of Consular Affairs brochure, Medical Information for Americans Traveling Abroad, available via the Internet at http://travel.state.gov.

OTHER HEALTH INFORMATION: Travelers should consider taking prophylaxis against malaria. Information on vaccinations and other health precautions may be obtained from the Centers for Disease Control and Prevention's international traveler's hotline at telephone 1-877-FYI-TRIP (1-877-394-8747); fax, 1-888-CDC-FAXX (1-888-232-3299); or CDC's Internet site at http://www.cdc.gov.

TRAFFIC SAFETY AND ROAD CONDITIONS: While in a foreign country, U.S. citizens may encounter road conditions that differ significantly from those in the United States. The information below concerning Burundi is provided for general reference only and may not be totally accurate in a particular location or circumstance.
Safety of Public Transportation: Poor
Urban Road Conditions/Maintenance: Poor
Rural Road Conditions/Maintenance: Poor
Availability of Roadside Assistance: Poor-nonexistent

For additional analytical, marketing, investment and business opportunities information, please contact
Global Investment & Business Center, USA
(202) 546-2103. Fax: (202) 546-3275. E-mail: rusric@erols.com

LOCAL AVIATION SAFETY: As a result of the ongoing conflict between government and rebel forces in Burundi, the U.S. Embassy has restricted U.S. Government personnel from flying in or out of Bujumbura during the hours of darkness.

Due to general safety concerns regarding African Airlines, a private commercial airline that flies between Bujumbura and destinations in Africa and the Middle East, the U.S. Embassy in Bujumbura recommends that its personnel not use this carrier.

AVIATION SAFETY OVERSIGHT: As there is no direct commercial air service at present, nor economic authority to operate such service between the U.S. and Burundi, the U.S. Federal Aviation Administration (FAA) has not assessed the Burundian Civil Aviation Authority for compliance with international aviation safety standards for oversight of Burundi's air carrier operations. For further information, travelers may contact the Department of Transportation within the U.S. at tel. 1-800-322-7873, or visit the FAA's Internet web site at http://www.faa.gov/avr/iasa/index.htm. The U.S. Department of Defense (DOD) separately assesses some foreign air carriers for suitability as official providers of air services. For information regarding the DOD policy on specific carriers, travelers may contact the DOD at tel. (618) 256-4801.

CRIMINAL PENALTIES: While in a foreign country, a U.S. citizen is subject to that country's laws and regulations, which sometimes differ significantly from those in the United States and may not afford the protections available to the individual under U.S. law. Penalties for breaking the law can be more severe than in the United States for similar offenses. Persons violating Burundian law, even unknowingly, may be expelled, arrested or imprisoned. Penalties for possession, use, or trafficking in illegal drugs in Burundi are strict, and convicted offenders can expect jail sentences and heavy fines.

CHILDREN'S ISSUES: For information on international adoption of children and international parental child abduction, please refer to our Internet site at http://travel.state.gov/children's_issues.html or telephone (202) 736-7000.

REGISTRATION/EMBASSY LOCATION: U.S. citizens are encouraged to register with the Consular Section of the U.S. Embassy in Bujumbura upon their arrival in Burundi and to obtain a list of the Embassy's emergency contact numbers and updated information on travel and security. The U.S. Embassy is located on the Avenue des Etats-Unis. The mailing address is B.P. 34, 1720 Bujumbura, Burundi. The telephone number is (257) 223-454, fax (257) 222-926.

For additional analytical, marketing, investment and business opportunities information, please contact
Global Investment & Business Center, USA
(202) 546-2103. Fax: (202) 546-3275. E-mail: rusric@erols.com

IMPORTANT INFORMATION FOR TRAVEL

GETTING THERE

AIR

The Belgian national airline, Sabena, which abandoned its weekly flights to Bujumbura in 1996, resumed flights in November 2000, but after an attack on its plane, it suspended the service indefinitely.
National airline: Air Burundi (state-owned).
Main airport: Bujumbura.
Airport tax: No departure tax.

SURFACE

There are good roads from Bukavu (Democratic Republic of Congo) and Kigali (Rwanda) to Bujumbura. Roads from Tanzania are generally in poor condition. Main port: Bujumbura (on Lake Tanganyika). Ferries operate from Kigoma (Tanzania), Kalenjie (DRC) and Mpulungu (Zambia). Dar es Salaam is the nearest sea port.

GETTING AROUND

NATIONAL TRANSPORT

Air: Air Burundi operates internal flights linking Bujumbura with Kinundo; aircraft can be chartered at Bujumbura.
Road: Most of the roads leading to provincial towns are surfaced. Unsurfaced roads elsewhere can be difficult in rainy season. Surfaced routes are being extended and local advice should be sought. Very little public transport available.

CITY TRANSPORT

Taxis: Available in Bujumbura.

CAR HIRE

Local firms only. International driving licence is required.

TIME

GMT plus two hours

GEOGRAPHY

Burundi is a landlocked country lying on the eastern shore of Lake Tanganyika, in central Africa, a little south of the Equator. It is bordered by Rwanda to the

For additional analytical, marketing, investment and business opportunities
information, please contact
Global Investment & Business Center, USA
(202) 546-2103. Fax: (202) 546-3275. E-mail: rusric@erols.com

north, Tanzania to the south and east, and by the Democratic Republic of Congo to the west.

CLIMATE

Equatorial around Lake Tanganyika (including Bujumbura); hot and humid with frequent winds with temperatures between 23-33 degrees Celsius (C). Temperate elsewhere with average temperature 20 degrees C. Rainy season from October-May (except brief dry period December-January), long dry season from June-September.

ENTRY REQUIREMENTS

PASSPORTS

Required by all.

VISA

Required by all.

CURRENCY ADVICE/REGULATIONS

No restrictions.

HEALTH (FOR VISITORS)

MANDATORY PRECAUTIONS

Yellow fever vaccination certificate if arriving from an infected area.

ADVISABLE PRECAUTIONS

Yellow fever vaccination is considered essential. Vaccinations for hepatitis A, polio, tetanus and typhoid are recommended. Malaria prophylaxis should be taken as risk exists throughout the country. Water precautions are essential except in major hotels. AIDS is widespread: 15 per cent seropositivity among adults in Bujumbura.

Seek advice on diphtheria, hepatitis B, meningitis and tuberculosis vaccinations. There is a rabies risk.

HOTELS

For additional analytical, marketing, investment and business opportunities information, please contact
Global Investment & Business Center, USA
(202) 546-2103. Fax: (202) 546-3275. E-mail: rusric@erols.com

Advisable to book in advance. Very little accommodation available outside Bujumbura. A 10 per cent tip is usual.

PUBLIC HOLIDAYS

FIXED DATES

1 Jan, 5 Feb, 1 May, 1 Jul, 15 Aug, 13 Oct, 21 Oct, 1 Nov, 25 Dec.

VARIABLE DATES

Ascension Day, Easter Monday.
Working hours

BANKING

Mon-Fri: 0800-1130; 1500-1600.

For additional analytical, marketing, investment and business opportunities information, please contact
Global Investment & Business Center, USA
(202) 546-2103. Fax: (202) 546-3275. E-mail: rusric@erols.com

SUPPLEMENTS

BASIC INDICATORS ON AFRICAN COUNTRIES – COMPARISON

Country	Area (´000 km)	Populat. Mllions	GNP per Capita (US$/ $EU)	Primary School Enrolmen	Adult Illiteracy Rate (%)	Life Expectancy (Years/Ans)	CPI Inflation (%)	GDP Growth (%)
		1997	1997	1996	1995	1997	1997	1997
Algeria	2382	29.5	1490	107	38	69	4.4	1.3
Angola	1247	11.6	340	74	47	48	111.1	7.6
Benin	113	5.7	380	76	63	56	3.6	5.6
Bostwana	600	1.5	3260	112	30	51	8.7	6.9
Burinka Faso	274	11.1	240	39	81	47	2.3	5.5
Burundi	28	6.4	180	49	65	48	31.2	0.4
Cameroon	475	13.9	650	85	37	57	1.5	5.1
Cape Verde	4	0.4	1090	135	28	66	8.7	3.0
Central African Rep	623	3.4	320	60	40	49	1.1	5.1
Chad	1284	6.7	240	65	52	48	5.6	6.5
Comoros	2	0.7	400	73	43	58	1.9	0.0
Congo	342	2.7	660	111	26	51	8.3	-1.9
Congo, Dem. Rep	2345	48.0	110	70	23	54	175.5	-5.7
Côte d´Ivoire	323	14.3	690	71	60	52	5.6	6.0
Djibouti	22	0.6	..	39	54	51	3.7	2.4
Eqypt	1001	64.5	1180	102	49	67	4.6	5.1
Equat. Guinea	28	0.4	1050	..	22	51	3.0	76.1
Eritrea	118	3.4	210	54	50	51	..	7.9
Ethiopia	1104	60.1	110	43	65	51	-3.7	5.6
Gabon	268	1.1	4230	..	37	56	4.0	4.1
Gambia	11	1.1	350	78	61	48	2.8	0.8
Ghana	239	18.3	370	76	36	59	27.9	4.2
Ghinea	246	7.6	570	50	64	47	1.9	4.8
Guinea Bissau	36	1.1	240	70	45	44	49.1	5.0

For additional analytical, marketing, investment and business opportunities information, please contact
Global Investment & Business Center, USA
(202) 546-2103. Fax: (202) 546-3275. E-mail: rusric@erols.com

Kenya	583	28.4	330	84	22	56	12.0	2.1
Lesotho	30	2.1	670	97	29	59	8.8	6.2
Liberia	111	2.5	..	33	62	55	10.0	..
Libya	1760	5.8	..	112	24	66	25.0	2.4
Madagascar	587	15.8	250	73	58	59	4.5	3.6
Malawi	119	10.1	220	133	44	41	9.1	5.1
Mali	1240	11.5	260	37	69	49	-0.4	6.7
Mauritania	1031	2.4	450	83	62	54	4.6	5.1
Maurutius	2	1.1	3800	107	17	72	6.9	5.0
Morocco	447	27.5	1250	84	56	67	0.9	-2.0
Mozambique	802	18.3	90	62	60	48	5.5	12.4
Namibia	823	1.6	2220	131	56	56	8.8	1.8
Niger	1267	9.8	200	29	86	49	2.9	3.4
Nigeria	924	118.4	260	87	43	53	8.2	3.9
Rwanda	26	5.9	210	94	40	43	12.0	10.9
Sao Tome &Principe	1	0.1	270	..	69	..	71.3	1.0
Senegal	196	8.8	550	69	67	52	1.7	5.2
Seychelles	0.3	0.1	6880	..	72	..	0.7	4.3
Sierra Leone	72	4.4	..	52	69	39	13.7	-20.2
Somalia	638	10.2	..	8	..	50	16.3	..
South Africa	1220	43.3	3400	116	18	66	8.6	1.7
Sudan	2506	27.9	280	53	54	56	46.7	4.6
Swaziland	17	0.9	1440	129	23	61	18.3	3.0
Tanzania	945	31.5	210	66	32	52	16.1	3.4
Togo	57	4.3	330	133	48	51	8.6	2.8
Tunisia	164	9.3	2090	114	33	70	3.6	5.4
Uganda	236	20.8	330	74	38	43	7.1	5.4
Zambia	753	8.5	380	88	22	44	24.8	3.5
Zimbabwe	391	11.7	750	113	15	49	18.8	3.2
Africa	30060	758.4	677	80	44	54	13.7	3.4

For additional analytical, marketing, investment and business opportunities
information, please contact
Global Investment & Business Center, USA
(202) 546-2103. Fax: (202) 546-3275. E-mail: rusric@erols.com

CONTACT IN BURUNDI

TELEPHONE AREA CODES

The international direct dialling (IDD) code for Burundi is +257, followed by area code (2 for Bujumbura), followed by subscriber's number.

USEFUL TELEPHONE NUMBERS

Police: 18, 19.

CHAMBERS OF COMMERCE

Chambre de Commerce et de l'Industrie du Burundi, BP 313, Bujumbura (tel: 22-280).

TRAVEL INFORMATION

Air Burundi, BP 2460, Avenue du Commerce, Bujumbura (tel: 23-460; fax: 23-452).
Bujumbura International Airport, PO Box 694, Bujumbura (tel: 23-707; 23-797; fax: 23-428).

NATIONAL TOURIST ORGANISATION OFFICES

Office National du Tourisme, 2 Avenue des Euphorbes, BP 902, Bujumbura (tel: 22-202, 22-023).

MINISTRIES

Ministry of Agriculture, Bujumbura (tel: 10-342; fax: 22-873).
Ministry of Commerce, Industry and Tourism, Bumjumbura (tel: 17-775; fax: 25-595).
Ministry of Communication with the Government, Bumjumbura (tel: 12-601; fax: 16-318).
Ministry of Community Development, Bumjumbura (tel: 13-098; fax: 24-678).
Ministry of Defence, Bumjumbura (tel: 19-994; fax: 25-686).
Ministry of Education, Bumjumbura (tel: 17-776; fax: 26-839).
Ministry of Energy and Mines, Bumjumbura (tel: 18-586; fax: 23-337).
Ministry of the Environment, Bumjumbura (tel: 21-649; fax: 28-902).
Ministry of Finance, Bumjumbura (tel: 17-918; fax: 23-827).
Ministry of Foreign Affairs and Co-operation, Bumjumbura (tel: 17-595; fax: 26-313).
Ministry of Health, Bumjumbura (tel: 18-200; fax: 29-916).

For additional analytical, marketing, investment and business opportunities information, please contact
Global Investment & Business Center, USA
(202) 546-2103. Fax: (202) 546-3275. E-mail: rusric@erols.com

Ministry of Human Rights, Law Reforms and Relations with the National Assembly, Bumjumbura (tel: 17-365; fax: 13-847).
Ministry of the Interior, Bumjumbura (tel: 12-480; fax: 23-904).
Ministry of Justice, Bumjumbura (tel: 10-595; fax: 22-148).
Ministry of Labour, Public Office and Professional Education, Bumjumbura (tel: 17-928; fax: 24-079).
Ministry of Peace Process, Bumjumbura (tel: 19-457; fax: 19-459).
Ministry of Planning, Development and Reconstruction, Bumjumbura (tel: 19-079; fax: 24-193).
Ministry of Public Works and Equipment, Bumjumbura (tel: 19-646; fax: 26-840).
Ministry of Repatriation of Displaced Persons, Bumjumbura (tel: 18-184; fax: 18-201).
Ministry of Social Action and Promotion of Women, Bumjumbura (tel: 10-376; fax: 16-102).
Ministry of Transport, Post and Telecommunications, Bumjumbura (tel: 10-462; fax: 26-900).
Ministry of Youth Sport and Culture, Bumjumbura (tel: 16-729; fax: 26-231).
Office of the President, Bumjumbura (tel: 17-806; fax: 26-424).

SELECTED GOVERNMENT CONTACTS

Ministère des transports, postes et télécommunications
B.P. 2000
BUJUMBURA
Telephone +257 22-2923
Telephone +257 22-3100
Telegram Minipostel Bujumbura
Telex 0903 5103 minitpt bdi
S.E. M. NGENDANGANYA Vedaste, Ministre des transports, postes et télécommunications

----

Direction générale des transports, postes et télécommunications
B.P. 2390
BUJUMBURA
Telephone +257 22-5422
Telegram Gentel Bujumbura
Telex 0903 5103 minitpt bdi
Fax +257 22-6900

M. Apollinaire Ndayizeye, Directeur général du Ministère des transports, postes et télécommunications

----

For additional analytical, marketing, investment and business opportunities information, please contact
Global Investment & Business Center, USA
(202) 546-2103. Fax: (202) 546-3275. E-mail: rusric@erols.com

Direction générale de l'Office national des télécommunications (ONATEL)
B.P. 60
BUJUMBURA
Telephone +257 22-3196
Telegram Dirgal Onatel Bujumbura
Telex 0903 5168 onatel bdi
Fax +257 22-6917
Ferdinand Ngendabanka, Directeur général de l'ONATEL
M. Siméon Cubwa, Directeur technique de l'ONATEL

M. J.M. Vianney Nishemezwe, Directeur commercial et d'exploitation de l'ONATEL

M. Emmanuel Minani, Directeur administratif et financier de l'ONATEL

M. Gérard Buname, Chef du Service planification et étude des projets de développement

Radiodiffusion du Burundi
B.P. 1900
BUJUMBURA
Telephone +257 22-3585
Telegram Radio Bujumbura
Telex 0903 5119

BURUNDI EMBASSIES

Missions Diplomatiques accréditées au Burundi	Adresse
Ambassade de R.P.Chine	Vugizo, Tél. (257) 22 43 07
Ambassade d'Egypte	Avenue Nzero / Kinindo, Tél. (257) 22 31 61
Ambassade des Etats-Unis d'Amérique	Avenue de la R.D.C., Tél. (257) 22 34 54
Ambassade de France	Boulevard de l'Uprona, Tél. (257) 22 28 54/ 22 64 64
Ambassade de Belgique	Boulevard de la Liberté, Tél. (257) 22 64 12 / 22 64 13
Ambassade de l'Etat de Vatican	Chaussée Prince Louis Rwagasore, Tél. (257) 22 23 26
Ambassade de la Libye	Avenue de Mai,

For additional analytical, marketing, investment and business opportunities
information, please contact
Global Investment & Business Center, USA
(202) 546-2103. Fax: (202) 546-3275. E-mail: rusric@erols.com

	Tél. (257) 24 39 67
Ambassade de la République Démocratique du Congo	Avenue de la R.D.C., Tél. (257) 22 69 16
Ambassade de la Russie	Boulevard de l'Uprona, Tél. (257) 22 60 98
Ambassade du Rwanda	Avenue de la R.D.C., Tél. (257) 22 68 65
Consulats accréditées aux Burundi	Adresses
Consulat du Sénégal	Avenue Mosso, Tél. (257) 22 96 83
Consulat des Iles Comores	Avenue du Stade, Tél. (257) 22 88 79
Consulat de la Corée du Sud	Boulevard de la Liberté, Tél. (257) 21 31 41 / 22 88 59
Consulat de la Roumanie	Avenue de France, Tél. (257) 22 52 41
Consulat d'Italie	Boulevard de l'Uprona, Tél. (257) 22 60 54 / 22 29 78
Consulat de Grèce	Avenue de Grèce, Tél. (257) 22 46 17
Consulat du Denmark	Route Aéroport, Tél. (257) 22 60 99
Consulat de Hollande	Boulevard de l'Uprona, Tél. (257) 22 23 58

For additional analytical, marketing, investment and business opportunities information, please contact
Global Investment & Business Center, USA
(202) 546-2103. Fax: (202) 546-3275. E-mail: rusric@erols.com

THE CROSS-BORDER INITIATIVE IN EASTERN AND SOUTHERN AFRICA[3]

EXECUTIVE SUMMARY

The Cross-Border Initiative (CBI) comprises a common policy framework developed by fourteen participating countries in Eastern and Southern Africa and the Indian Ocean, with the support of four co-sponsors; the International Monetary Fund, the World Bank, the European Union, and the African Development Bank. The participants are Burundi, Comoros, Kenya, Madagascar, Malawi, Mauritius, Namibia, Rwanda, Seychelles, Swaziland, Tanzania, Uganda, Zambia, and Zimbabwe; Mozambique has also indicated its intention to join. The policy framework aims to facilitate cross-border economic activity by eliminating barriers to the flow of goods, services, labor, and capital, and to help integrate markets by coordinating reform programs in several key structural areas, supported by appropriate macroeconomic policies. The initiative places the responsibility for determining how to implement the agreed policy measures at the national level.

The **four key elements of the Initiative** are:

- liberalizing foreign exchange systems by eliminating restrictions on current account transactions and certain capital transactions, and establishing unified interbank spot foreign exchange markets;
- dismantling nontariff barriers on imports and exports, eliminating tariffs on trade between CBI participants, and lowering tariffs on a nonpreferential (MFN) basis to agreed or lower levels;
- strengthening domestic financial markets by, inter alia, improving prudential and supervisory capacity of central banks; and
- simplifying and liberalizing investment procedures.

The purpose of this paper is to take stock of the achievements under the CBI in each of the four areas mentioned above. The paper takes into account recent developments through end-December 1998. Regarding the **liberalization of foreign exchange systems**, most countries had removed restrictions on current account transactions by end-1998. In addition, a handful of countries liberalized substantially capital account transactions while the remaining countries took partial steps to ease such controls, including those affecting equity investments among the participating countries. On the **exchange rate regime**, most countries met the CBI objective of introducing a flexible exchange rate system within the context of a unified inter-bank foreign exchange market.

---

[3] Jose Fajgenbaum, Robert Sharer, Kamau Thugge, and Hema DeZoysa July 14, 1999

For additional analytical, marketing, investment and business opportunities information, please contact
Global Investment & Business Center, USA
(202) 546-2103. Fax: (202) 546-3275. E-mail: rusric@erols.com

On **trade liberalization and facilitation**, significant but uneven progress was achieved. Many of the participating countries made substantial progress toward meeting the CBI targets on tariffs. Although, none of the countries fully eliminated intraregional tariffs, virtually all countries implemented preference margins for other CBI participants ranging between 60—80 percent. Progress on MFN liberalization was mixed; (i) three countries met the target of lowering the maximum tariff rate to 20—25 percent; (ii) six countries met the target of reducing the number of nonzero tariff bands to no more than three; and (iii) three countries where data are available, met the target of reducing their weighted average tariff rates to no more than 15 percent. Nevertheless, tariff exemptions remained widespread, including for imports by governments, parastatals, nongovernmental organizations, and for goods related to foreign-financed projects and those under the various investment codes. The pace of trade reform reflected, in part, concerns on the potential adverse impact on fiscal revenue.

Notable progress was achieved in reducing **nontariff barriers** to imports. Most countries eliminated import quotas and bans, as well as import licensing requirements. Moreover, the monopoly power previously exercised by state marketing boards or state controlled enterprises in regard to exporting, importing, and price setting was significantly reduced in most of the countries. Although export duties and export marketing monopolies remained in place in about half the countries, only a few countries continued to maintain export restrictions. Finally, substantial progress was also achieved in some key areas of **trade facilitation**, including implementing the harmonization of road transit charges, and the introduction of the Road Customs Transit Document and of a single goods customs declaration form.

Good progress was made in reforming the **domestic financial sectors to** improve their efficiency. Most countries moved to the use of indirect monetary instruments to control monetary aggregates, and administered interest rates were phased out and replaced with market-based mechanisms. Increased attention was devoted to strengthening the powers of central banks to enforce prudential regulations and to provide autonomy in conducting monetary policy. All CBI countries had either adopted or were in the process of adopting Basle capital adequacy standards, and several countries required that the capital ratio be above the minimum 8 percent of risk-weighted assets. In addition, most of the countries had prudential limits on connected/single borrower transactions, as well as on single/aggregate foreign exchange exposures. There was a substantial increase in the number of banks in some countries, including a significant presence of foreign owned banks, but in other countries, the degree of competition in financial markets was still limited to a few operators.

Progress was made in the area of **investment deregulation**. There was substantial simplification of approval procedures (particularly through the

For additional analytical, marketing, investment and business opportunities information, please contact
Global Investment & Business Center, USA
(202) 546-2103. Fax: (202) 546-3275. E-mail: rusric@erols.com

establishment of a one-stop investment approval authority). The publication of investment codes was completed by ten participants, and substantive progress made in the remaining countries. However, with the exception of a few countries, most of the investment codes included some form of tariff exemptions. There was slow progress in concluding double taxation agreements, in the cross-listing of stocks, and in **facilitating labor mobility** (visa protocol, residence/work permits, and short-term entry permits).

I. INTRODUCTION

1. As described in earlier papers[1], the Cross-Border Initiative (CBI) comprises a common policy framework developed by fourteen participating countries in Eastern and Southern Africa and the Indian Ocean[2], with the support of four co-sponsors—the Fund, the World Bank, the European Union (EU), and the African Development Bank. The policy framework aims to facilitate cross-border activity by eliminating barriers to cross-border flows of goods, services, labor, and capital, as well as to integrate markets through a coordination of reform programs in the areas of trade, exchange systems, domestic banking and payment systems, and investment regulations, supported by appropriate macroeconomic policies. The CBI has avoided the creation of new institutions, placing responsibility at the national level for the design and implementation of measures to support the agreed policy framework.

2. To this end, a set of "core" measures were articulated in a Concept Paper[3], which was adopted at the First CBI Ministerial Meeting in Uganda in August 1993 (Box 1). A Second Ministerial Meeting, held in Mauritius in March 1995, endorsed a "Road Map" for further trade liberalization that included the elimination of tariffs on intraregional trade and the convergence of external tariffs to a trade-weighted average of 15 percent, both by October 1998. At the Third Ministerial Meeting, held in Zimbabwe in February 1998, the participating countries decided to continue and broaden the CBI, and agreed that the future focus should emphasize investment facilitation issues, and the harmonization of national and regional policies toward a conducive environment for efficient investment and trade flows. [4]

3. Under the CBI, each participating country was expected to: (i) create a Technical Working Group (TWG) comprised of representatives of the public and private sectors that would identify and report on the main impediments to the cross-border activities outlined in the Box, and would suggest a common program of action to be implemented at the national level; (ii) establish a Policy Implementation Committee (PIC), comprised of officials with the authority to design and implement a specific program of policy measures[5]; and (iii) complete a Letter of CBI Policy (LCBIP) specifying the steps that the country would take to

For additional analytical, marketing, investment and business opportunities information, please contact
Global Investment & Business Center, USA
(202) 546-2103. Fax: (202) 546-3275. E-mail: rusric@erols.com

implement the various measures, including regulatory changes and a timetable which would be endorsed by the co-sponsors. [6]

4. As one of the co-sponsors, the Fund's role was to ensure that each LCBIP was consistent with progress toward a stable macroeconomic framework. The CBI objectives and the schedule of implementation of the various measures have been featured in staff discussions in the context of Article IV consultations and use of Fund resources, and have been taken into account in considering technical assistance requests. For countries undertaking structural adjustment in the context of Fund-supported programs, actions included in the LCBIPs have been built in, and coordinated with, the adjustment program. The CBI has also been featured in staff discussions with nonparticipating countries to apprise them of emerging policy trends with wider implications.

5. The purpose of this paper is to take stock of the achievements of the CBI since its inception in 1993. It is, of course, important to mention that measures in areas such as improving financial intermediation were underway before the CBI began and were undertaken for domestic reasons rather than considerations regarding regional cooperation and harmonization. Section II describes progress in implementing the measures specified in the four areas of the CBI policy framework as of December 1998—foreign exchange systems, trade regimes, domestic banking and payments systems, and investment regulations. Finally, Section III discusses the remaining agenda and the issues to be addressed.

Box. Key Elements of the CBI Framework

Exchange Systems

- Complete elimination of restrictions on current account transactions, and relaxation of restrictions for some capital transactions to liberalize direct investment and investment in regional equity markets.
- Establish unified interbank spot-foreign exchange markets by 1996.

Trade Liberalization and Facilitation

- Dismantle nontariff import barriers on a most-favored-nation (MFN) basis. Short negative lists for reasons of health and security could be retained. Where immediate elimination is not feasible, participants should agree with the Fund on a schedule for their removal, normally within one year.
- Eliminate all quantitative restrictions on exports to all countries, except for a short negative list.
- Eliminate tariffs on intraregional trade by October 1998 for products originating in the CBI area.
- Aim at a harmonized external tariff with no more than three nonzero

---

For additional analytical, marketing, investment and business opportunities information, please contact
Global Investment & Business Center, USA
(202) 546-2103. Fax: (202) 546-3275. E-mail: rusric@erols.com

bands, a maximum rate of 20—25 percent, and a weighted average rate of 15 percent by October 1998.

- Implement harmonized transit charges and introduce: a road customs transit document, a single goods declaration document, and a bond guarantee scheme.

Domestic Banking and Payments Systems

- Strengthen regulatory and prudential functions of central banks and domestic financial markets.
- Eliminate impediments to entry by regional and extraregional financial institutions, and enable specialized financial institutions—including offshore banking facilities—to participate in providing equity and export credit facilities.

Investment Regulations

- Simplify and liberalize investment approval procedures; consolidate investment codes and all regulations into a single published document.
- Establish one-stop investment centers to process investment applications within 45—60 days, with automatic approval in the absence of valid objections.
- Process residence and employment permits within four weeks; relax or eliminate visas on a reciprocal basis; allow freer movement in border areas.
- Authorize stock exchanges to list and trade equities from other stock exchanges in the region.

II. POLICY IMPLEMENTATION AND ISSUES

A. Liberalization of Foreign Exchange Systems

Developments

6. Under the CBI framework, participants are expected to eliminate exchange restrictions on current account transactions in a nondiscriminatory manner and to relax certain types of capital transactions. The liberalization of the capital account referred principally to transactions associated with long-term, non-debt-creating, foreign direct investments (FDI) rather than to short-term capital. The main focus of the reform was to improve the regulatory environment for investments, both domestic and foreign; progressively harmonize investment incentives; and encourage investment in regional equity markets (see Section D below). In light of the fragility of the domestic financial system (elements of which were to be

For additional analytical, marketing, investment and business opportunities information, please contact
Global Investment & Business Center, USA
(202) 546-2103. Fax: (202) 546-3275. E-mail: rusric@erols.com

addressed within the Initiative; see Section C), the liberalization of short-term capital inflows was not perceived to be a priority. In regard to foreign exchange markets, the objective was to establish unified, interbank spot-exchange markets no later than 1996. Such markets would, in turn, set the stage for more diversified operations, including forward cover, and liberalization of foreign currency accounts.

7. With regard to the removal of exchange restrictions on current account transactions, 12 of the 14 CBI countries have accepted the obligations under Article VIII, sections 2, 3, and 4 as of December 1998 (compared with only two in 1993) (Table 1)[7]. Regarding the capital account, Kenya, Malawi, Mauritius, Uganda, and Zambia have substantially liberalized capital account transactions, while Comoros and Madagascar have taken steps to ease controls, including on the repatriation of portfolio outflows. Tanzania and Zimbabwe also took steps in the latter regard.

8. Exchange arrangements vary widely, with 9 participating countries maintaining a floating exchange rate system in the context of unified interbank exchange markets (Tables 2 and 3)[8]. Controls on foreign currency accounts for residents and foreign entities have been lifted, with the exception of Burundi, Comoros, Namibia, Seychelles, Swaziland, and Zimbabwe. Finally, although some progress has been made over the last three years in easing foreign exchange repatriation and surrender requirements, most countries continue to impose such controls (Table 4). Competition in foreign exchange markets has also been enhanced with the licensing of nonbank foreign exchange bureaus in nine countries. Forward cover through commercial banks and other authorized dealers is available in nine countries. In addition, Kenya, Tanzania, and Uganda (the East African Cooperation (EAC) countries) have agreed that their respective currencies be fully accepted within the EAC countries, and that the currencies be quoted by banks and foreign exchange bureaus.

B. Trade Liberalization and Facilitation

Developments

9. The CBI framework called for a coordinated and time-bound reduction of trade barriers at the regional level, and with third countries on an MFN basis. The specifics of the trade reform agenda and the timetable for implementation included: (i) effective October 1995, increasing from 60 percent to 70 percent the intraregional tariff preference for countries that had not yet done so; (ii) elimination of tariffs on intraregional trade by October 1998, with an increase in the preference rate to 80 percent by October 1996 and to 90 percent by 1997; and (iii) a harmonized external tariff to be adopted by October 1998 consisting of no more than three nonzero bands, a trade weighted average tariff rate of no

For additional analytical, marketing, investment and business opportunities information, please contact
Global Investment & Business Center, USA
(202) 546-2103. Fax: (202) 546-3275. E-mail: rusric@erols.com

more than 15 percent, and a maximum rate of 20—25 percent[9]. With regard to nontariff barriers (NTBs), countries were expected to dismantle import licensing requirements and similar NTBs on an MFN basis, except for a short "negative list" for noneconomic reasons such as security, health, and environment. Quantitative restrictions on exports to all countries were to be eliminated, except for a small negative list for the same noneconomic reasons.

10. By end-December 1998, many of the participating CBI countries had either met or made substantial progress toward meeting CBI targets for trade liberalization (Tables 5 and 6). Significant progress on tariff reduction on intraregional trade was achieved. Although, none of the countries met the target for eliminating intraregional tariffs by end-December 1998, Kenya, Madagascar, Tanzania, Uganda, and Zimbabwe, had implemented an 80 percent preference margin, while Burundi, Comoros, Malawi, Mauritius, Rwanda, and Zambia had increased the preference margin to 60—70 percent. Moreover, Kenya, Tanzania, and Uganda have indicated a desire to accelerate tariff reductions on trade between them, in the context of the EAC Agreement. Namibia and Swaziland could not change their preference margins because they are members of the Southern African Customs Union (SACU). Seychelles has not made any progress on increasing the preference margin.

11. Regarding the reduction of the maximum tariff rate, Kenya, Uganda, and Zambia met the CBI target of 20—25 percent by end-December 1998 [10]. In addition, Madagascar, Malawi, and Tanzania reduced their maximum rates to 30 percent, while Comoros and Rwanda lowered theirs to 40 percent. Although some reductions have taken place in the remaining six countries, the maximum rates remain high in Mauritius, Namibia, and Swaziland (in the range of 70—80 percent); and substantially higher in Burundi and Zimbabwe (100 percent), and Seychelles (200 percent).

12. Comoros, Kenya, Madagascar, Rwanda, Uganda, and Zambia met the target of reducing the number of nonzero bands to no more than three, by end-December 1998—Uganda's two tariff bands went beyond the target. Burundi, Malawi, and Tanzania had 4—5 tariff bands, and the least amount of progress was recorded in the cases of Mauritius, Seychelles, and Zimbabwe with 8, 9, and 17 bands, respectively, and the SACU countries which continued to have multiple tariff bands.

13. Information on the weighted average tariff rate is not available for all countries. Among the countries with such information, the CBI target of an average tariff rate of no more than 15 percent was met with substantial margins in Kenya, Uganda, and Zambia. Using the more widely available unweighted average tariff rate, six countries (Malawi, Namibia, Rwanda, Swaziland, Uganda, and Zambia) have averages that are either around or below 15 percent. Kenya

For additional analytical, marketing, investment and business opportunities information, please contact
Global Investment & Business Center, USA
(202) 546-2103. Fax: (202) 546-3275. E-mail: rusric@erols.com

and Madagascar had unweighted average rates of about 18 percent, and the rest of the countries had unweighted average rates ranging from 21.8 percent (Tanzania) to 35 percent (Burundi). Limited progress was made in reducing other duties and charges (ODCs) and in amalgamating them into the basic tariff structure, mainly because of revenue concerns. Malawi, Seychelles, Tanzania, and Zambia met the CBI objective, while Burundi, Comoros, Namibia, Rwanda, Uganda, and Zimbabwe had ODCs below 15 percent, and Madagascar and Mauritius had ODCs of up to 40 percent and 400 percent, respectively.

14. Although notable progress was achieved in reducing import NTBs, particularly those related to bans, quotas, and licensing requirements, the record on dismantling state monopolies and eliminating discriminatory taxes and reducing tariff exemptions has been mixed (Table 7 and 8). The CBI countries have eliminated all import quotas and bans, with the exception of Namibia (which has quotas for imports of used cars and clothing, and seasonal bans on some agricultural products), Uganda (which has a ban on cigarettes that is expected to be eliminated by July 1999), Seychelles (which has semiannual quotas on all imports) and Swaziland (which maintains seasonal bans on some agricultural products). Import licensing requirements have been eliminated in most CBI countries, with the exception of Namibia, Seychelles, and Zimbabwe. The monopoly power previously exercised by state marketing boards or state controlled enterprises with regard to exporting, importing, and price setting was significantly reduced in all countries with the exception of Comoros, Mauritius, Namibia, Seychelles, Swaziland, and Tanzania. Similarly, progress was mixed in eliminating discriminatory higher rates of excise duty and/or value-added tax on certain imports which remain in half of the CBI countries (Burundi, Kenya, Mauritius, Seychelles, Tanzania, Uganda, and Zambia). Tariff exemptions remain widespread, including for imports by governments, parastatals, nongovernmental organizations, and for goods related to foreign-financed projects and those under the various investment codes.

15. Substantial progress was achieved in reducing impediments to exports (Table 9). By end-December 1998, only Zambia and Zimbabwe maintained export bans and quotas, respectively, while export licenses were required in only three countries (Kenya, Namibia, and Zimbabwe). Export duties remained in place in Burundi, Comoros, Rwanda, Swaziland, Tanzania, and Zimbabwe, while Burundi, Namibia, Seychelles, Swaziland, and Zimbabwe still maintained marketing monopolies.

16. Substantial progress was achieved in some key areas of trade facilitation. With the exception of the SACU countries (Namibia and Swaziland) and the island economies, the rest of the CBI countries implemented the harmonization of road transit charges, and introduced the Road Customs Transit Document (Table 10)[11]. In addition, a single goods customs declaration form was introduced

For additional analytical, marketing, investment and business opportunities
information, please contact
Global Investment & Business Center, USA
(202) 546-2103. Fax: (202) 546-3275. E-mail: rusric@erols.com

by most countries, except in Burundi, Malawi, and Rwanda, where information is not available. In contrast, however, no country had yet introduced a bond guarantee scheme by the end of the CBI period.

Assessment of progress

17. The extent of trade liberalization achieved in the CBI countries can be assessed using an index of aggregate trade policy restrictiveness.[12] Under the CBI, considerable progress has been made in trade reforms, mainly in the context of adjustment programs supported by the Fund and the World Bank. Five countries moved to open trade regimes, compared to zero at the inception of the initiative; another three countries had moderately restrictive trade regimes, the same number as at the beginning of the initiative; and the remaining six countries continued to have relatively restrictive trade regimes (Figure 1 and Table 11).

18. Based on the index, the most ambitious reformers were Kenya, Madagascar, Malawi, Rwanda, Uganda, and Zambia, as they reduced their restrictiveness ratings by 4—5 points and achieved open trade regimes (except Kenya which moved from the restrictive to the moderate category). In contrast, Burundi, Comoros, Seychelles, and Zimbabwe made no progress in trade liberalization; moreover, Seychelles and Zimbabwe continued to have a rating of "10" on the index.

19. As a group, the CBI countries reduced their rating on the index by an average of 2.4 points compared to 1.7 for a select group of non-CBI African countries.[13]

For additional analytical, marketing, investment and business opportunities information, please contact
Global Investment & Business Center, USA
(202) 546-2103. Fax: (202) 546-3275. E-mail: rusric@erols.com

As a result, although the CBI countries had more restrictive trade regimes at the beginning of the Initiative, by end-1998 their trade regimes were, on average, less restrictive (5.9) than those of the select group of non-CBI countries (6.2). However, the CBI countries still remain, on average, markedly more restrictive than countries in other regions. While 43 percent of the CBI countries would be classified as having highly restrictive trade regimes, only 17 percent of the economies of the rest of world (excluding non-CBI African countries) would be classified as highly restrictive (Figure 2). Similarly, only 36 percent of the CBI countries would be classified as open compared with 52 percent for the rest of the world. Of course, the rating for the rest of world masks a wide dispersion among the various regions of the world, with industrialized countries as a group having the lowest rating of 4 and the Middle Eastern countries having the highest rating of 5.5, compared with 5.9 for CBI countries.[14] It is important to note that good practice countries (Chile, Colombia, New Zealand, and Singapore) have a rating of 1.5, and that Uganda and Zambia, with ratings of 2, are very near this level.

FACTORS INFLUENCING ACHIEVEMENT OF CBI TRADE REFORM OBJECTIVES

For additional analytical, marketing, investment and business opportunities information, please contact
Global Investment & Business Center, USA
(202) 546-2103. Fax: (202) 546-3275. E-mail: rusric@erols.com

20. Several reasons have been cited for the delay in implementing trade policy reforms. These included: civil unrest (Burundi, Comoros and Rwanda); the concern about potential adverse impact of trade reform on government revenues (Comoros, Tanzania and Zimbabwe) and hence on macroeconomic stability; and membership in other regional trading arrangements (RTAs). The fiscal impact of trade reform depends on the nature of the reforms introduced and the specific circumstances of the country.[15] In order to offset any possible adverse effect on revenues, the reduction in tariffs should be accompanied by a tariffication of NTBs on imports and exports, and the elimination of tariff exemptions. However, even in those circumstances where trade liberalization might lead to a short-term loss in revenues, the appropriate response should be to adopt offsetting measures—if on the revenue side preferably by less-distorting and more broad-based taxes that are applied equally to both imports and domestic production.

21. The excessive number of RTAs which the CBI countries are members may indeed have interfered with the pace of trade liberalization. As shown in Figure 3 and Table 12, the CBI countries are members of five different RTAs: the Common Market for Eastern and Southern Africa (COMESA), EAC, IOC, SACU, and the Southern Africa Development Community (SADC). These countries are faced with conflicting obligations, different and uncoordinated strategies, inconsistent external liberalization goals, and different and conflicting rules and administrative procedures. For example, under the COMESA Treaty, 80 percent preferences were to have been provided by the member states to each other by 1998 and 100 percent by 2000. In contrast, under the more accelerated CBI framework, the complete elimination of intra-CBI tariffs was envisaged to take place by end-October 1998. As for the SADC, intraregional preferences are also envisaged, but over eight years beginning in 2000.

C. REFORM OF THE DOMESTIC FINANCIAL SECTOR

DEVELOPMENTS

22. The development of a sound financial sector and efficient payment systems are viewed as essential for increasing cross-border flows and market access. To ensure the soundness of financial institutions, the CBI framework called for intensified efforts to improve prudential and supervisory capacity of central banks so as to encourage development of the commercial banking sector and other financial institutions, and to strengthen the domestic payments system. Additional measures included developing foreign trade financing instruments and establishing correspondent banking relationships within the region.

23. At the commencement of the Initiative, virtually all CBI countries relied on bank-by-bank credit ceilings and administered interest rates as key instruments of monetary policy. Government interference was prevalent, through directed

For additional analytical, marketing, investment and business opportunities
information, please contact
Global Investment & Business Center, USA
(202) 546-2103. Fax: (202) 546-3275. E-mail: rusric@erols.com

credit allocations, heavy borrowing from central banks to finance large fiscal deficits, and maintenance of negative real interest rates. With respect to the institutional structure, a proper legal framework for the independence of central banks was largely absent, entry by domestic and foreign commercial banks was restricted and led to concentrated ownership structures, and regulation and supervision were inadequate to ensure the soundness of financial institutions.

For additional analytical, marketing, investment and business opportunities information, please contact
Global Investment & Business Center, USA
(202) 546-2103. Fax: (202) 546-3275. E-mail: rusric@erols.com

24. Despite the variety of problems, there has been good progress in improving the efficiency of the financial system. In the banking system, direct monetary

For additional analytical, marketing, investment and business opportunities information, please contact
Global Investment & Business Center, USA
(202) 546-2103. Fax: (202) 546-3275. E-mail: rusric@erols.com

instruments in the form of individual bank credit ceilings and selective credit controls have been phased out in all countries except Comoros; most countries now use indirect monetary instruments such as open market operations, changes in liquidity requirements, and standing discount facilities (Table 13).[16] Administered interest rates have been phased out and replaced with market-based mechanisms in almost all countries except Comoros and Seychelles.[17]

25. Financial market developments can also be gauged by the presence of active primary and secondary markets for public debt instruments, an interbank money market, and a stock exchange. Most CBI countries, with the exception of Comoros, Rwanda, and possibly Burundi have fairly active primary markets for government and central bank securities with weekly auctions, and/or tap sales between auctions. The existence of secondary markets is more limited, with active markets being present only in Kenya, Malawi, Zambia, and Zimbabwe. Secondary markets have been slow to develop, owing in part to the existence of high liquidity requirements, the lack of infrastructure and capacity, as well as lingering doubts about the soundness of some banks. The latter factor has confined active interbank markets to Kenya, Malawi, Mauritius, Namibia, Zambia, and Zimbabwe. Stock exchanges exist in several countries, but it could be argued that only the stock exchanges in Kenya, Namibia, Zambia, and Zimbabwe are relatively active.

26. Attention has also been devoted to central banks' powers to enforce prudential regulations. To this end, legislation was enacted or revised during 1993—98 in Madagascar, Namibia, Seychelles, Swaziland, Uganda, and Zambia (Table 14). In Comoros and Zimbabwe, the supervisory and regulatory role continues to be shared by the government and the central bank. In principle, central banks have full autonomy in most countries, except in Comoros, Kenya, Tanzania, and Zambia, where autonomy is partial.[18]

27. Roughly half the CBI countries have either fully or substantially implemented financial sector reform programs. An evaluation of the development of foreign trade instruments and the removal of impediments to entry indicate that considerable progress has also been achieved in the majority of countries. The increased focus on financial sector reform issues has also coincided with an expansion of financial markets in most of the countries. Thus, the number of commercial banks has increased to more than 50 in Kenya; 21 in Zambia; 20 in Uganda and 18 in Tanzania. At the same time, all countries with the exception of Comoros and Malawi have foreign banks operating in their countries; and Kenya, Malawi, Tanzania, and Uganda have taken measures to reduce government ownership or privatize state-owned banks and to review existing licensing procedures before licensing additional new banks. The payment system appears to be satisfactory in ten of the participating countries although efficiency is high in only a few (Mauritius, Namibia, and Swaziland).

For additional analytical, marketing, investment and business opportunities information, please contact
Global Investment & Business Center, USA
(202) 546-2103. Fax: (202) 546-3275. E-mail: rusric@erols.com

ASSESSMENT OF PROGRESS

28. Despite recent progress in several areas, the degree of competition in financial markets in a number of countries remains limited to a few operators, and there is only a thin supply of financial instruments. The market for treasury and central bank bills remains narrow in most of the participating countries, to the extent that the frequent reason attributed to the lack of secondary markets in public debt is the absence of a sufficient amount of outstanding public paper. In this context, changes in reserve and liquidity ratios have been extensively used as the preferred monetary instrument. Such uses (together with the high level of nonperforming loans) are often cited as contributing to the wide spreads between deposit and lending rates.

29. Supervisory practices have improved significantly in most of the CBI countries. All CBI countries have either adopted or are in the process of adopting the Basle standard for capital adequacy requirement of 8 percent; and in several countries the capital ratio is above the minimum requirement. Most of the countries have prudential limits on connected/single borrower transactions, as well as on single/aggregate foreign exchange exposures.

D. REFORM OF INVESTMENT REGULATIONS

30. Another major objective of the CBI involved reforming the regulatory environment for direct investments, and the progressive harmonization of the structure of investment incentives. In regard to the regulatory environment, participating countries agreed to simplify and codify all investment-related regulatory provisions into a single published document that would be widely available; establish one-stop investment centers that would process all applications between 45 days and 60 days; and grant automatic approval in the absence of objections at the end of that period. Other specific measures called for participants to conclude avoidance of double taxation agreements on a bilateral basis; authorize the cross-listing of stocks from other exchanges in the region; and expedite the processing of residence and work permits, and relax visa requirements for investors. In addition, participating countries were expected to become members of the Multilateral Investment Guarantee Agency, and where necessary, of bilateral investment guarantee agencies such as Overseas Private Investment Corporation. The ratification of a suitable amended form of the Multilateral Industrial Enterprise Charter was also encouraged.[19]

31. Overall progress in the area of investment deregulation has been mixed. There has been almost full liberalization of approval procedures (in particular establishing a one-stop investment approval authority), and the publication of investment codes has been completed by 10 participants, and the remaining countries have made substantive progress (Table 15). However, with the

For additional analytical, marketing, investment and business opportunities information, please contact
Global Investment & Business Center, USA
(202) 546-2103. Fax: (202) 546-3275. E-mail: rusric@erols.com

exception of a few countries, most of the investment codes include tariff exemptions. With regard to the statute of limitation, only 6 participants have fully implemented it. There has also been slow progress with regard to double taxation agreements and cross-listing of stocks.

32. Overall progress in regard to the facilitation of labor market issues (visa protocol, residence/work permits, and short-term entry permits) has also been mixed. Most of the non-island economies have taken action on short-term entry permits for border residents, while the EAC countries—Kenya, Tanzania, and Uganda—no longer require visas for their citizens to travel between their countries. There has been little progress in the processing of residence and work permits except for Kenya, Namibia, Tanzania, Uganda, and Zambia.

III. THE REMAINING AGENDA

33. In the context of a gradual return to macroeconomic stability, good progress has been achieved in most of the CBI countries in the liberalization of exchange systems over the last few years. This is reflected in the widespread elimination of restrictions on external current transactions, the shift towards market-based exchange rates, and the move (mainly in respect of inflows) towards liberalizing external capital transactions related largely to FDI. The movement towards liberalization, moreover, has reduced reliance on direct controls, and correspondingly increased the role of macroeconomic policies. In particular, macroeconomic policies have become the key instruments in promoting exchange rate stability and containing inflationary pressures. Some countries, however, still need to remove the remaining restrictions on current account transactions. To strengthen investor confidence and the export environment there is also the need to further liberalize capital account transactions on FDI and to liberalize foreign exchange repatriation and surrender requirements.

34. Although some of the CBI countries have made significant progress in trade liberalization going well beyond the CBI objectives to achieve open trade regimes, others continue to have either moderately or highly restrictive trade regimes. Ideally, the countries classified as having moderately to highly restrictive trade regimes need to move to open trade regimes, say, over the next three years. Moreover, countries should continue to persevere with trade reform by lowering their maximum tariff rates to no more than 15 percent (in line with the current maximum rate for Uganda), and reducing the number of nonzero tariff bands to 2 or 3 and their unweighted average tariff rates to no more than 10 percent over the medium term.

35. The continuing existence of other duties and charges outside the basic tariff structure needs to be eliminated. The amalgamation of these charges into the tariff structure would reduce its complexity and improve its transparency and

For additional analytical, marketing, investment and business opportunities information, please contact
Global Investment & Business Center, USA
(202) 546-2103. Fax: (202) 546-3275. E-mail: rusric@erols.com

efficiency. With regard to NTBs, much remains to be done, especially in the areas of state monopolies and discriminatory taxes. Given that NTBs are the most distortionary aspects of a trade regime, the future agenda should focus attention on eliminating them as a priority. By making the trade regimes more transparent and less distorted, such an agenda would help make these economies more efficient and competitive. More determined efforts will be needed to eliminate or reduce sharply tariff exemptions. This would serve the purpose of strengthening the fiscal position and introducing more transparency into the trade regimes.

36. The difficulties caused by overlapping RTAs needs to be addressed. Ideally, while trade liberalization should be undertaken on an MFN basis, the extension of tariff preferences to other members of RTAs is likely to enhance trade creation and lessen trade diversion, if accompanied by liberalizing on an MFN basis. In this light, it would be important that the overlapping regional trade arrangements in Eastern and Southern Africa (see Annex I) harmonize the various goals and objectives of the different RTAs, coordinate them more efficiently, and make their objectives more internally consistent so as to (i) avoid negating some of the potential gains from regionalism and undermining the potential improvement in the investment climate that arise from a larger market and improved transparency; (ii) introduce common and simple (rather than conflicting) rules of origin into the trading process; (iii) prevent costly duplication of administrative effort; and (iv) reinforce the reform momentum by consolidating the political capital needed to pursue reforms. CBI participants should make every effort to achieve these goals and accelerate the ongoing efforts at trade facilitation.

37. As a practical matter, rationalizing the current multiple RTAs would be facilitated by accelerating reduction of external tariffs on an MFN basis and removing NTBs. Such an action by one country, or group of countries, could increase the pressure on others to follow suit to prevent intraregional trade and investment from being diverted away from them. In addition, more frequent contacts between all the countries in the region might provide a forum for discussion on adopting a common set of objectives, adopting common rules and regulations and reducing administrative complexity, and for resolving policy disagreements. For example, it would be useful to explore the possibility of inviting COMESA and SADC to join the CBI Steering Committee. Rationalization of the multiple RTAs would enlarge markets, improve transparency, and reduce administrative costs, thus providing a better climate for trade and investment.

38. Despite recent progress in several areas, much work also remains to be done to develop the financial systems to achieve the objectives of the CBI. The authorities need to work toward increasing competition in the financial system by accelerating the pace of privatization of banks, in a transparent manner, and by granting further autonomy to central banks—legally and in practice. Further,

For additional analytical, marketing, investment and business opportunities information, please contact
Global Investment & Business Center, USA
(202) 546-2103. Fax: (202) 546-3275. E-mail: rusric@erols.com

macroeconomic stability and the resulting lower inflation rate will ensure that real interest rates are positive and help raise financial savings, and thus the development of money and capital markets. There is also the need to strengthen regulation and supervision to help achieve financial system soundness, which is an important element for macroeconomic stability. The introduction of a transparent safety net, such as a well defined and limited deposit insurance scheme, rather than reliance on blanket government guarantees, would help increase market discipline. It should be pointed out that the prevalence of state-owned banks makes it hard to credibly refuse to bail out such banks in case of failure.

39. Increased investment (both domestic and foreign) in participating countries is crucial for real per capita economic growth and diversification. As mentioned earlier, the Third Ministerial Meeting held in Zimbabwe (February 1998) requested the co-sponsors to prepare a Road Map for Investment Facilitation to be discussed at the Fourth Ministerial Meeting to be held in 1999. The paper outlining this road map, which has now been finalized by the co-sponsors, indicates that while there has been an upturn in the average real per capita growth in recent years, growth in sub-Saharan Africa and the CBI countries needs to be raised and diversified to ensure a significant improvement in living standards in the near future. To this end, gross investment in the CBI countries needs to be increased to at least 25 percent of GDP, as suggested by the Global Coalition for Africa. Foreign direct investment, which had increased only marginally compared to other developing countries, should be allowed to play an important role in this process. The main lessons of experience drawn by the Paper are that investor confidence is linked not only to the perception of the robustness of reforms, but also to their consistent implementation over time; that reform efforts (which usually take a long time) have not been consistent and sustained enough to regain investor confidence; and that a concerted effort is needed, over an extended period, to firmly establish improved general conditions for attracting investment and build a better image. The Paper identified eight essential conditions for attracting investment: political stability, good governance, macroeconomic reform and stability, trade liberalization, exchange system liberalization, market integration, investment deregulation, and consistency in policy application. Since it would not be feasible to tackle all aspects of investment facilitation at one and the same time, the Paper suggests immediate actions in selected priority areas. They consist of actions to accelerate implementation of the CBI trade reform agenda; investment promotion at the regional and national level; selective legal and judicial reforms; selective tax reforms; and steps to raise awareness and spur the private sector to deliver improvements in services and performance.

40. In implementing the remaining agenda, participation of the private sector through the TWGs will continue to be important. Experience under the CBI

For additional analytical, marketing, investment and business opportunities information, please contact
Global Investment & Business Center, USA
(202) 546-2103. Fax: (202) 546-3275. E-mail: rusric@erols.com

suggests that the TWGs have emerged as a crucial part of the CBI process by contributing to ownership and effective implementation of reforms.

ANNEX 1

REGIONAL ORGANIZATIONS IN EASTERN AND SOUTHERN AFRICA, AND THE INDIAN OCEAN

A. THE COMMON MARKET FOR EASTERN AND SOUTHERN AFRICA (COMESA)

41. The COMESA was established in November 1993, superseding the Preferential Trading Agreement (PTA) for Eastern and Southern African states.[20] The aims and objectives of the COMESA Treaty and Protocols are to facilitate the removal of structural and institutional weaknesses of its members through the creation and maintenance of:

- a full free trade area guaranteeing the free movement of goods and services produced within the COMESA region, and the removal of all nontariff barriers;
- a customs union under which goods and services imported from non-COMESA countries will attract a single tariff rate;
- the free movement of capital and investment supported by the adoption of common investment practices;
- a gradual establishment of a payments union based on the COMESA Clearing House, and the eventual establishment of a common monetary union; and
- the adoption of common visa arrangements, leading eventually to the free movement of bona fide persons.

42. The fulfilment of the complete COMESA mandate is regarded as a long-term objective. To become more effective as an institution COMESA has defined its priorities over the next 3—5 years as being "The Promotion of Regional Integration Through Trade and Investment." Under the COMESA program, activities in respect of trade liberalization, trade facilitation, payments systems, institutional support, competition policy, investment road maps, strengthening the private sector, and immigration and free movement of persons will be undertaken.

43. The COMESA program includes the establishment of a Free Trade Area (FTA) by the year 2000, to be achieved by the annual reduction of intra-COMESA tariffs. As of end-December 1998, eight countries had achieved a reduction of 80 percent, and six other countries achieved reductions of 60—70 percent. All COMESA countries have reiterated their commitment to achieve a FTA by October 2000, and over half are in a position to make such a transition

For additional analytical, marketing, investment and business opportunities information, please contact
Global Investment & Business Center, USA
(202) 546-2103. Fax: (202) 546-3275. E-mail: rusric@erols.com

without having to effect large additional preferences. Member countries have also agreed to adopt a formula on the rules of origin for preferential trade that require the local content to be not less than 35 percent of the ex-factory cost of the goods. COMESA member states have further agreed to establish a customs union with a common external tariff (of 0 percent, 5 percent, 15 percent, and 30 percent) by 2004. In the area of trade facilitation, the COMESA Secretariat is implementing a program to improve the transport and communications systems of the region. These include the adoption of Harmonized Road Transit Charges, a Yellow Card (vehicle insurance) Scheme, Customs Bond Guarantee Scheme, and an Advance Cargo Information System. To provide the required financial infrastructure and service support, COMESA has created specialized institutions in the form of a Trade and Development Bank, a Reinsurance company, and the COMESA Clearing House.[21] Institutional support in the form of a Court of Justice, formally created in June 1998, establishes COMESA as an institution with rules which can be enforced through a court of law. The Court will adjudicate and arbitrate on, inter alia, unfair trade practices, interpretation of the treaty, and ensuring that members comply with agreed decisions. In regard to immigration and the free movement of persons, four countries are already in full compliance, while others have committed themselves to fully implementing the protocol. The protocol on the free movement of persons will be implemented in several stages, with the first stage—the removal of visa requirements—to be completed by the year 2000.

B. THE SOUTHERN AFRICAN DEVELOPMENT COMMUNITY (SADC)[22]

44. In August 1992, a formal treaty providing for the establishment of SADC was adopted, superseding the Southern African Development Coordination Conference (SADCC).[23] This treaty called for the broadening of cooperation among member states in 20 sectors, including transport, health, tourism, mining, and water.

45. The SADC Trade and Development Protocol, signed in August 1996, seeks to establish a SADC Free Trade Area eight years after ratification and the gradual elimination of tariffs and NTBs to trade in the interim. The Protocol has been ratified by only five member states. Others are in agreement on a tariff liberalization program, currently being negotiated by the 11 original signatories of the Trade Protocol. This program is less ambitious than the one agreed by its own member countries under the CBI and under the COMESA. Current proposals call for the removal of all intraregional tariffs within eight years, but do not cover the liberalization of trade with non-SADC countries. Also, unlike agreements under the CBI, proposals regarding trade liberalization among SADC countries allow for special treatment of so-called "sensitive products" (in agriculture, agro-industry, and manufacturing), involving a slower phase-in for import tariff reductions. Moreover, some of the proposals being considered leave

For additional analytical, marketing, investment and business opportunities information, please contact
Global Investment & Business Center, USA
(202) 546-2103. Fax: (202) 546-3275. E-mail: rusric@erols.com

open the possibility of excluding some goods/sectors altogether from the trade liberalization exercise.

46. South Africa, on behalf of its partners in the South African Customs Union (SACU),[24] has offered to reduce its tariffs at a faster pace than non-SACU SADC countries, although a number of "sensitive" goods—dairy products, wheat, sugar, cotton, fabrics, leather footwear, and vehicles—will be subject to a slower liberalization process. Negotiations within SADC are being held each month under a Trade Negotiating Forum framework. The aim is to reach agreement on a full schedule of tariff reductions before the SADC Summit in August 1999.

C. SOUTHERN AFRICAN CUSTOMS UNION (SACU)

47. The Southern African Customs Union (SACU) was established in 1910 between the newly established Union of South Africa and the separate protectorates of Botswana, Lesotho, and Swaziland. The agreement was renegotiated in 1969 to reflect increases in the partner country shares of regional imports. Namibia became a member of SACU in 1990. The aims of the SACU are to encourage economic development and diversification, in particular in the less-advanced member countries, and afford all parties equitable benefits arising from intra-Union and international trade. The Customs Union Commission, comprising representatives of all the contracting parties, is the supreme consultative body of SACU and meets annually.

48. Under the SACU agreement, members apply the customs, excise, sales, antidumping, countervailing and safeguard duties, as well as related laws, set by South Africa, to goods imported to the common customs area from third countries outside the Union. A SACU member may enter separately into, or amend, trade agreements with a country outside the common customs area, provided the terms of such agreements or amendments do not conflict in any way with the provisions of the SACU agreements. Members may not impose duties or quantitative restrictions on goods grown, produced or manufactured in the SACU area and they may not impose any duties on importation, from any other member, of goods which were imported from outside the common customs area. Each member has its own legislation on quantitative restrictions on goods imported from outside the SACU area. Members, other than South Africa, may, following consultations, apply additional duties or increase duties for protection of infant industries. Rebates, refunds, and drawbacks granted by member countries must be identical, except in specified circumstances. Exceptional trade restrictions by a member may also be justified. There are marketing arrangements under which agricultural imports from other SACU countries may be restricted.

For additional analytical, marketing, investment and business opportunities information, please contact
Global Investment & Business Center, USA
(202) 546-2103. Fax: (202) 546-3275. E-mail: rusric@erols.com

49. All customs, excise, sales and additional duties collected by SACU members are pooled and distributed to members. The shares of BLNS countries are determined on the basis of a revenue-sharing formula and the residual is allocated to South Africa. The original 1910 revenue sharing formula was based on the respective contribution of the BLNS countries to total imports into, and consumption of excisable goods produced within, the SACU area. The 1969 formula provided for an enhancement factor of 42 percent of the shares of the BLNS countries; this factor was introduced to compensate the BLNS countries for negative effects resulting from their participation in SACU. These effects were: (i) the price-increasing effect of the customs union for the BLNS countries and the implicit protection for South African industry; (ii) the industrial polarization resulting from the tendency of industries to locate within the customs union to choose sites in South Africa; and (iii) the loss of fiscal discretion experienced by the BLNS partners because South Africa retained tariff-setting power for the region. Nontariff barriers applied by South Africa also had a negative effect on the size of the revenue pool. Subsequently, the revenue sharing formula was renegotiated in 1975 and a "stabilization factor" was added in 1978, operating retrospectively to 1974/75, to reduce fluctuation in the revenue shares accruing to the BLNS countries. The stabilization factor was centered on a mean of 20 percent of the tax base, with a lower bound of 17 percent and an upper bound of 23 percent. The tax base refers to the sum of duty-inclusive imports, c.i.f., and excise tax-inclusive value of goods produced in the Union and consumed in a particular BLNS country.

D. COMMISSION FOR EAST AFRICAN COOPERATION (EAC)

50. The EAC between Kenya, Uganda, and Tanzania was established in November 1993, and is the most recent in a long line of regional integration arrangements between these three countries.[25] Through regional cooperation, the EAC seeks, inter alia, to:

- strengthen and consolidate cooperation in agreed fields with a view to bringing about equitable development among member states;
- establish a single market and investment area in the region; and
- promote sustainable utilization of the region's natural resources and effective protection of the environment.[26]

51. The main policy organs of the EAC are: the Summit of the Heads of State, the Permanent Tripartite Commission, the Coordination Commission, and the Secretariat. Since the launching of the EAC, the Tripartite Commission has concentrated on the identification and elimination of physical and policy related constraints, which could slow progress in the establishment of a single market and investment area. Accordingly, much of the work has focussed on formulation of programs to ease the movement of people, goods, services and capital;

For additional analytical, marketing, investment and business opportunities information, please contact
Global Investment & Business Center, USA
(202) 546-2103. Fax: (202) 546-3275. E-mail: rusric@erols.com

provide adequate and reliable basic infrastructure; harmonize standards, specifications, trade documentation and investment policies; harmonize macroeconomic and sectoral policies; provide trade financing and other facilities ancillary to the growth of exports; and achieve convertibility of the three East African currencies.

52. As a result of these activities, the EAC has achieved (i) full convertibility of the three East African currencies within the region; (ii) full liberalization of the external current account, and progress towards liberalization of the capital account; (iii) holding of pre- and post-budget consultations in order to harmonize monetary and fiscal policies; (iv) synchronization of the budget day of the three member countries; (v) development of a macroeconomic framework for the region to guide countries towards economic convergence; (vi) launching of the EAC Development Strategy, 1997—2000, which provides for guidelines for economic and social development; (vii) formation of an East African Securities Regulatory Authority to facilitate the establishment of an East African Stock Exchange and cross-listing of stocks; (viii) formation of East African Business Council, comprising private sector organizations to promote cross-border trade and investments; and (ix) the execution of tripartite agreements for the avoidance of double taxation, road transport, and inland waterways. In addition, efforts are underway to eliminate internal tariffs by July 1, 2000, for the launching of an East African passport, and the identification of a EAC designated transport network.

E. THE INDIAN OCEAN COMMISSION (IOC)

53. The IOC was established in December 1982 by Madagascar, Mauritius, and Seychelles, with the objective of promoting cooperation in trade, agriculture, fishing and ecosystem conservation, as well as cooperation in the cultural, scientific, technical and educational areas. While the IOC has developed a wide variety of regional programs, cooperation in the economic sector has been a priority, as reflected in the implementation of an Integrated Regional Program for Development of Trade (PRIDE)[27].

54. The overall objective of PRIDE is to strengthen regional trade integration, specifically by lifting the technical and financial constraints on the private sector of its members. PRIDE is expected to increase business competitiveness, enhance the quality of traded goods, and improve the availability and reliability of trade data. PRIDE has two main components: a macroeconomic component consisting of a general framework of actions to liberalize trade in goods and services, investment, capital movements, and the movement of people;[28] and a microeconomic component aimed at facilitating business contacts and partnerships such as participating in trade exhibitions and organizing trade missions.

For additional analytical, marketing, investment and business opportunities
information, please contact
Global Investment & Business Center, USA
(202) 546-2103. Fax: (202) 546-3275. E-mail: rusric@erols.com

55. As the IOC member states are also members of COMESA, they subscribe to the trade integration strategy of COMESA. The IOC has also been actively involved in all the preparatory meetings of the CBI, and expects to be involved in its implementation, particularly in those areas that fall within its purview.

BIBLIOGRAPHY

International Monetary Fund, 1994, "Initiative for Promoting Cross-Border Trade, Investment, and Payments in Eastern and Southern Africa" SM/94/91 (Washington: International Monetary Fund).

——, 1996, "The Cross-Border Initiative in Eastern and Southern Africa" SM/96/94 (Washington: International Monetary Fund).

——, 1997, "Trade Liberalization in Fund-Supported Programs" EBS/97/113 (Washington: International Monetary Fund).

——, 1998, "Revenue Implications of Trade Liberalization" SM/98/254 (Washington: International Monetary Fund).

Mehran, Hassanali, and others, 1998, Financial Sector Development in Sub-Saharan African Countries, IMF Occasional Paper No. 169 (Washington: International Monetary Fund).

---

1 - Detailed background information (including on the principles underlying the CBI) was provided in "The Cross-Border Initiative in Eastern and Southern Africa" (SM/96/94, March 14, 1996), and "Initiative for Promoting Cross-Border Trade, Investment, and Payments in Eastern and Southern Africa" (SM/94/91, April 8, 1994).

2 - Comprising Burundi, Comoros, Kenya, Madagascar, Malawi, Mauritius, Namibia, Rwanda, Seychelles, Swaziland, Tanzania, Uganda, Zambia, and Zimbabwe. Recently, Mozambique has expressed its intention of joining the CBI.

3 - See SM/94/91 (Annex).

4 - The Meeting also requested the co-sponsors to prepare a Road Map for Investment Facilitation to be discussed at the Fourth Ministerial Meeting to be held in October 1999.

5 - The TWGs are to act as advisory committees and complement the policy work of the PICs.

6 - LCBIPs had to be completed before end-1995. However, LCBIPs have been agreed for all member countries, except for Burundi and Rwanda.

7 - The remaining two countries—Burundi and Zambia—have expressed the intention of accepting the obligations under Article VIII in the near future.

8 - Although Namibia and Swaziland, as members of the Common Monetary Area (CMA), peg their respective currencies to the South African Rand, an interbank market exists for the determination of forward rates. Comoros has a fixed exchange rate vis-à-vis the French franc, and since January 1, 1999, the Euro. Burundi's franc, and Seychelles' rupee are pegged to baskets of currencies of their main trading partners.

9 - In contrast to a common external tariff structure, the harmonization of external tariffs implies some flexibility for countries to establish their own tariff schedule, while agreeing with its regional partners on parameters such as the number of tariff bands and maximum and average tariffs.

10 - However, Kenya has "stand-by" tariffs on certain imports on top of regular tariffs.

11 - Since these measures were intended to facilitate land-based transportation, Madagascar,

For additional analytical, marketing, investment and business opportunities information, please contact
Global Investment & Business Center, USA
(202) 546-2103. Fax: (202) 546-3275. E-mail: rusric@erols.com

Mauritius, and Seychelles were not required to enact them. As for the SACU countries, the timing for the implementation of these measures depended on discussions with South Africa.

12 - This index combines measurements of the restrictiveness of tariffs and nontariff barriers, with a rating of "1" denoting the most open trade regime, and a rating of "10" the most restrictive. For purposes of analysis, countries with a rating of 7—10 were considered "restrictive"; rating of 5—6 "moderate"; and rating of 1—4 "open." For a more detailed description of the index, see "Trade Liberalization in Fund-Supported Programs," Annex I, EBS/97/113.

13 - The select group included non-CBI African countries which had medium-term adjustment programs supported by the Fund in the early to mid-1990s. Comprehensive estimates of the restrictiveness rating for non-CBI African countries in 1993 are not available.

14 - Five CBI countries have trade regimes that are as or less restrictive than that of the average industrial country.

15 - For a detailed analysis see "Revenue Implications of Trade Liberalization," SM/98/254 (November 17, 1998).

16 - See also "Financial Sector Development in Sub-Saharan African Countries," Occasional Paper 169 (1998), Appendix.

17 - Namibia and Swaziland, as members of the CMA, are heavily influenced by interest rate developments in South Africa, although differentials exist between rates in these two countries and South Africa due to differences in reserve and liquidity requirements.

18 - In practice, however, even the central banks with full autonomy face substantial interference from other branches of government.

19 - The need for its ratification has been overtaken by recent economic reforms such as improvements in investment related legislation which generally removed discrimination against foreign direct investment.

20 - At its inception COMESA had 10 members: Ethiopia, Kenya, Lesotho, Malawi, Mauritius, Somalia, Swaziland, Uganda, Zambia, and Zimbabwe. Since that time its membership has expanded to 21 members with the addition of Angola, Burundi, the Democratic Republic of the Congo, Comoros, Djibouti, Egypt, Eritrea, Madagascar, Rwanda, Sudan, Namibia, Seychelles, and Tanzania, and the withdrawal of Lesotho and Somalia. Mozambique was a member for part of the period.

21 - With the direct availability of foreign exchange to firms and importers, the utilization of the Clearing House has declined. A restructuring of the Clearing House is being considered so that it can improve the management of risk in cross-border payments, including a facility to provide guarantees against political risk.

22 - At its inception SADC had nine members: Angola, Botswana, Lesotho, Malawi, Mozambique, Swaziland, Tanzania, Zambia and Zimbabwe. Since then, five countriesCthe Democratic Republic of the Congo, Mauritius, Seychelles, Namibia, and South Africa have joined the Community.

23 - The SADCC was set up as a rather informal organization by the "frontline" countries with the objective of reducing economic dependence on South Africa. For the most part, the focus of the SADCC activities was on the implementation of projects.

24 - Consisting of South Africa and the BLNS (Botswana, Lesotho, Namibia, and Swaziland) countries.

25 - Consisting of the East African High Commission (1948—1961), the East African Common Services Organization (1961—1967), and the East African Community (1967—1977).

26 - To define in clearer terms how cooperation is to proceed, the Heads of State at the last Summit (April 1997), directed that a Treaty to upgrade the current cooperation agreement be prepared, thereby making regional integration more sustainable. It is expected that this Treaty will be signed by July 1999.

27 - Programme Regional Intégré de Développement des Echanges.

28 - Consensus was recently achieved in agreeing on the rules of origin adapted from the COMESA model.

For additional analytical, marketing, investment and business opportunities information, please contact
Global Investment & Business Center, USA
(202) 546-2103. Fax: (202) 546-3275. E-mail: rusric@erols.com

Burundi

AFRIQUE DE L'EST ET
CORNE DE L'AFRIQUE

EASTERN AFRICA AND
HORN OF AFRICA

 27 824

 6 315 619

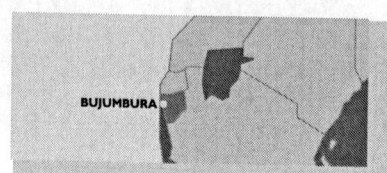

BUJUMBURA

Economic indicators

GNP per capita
€ 110 (1996)

European imports from...
46 967 270 (1997)
Coffee **87%**

European Exports to...
€ 40 997 110 (1997)

Debt service / exports
27.8% (1995)

Social indicators

Population growth rate
2.6% (1995-96)

Primary schooling rate
69.1% (1996)

Secondary schooling rate
8.4% (1996)

Urbanisation rate
8% (1996)

The Tutsi minority has held power under President Buyoya since 1996 although the internal war between the Tutsis, supported by the army, and the majority Hutu group has continued. The Commission suspended development co-operation with Burundi in 1997 because of the security situation; only humanitarian aid continued. Its policy has been to support initiatives for a negotiated peace acceptable to all parties to the conflict, in particular, the Arusha peace process led by former President Nyerere of Tanzania. Mr Aldo Ajello, the EU Special Envoy to the Great Lakes, continued his work of peace-maker throughout the year both in the Region and in Europe, the United Nations etc.

There was no development co-operation following the suspension of 1997 until July 1998. Professor Pinheiro then promised that there would be a gradual resumption of aid, in view of signs of progress with the peace talks and in order to encourage the Burundi Government to continue this process. A chargé d'affaires was nominated by the Commission to work on recommencing Commission development programmes and he took up his post on 30.10.98.

However, in pursuance of its wish to further the peace process, in 1998 the Commission allocated € 500,000 to the Arusha peace process, and some € 834,000 to the Inter-Parliamentary Union to work with the National Assembly, both sums coming from the budget line for human rights and democracy. Furthermore, ECHO continued its programmes providing some €7 million in 1998, plus € 3.65 million in Regional funds.

As regards the Commission's current programme for Burundi, the priority is to alleviate the considerable suffering of the Burundi people of the past years. Therefore, a new rehabilitation programme is being prepared using 7th EDF, whilst the suspended 7th EDF health and micro-project programmes are being revived. Operations to advance internal peace, such as funding law reform, human rights, prisons etc. will also be considered for funding.

FED EDF + budget

dotations en millions €
allocations in € million

budget

autres fed + bei
others fed + eib

pin (dotation pour 5 ans)
nip (envelope for 5 years)

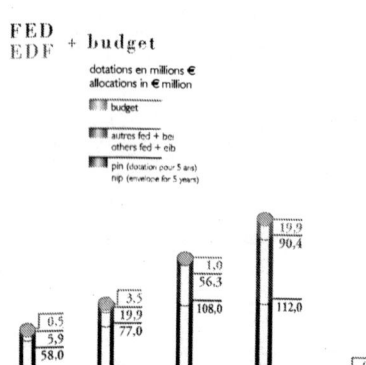

FED EDF — **répartition sectorielle du PIN** en % de la dotation totale / **sectoral breakdown of NIP** % of the total envelope

développement rural/pêche
rural development/fishing

transport et communications
transport and communications

secteurs sociaux
social sectors

autres
others

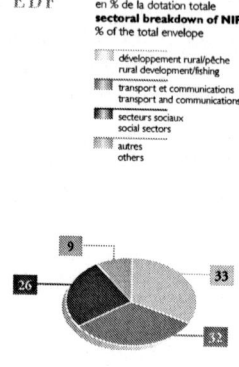

FED EDF 4-5-6-7-8

paiement par instrument
payments by instrument

stabex   divers / various

FAS / SAF   PIN / NIP

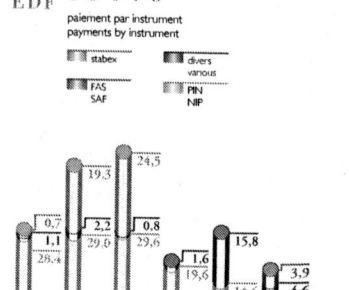

Printed in the United Kingdom
by Lightning Source UK Ltd.
102992UKS00001B/29-30